RULING FROM HORSEBACK

Portrait of Soni. Reproduced with permission from the collection of David Kidd, Ashiya City, Japan. The inscription on the label of the portrait's outer mounting reads: "Great Minister So, wearing otter-skin-edged, brocade-sleeve court gown; age fifty-five <u>sui</u>. Imperial presentation; the twelfth year of the Shun-chih reign." See David Kidd, "Ritual and Realism in Palace Portraiture," <u>Oriental Art</u> 19, no. 4 (Winter 1973): 421-28.

RULING FROM HORSEBACK

Manchu Politics in the Oboi Regency 1661–1669

ROBERT B. OXNAM

The University of Chicago Press
Chicago and London

Robert B. Oxnam is associate professor of history at
Trinity College, Hartford, Connecticut.

The University of Chicago Press, Chicago 60637
The University of Chicago Press, Ltd., London

Library of Congress Cataloging in Publication Data
Oxnam, Robert B.
    Ruling from horseback: Manchu politics in the Oboi
Regency, 1661-1669.

    Based on the author's thesis, Yale, 1969
    Bibliography: p.
    1. China—History—K'ang-hsi, 1662-1722. I. Title.
DS754.2.095   951'.03   74-10343
ISBN 0-226-64244-5

To Barbara

Contents

Acknowledgments

I am deeply indebted to Jonathan Spence for inspiring me to write this book and for his superb guidance in my research and writing. I have depended heavily on his insights into the early Ch'ing period and on his methodology in dealing with source materials.

The late Mary Wright was a source of great personal and scholarly assistance in the course of my experience as a graduate student at Yale University. I was but one of many whose lives both as Chinese historians and as individuals were deeply affected by her talents and human understanding. Those of us fortunate enough to have studied under her will always remember her for her unique combination of warmth and high scholarly standards.

I benefitted considerably from the meticulous review of my manuscript by Robert Kapp, and many of his comments have been incorporated into this book. I would like to thank Donald Price, Beatrice Bartlett, Andrew Chia, George Cooper, Douglas Payne, and Vera Morrissey for reading copies of my work and for making valuable suggestions. Wan Wei-ying, during his tenure as Curator of the East Asian Collection at Yale University, provided expert and untiring assistance in finding works relevant to my research. Similarly, I received invaluable help from the Harvard-Yenching Library staff, who guided me in using that rich collection of materials on East Asian history. My deep appreciation is due to two people who offered considerable help in translating some early Ch'ing documents: Parker Huang of the Institute of Far Eastern Languages at Yale, and Kiyoshi Matsumi of Trinity College. Several specialists on the early Ch'ing period, particularly John Wills, Jr., John Watt, Lawrence Kessler, David Farquhar, and Silas Wu, receive my thanks for making important bibliographic suggestions.

I would like to thank all those at Yale University in the Department of History, the Institute of Far Eastern Languages, and the Colloquium on East Asian Studies for their aid in my studies. A great deal of the research and some of the writing of thes book were accomplished in my dissertation for the Department of History at Yale under the title of "Policies and Factionalism in the Oboi Regency, 1661-1669." Generous financial support for research and typing of the manuscript for this book was provided by Trinity College. Patricia McDonald and Carol Steiman did an excellent job typing the manuscript.

Finally, I bear a heavy debt of gratitude to my wife, Barbara, who took considerable time from her own graduate work to make extensive comments on style and structure.

R.B.O.

Trinity College
Hartford, Connecticut

Abbreviations

CS	Ch'ing-shih
CSK	Ch'ing-shih kao
CSLC	Ch'ing-shih lieh-chuan
HT	Ch'in-ting ta-Ch'ing hui-tien (1899 edition)
HT (1690)	Ch'in-ting ta-Ch'ing hui-tien (1690 edition)
HTSL	Ch'in-ting ta-Ch'ing hui-tien shih-li
KCCH	Kuo-ch'ao ch'i-hsien lei-cheng
KH Shih-lu	Ta-Ch'ing Sheng-tsu Jen huang-ti shih-lu (Veritable Records of the K'ang-hsi Reign)
MCSL	Ming-Ch'ing shih-liao
PCST	Pa-ch'i Man-chou shih-tsu t'ung-p'u
PCTC	Pa-ch'i t'ung-chih (1739 edition)
PCTC (1795)	Pa-ch'i t'ung-chih (1795 edition)
SC Shih-lu	Ta-Ch'ing Shih-tsu Chang huang-ti shih-lu (Veritable Records of the Shun-chih Reign)
T'ai-tsung Shih-lu	Ta-Ch'ing T'ai-tsung Wen huang-ti shih-lu (Veritable Records of the T'ai-tsung Reign)

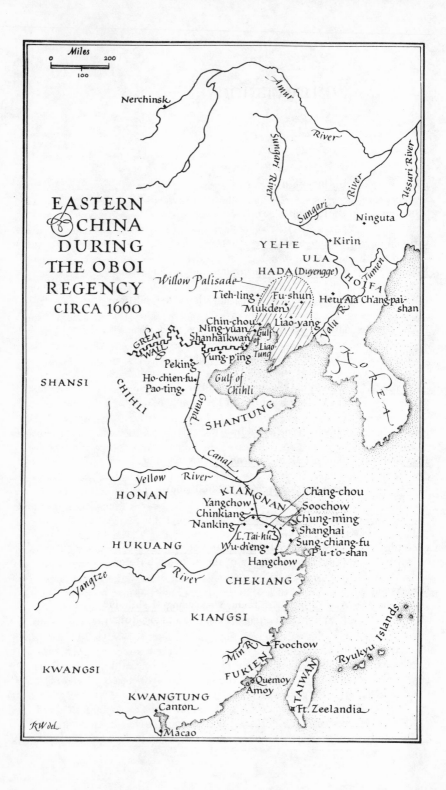

Miles
0   100   200

Nerchinsk

Amur River
Sungari River
Ussuri River
Sungari River

Ninguta

EASTERN CHINA DURING THE OBOI REGENCY CIRCA 1660

YEHE
Kirin
ULA
HADA (Duyengge)
HOIFA

Willow Palisade

T'ieh-ling   Fu-shun
Mukden   Hetu Ala   Ch'ang-pai-shan

Chin-chou   Liao-yang
Ning-yuan   Gulf
Shanhaikwan   of
Liao-   Tung
Yung-p'ing

KOREA

Valu R.
Tumen

GREAT WALL

Peking
Ho-chien-fu
Pao-ting

SHANSI

CHIHLI

Grand

Gulf of Chihli

SHANTUNG

Canal

Yellow River

HONAN

KIANGNAN
Ch'ang-chou
Yangchow   Soochow
Chinkiang   Ch'ung-ming
Nanking   Shanghai
L. Tai-hu   Sung-chiang-fu
Wu-ch'eng   P'u-t'o-shan
Hangchow

HUKUANG

Yangtze River

CHEKIANG

KIANGSI

Min R.   Foochow

Ryukyu Islands

KWANGSI

FUKIEN
Quemoy
Amoy

TAIWAN

KWANGTUNG
Canton

Ft. Zeelandia

Macao

R.W.del.

1   Introduction

In the evening of 5 February 1661 it was announced that the twenty-two-year-old monarch of the Ch'ing dynasty, who had ruled since 1643 under the reign-title Shun-chih, had died in one of the palaces in that section of Peking called the Forbidden City. Shortly after his death the emperor's Imperial Will (i-chao) was read to the great Manchu and Chinese officials of the empire: the young prince Hsüan-yeh, then only seven years of age, was to succeed as emperor under the reign title K'ang-hsi; and during his minority, four Manchu regents—Soni, Suksaha, Ebilun, and Oboi—were to direct affairs of state. In addition, the emperor used his Will to castigate himself for a variety of sins: luxurious self-indulgence; reliance on corrupt eunuchs and officials; failure to depend on his Manchu military personnel; and rejection of the guidance of his mother, the Grand Empress Dowager Hsiao-chuang.

On the surface the transition of power proceeded smoothly. The Shun-chih Will had named a new emperor, a new regency, and had advised the new rulers about the pitfalls of imperial behavior. However, just as many Chinese statesmen of the time must have suspected, it is now thought that much of the Shun-chih Will was a blatant forgery accomplished by the Grand Empress Dowager and the four future regents (see appendix 1).

The Grand Empress Dowager and the new regents had been annoyed by the Shun-chih Emperor's unwillingness to rely on them for advice during his reign and by the emperor's attraction to Chinese officials and to the Chinese way of life in general. Much of the Imperial Will was not the last statement of a dying monarch, but was a harbinger of the policies and personalities which governed China during the so-called Oboi regency (1661-69). For the first five years of the regency these Manchus governed collectively, issuing edicts and making decisions which suited their ideal of a Manchu-dominated Chinese empire. After 1666, however, one of the regents, Oboi, managed to concentrate power in his own hands and to eliminate the influence of the other regents. In the years 1667-69 the young K'ang-hsi Emperor, assisted by the Grand Empress Dowager and several Manchu advisers, sought to assert personal control over the Ch'ing state and restrain the ambitious Oboi. Eventually, in June 1669, the emperor arrested Oboi and put an end to his faction of relatives and supporters.

The Oboi regency, named after the most ruthless and infamous of the four regents, was a significant transitional period in modern Chinese history. The regency occurred in the formative years of the Ch'ing dynasty (1644-1912), two decades after the Manchu conquest of Peking but before the reigns of the well-known emperors of the High Ch'ing period, K'ang-hsi, Yung-cheng, and Ch'ien-lung. During the seventeenth century, and particularly in the Oboi regency, the Manchus confronted the dilemma of maintaining their power and preserving Manchu traditions while governing a Chinese state and society. The four regents were the last Ch'ing rulers who had actually participated in the campaigns that led to the Manchu conquest in 1644. Although all of them brought some experience in civil administration to the regency, their primary values had been shaped on the battlefields of southern Manchuria and northern China. They had been rugged field-grade officers for thirty years before their regency, winning fame and rewards for consistent military success. They prized courage, efficiency, and obedience. They recalled with pride the militant and authoritarian regimes of Nurhaci and Abahai, founders of the Manchu state. They distrusted the Chinese scholar-official class, whose lifestyle seemed weak and effeminate and whose political allegiances often rested with the deposed Ming dynasty.

And yet the vast empire which the four regents ruled in the 1660s was predominately Chinese in population and cultural tradition. The Manchus constituted a tiny minority of a few hundred thousand—a "barbarian" minority from a Chinese perspective—ruling over one hundred fifty million Chinese subjects. The regents also inherited a political system which was heavily Chinese both in its institutions and officialdom. The Ch'ing decisions to adopt much of the Ming administrative structure and to retain many of the Ming statesmen were made by Abahai in the 1630s and Dorgon in the 1640s. It was evident that the regents would have to work within and around the constraints of a Chinese sociopolitical order. The politics and policies of the Oboi regency, therefore, were charged with tension between the regents' quest for Manchu supremacy and the powerful force of sinification to which several non-Chinese dynasties had succumbed in the past. In this setting Chinese and Manchus alike played out their politics around the imperial throne in Peking.

This book explores the Oboi regency in light of this tension between Manchu and Chinese visions of the early Ch'ing dynasty. It examines the forces of sinification and Manchu dominance in evaluating the origins of the Oboi era, the key decisions and episodes of the 1660s, and the factional clashes which marked the demise of the regency and the rise of the K'ang-hsi Emperor. "Sinification" is defined as the overriding commitment of a ruling group to governance by Chinese institutions, Chinese officials, and Chinese ideology. "Manchu dominance," on the other hand, is an overriding commitment to governance by Manchu institutions, officials, and ideology. This interpretive dichotomy is attractive because it has figured prominently in the historiography concerning the Manchu conquest and the early Ch'ing era; if approached with some caution, the dichotomy continues to suggest valid insights into the process of Manchu acculturation in the seventeenth century. Yet an obsession with these terms—in particular the tendency to view this period as either fully "sinified" or "Manchu-ized" (for lack of a better term)— can lead to serious distortions. As political power changed hands in the post-conquest era, there were frequent shifts across the spectrum from sinification to Manchu dominance, and political figures often exhibited characteristics of both extremes in various mixtures. When one begins to investigate these mixtures, factors like personality idiosyncrasies, ambition, factional and clan ties, intelligence, political experience, and personal animosities are interlaced with Chinese and Manchu orientations, thus complicating the historian's task while moving us towards a closer approximation of reality.

Keeping in mind these qualifications, it seems appropriate to begin with a brief historiographical review, exploring some previous interpretations of the rise and development of the Manchu dynasty. The Oboi period, it must be noted at the outset, has been virtually untouched by Western historians, except for a few valuable biographies in Eminent Chinese of the Ch'ing Period, edited by Arthur Hummel in the early 1940s. And with the exception of brief overviews of the regency by some Chinese historians (most notably Meng Sen and Hsiao I-shan), the Oboi era is tabula rasa in the writings about early Ch'ing history in any language. But what the historian lacks in previous interpretations of the regency is more than compensated by the rich resources he finds in the official chronicle of the Ch'ing dynasty, the "Veritable Records" (shih-lu), in which thirty chapters (chüan) are devoted to the Oboi regency, amounting to over 1700 pages in the original version. In this chronicle one finds a day-by-day record of the imperial court: memorials received from provincial officials and military commanders; imperial rescripts and notations appended to the memorials by the regents; edicts and proclamations issued by the regents in the name of the K'ang-hsi Emperor; and considerable information about financial and judicial developments in Peking and throughout the empire. Complementing the "Veritable Records" are an array of encyclopedias, biographical collections, histories of the military structure, provincial and local gazetteers, and a variety of institutional studies. Although most of these resources lack the informality and color of the memoirs, letters, and diaries that play such an important role in the writing of Western history, their strong points are comprehensiveness and detail.

Relying on these resources, but in the absence of previous studies of the 1660s, one is forced to look further into the historiography of the early Ch'ing period for interpretations which might be applicable. This search soon reveals the "sinification versus Manchu dominance" controversy. The sinification approach has deep roots in the traditional Chinese concept of a world order. In its idealized and simplified form —a form often more suited to the writing of history than to the reality of history—the traditional concept was sinocentric: the emperor, "Son of Heaven" (t'ien-tzu), ruled the entire known world ("all under Heaven" or t'ien-hsia), and thus China was not a nation in modern parlance, but rather the axis mundi or "Central Kingdom" (chung-kuo), whose political and cultural influence was all-pervasive. Again speaking ideally, the non-Chinese peoples and states on the perimeter of China proper were expected to pay homage to the Central Kingdom by sending regular tribute missions to the imperial capital, thus performing the kowtow to Chinese superiority and keeping the emperor informed of developments in their tribes and kingdoms. It was expected that the "barbarians" (i) would remain docile beneath the Chinese influence, that the emperor could use a "loose reins" policy (chi-mi) of negotiation, marriage ties, and imperial gifts to placate the non-Chinese groups. It was hoped that these approaches would pit the barbarians against one another and prevent their consolidation into a larger military and political confederation which could contend for the Chinese throne. Ultimately the emperor might be forced to resort to warfare, and thus frontier garrisons were established to provide regular surveillance and a quick response if the conditions demanded it. [1]

But of course this system, which seldom worked with the pristine simplicity suggested above, often broke down completely when China was overrun by non-Chinese conquerors who established their own dynasties. Beginning with the Chou dynasty more than a millenium B.C. and culminating in the Manchu conquest of the seventeenth century A.D., non-Chinese ruled all or part of the empire for almost one-half of recorded Chinese history. In the most recent millenium of Chinese history the fraction exceeds one-half by a considerable margin with the Khitan Liao dynasty (947-1125), the Jürched Chin dynasty (1122-1234), the Mongol Yüan dynasty (1271-1368), and the Manchu Ch'ing dynasty (1644-1912). How could the Chinese explain the fact that their world order had been so frequently subverted by the barbarians supposedly under its constraints? The answer was found in the sinification theory. Traditional Chinese literati argued that, while there were defects in frontier policy which permitted barbarian armies to topple Chinese dynasties, the barbarians' ability to govern China depended on accepting the Chinese political structure and its Confucian ideological underpinning. A venerable Chinese saying observes that "though the empire can be conquered on horseback, it cannot be ruled from horseback" (t'ien-hsia sui te-chih ma-shang, pu-k'o-i ma-shang chih). This theory of sinification, in addition to offering solace to Chinese scholar-officials confronting the dilemma of barbarian rule, had a strong basis in the histories of non-Chinese dynasties. All of the dynasties mentioned above,

---

1. These concepts, their derivation, and their relevance for imperial Chinese history are carefully studied in the following two works: Fairbank, Trade and Diplomacy, esp. vol. 1, part 1; and idem, Chinese World Order.

[All books and articles cited in this volume, and all abbreviated titles, are listed alphabetically in Works Cited.]

for instance, eventually adopted substantial aspects of the Chinese political structure, court ritual and ideology, and even language and cultural pursuits.

The sinification interpretation has enjoyed a strong revival in twentieth-century Western sinology. Owen Lattimore and Franz Michael have sought to discover the role of sinification in the pre-conquest governments and societies of non-Chinese invaders. Lattimore's Inner Asian Frontiers of China gives us great insights into the "marginal areas" on the northern and western periphery of the Chinese empire in which many of the invasions were born. Frequently in these marginal areas—and southern Manchuria in the sixteenth and seventeenth centuries is among Lattimore's endless examples—there was a political, economic, and cultural intermingling which set the stage for conquest. Given strong leadership, assistance from Chinese advisers, and a composite economic base which included agriculture, a new centralized administrative order and military structure could emerge. In very summary form, this is Lattimore's interpretation of the rise of Nurhaci and Abahai, the emergence of a Manchu state and military organization, and the conquest of China in the mid-seventeenth century.[2] It is an interpretation which is based on partial sinification, a mixing of Chinese and non-Chinese elements, to produce the ingredients for conquest.

Franz Michael takes a stronger stand in favor of pre-conquest sinification while applying Lattimore's general thesis to the rise of the Manchus in his Origin of Manchu Rule in China. Published in 1942, it was a pioneering work, and most of his observations remain useful thirty years later, even after a great deal of new primary material has been published. Michael's discovery of Abahai's sinified bureaucracy in Mukden in the 1630s; his discussion of the role of Chinese advisers in the service of Nurhaci and Abahai; his emphasis on the administrative role of the Manchu banner system; and his reflections about Manchu clan struggles continuing after the conquest—all stand as key insights into the early Ch'ing period. My own differences with Michael's interpretation, therefore, stem not from these specific elements but rather from his heavy emphasis on the importance of Chinese influence, an emphasis clearly indicated in one of his conclusions: "It was the Chinese system, Chinese officials, and Chinese ideas that enabled the Manchus to conquer China."[3] I suggest that this view overemphasizes the sinification of the Manchus both before and after the conquest, and thus

---

2. Lattimore, Inner Asian Frontiers. See especially chapters 5, 16, and 17.

3. Michael, Origin of Manchu Rule, p. 79. Others have questioned Michael's emphasis on the Ming model for the origins of the Manchu banner system and other aspects of the early Manchu state; see, for instance, Farquhar, "Origin of the Manchus' Mongolian Policy." Michael does qualify his general conclusion somewhat in a later chapter by observing Abahai's reliance on Chin precedents and by noting the general Manchu fear of assimilation, but nevertheless he continues to underscore the total Manchu adoption of the Chinese political structure and ideology (Michael, Origin of Manchu Rule, pp. 99–108).

misses the ongoing tension between sinification and Manchu dominance, a phenomenon which lasted well into the K'ang-hsi reign. It also underplays the enduring importance of pre-conquest Manchu institutions, the political leadership of the Manchus, and the widespread commitment of Manchus to their tradition. These points will be developed in chapters 2–7 as we explore the origins of the Oboi regency, both before and after the conquest of 1644, and investigate the key policies of the regency.

The other major interpretation of the Manchu conquest is derived from the strident anti-Manchu literature of Chinese revolutionaries in the era of the 1911 Revolution. A common theme in the revolutionary press of the period was anti-Manchu racism. Tsou Jung's famous book, The Revolutionary Army (Ko-ming chün), reflects this trend clearly: "Sweep away thousands of years of despotism, cast off thousands of years of slavishness, exterminate the five million bestial Manchus, wash away the humiliation of 260 years of oppression and sorrow, cruelty, and tyranny, turn the Chinese soil into a clean land and all the sons and grandsons of the Yellow Emperor into George Washingtons."[4] The anti-Manchu fever spread not only through the ranks of radicals, but also to many reformers as well, the cultivated and articulate Liang Ch'i-ch'ao being perhaps the best example. Liang reprinted and distributed thousands of copies of Wang Hsiu-ch'u's "A Memoir of a Ten Days' Massacre at Yangchow" (Yang-chou shih-jih chi), which described in graphic detail the rapes, executions, and looting which are alleged to have occurred when the Manchu army took Yangchow (20–29 May 1645).[5] The Manchus were thus stereotyped and vilified. They were, in the eyes of many revolutionaries, barbarian reactionaries when it came to domestic reform, and cowardly traitors when it came to foreign affairs. As the revolutionaries' scapegoat for the preceding century of troubles, the

---

4. Translation from Rankin, Early Chinese Revolutionaries, p. 18. The strong anti-Manchu propaganda of the Ming loyalist movements in the seventeenth century was revived by secret societies in the early part of the nineteenth century. The Triads in particular relied heavily on the slogan "overthrow the Ch'ing and restore the Ming" (fan-ch'ing fu-Ming) in their ritual and propaganda. See Novikov, "Anti-Manchu Propaganda," pp. 49-63.

Michael Gasster has provided an excellent review of anti-Manchu themes in T'ung-meng-hui writings of the pre-1911 Revolution period. By examining the T'ung-meng-hui program and the writings of Wang Ching-wei in particular, Gasster has pointed out three aspects of the anti-Manchu propaganda: "First, they had conquered China by military force, plundering widely and slaughtering wantonly, and once in power they had carried out discriminatory policies that relegated the Chinese people to an inferior position in society and had visited upon them a host of other oppressive measures. Second, they were foreign barbarians, an inferior race. Third, they were now attempting to perpetrate a gigantic hoax by posing as reformers who wanted to save China, chiefly by introducing constitutionalism" (Gasster, Chinese Intellectuals, p. 69; see also pp. 65-105, passim).

5. See Chang Hao, Liang Ch'i-ch'ao and Intellectual Transition, pp. 126-27. A translation is available: Wang Hsiu-ch'u, "Memoir of a Ten Days' Massacre."

Manchus were a useful target: they could be easily identified as the
cause of China's ills, and could serve as a negative rallying point for
the various revolutionary movements in China and Japan.

Several scholars, in addition to Lattimore and Michael, have raised
opposition to this portrayal of the Manchus. Mary Wright has shown the
emergence of a "Sino-Manchu amalgam" in the eighteenth and nineteenth
centuries, the joint struggle of Manchus and Chinese against rebellion
and imperialism in the mid-nineteenth century, and the existence of
prominent reformers among the Manchus in the decade preceding the
Revolution of 1911. While Wright has agreed that there were indeed
some reactionaries among the Manchus at the end of the Ch'ing, and
that the effort of Prince Ch'un to revive the Manchu power in government gave some credence to the anti-Manchu propaganda in the 1908–
11 period, she has concluded that the revolutionaries greatly overstated
their case.[6] Nevertheless, the thesis that the Manchus were reactionaries and traitors has been perpetuated in both Kuomintang and Commu-
nist writings about the late Ch'ing period, and has colored much of the
popular thinking about the Ch'ing dynasty.[7]

For our purposes, most of the arguments of the anti-Manchu movement of the early twentieth century have limited value except as an explanation for previous historical writings about the early Ch'ing period.
Even the conclusion that the Manchus were ruthless and rapacious invaders—a conclusion supported by abundant evidence from the 1640s
and 1650s—must be modified by observing the role of Chinese commanders and Chinese troops in the conquest of the Chinese empire. The
anti-Manchu propagandists did not reveal the violent episodes perpetra-
ted by Chinese bannermen like Hung Ch'eng-ch'ou, Shang K'o-hsi, and
Wu San-kuei. Nor did the propagandists dwell on the fact that the Ming
dynasty fell to Chinese rebels, most notably Chang Hsien-chung and Li
Tzu-ch'eng, before the Manchu conquest occurred. The policy of terror adopted by Chang Hsien-chung in Szechwan during 1645–46 surely
rivals the massacres in the central coastal region among early Ch'ing
horror stories.[8] Brutality was a characteristic of the times, not restricted ethnically to the Manchus, but openly practiced by both Chinese
and Manchus in this turbulent era of dynastic collapse.

There is only one facet of the anti-Manchu literature which, if politically defused and chronologically limited to the early Ch'ing period,
has validity as an antidote to the sinification approach. In the twenty-
five years following the conquest of 1644, and particularly during the
Dorgon and Oboi regencies, it is quite true that Chinese were frequently oppressed in the interest of consolidating and protecting Manchu rule.

6. See Wright, Last Stand of Chinese Conservatism, pp. 51-56; and idem,
China in Revolution, pp. 21-23. Also see Gasster, "Reform and Revolution,"
pp. 72-77.

7. Wright, Last Stand of Chinese Conservatism, p. 51.

8. See Parsons, Peasant Rebellions, pp. 176-78.

There is ample evidence of forceful removal of Chinese commoners
from their lands to accommodate Manchu military policies, of harsh
retaliation against presumed threats against Manchu rule from Chinese
scholar-officials, and of the promotion of Manchu officials and Manchu
institutions over their Chinese counterparts. Manchu dominance and
its corollary, the submission of Chinese, was the central point behind
most policies of the early 1660s. But a major theme in this book is
that the Oboi period represented the extreme expression of Manchu-
oriented governance in the early Ch'ing dynasty, that it was—if we may
adapt the title of Mary Wright's famous work—the "last stand of Manchu conservatism." The K'ang-hsi Emperor, though he maintained his
Manchu loyalties and relied heavily on Manchu advisers, labored to
overcome the legacy of his regents; in doing so he laid the foundations
for the "Sino-Manchu amalgam" of the late Ch'ing. In short, while the
revolutionary propaganda may give us a clue about Manchu politics
shortly after the conquest, it tells us more about the revolutionaries
than about the Manchus in the early twentieth century.

We encounter sinification and Manchu dominance, therefore, in the
years when they were real and live options, when the political world of
imperial China was unstable and uncertain of its future course. While
it is the historian's role to bring retrospective order to the events of
the past, we must not overlook the turmoil and anxieties of this era.
The late Ming rebellions and the conquest battles of the Manchus destroyed huge amounts of cultivated land and brought death to millions
of Chinese. A fairly good indication of the extent of devastation is found
in the land tax registers which report the amount of arable land which
can be taxed by the imperial government. In 1602 the registers recorded 1,161,894,881 mou (or 176,000,000 acres), but by 1645 the total had
plummeted to 405,690,504 mou (or 66,800,000 acres).[9] Fighting continued long after the Ch'ing defeated the last Ming loyalist in Burma in
1662; under the reign of K'ang-hsi, China experienced another half-century of massive military operations. In two of these military struggles,
the rebellion of the feudatory princes in south China and the invasions
of Galdan and his Ölöd Mongols, K'ang-hsi's troops were fighting for
the very existence of the Ch'ing dynasty. His success paved the way to
the relative peace of the eighteenth century, but that peace was bought
by the blood and anxiety of the seventeenth century.
    Intensifying this military insecurity were the variety of Chinese re-
sponses to the Manchu conquest. Some Ming military officers, as observed earlier, surrendered themselves and their troops to the Manchus prior to 1644. Enrolled as Chinese bannermen in the Manchu military structure known as the eight-banner system (pa-ch'i chih-tu),

9. See Ho, Studies on Population of China, p. 102. Also see appendix 4 of
this volume. Late Ming and early Ch'ing registration problems may also account
for some of this drop in registered tax lands.

these Chinese provided considerable assistance in planning and executing the conquest. Several Ming officials in the metropolitan and provincial bureaucracies, while serving their dynasty until 1644, quickly surrendered after the Manchus took Peking. These officials, responding to Dorgon's offer of amnesty and continued political office, were later named "two-dynasty officials" (er-ch'en) by Ch'ien-lung, who sought a new definition of loyalty. But many Ming civil officials, military officers, and scholars refused to accept service under the Manchus, and thousands perished supporting Ming princes in central and southern China in the decade after the conquest. Survivors from the ranks of the Ming loyalists included outstanding philosophers like Huang Tsung-hsi, Wang Fu-chih, and Ku Yen-wu, who steadfastly refused official posts in the Ch'ing dynasty and devoted their lives to scholarship instead. Some of the loyalist survivors continued their struggle against the Manchus long after the conquest, relying primarily on concealed attacks in their prose and poetry.

It is against this background of military insecurity and the variety of Chinese responses to the Ch'ing conquest that we must explore the policies of the Oboi period. Of great importance to our understanding of the regents' response to these conditions is that they had themselves fought the battles of conquest under Abahai and Dorgon. It was their victory. This outlook sparked their criticism of post-conquest developments and it defined the range of political alternatives open to them in the 1660s. A single question seems to have pervaded their political thinking: "What did we fight for?" Politics was the extension of warfare into another arena, and the regents seldom concealed this notion. In expressing these views, however, the regents were not speaking for themselves alone, but rather for a Manchu conquest elite with whom they had close connections.

Since this term, "Manchu conquest elite," will be often used in explaining various facets of the Oboi regency, a brief definition may help at this point. The term is meant to denote an elite corps of Manchu officers and is restricted in time to the period from the 1600s through the 1660s. The Manchu conquest elite includes the Imperial Clansmen, officers in the Imperial Household and the Imperial Bodyguard, and all Manchus holding the rank of company captain (tso-ling) and above in the banner system. The upper echelons of this elite were the Imperial Princes, the Ministers of the Imperial Household, the Chamberlains of the Imperial Bodyguard, the lieutenant-generals and deputy lieutenant-generals of the Manchu banners, and all Manchus holding high metropolitan office. It was a small elite, comprising fewer than two thousand individuals who resided in the Peking area when not on campaigns, garrison duty, or hunts. Almost all of them had fought in the military operations related to the conquest; and the majority were limited in background and language to their Manchu tradition. While a few of this Manchu conquest elite had civil bureaucratic experience and close contact with regular Chinese officials, most came from purely military backgrounds and their most frequent Chinese associates were Chinese banner officers.

The four regents of the 1660s represented the upper echelons of this elite, and they shared the esprit which came from commanding the Manchu cavalry and infantry. Contrary to the Chinese tradition, they were committed to military control over political institutions; in the early Ch'ing context, this meant the dominance of the Manchu conquest elite over the Chinese official and local elites. Military control meant reviving the importance of pre-conquest Manchu institutions, particularly the Council of Deliberative Officials (i-cheng ta-ch'en), a cabinet of Manchu commanders which had figured prominently under Abahai. It meant exaggerating the weaknesses of the Ming dynasty, implying that the corruption of the late Ming proved the inherent weakness of Chinese institutions without appropriate military supervision. Finally, it meant an effort to spread Manchu martial values beyond the Chinese bannermen to the Chinese officials and commoners of the empire. In this venture, the regents found their power in the Manchu banner system; their authority was derived from their own interpretation of the legacy of Nurhaci and Abahai, and from the support of the Manchu conquest elite.

The regents' mission took on a sense of urgency in the 1660s, for they were older men (we do not know their exact ages, but it is likely that they were in their late fifties or sixties), as were most of the others in the upper ranks of the Manchu conquest elite. A new generation of Manchus was emerging whose military training and experience was complemented by greater familiarity with Chinese language, culture, and political traditions. Several Manchus, for example, successfully passed the highest level of the Chinese civil service examination in the 1650s and received the degree of chin-shih ("presented scholar"). The regents reacted strongly against these tendencies, and perhaps the psychohistorian would tell us that the regents were equating their own approaching deaths with the death of the Manchu conquest. [10] But lacking the expertise or the evidence to support this latter notion, I will only suggest that the regents, and much of the Manchu conquest elite, were experiencing the anxieties of a generation gap. They could see the emergence of sinification among some of the Manchu youth, and they surely saw it in the policies of the young Shun-chih Emperor who preceeded them. The only cure, from the regents' point of view, was a heavy dose of Manchu authoritarianism for the edification of Chinese and Manchus alike.

The regents were not alone among the early Ch'ing sovereigns in their authoritarian approach to policymaking. The regimes of the K'ang-hsi, Yung-cheng, and Ch'ien-lung emperors have been described by Harold Kahn in language that well echoes the regents' concerns:

10. This theory has been proposed as an explanation for Mao Tse-tung's role during the Chinese Cultural Revolution of 1966-69; see Lifton, Revolutionary Immortality.

[Their] _forte_ was action, organization, and vigorous exercise
of the imperial prerogatives. Perhaps more than previous dynasties, they recognized the potentialities and made the most of
their position. And if their pronouncements on rulership do not
enrich the corpus of Confucian state doctrine, they do reveal the
concerns of tough-minded authoritarians bent on defining their
power in terms that could not fail to impress even the most ob-
tuse bureaucrat. . . . The task was to exorcise the specter of
destructive Ming factionalism, rationalize the Manchu overlord-
ship, assert the primacy of the emperor in matters of taste, administration, and policy, and carefully circumscribe the sphere
of official criticism—in effect, to neutralize the power of officialdom.[11]

So far the description fits the regents perfectly, but Kahn goes on to
point out that these three emperors were, at least nominally, Confucian
idealists. They had been schooled in the "historical models of imperial
perfection" and they "aspired to the same perfection."[12] How different
were the regents of the K'ang-hsi Emperor who rested content in their
role as Manchu authoritarians and who dispensed with even the facade of
Confucian idealism. For them the imperial institution could be stripped
of its Confucian vestments and used to fulfill and protect Manchu interests.

A related characteristic of the High Ch'ing emperors—one which
several historians have observed—was their penchant for "direct, ver-
tical rule."[13] These emperors sought to cut through routine bureaucratic channels and, in the interests of efficiency and information, to
confront officials individually and directly. Through an enormous expenditure of energy and time, they endeavored to exercise personal rule
over the huge and cumbersome bureaucracy, to move from specific encounters to more general policies, and to restore the ideal of rule by
human relations and moral example. Once again, the regents shared
only part of this approach to Ch'ing governance: they were committed
to governmental efficiency. By reforming institutions and personnel
policies, the regents tried to foster better communication between themselves and their officials and ultimately to instill greater obedience to
Manchu rule. But here they were limited by almost total reliance on
their Manchu associates and Chinese bannermen and by their unfamil-
iarity with the Chinese officialdom and society. The regents, having
just left a period in which Chinese were the enemy, were not inclined
to engage in prolonged personal encounters with their regular Chinese

---

11. Kahn, _Monarchy in the Emperor's Eyes_, pp. 7-8.
12. Ibid., p. 8.
13. This term and its implications are taken from Wakeman, "High Ch'ing."
Similar observations are found in Spence, _Ts'ao Yin_, and Silas Wu, _Communi-
cation and Imperial Control_.

officials. Instead, the regents ruled by law and military force and
seldom tried face-to-face suasion with those outside their immediate
group of associates.

Given the regents' attachment to law and force, can we identify their
approach to governance with the legalist and authoritarian tradition in
Chinese history? At a fairly high level of abstraction, the regents do
seem to reflect certain aspects of this tradition. They were tough and
autocratic not just because they came from rigidly disciplined Manchu
backgrounds, but also because they felt that the times called to authoritarianism. The memories of the late Ming and the Shun-chih reign
were irksome to the regents both because they were dominated by Chinese and because they exemplified weak imperial guidance and corrupt
government. Like many founding emperors—Ch'in Shih-huang-ti and
Ming Hung-wu, for example—the regents felt that toughness was a good
antidote to the decay and chaos which preceded their reigns.

When one probes beneath this level of abstraction, however, and
examines the policies and motivations of the regents in more detail,
the parallels to traditional legalism are less distinct. The regents
were locked, by their experience and inclination, to Manchu tradition
and Manchu precedent. They did not see themselves as heirs of any
Chinese tradition, legalist or Confucian. Ming Hung-wu was the hero
of the Shun-chih Emperor, not of the regents in the 1660s.[14] To them
almost anything defined by the adjective "Ming" had to be approached
with utmost caution and suspicion. Just as legalism has limited value
in explaining the motivations of the regents, it is of minimal use in understanding the nature of their policies. The regents were authoritarians, to be sure, but their authoritarianism manifested itself differently
as the regents dealt with various institutions, personnel, and problems.
They acted as sophisticated reformers when restructuring Manchu political institutions, but as harsh critics when drastically altering the
Chinese bureaucratic structure. They were conservatives in their foreign and military policies, dutifully preserving the precedents of the
pre-conquest period, and content to consolidate post-conquest gains without risking any dangerous new ventures. They were militant autocrats
when they turned to provincial China, brooking no opposition and vigorously
promoting obedience to Manchu rule. We shall comprehend this multi-
faceted authoritarianism, therefore, only by seeing it in the context of the
early Ch'ing period and understanding its dependence on the Manchu heritage. Insistence on a "legalist" or "dynastic cycle" interpretation of the
Oboi regency obscures the complex web of motivations and actions which
occurred in this period. Such an interpretation also frustrates comparisons between the "authoritarian" regents and the "authoritarian" emperors
who followed them. In misses the fact that the regents' passionate attachment to the Manchu tradition limited their political options. By contrast,

14. See chapter 3 for Shun-chih's evaluation of previous emperors and his
conclusion that Ming Hung-wu was the finest emperor in Chinese history.

the High Ch'ing rulers mixed passion with perspective: the Manchu heritage was not only a source of identity, but also offered a useful viewpoint from which they could oversee major reforms. Such reforms augmented the poser of Ch'ing emperors, but they also moderated Sino-Manchu tensions and put the Ch'ing dynasty on a more stable foundation.

Interwoven with the various factors mentioned previously—the tension between sinification and Manchu dominance, the anxieties of the conquest era, the role of the Manchu conquest elite, and the question of authoritarianism—is the matter of factionalism. Factionalism was rampant in seventeenth-century politics, and there were factions around emperors, around eunuchs, around military strongmen, and around regents. During the first quarter-century after the conquest, no fewer than six factions successively came to power in Peking: the Dorgon faction (1643-50), the Jirgalang faction (1651-52), the Shun-chih faction (1653-61), the Joint Regents' faction (1661-66), the Oboi faction (1667-69), and the Songgotu-Mingju faction (1669-early 1670s). Severe policy shifts accompanied each new regime in power, leaving the historian with a relatively clearcut progression, but augmenting the anxieties for Chinese and Manchu statesmen of the time.

The prevalence of factionalism in the early Ch'ing period raises some questions about authority and power in the politics of imperial China. During most dynasties a compromise was developed between the altruistic Chinese concept of sovereignty and the factional allegiances which perpetuated imperial power. Theoretically, the legitimacy of an emperor (or of his regents) was determined by holding the "heavenly mandate" (t'ien-ming) and by providing protection, prosperity, and justice for all subjects. The formation of factions (tang) was generally forbidden on the grounds that factional interests were selfish and tended to restrict the proper exercise of imperial prerogatives. The Ch'ing dynasty was no exception, and injunctions against factionalism were issued from the Shun-chih reign on, capped by Yung-cheng's obsession with this matter in the 1720s. Nevertheless, most rulers exempted themselves from their own admonitions and relied on some degree of factional support to guarantee their power. Imperial relatives, palace assistants, and powerful civil and military officials often developed close and informal ties with their sovereign. A symbiotic relationship ensued as the ruler and his factional allies protected the interest of one another, while using proclamations and often force to discourage the formation of other cliques which could contend for political power.

The six factions which we shall explore offer important insights into the early Ch'ing political world and into the major personalities of the period. They all aspired to ultimate political control, achieved it for a time, and then lost influence to new contenders. In every instance except the Shun-chih faction, the leaders were men of unbridled ambition. They struggled in a world in which politics and war bore strong similarities. Not only were many politicians drawn from the ranks of professional soldiers, but the stakes were the same. The victors could rise to absolute power in a despotic system; while for the vanquished, the mildest penalty was humiliation and loss of rank; more often it was death.

The theme of sinification versus Manchu dominance must be observed against this backdrop of factionalism. In fact, in the two short-lived Jirgalang and Oboi factions, the brutal struggle for political power precluded them from taking a forthright stand on this larger issue. In the case of the other four factions, which maintained a somewhat longer hold over the Ch'ing hierarchy, the theme emerged more clearly as these regimes had sufficient opportunity to register their positions across the spectrum of sinification and Manchu dominance. It is clearest of all, however, in the policies of the Joint Regents' faction of Soni, Suksaha, Ebilun, and Oboi, in their period of collective governance spanning the years 1661-66. They sought to create an order in which the Manchu system, Manchu officials, and Manchu ideas held undisputed control over Ch'ing China. And thus we have an intriguing variation on the Chinese saying previously mentioned: "Though the empire can be conquered on horseback, it cannot be ruled from horseback." Because these regents, despite the fact that the conquest appeared to be over, seemed determined at times to climb back into the saddle.

2   The Genesis of the Regency, I: 1580–1643

For the historian, as for the Joint Regents' faction, the Imperial Will of the Shun-chih Emperor, issued in 1661, offers a fitting overture to the regency. The Will, enumerating fourteen "sins" of the Shun-chih Emperor, began in the following fashion:

Having, myself, only very limited virtues, I hand on the great inheritance which I held for eighteen years. Since I personally took over the government, I have been unable to imitate the majestic examples of T'ai-tsu [Nurhaci] and T'ai-tsung [Abahai] in making laws and regulations and in choosing men for administrative posts. Because I have procrastinated and been negligent in my duties, I have gradually come to practice the customs of the Chinese. The pure and honest old system [of the Manchus] has been changed daily. Because of all this the dynasty's government has not reached its potential and the peoples' livelihood has not been improved. This was one of my sins.[1]

While it is uncertain whether this section of the Imperial Will was forged, like much of the rest of the document (see chapter 3 and appendix 1), the regents could not have asked for a better statement of their position. Nurhaci and Abahai were restored to heroic status. The Shun-chih Emperor was portrayed as a whining incompetent. And the regents could begin hammering out their decisions as proud representatives of the Manchu conquest elite.

The Shun-chih Will thus points in two directions: toward the future policies of the Joint Regents' faction, but also back to the reigns of Abahai and Nurhaci. It is in this Manchu past that our story begins, with the families who produced the four men who comprised the Joint Regents' faction. The regents all traced their genealogies to the time of Nurhaci in the late sixteenth and early seventeenth centuries, when their forebears were prominent warriors and, in some cases, major factors in the early Manchu political structure and cultural tradition. The regents themselves emerged as active figures in the 1620s and 1630s, working their way to the upper ranks of the conquest elite while also developing the individual skills and characteristics which would differentiate their roles in the post-conquest period. This chapter, therefore, deals with the early experiences and values which have a general bearing on the

1. SC Shih-lu, ch. 144, pp. 2a-b.

Oboi regency; the next chapter is concerned with the more specific
events which occasioned the formation of the Joint Regents' faction in
the period of 1644-61.

FOUR FAMILIES IN THE REIGN OF NURHACI

Nurhaci (1559-1626) was a member of the Aisin Gioro clan, later the
Ch'ing imperial clan, which held a hereditary tribal chieftanship in the
Chien-chou group of Jürched peoples. Although his ancestry can be
traced back to the early fourteenth century (perhaps even earlier to the
Yüan dynasty), the direct context for the rise of Nurhaci is found in the
late sixteenth century. At this time the Chien-chou Jürched lived in
the area north of the Yalu River and east of the Liaotung agricultural
basin which was populated by Chinese. In 1574 Nurhaci's grandfather
and father, Giocangga and Taksi, allied themselves with the Ming general Li Ch'eng-liang, and together they attacked and captured Wang Kao,
leader of a large group of Chien-chou Jürched known as the Right Branch.
In late 1582 the alliance of Li, Giocangga, and Taksi was revived as they
jointly moved on Wang Kao's son, Atai. During the attack, both Giocangga and Taksi were killed, probably in the course of the battle, but
possibly by Li Ch'eng-liang seeking to eliminate several Chien-chou
chieftains in a single operation. Nurhaci chose to believe the latter
interpretation and, like Chinggis Khan four centuries earlier, began
his career as conqueror by seeking to avenge the deaths of his forebears. For the time being he concentrated his efforts on various Jürched tribes and chieftains on the pretext of eliminating those who had
complicity in the deaths of his father and grandfather. Until 1618 Nurhaci maintained ties with the Ming, sometimes going personally on tribute missions to the Ming court, where he received silver in return for
presents of furs, pearls, and ginseng.[2]

From the early 1580s to the late 1610s, Nurhaci gradually extended
his grasp over the Chien-chou tribes and the Hai-hsi Jürched tribes to
the north. The four main Hai-hsi tribes submitted only after prolonged
warfare: the Hada tribe was conquered in 1601; the Hoifa in 1607; the
Ula in 1613; and the Yehe, the northernmost tribe of the Hai-hsi group,
in 1619. These were perilous years for Nurhaci, and more than once
he narrowly escaped assassination attempts.[3] But Nurhaci persisted,

---

2. Information in English on early Manchu history and the rise of Nurhaci is
found in Michael, Origin of Manchu Rule; relevant biographies in Hummel; Wada,
"Some Problems Concerning the Rise of T'ai-tsu." I have not attempted a detailed analysis of this period, but further information can be found in the Japa-
nese and Chinese language works of Wada, Kanda, and Meng; some of these are
cited later in this book. Nurhaci's practice of sending tribute missions to the
Ming court was halted in 1609.

Other new information concerning the preconquest history of the Manchus
may be found in Ch'en Chieh-hsien, "The Value of the Early Manchu Archives";
Li, "Analysis of Questions Relating to the Imperial Succession"; and Ch'en Chieh-
hsien, "Chiu Man-chou tang shu-lüeh."

3. See Wada, "Some Problems Concerning the Rise of T'ai-tsu."

and at his heavily fortified ancestral town of Hetu Ala (later Hsing-ching, about a hundred miles east of Shen-yang or Mukden), he established his base of operations and began to lay the military, administrative, and economic groundwork for the later moves against the Ming itself.[4] In 1607 he took the title "Wise and Respected Emperor" (Sure Kundulen Khan) from Mongol tributaries who had come to Hetu Ala, thus indicating his grander imperial visions for the first time.[5] As he labored to weld the tribes into a strong Manchu military machine, Nurhaci relied on the loyal support of several Manchu families who assisted and complemented the efforts of those in the imperial Aisin Gioro clan.

Three of the regents' families began their service under Nurhaci before the turn of the seventeenth century. Oboi's grandfather was Solgo, a member of the Guwalgiya clan and a tribal leader. In 1588 Solgo led five hundred of his tribesmen to join Nurhaci, thus linking his fortunes with the young leader and providing Nurhaci one of the toughest warrior families of the day. Solgo's second son, and Oboi's uncle, was Fiongdon (1564-1620), who rose to become one of Nurhaci's chief generals and councillors. After exposing a plot against the leader's life, Fiongdon was given Nurhaci's eldest granddaughter as a wife and was appointed a judge (jarguci) with the responsibility of arbitrating disputes. In 1615 Fiongdon was named one of the "five high officials" (wu ta-ch'en), who ranked immediately behind the eight imperial princes (beile) and assisted Nurhaci and the princes in governmental deliberations. A year later, in recognition of his successes on the battlefields, Fiongdon was appointed commander of the left-wing army, and led the attacks against the Ming in 1618-19. A biographer has observed that "Fiongdon was generally conceded to have been Nurhaci's most valuable associate, and successive emperors down to the Ch'ien-lung period outdid one another in paying him honor."[6] Oboi's father, Uici (d. 1635?), was an illustrious soldier in his own right, though somewhat overshadowed by the fame of his elder brother. He was instrumental in several campaigns against Mongol tribes and Ming detachments in the years 1624-34; and Abahai eventually appointed him commander of the guard units left at the Manchu capital when the main force was engaged elsewhere. When Uici retired in 1634, he was recognized as an Eminent Statesman, given servants, and assigned a captain as his personal attendant.[7]

Ebilun's father, Eidu (1562-1621), was a contemporary of Fiongdon, and their careers bear strong similarities. Eidu's family was of the Niohuru clan which had settled in the eastern section of the Ch'ang-pai-shan (the Long White Mountains, considered the sacred home of the Manchu ancestors). His parents were murdered in a feud when Eidu was a

4. Prior to 1603 Nurhaci's capital was Hulun Hada, located to the southwest of Hetu Ala.

5. See Farquhar, "Origins of the Manchus' Mongolian Policy."

6. Hummel, p. 247.

7. Biographies of Uici are found in CSLC, ch. 4, pp. 8b-9a; PCTC, ch. 135, pp. 22a-23a.

child, and he escaped under the protection of a neighbor. According to
one story, when Eidu was twelve he killed the murderer and then found
shelter in the home of his aunt, the wife of a Jürched tribal chieftain.
In 1580 Nurhaci stopped at the chieftain's home and was greatly impressed by the eighteen-year-old Eidu. Eidu was placed in Nurhaci's
service and remained a close comrade for the duration of his life.
Like Fiongdon, Eidu distinguished himself in several battles and was,
in 1615, appointed one of the "five high officials" in Nurhaci's administration. Indicative of the stern military paternalism with which Eidu
raised his family was his treatment of his insolent second son, Daki,
who was married to one of Nurhaci's daughters. As George Kennedy
has phrased it: "one day, at a family banquet to which all his sons were
gathered, he seized the arrogant Daki and, drawing his dagger, addressed the assembly on the duty of respect toward superiors. Then,
warning them that all who disobeyed would 'spill their blood on the same
dagger,' he led Daki into a side room and put him to death. This un-
natural act made a profound impression on Nurhaci who called Eidu his
most patriotic officer."[8] Prior to his death in 1621 Eidu served as a
high-ranking officer in the Manchu military, and captured several Ming
fortresses. In addition to his many honors, Eidu had been given one of
Nurhaci's sisters as his wife.[9]

Although less is known about Soni's father, Sose, than about the families of Oboi and Ebilun, circumstantial evidence points to an interesting variant on the loyal warrior pattern. In Ch'ing biographical collections, Sose and two of his sons, Soni and Hife (d. 1652), are closely
associated with the development of the Manchu language under Nurhaci.
The family was of the Heseri clan and were members of the Hai-hsi
Jürched tribe known as the Hada. They originally lived in the village
of Duyengge, to the northwest of Hetu Ala. Duyengge was also the ancestral home of Erdeni (d. 1623), founder of the Manchu written language. Perhaps because Duyengge was located fairly close to the Chinese population in the south Manchurian plain and to the Mongol tribes
of western Manchuria, Erdeni developed knowledge of the Chinese and
Mongol languages. When he joined Nurhaci, probably in the 1590s, Erdeni was appointed an interpreter and given the title of "teacher" (baksi).
In 1599 Nurhaci ordered Erdeni to establish a Manchu written language
so that the Jürched would no longer have to rely totally on the Mongol
language. Erdeni then began to create the Manchu language on a modified form of the Mongol alphabet.[10]

Although Erdeni was to leave a lasting impression on Manchu culture because of his newly developed language, he himself was executed

8. Hummel, p. 221.
9. Biographies of Eidu are found in Hummel, p. 221, and CSLC, ch. 4, pp.
1b-3a.
10. Even after the creation of a Manchu langauge, the Jürched continued to
rely heavily on ideas and institutions derived from the Mongol language and experience. See Farquhar, "Origins of the Manchus' Mongol Policy."

by Nurhaci in 1623 on a charge of accumulating and stealing valuables.
But Abahai, deciding to rescue Erdeni's reputation, ordered that he
would be posthumously attached to the Heseri clan, into the family of
Sose, Soni, and Hife.[11] Since we do know that these three had facility
in Chinese, Mongol, and Manchu languages, Abahai's action would seem
to imply that they may also have been involved in the early stages of the
Manchu written language. Sose probably surrendered his family to Nurhaci during the 1599-1601 wars against the Hada tribe, and possibly assisted his fellow villager Erdeni from that time forth. In any case, the
linguistic abilities of Hife and Soni were to have decisive influence on
their later careers in Abahai's civil bureaucracy.[12]

In contrast to the families of the other regents, Suksaha's family belonged to the Yehe tribe of the north, which put up a prolonged struggle
against Nurhaci before finally submitting in 1619. Suksaha's father,
Suna (d. 1648), was related to one of the key figures in the resistance
to Nurhaci, the prince Gintaisi (d. 1619). Gintaisi tried desperately to
hold off the Nurhaci onslaught, and allied himself with Mongols, various
Jürched tribes, and even with Ming garrison troops in his valiant but
futile effort.[13] After Gintaisi's death, Suna and many other Yehe leaders surrendered to Nurhaci and were enrolled in his military organization. Suna had a checkered career after his surrender. It began well
enough as Suna married an imperial princess, received a company command, and led several successful assaults against Ming forces in Liaotung, Mongol tribes, and Korean troops south of the Yalu River. But
he seems to have had a vicious streak. In 1628 he led a detachment
against some Chahar Mongols, who quickly surrendered and promised
allegiance to the Manchus. Instead of dealing with them peacefully,
Suna executed the Mongol males and captured their wives and concubines. For this ruthless slaughter he was severely reprimanded but
was permitted to keep his ranks. On another occasion, after a successful attack on Ming towns north of the Great Wall, Suna was accused of
hiding the population registers (perhaps to conceal yet another incident
of mass murder) and was stripped of his ranks. Still later he was appointed to the highest command of all, a lieutenant-generalship in the
Mongol Plain White Banner. In this post he successfully led his troops
against the Ming in Chihli province and against several Korean towns.
But on one of the Korean expeditions, Suna disobeyed orders and returned by an improper route (probably to engage in looting on the side);
for this he lost his command and was reduced to the rank of company
captain, a post he held until his death in 1648.[14]

11. See Erdeni biography in Hummel, p. 226.
12. What little information is available about Sose is found in the biographies
of Soni and Hife; see CSLC, ch. 4, p. 11a; ch. 6, p. 14a. Further information
about the role of Soni and Hife, particularly about their language expertise, will
be found later in this chapter.
13. Gintaisi biography in Hummel, pp. 269-70.
14. Biographies of Suna are found in CSK, lieh-chuan 36, pp. 3b-4a; PCTC,
ch. 156, pp. 20a-22b.

The families of the four regents, therefore, contributed a range of talents to Nurhaci's cause. Suksaha's father, like most of the conquest elite, served the emerging Manchu nation as a military officer. The families of Oboi and Ebilun, in addition to their famous military activities, were also close associates of Nurhaci and assisted in the administration of the emerging Manchu state. Soni's family, because of their linguistic abilities, helped to codify the Manchu traditions in law and history. Much of Nurhaci's success can be attributed to his recognition and cultivation of such talents. What permitted Nurhaci and, later, Abahai, to use the support of families like those of the four future regents so effectively was the Manchu eight-banner system in which these families were enrolled. This system, which had similarities to Mongol organizations but which probably developed independently,[15] was instituted by Nurhaci in 1601. In that year Nurhaci organized his troops into companies of 300 men (called niru, and later changed to the Chinese, tso-ling), which were in turn attached to four larger units known as banners (gūsa, later changed to the Chinese, ch'i). These banners were distinguished by their yellow, white, blue, and red flags. As his fighting forces increased, Nurhaci developed new companies, still at the same size of 300 men, and attached them to the various banners. In 1615 he added four more banners to make a total of eight, the new ones maintaining the original colors but being distinguished by borders on the flags. Like all other Manchu families under Nurhaci, those of the future regents were included in this eight-banner system.[16] Ebilun and Oboi were attached to the Bordered Yellow Banner; Soni to the Plain Yellow Banner; and Suksaha to the Plain White Banner.

Although we know nothing about the early lives of these four Manchus (not even their dates of birth), it is certain they devoted much of their youth to military training within their banner units. Here they spent years of arduous practice, both on the training fields and on hunts, learning to use the formidable Manchu arsenal, which included swords, daggers, spears, axes, and, most importantly, the bow and arrow. The Manchu bow was short and compact, recurved in design for extra cast, and propelled a wooden arrow with an iron ferrule. It probably was very effective at short range when used by the footsoldier, but was especially suited for deployment on horseback. Much of the bannermen's training centered on shooting arrows from horseback, endeavoring to strike fixed targets or to bring down game such as the deer which were plentiful in central Manchuria. In the hunts banner companies stalked game in units, under the orders of battlefield commanders. This preparation in Manchu martial arts readied the young Manchus for the great

15. See Farquhar, "Origins of the Manchus' Mongol Policy."
16. Useful introductions to the origin and evolution of the banner system are found in: Hummel, p. 596; PCTC, ch. 1, passim; Fang, "Early Manchu Military Forces"; Meng, "Pa-ch'i chih-tu k'ao-shih"; Spence, Ts'ao Yin, pp. 2-18; Lee, Manchurian Frontier, pp. 24-46; Ch'en Wen-shih, "Man-chou pa-ch'i niu-lu."

battles ahead, while it also toughened them into stern and proud disci-
plinarians, forging the military values of the Manchu conquest elite.

But the banner system was more than a military organization. It
was also the basic Manchu administrative structure and was later expanded to include Mongols and Chinese as well. Enrolled in the company (niru) were the common soldiers and their families. Company
registers monitored the overall growth of Manchu population, while also
recording the size of the Manchu army. The company registers, therefore, facilitated·control of the entire populace and provided an accurate
basis for distributing wages and land grants. At the top of Nurhaci's
banner system were eight princes (beile), who were selected from among
his own sons. Each prince was entrusted with the military and civil affairs of those under one of the banners. Nurhaci also ordered these
eight princes to meet together to discuss major military and political
policies; collectively they were known as "the princes who deliberate on
government" (i-cheng wang). Beneath this superstructure of princes,
Nurhaci established the beginnings of a Manchu civil and judicial administration. In 1615 he appointed the previously mentioned "five high
officials," including Eidu and Fiongdon, and also "ten judges" (shih cha-
er-ku-ch'i; Manchu, jarguci). These subordinate appointees were collectively called "the high officials who deliberate on government" (i-
cheng ta-ch'en).[17]

By building this structure over the banner system, under the joint

17. The development of Nurhaci's systems of deliberative princes and deliberative officials was a complicated and often confusing process. Several works
have sought to untangle this matter: Fu Tsung-mao, Ch'ing-tai Chün-chi ch'u,
pp. 1-12; Wu, Communication and Imperial Control, pp. 1-19; Kanda, "Shinsho
no gisei daijin ni tsuite"; Kanda, "Shinsho no bairoku ni tsuite"; Ch'en Chieh-
hsien, "Hou-Chin ling-ch'i pei-le"; and Corradini, "Civil Administration."

There is disagreement as to whether or not the appointment of the "five high
officials" marked the real beginnings of a bureaucratic administration under the
Manchus. Fu Tsung-mao has argued in the affirmative, believing that the later
institution known as the Council of Deliberative Officials (i-cheng ta-ch'en) can
be traced directly to this source. Se Fu Tsung-mao, Ch'ing-tai Chün-chi ch'u,
p. 54. Other historians, however, place the direct antecedents of the Council of
Deliberative Officials under the last years of Nurhaci's reign and the beginning
of Abahai's reign in the 1620s. See Silas Wu, Communication and Imperial Control, pp. 10-11; Michael, Origin of Manchu Rule, p. 67. My own feeling is that
Nurhaci's administrative structure indicates some kind of commitment to a bureaucratic system, and that the question of whether or not the five high officials
were the direct antecedent of the Council of Deliberative Officials is of less importance.

There is also some contradictory evidence about the dates of appointment
and the numbers of high officials under Nurhaci. In 1599 Nurhaci is reported to
have given daughters of his "six high officials" (liu ta-ch'en) to those who had submitted to his rule and had come to pay tribute. See Man-chou shih-lu, pp. 107-8.
In 1613 there is a record of four younger brothers among the sons of Nurhaci discussing matters with the "five high officials" (wu ta-ch'en). See Man-wen lao-
tang, 1:28-29. In 1616 Nurhaci is recorded as having selected "eight high officials"

supervision of the princes and with the assistance of the high officials,
Nurhaci envisioned a relatively open and collective approach to governance. Nurhaci experienced severe difficulties in finding a suitable
successor and thus, in 1622, advised his sons to perpetuate the collective approach after his death:

> Do not choose a strong, vigorous ruler when I die. If the ruler is
> strong and vigorous, he will only respect his own ability and will
> possibly be rejected by Heaven. No matter how wise he is, he will
> fail in propagating his wisdom to the commoners. You, eight sons,
> will be the eight princes. If the eight sons discuss matters in a
> council, there will be no confusion. Find a man whom you, the
> eight princes, will not oppose, and select him to succeed your fa-
> ther. Should he not accept your words and act against your wishes,
> replace him with one who does go along with all of you. On that
> matter you should talk a great deal. [18]

Nurhaci's ideal of collective administration was to be quickly eliminated by his son and successor, Abahai, who established himself as a
strong personal ruler. But the ideal was to enjoy a brief revival under
the collective government of the Joint Regents' faction in the early 1660s.
It is quite possible that the regents recalled Nurhaci's approach; for even
if they themselves had not been close enough to watch Nurhaci in action,
at least Oboi and Ebilun had learned about his methods through their
relatives, Fiongdon and Eidu, who were among the "five high officials."
The regents often spoke of the need to restore the "old systems of Tsu
and Tsung," and perhaps this was part of what they had in mind.

It must be remembered that the future regents were very young men
under the reign of Nurhaci (Suksaha was probably still a child) and that
this was a time for listening, learning, and training. Only Soni, the
eldest of the regents, experienced much military action and administrative service before the 1630s. Under Nurhaci, in addition to some
work as a translator and interpreter, Soni was appointed to the post of
Imperial Bodyguard of the first rank. This post, which was later to

---

and "forty judges" to oversee the domain and prevent injury to the commoners.
See Man-wen lao-tang, 1:54. What this may mean is that Nurhaci's administrative system emerged over the whole period from 1599 to 1626, changing its size
and function; further research on the early Manchu state might well indicate that
the system was quite flexible and shifted as Nurhaci perceived his changing needs.

18. Man-wen lao-tang, 2:554. Another version is found in the Man-chou
shih-lu; see Silas Wu, Communication and Imperial Control, pp. 11, 155. Nurhaci's directive goes on to urge the princes to appoint other officials after his
death: eight Manchu high officials, eight Chinese high officials, and eight Mongol
high officials; similarly, eight judges from each of the three ethnic groups are to
be placed under the control of the high officials; and finally, eight secretaries
from each of the groups are also to be established (Man-wen lao-tang, 2:555-56).
The succession issue is discussed later in this chapter.

figure importantly in imperial politics, permitted Soni fairly close contact with the ruler, and thus his name should probably be added to those
of Oboi and Ebilun with personal recollections of politics in the Nurhaci
period. As an Imperial Bodyguard, Soni also accompanied banner troops
on a few expeditions in the 1620s.[19] The other three future regents did
not receive important military posts until the middle and later years of
the Abahai reign. Oboi started his military career as a lieutenant in
the Guards Division (hu-chün) which protected the imperial capital. His
first line command, however, did not come until 1633, when he was appointed a major in his own Bordered Yellow Banner.[20] In 1634 Ebilun
inherited his father's title, viscount of the first class, and was concur-
rently made an Imperial Bodyguard. A year later Ebilun was given servants and property and was appointed a company captain in the Bordered
Yellow Banner. Ebilun seems to have fared best in his initial appointments because, in an era when many Manchu ranks and titles were hereditary, his father Eidu had achieved very high status.[21] Suksaha, the
youngest of the four, did not receive his first commission until the very
end of Abahai's reign, when he was selected as a company captain in the
Plain White Banner.[22]

But while the four young Manchus had to wait impatiently for their
first commands, they must have been enthusiastic about the turn of
events during the later years of Nurhaci's reign. In 1616 Nurhaci declared himself emperor of the Later Chin (Hou Chin) dynasty, thus linking himself with the earlier Jürched Chin dynasty (1122-1234) and implying his intention of conquering the Ming. For his reign title, Nurhaci selected "Heavenly Mandate" (T'ien-ming), again with unmistakable
implications. Two years later, in 1618, Nurhaci formally severed relations with the Ming court by announcing his "seven grievances" against
the Ming: the grievances included the murder of his father and grandfather, and the provision of assistance to the Hada and Yehe tribes a-
gainst him. In the same year Nurhaci's banner forces finally broke out
of the Jürched tribal areas and began to move west and south into the
Manchurian plain inhabited by Chinese farmers. After a series of successful battles against the Ming forces under the command of General
Yang Hao, the Manchus took Fu-shun, Liao-yang, and Shen-yang (later
called Mukden). The latter became Nurhaci's new capital in 1625 and
was the Manchu base of operations until Peking fell in 1644. The entire
Liaotung region soon was in Nurhaci's control, and he held the Manchurian plain except for the two-hundred-mile stretch from the top of the
Gulf of Chihli, guarded by the Ming fortresses at Chin-chou and Ning-
yüan, south to the Great Wall at Shanhaikwan. Some captured Chinese
soldiers were very helpful in Nurhaci's consolidation of this area, most

19. CSLC, ch. 6, pp. 14a-b.
20. Ibid., ch. 6, p. 9b.
21. Ibid., ch. 6, p. 17a; Hummel, p. 219.
22. CSLC, ch. 6, p. 4b.

notably Li Yung-fang (d. 1634), who had surrendered at Fu-shun in 1618 and eventually became a brigade-general in the Manchu army.[23]

Nurhaci's advance into the Manchurian plain was of great strategic importance, but it also had economic and social consequences. This rich agricultural basin provided food and land for his troops, and Chinese captives to do the farming and provide military supply services.[24] Before this conquest, the Chien-chou Jürched had existed on a mixed economy consisting of food-gathering, hunting and fishing, animal husbandry, and agriculture. The Jürched had practiced farming as early as the fifteenth century, acquiring tools, oxen, and techniques from both the Koreans and the Ming in return for trade and tribute. Before the advent of Nurhaci, however, the Chien-chou Jürched had lacked the stability, organization, and geographical location to develop a predominantly agrarian economy. Instead they had hunted for many varieties of game in the Chien-chou area: fox, sable, leopard, tiger, deer, and squirrel; they had traded ginseng, pearls, and several products of household industries (silverwork, woodwork, deerskins, and embroidery); and they had raised domesticated animals, including swine, chickens, ducks, and sheep. Iron founderies had been established by the Jürched in the latter half of the sixteenth century, and Nurhaci had made considerable use of weapons produced in his ironworks at Hetu Ala.

Although these earlier forms of livelihood were perpetuated by tribespeople who remained in central and northern Manchuria,[25] the acquisition of the Manchurian basin brought a rapid and widespread shift of the Manchus to an agrarian economy. According to one estimate, in taking the two towns of Hai-chou and Liao-yang in 1621, Nurhaci gained over 1,500,000 mou of farm land, or roughly 300,000 acres.[26] This figure can probably be multiplied several times to determine the total arable acreage under the Manchus in the pre-conquest period. It has also been estimated that the total Manchu population which migrated to the agrarian basin during these years amounted to about 400,000 to 500,000 persons, while the Chinese populace under their control may have been four or five times that number.[27] The captured Chinese were forced to wear the queue according to the Manchu tradition, and were enslaved to their Manchu conquerors. The farm lands and the Chinese slaves were distributed to the bannermen according to household size and military rank.

23. For descriptions of Nurhaci's battles against the Ming, see Hsiao I-shan, 1:73-107; Hummel, p. 597. On Li Yung-fang, see Michael, Origin of Manchu Rule, pp. 70-72; Hummel, p. 499.

24. This brief survey of the Manchu economy and society in the 1620s relies mainly upon the following: Ch'en Wen-shih, "Ch'ing-jen ju-kuan ch'ien ti nung-yeh sheng-huo"; Wang Chung-nan, Ch'ing-shih tsa-k'ao, pp. 1-39; and Liu, Ch'ing-ch'ao ch'u-ch'i ti pa-ch'i ch'üan-ti.

25. See Lee, Manchurian Frontier, pp. 1-23, passim.

26. Wang Chung-han, Ch'ing-shih tsa-k'ao, pp. 7-8.

27. Ibid., p. 22.

In the span of forty years, therefore, Nurhaci brought together the Jürched tribes, organized them into the powerful banner system, started the operations against the Ming, and provided the essential economic foundation for the conquest. In all of these accomplishments, he had relied heavily on his prominent Manchu families, including those of Soni, Suksaha, Ebilun, and Oboi. Nurhaci might have died a proud and contented man, but in 1626 he met his greatest military defeat. Early in that year, he led his main force across the Liao River to attack the city of Ning-yüan, only a hundred miles from the Great Wall of China. The Ming commander was the capable general, Yüan Ch'ung-huan (1584-1630), who had carefully fortified the city in 1623. When the Manchus attacked, Yüan and his troops were able to repel them, in part because the Ming had deployed a new and fearsome weapon, the cannon. The Ming cannon, developed with the assistance of Jesuits, were coordinated by Yüan Ch'ung-huan's Fukienese cook. The Manchus were forced to retreat. Nurhaci, having sustained a minor wound but a great blow to his pride, died seven months later.[28]

Nurhaci's death prompted the first of many succession crises in the early history of the Manchu dynasty.[29] Although it is unlikely that any of the four future regents participated directly, they probably observed the events and learned much about the brutality of Manchu politics. Shortly after Nurhaci died, four senior princes (ssu-ta-beile) emerged as the dominant figures in Shen-yang: Daišan (1583-1648), Amin (d. 1640), Mangultai (1587-1633), and Abahai (1592-1643). To secure their position, these senior princes forced the suicide of Nurhaci's third wife, Empress Hsiao-lieh; they feared that through her influence her sons, Dorgon (1612-1650), Dodo (1614-1649), and Ajige (1605-1651), might successfully challenge their rule. Then, taking control of two banners, the Bordered Yellow and the Plain Yellow, Abahai began his rise to absolute control. In 1629 he eliminated the practice by which the senior princes took monthly turns in administering the Manchu state. In 1630 he imprisoned Amin on the charge of having abandoned the recently conquered town of Yung-p'ing; Amin was to spend the remaining ten years of his life in prison. Then, after Manggultai died in 1633, Abahai declared him a traitor, and placed Manggultai's Plain Blue Banner under his own control. By this time Abahai had risen to the status of an em-

---

28. Hummel, pp. 597, 686, 954.

29. A primary reason for so many succession struggles in the early Ch'ing is that the Manchus employed two different systems for succession to the throne. Most of the early Manchu emperors did name a successor but encountered difficulties with the heir apparent; thus they were forced to the second system, in which a successor would be determined by the emperor's sons after his death. Nurhaci first named Surhaci (1564-1611) but later deposed and executed him. For a useful study of these matters, see Ch'en Chieh-hsien, Man-chou ts'ung-k'ao, pp. 79-93.

peror, and was able to enforce his claims through the control of three
of the eight banners.[30]

FOUR MANCHUS IN THE REIGN OF ABAHAI

Abahai's reign brought the Manchus to the brink of the conquest. His
rule was characterized by the expansion of imperial power and the subordination of the influence of the princes, the military and diplomatic
extension of Manchu control over Korea and Mongolia, and the creation
of the military and civil institutional framework for the invasion of Ming
China. Now, during the 1630s and early 1640s, we can observe the direct involvement of the future regents and their relatives in these several aspects of Abahai's regime. For three of these Manchus—Soni,
Ebilun, and Oboi—Abahai's quest for strong imperial control had the
effect of promoting their careers. The three were all officers in imperial banners (the Plain and Bordered Yellow Banners) and thus received special trust and close attention from the emperor. In seeking
to break the influence of the princes, moreover, Abahai came to rely
heavily upon the high-ranking officers in the Manchu banners for policymaking deliberations. Although the four Manchus never entered the inner circle of Abahai's advisers, they surely gained a new sense of self-
esteem and prestige as Manchus outside the imperial clan became architects of Ch'ing policies and of the conquest itself.

The battles of Abahai constitute a remarkable military success story.
By 1634 he had subdued the Chahar Mongols, the strongest of the Inner
Mongolian tribes. In 1638 he personally led a Manchu expeditionary
force to Korea and within a month was able to overcome the armies of
the king of the Korean Yi dynasty. Korea, a traditional tributary of
China, acknowledged Manchu sovereignty and began sending annual tribute to Mukden. Meanwhile, in a series of major battles and hundreds
of raids, Manchu troops broke the last defenses of the Ming in Liaotung
and made several forays through the Great Wall into the Ming provinces
of Shansi, Chihli, and Shantung. The Ming, severely weakened by court
factionalism and rebellions, tried in vain to stave off the Manchu assault by sending troops and supplies to southern Manchuria. The final
campaign took place in 1641-42 at the cities of Chin-chou and Sung-shan,
where Abahai defeated the remainder of the Ming garrison forces under
the command of generals Tsu Ta-shou and Hung Ch'eng-ch'ou. By the
time of his death in 1643, Abahai's territory extended close to the city
of Shanhaikwan, where the Great Wall meets the sea. Surrendered

---

30. A good introduction to this complicated succession struggle, which I have
only briefly mentioned here, can be found in the relevant biographies in Hummel.
A careful treatment of the succession of Abahai is Okada, "Ch'ing T'ai-tsung chi-
wei k'ao-shih." Also see: Kanda, "Shinsho no bairoku ni tsuite"; Ch'en Chieh-
hsien, "Hou-Chin ling-ch'i pei-le ltteh-k'ao"; and Meng, "Pa-ch'i chih-tu k'ao-
shih."

troops had greatly increased the size of the Manchu military organization: in 1634 eight Mongol banners had been added, and in 1642 eight Chinese banners.[31]

Oboi was a prominent figure in many of Abahai's battles and had the most illustrious military career of the future members of the Joint Regents' faction. After participating in the operations against the Chahar Mongols in 1633-34, Oboi achieved real fame in 1637 for leading an attack on Ming troops stationed on P'i-tao Island near the mouth of the Yalu River. P'i-tao Island, well-defended by cliffs, was a major Ming base for operations into Liaotung and was supplied by shipments from Shantung. Before the attack the Manchu prince Ajige called together his commanders and asked them about tactics for taking the island. Oboi and another major, Junta, asked to be placed in the vanguard of the army. They are reported to have said to Ajige, "If we fail to take the island, then you will never see us again." The army was then ferried across the water and encountered strong resistance from the fortifications on the cliffs. When it seemed that there was no one among the officers who dared lead the climb, "Oboi gave a loud cry, jumped up, and ran forward. Disregarding the arrows, he charged straight ahead and entered combat on his own. Junta followed him. The Ming forces were dispersed and subsequently he controlled the island. T'ai-tsung [Abahai] considered control over this island as important as taking a large city."[32] For this victory Abahai bestowed on Oboi the rank of baron and the honorary title "hero" (baturu). After this auspicious beginning, Oboi went on to gain further renown at the battles of Chin-chou and Sung-shan. Along with the prince Jirgalang and others, Oboi's troops surrounded the walls of Chin-chou in 1641. As a Ming relief force began to approach the city, the soldiers within the city attacked, hoping to defeat the Manchus with pressure from both the front and the rear. Once again Oboi proved himself an adept commander by leading his troops into combat without waiting for orders or for supplies. Although the ensuing battle was fiercely contested, Oboi managed to win a key victory. Later at Sung-shan, when the Ming forces were again trapped in a town, Abahai calculated that his foes would try to escape

31. Detailed accounts of the battles of Abahai are found in Hsiao I-shan, 1: 108-219. For discussions of the establishment of Mongol and Chinese banners, see: Spence, Ts'ao Yin, pp. 2-7; Meng, "Pa-ch'i chih-tu k'ao-shih," pp. 28-92, passim. Soni and his brother Hife helped to supervise the division of Chinese troops into four banners in 1639 (T'ai-tsung shih-lu, ch. 47, pp. 10a-11a).

32. CSLC, ch. 6, p. 10a. For further information about P'i-tao Island, see Hummel, pp. 568, 635; Rockhill, China's Intercourse with Korea, p. 22. The account of Oboi's military career under Abahai is taken primarily from CSLC, ch. 6, pp. 9b-12b. Other biographies of Oboi are: Hummel, pp. 599-600; CSK, ch. 255, pp. 7a-9a; PCTC (1795), ch. 137, pp. 14b-24a; PCST, ch. 1, pp. 6a-b. In 1642 Oboi was appointed to the post of captain-general in the Guards Division (T'ai-tsung shih-lu, ch. 61, p. 7b).

at night. Oboi was ordered to hold a position on the flank. When night fell and the enemy made their expected effort to escape, Oboi quickly followed, slaughtering and capturing many of the fleeing troops.

Oboi's military career was highly successful, but he was only one of four sons of Uici who found glory on the battlefields of southern Manchuria. His brothers, Baha, Jobtei, and Murma were exceptional commanders and engineered many victories in the Abahai and Shun-chih reigns. Both Baha and Jobtei were appointed to the Council of Deliberative Officials and both became chamberlains of the Imperial Bodyguard. Jobtei also served as lieutenant-general of the Manchu Bordered Yellow Banner. Murma was given his brother's post of lieutenant-general in 1660 and became president of the Board of Works in the same year.[33] During the 1660s Oboi was able to exploit his family's influence and his brothers' military and civil posts to his personal advantage. Oboi and his three brothers became leading figures in the factionalism that plagued the Manchu court in the early K'ang-hsi reign.

Compared to Oboi, Suksaha and Ebilun saw more limited military action before the conquest. Both fought in the Chin-chou and Sung-shan campaigns and were rewarded for their services. These were the first major battles for the young Suksaha. In 1643 Ebilun accompanied the Manchu prince Abatai in his foray into Ming China. They crossed through a breach in the Wall, swept through the metropolitan province of Chihli, and went all the way to northwestern Shantung. Ebilun was credited with the conquest of several towns in the mission, including that of Hsia-ching in Shantung province. They must have been satisfying missions for Ebilun because he had suffered disgrace in the late 1630s and had not been restored to rank until 1641. In 1637 Ebilun had been involved in a criminal case involving his niece, the daughter of one of his brothers, Turgei. The niece, who was childless in her marriage to a Manchu officer, had tried illegally to adopt a child and treat her as her own daughter. When Ebilun was called to testify, he did not give the facts accurately and instead tried to conceal his niece's guilt. For this he lost both his hereditary rank and his captaincy for a period of four years.[34]

---

33. Biographies of Murma in CSLC, ch. 4, pp. 9a-b; CSK, ch. 255, pp. 8a-b; PCTC (1795), ch. 135, pp. 23a-24b; PCST, ch. 1, p. 6b. Biographies of Jobtei in PCTC (1795), ch. 137, pp. 10b-14b; PCST, ch. 1, p. 5a. Biographies of Baha in CSLC, ch. 6, pp. 12b-13a; PCTC (1795), ch. 137, pp. 28b-31b; PCST, ch. 1, p. 6a.

34. See biographies of Suksaha in CSLC, ch. 6, pp. 4a-b; CSK, ch. 255, pp. 3b-6a; KCCH, ch. 264, pp. 34a-37a; PCTC (1795), ch. 158, pp. 14b-20a; PCST, ch. 22, pp. 3b-4a; Hummel, pp. 218, 600. On Ebilun: CSLC, ch. 6, pp. 17a-18a; Hummel, pp. 219-21; CSK, ch. 255, pp. 6a-7a; KCCH, ch. 269, pp. 41a-43a; PCTC (1795), ch. 137, pp. 24a-28b; PCST, ch. 5, pp. 7a-b; Ch'ien I-chi, Pei-chuan chi, ch. 5, pp. 2a-3a.

On the case involving Ebilun's niece, see CSLC, ch. 6, p. 17a; Hummel, p. 219; PCTC (1795), ch. 135, p. 33b. Turgei was a well-known commander under Abahai and was the best military officer of Eidu's sixteen sons. See Hummel, pp. 221-22; PCTC (1795), ch. 135, pp. 31a-35a.

Although Soni engaged in considerable fighting under Abahai, his most famous moment was a diplomatic victory. In 1628 he was sent on a mission to Ooba, the khan of the Korcin Mongols. Although Ooba had accepted one of Abahai's daughters as his wife in order to seal his vassalage to the Manchus, he had been delinquent in providing troops for his Manchu overlords, and it was rumored that he had made furtive contacts with the Ming. Soni was given the responsibility of upbraiding the khan for his disobedience. When Soni first arrived in the territory of the Korcin Mongols, Ooba feigned illness and refused to meet with him. Then Soni informed one of Ooba's functionaries that he had orders to sacrifice Ooba's wife, the daughter of Abahai, thereby severing all relations with the Korcin Mongols and, in effect, declaring war. Soni's strategy worked and Ooba, in alarm, admitted Soni to his tent and said, "Forgive me. I must make a humble apology and confess my guilt. The anxiety is more than I can bear." Soni replied, "The Emperor's influence extends across Heaven and Earth. If you truly confess your evil and extend allegiance to the dynasty, we will certainly conceal your guilt and take pity on you." Ooba then kowtowed and gave his allegiance to the dynasty.[35] Soni's linguistic abilities and his native resourcefulness had thus prevented the Manchus from undertaking yet another military operation.

The career of Soni provides a convenient bridge to the other side of Abahai's reign, his political activities and institutions. In 1629 Abahai created his first specialized civil institution, the Literary Office (wen-kuan). Among his initial appointments to the Literary Office were the famous translator, Dahai (d. 1632), as well as Soni and Hife. One of their duties was to continue Dahai's pioneering efforts in the translation of Chinese works into Manchu; Dahai had already translated some Chinese books on military science and also portions of the penal code in the Ming Statutes (Ta-Ming hui-tien). They were also expected to keep a careful record of Manchu history and the events at the Shenyang court. Those in the Literary Office, called "scholars" (ju-ch'en) or "literary officials" (wen-ch'en), frequently translated state documents from Korean or Chinese into Manchu, and were sometimes commissioned to accompany the troops in order to give commands to surrendered Mongols or Chinese.[36]

---

35. CSLC, ch. 6, p. 15a.
36. On the establishment of the Literary Office and the appointment of Dahai, Soni, and Hife, see: T'ai-tsung shih-lu, ch. 5, pp. 11b-12a; Hummel, p. 213; CSLC, ch. 4, p. 11a. Communication with the enemy, through both written and verbal instructions, was a well-established practice for the Manchus during the early 1630s. CS, 1 (pen-chi): 16-18, passim. On 26 May 1630, Soni and several other "literary officials" were ordered to remain in recently conquered Chinese cities in order to supervise the Ming leaders and commanders (T'ai-tsung shih-lu, ch. 6, pp. 23a-b).
On 25 February 1631, Abahai paid a visit to the Literary Office and perused a copy of Dahai's translation of the Chinese Military Classic (wu-ching). He was

By establishing the Literary Office, Abahai had begun to demonstrate his growing conviction that language, history, and bureaucratic organization were important tools for conquest. Abahai had a sophisticated and broad-ranging political mind. He brought perspective and moderation to his overall objectives of military success and strong personal control. He also had a sense of the importance of timing. Frequently during the 1630s he resisted heavy pressures from close advisers, both Manchu and Chinese, to launch an immediate, all-out invasion of the Ming. Abahai thanked his advisers for their opinions and confidence, but warned them that the Manchus were not yet ready to undertake the ultimate venture.[37] Readiness to Abahai implied more than military preparation. It also meant a deep knowledge of the society and government of the Ming enemy, and the development of leadership and institutions which would sustain Manchu rule in that alien environment. The structures and techniques which Abahai created around these beliefs had a lasting impact on the Manchu conquest elite; they were central to our regents' vision of "the pure and honest old system." There were three aspects to what the regents would later call "the majestic example" of Abahai: the juxtaposition of Manchu and sinified institutions; the role of Chinese officers and advisers; and Abahai's concept of the Manchu historical mission.

In the years 1631-37 Abahai created the basic Ch'ing governmental structure on a mixture of institutions drawn from Manchu and Chinese sources. The most important organization was Abahai's policymaking body known as the Council of Deliberative Officials (i-cheng ta-ch'en). The Council was clearly a Manchu institution and had no Chinese analogue. The origins of the Council can be traced to the governmental systems of the later years of Nurhaci's rule in which Manchu princes had cooperatively governed the state with assistance from Manchu military leaders. Shortly after his father's death, Abahai expanded Nurhaci's system by appointing "eight high officials" (pa-ta-ch'en), one for each of the eight banners, who would sit with the princes in governmental deliberations. Then, on 23 March 1637, he formally established the Council of Deliberative Officials and limited its membership to the eight lieutenant-generals (tu-t'ung) and the sixteen deputy lieutenant-generals (fu tu-t'ung) who directly administered the affairs of the Manchu banners. The princes were explicitly excluded from the Council on the grounds that they were generally away from Mukden on

---

especially taken by a passage in which ancient Chinese generals are reported to have thrown wine sediments in rivers for the restorative effects such water would have for their troops. Abahai then issued an edict which noted the affection ancient Chinese leaders showed their troops and which deplored atrocities committed by one of his own Manchu commanders (T'ai-tsung shih-lu, ch. 8, pp. 5a-6a).

37. For pressures on Abahai to begin the final assault on the Ming, see T'ai-tsung shih-lu, ch. 12, pp. 3a-5b, and ch. 22, pp. 21b-23b.

military operations. One of the first members of the Council was Oboi's brother, Baha; thus the family tradition of close service to the ruler, begun by Fiongdon, was preserved. Through the creation of the Council, Abahai circumvented the political power of the other princes, and rested his administration on the top Manchu officers outside the imperial clan. His personal influence was thus enhanced, while the principle of military control over government was maintained. From this beginning, the Council of Deliberative Officials served as the institutional nucleus of Manchu rule throughout much of the seventeenth century, and particularly under the regime of the Joint Regents' faction in the early 1660s.[38]

Another Abahai institution, strictly Manchu in origin and of considerable importance to the Oboi period, was the Li-fan yüan (Court of Colonial Affairs). Established in 1638 as an expanded version of the earlier Mongol Office (Meng-ku ya-men), the Li-fan yüan was entrusted with the management of relations between the Ch'ing and the recently subdued Mongol tribes to the north and west. After the conquest the Li-fan yüan became an integral part of the Ch'ing foreign affairs administration, and its responsibilities extended to Tibet and Sinkiang as well as Mongolia. The Ch'ing Li-fan yüan, therefore, gave special attention to these regions; while the Board of Rites (li-pu), which had handled all foreign affairs under the Ming, was limited to dealings with the tributaries of East and Southeast Asia. The regents, as we shall see later, were strongly committed to this bifurcated outlook on foreign policy, and paid special attention to the Li-fan yüan.[39]

Juxtaposed to these Manchu institutions were three other organizations which Abahai modified from Chinese models. These organizations, which performed functional tasks as opposed to having deliberative responsibilities like those of the Council of Deliberative Officials, were: the Six Boards (liu-pu), established in 1631; the Censorate (tu-ch'a-

38. The edict of 1627 establishing the "eight high officials" (these were really the predecessors of the lieutenant-generals and were called by their Manchu name, gusai ejen) is found in T'ai-tsung shih-lu, ch. 1, pp. 11a-12a. At the same time Abahai named sixteen other officials to provide assistance in governmental deliberations at the capital, and sixteen others to accompany troops on campaigns and adjudicate any disputes (ibid., ch. 1, pp. 11a-12a). The 1637 edict establishing the Council of Deliberative Officials is found in ibid., ch. 34, pp. 23a-26b. An excellent review of the evolution of the Council is found in Silas Wu, Communication and Imperial Control, pp. 1-19. For other information, see note 17 of this chapter. The Council of Deliberative Officials will receive further attention in this book in chapters 3, 4, 8, and 9. For Baha's appointment to the Council under Abahai, see Kanda, "Shinsho no gisei daijin ni tsuite," pp. 175-76. Kanda has noted that Abahai's Council numbered twenty-seven men, with three appointments in addition to the twenty-four ex officio members.

39. On the development and functions of the Li-fan yüan, see Fairbank and Teng, Ch'ing Administration, pp. 130-35; Mancall, Russia and China, pp. 4-8. The earliest reference to the Mongol Office I have found is 1636. See Tayama, Shin-jidai ni okeru Moko no shakai seido, p. 90, n. 11.

yüan), established in 1636; and the Inner Three Departments (nei-san-
yüan), also in 1636. The Six Boards and the Censorate directly bor-
rowed Chinese names, while the Inner Three Departments, lacking Chinese antecedants in name, replicated some of the functions of the Ming
Grand Secretariat (nei-ko) and Hanlin Academy (han-lin yüan). In all
three instances, Chinese advisers were instrumental in encouraging
Abahai to establish these institutions and in carrying out details related
to their establishment.[40] Abahai had several objectives in mind as he
created these agencies. As Franz Michael has clearly indicated, Abahai needed effective organization to rule his growing territory and population and the Chinese models were close at hand.[41] As the time for
the invasion approached, Abahai also wanted a governmental system
that would prove attractive to increasing numbers of Ming bureaucrats.
Finally, he made these moves in order to provide a training ground for
Manchu officials who could hold the top governmental positions after the
conquest was complete.

In the Six Boards, the most prominent of these three institutions,
there were significant differences from the Ming system. When Abahai
first established the Boards in 1631, six imperial princes were assigned
to head them, each given the responsibility of "managing the affairs" of
one of the boards (kuan pu-shih). Beneath them were four presidents
(ch'eng-cheng) for each board, two of whom were Manchus, one Mongol,
and one Chinese. Ebilun's brother, Turgei, was appointed in 1631 as
one of the first presidents of the Board of Civil Office. Under the presidents were fourteen vice-presidents (shih-lang): eight Manchus, four
Mongols, and two Chinese. Still lower were a variety of clerks and
readers, including Soni, who was appointed to the post of clerk (ch'i-
hsin-lang) in the Board of Civil Office in 1631.[42] The major point here
is that, while the Six Boards were Chinese in name, Abahai's appointments were predominantly Manchu. In 1638 he continued this trend by
limiting the presidents to one per board, all of whom were Manchu; under them were several vice-presidents (called ts'an-cheng at this time),
most of whom were Manchus and Chinese military officers.[43] As we
shall see in the next chapter, Dorgon was to draw much of his post-

---

40. The edicts establishing these bodies are found in T'ai-tsung shih-lu, ch.
9, pp. 11b-12b; ch. 28, pp. 2a-3a; and ch. 29, pp. 6a-7a. Also see Hummel,
pp. 231-32, 592-93. A diligent effort to reconstruct the original edict creating
the Six Boards is Kuang-lu and Li, "Lao Man-wen yüan-tang yü Man-wen lao-
tang," pp. 148-65.

41. Michael, Origin of Manchu Rule, p. 77.

42. See Kuang-lu and Li, "Lao Man-wen yüan-tang yü Man-wen lao-tang,"
pp. 154-57; T'ai-tsung shih-lu, ch. 9, pp. 11b-12b.

43. This new structure applied not only to the Six Boards, but also to the
Censorate and Li-fan yüan as well; collectively these agencies were called the
Eight Offices (pa ya-men). The edict is in T'ai-tsung shih-lu, ch. 42, pp. 21b-
24a. Soni continued to have a functional position in the newly organized Board of
Civil Office (ibid., ch. 42, p. 21b).

conquest bureaucracy from these appointments in the later years of
Abahai's reign.

Like the Six Boards, the Inner Three Departments played no deliberative role, but served rather as a functional support for the emperor. The Inner Three Departments, an expanded version of the Literary Office, consisted of the following subdivisions: the Department
of Dynastic History (kuo-shih yüan), in charge of keeping the court
chronicle, compiling books of history, and offering comments about
imperial proclamations; the Department of the Secretariat (mi-shu
yüan), in charge of documents relating to diplomatic missions and of
matters concerning imperial edicts and funerary odes; and the Department of Literature and Conduct (hung-wen yüan), in charge of giving
lectures on morality to the emperor, of tutoring the emperor's sons,
and of all matters related to virtuous conduct. Heading the Inner Three
Departments were four Grand Secretaries (ta-hsüeh-shih), two Manchu
and two Chinese; Soni's brother, Hife, was one of the first Manchus to
hold this post. The number of Grand Secretaries was reduced to three
in 1638, two Manchus and one Chinese, and remained that way until after the conquest in 1644. The Chinese Grand Secretary was Fan Wen-
ch'eng (1597-1666), who had surrendered to the Manchus in 1629 and
had provided assistance in developing some of the functional institutions;
the Inner Three Departments thus offered Abahai a convenient post for
lodging this valuable adviser. [44]

Of all the pre-conquest governmental agencies, the Censorate appears to have been the least influential. At first it consisted of a single
Chinese official, Chang Ts'un-jen (d. 1652), who was designated as
president (ch'eng-cheng) of the Censorate in 1636. Chang took his post
seriously and shortly after assuming office presented a long memorial
citing corruption in Manchu government and rebuking the emperor for
some of his appointments. Chang was apparently operating under the
traditional Chinese notion of loyalty (chung), whereby the truly loyal
official criticized the behavior, the policies, and the officials of his
sovereign. Abahai, however, equated loyalty with obedience, and
snapped back at his censor, "I have never heard such vilification as
the words and accusations presented in this memorial."[45] In 1638 a
Manchu president was appointed to the Censorate, and Chang Ts'un-jen
was relegated to a vice-presidency along with one other Chinese and

---

44. A useful introduction to the Inner Three Departments and the Ch'ing Grand
Secretariat is Silas Wu, Communication and Imperial Control, pp. 15-17. Wu
properly observes that this institution held a rather low status in the Manchu bureaucracy and barely resembled the powerful Grand Secretariat of the early Ming
period. Also see Hummel, pp. 231-32, 592-93; T'ai-tsung shih-lu, ch. 28, pp.
2a-3a; CS, 4:2446-47; Hsieh Pao-chao, Government of China, pp. 275-76.

45. T'ai-tsung shih-lu, ch. 30, p. 4b; Chang's memorial is ibid., ch. 30,
pp. 2a-4a. Also see ibid., ch. 29, pp. 6a-7a, 9a.

two Manchus. The Censorate, moreover, was listed at the bottom of the institutional hierarchy beneath the Li-fan yüan. [46]

Here, then, was the "majestic example" which the regents saw in Abahai's governmental structure: policies were determined by the Emperor and his Manchu Council of Deliberative Officials. The remainder of the bureaucracy was a mixture of Manchu and sinified institutions and a similar mixture in personnel, with Manchus dominating the top-ranking posts. Abahai had created a judicious balance between his interests in personal and Manchu control and his need for a governmental system which would appeal to the Chinese, train more Manchus for administrative work, and take over power quickly and efficiently when the Manchus entered Peking. To adapt a popular phrase of the late nineteenth century, the essence (t'i) of Abahai's political structure remained Manchu, while modifications of Chinese institutions were employed for their practical use (yung).

Another legacy to the future regents was Abahai's approach to the use of Chinese in his administration. As observed earlier, Abahai did rely on a few carefully selected Chinese collaborators as imperial confidants and advisers. The best example is Ning Wan-wo (d. 1665), who, until he was cashiered for gambling in 1635, served Abahai as a military officer, interpreter, protocol consultant, and close adviser on military strategy and administrative structure.[47] Also among Abahai's close associates, in addition to the previously mentioned Li Yung-fang and Fan Wen-ch'eng, were some surrendered Ming officers like Keng Chung-ming (d. 1649), K'ung Yu-te (d. 1652), and Shang K'o-hsi (d. 1676). From the early 1630s onward, these men not only led their surrendered troops to victories against Mongols and Chinese, but they also offered opinions on military strategy to Abahai. Having been forced to surrender in a period of weakening Ming military power, they knew well its flaws and were able to provide valuable first-hand information to the Manchu ruler. [48]

The great majority of Chinese in the service of Abahai, however, did not enjoy such close contact with the Manchu leader, but rather fought for him in the ranks of the Chinese banner forces. Chinese troops subject to the Manchus expanded considerably under Abahai; they were formally established in eight banners in 1642, and amounted to 177 companies by 1644.[49] The officers of the Chinese banners were given ranks identical to their Manchu counterparts, ranging from company captains at the bottom to lieutenant-generals at the top. These were the Chinese with whom the Manchu conquest elite had its closest associations and on whom the Manchus would rely heavily after the conquest for both military

46. For appointments to the Censorate in the 1638-43 period, see PCTC (1795), ch. 118, pp. 3a-9a.

47. Hummel, p. 592.

48. Biographies of Keng Chung-ming, K'ung Yu-te, and Shang K'o-hsi can be found in ibid., pp. 416-17, 435-36, and 635-36.

49. Fang, "Early Manchu Military Forces," pp. 208-9.

and civil service. Few of these Chinese bannermen had held posts in
the regular civil service. Instead they had worked up through the ranks
of the Ming military until they were sent to Liaotung, where their Ming
careers terminated in battlefield disasters. Having selected surrender
over death, their only hope for fresh careers was to exhibit complete
obedience to the Manchus and bring military success to the conquerors.
In the eyes of the Manchu conquest elite, these banner officers constituted ideal Chinese, whose values and experiences approximated their
own.

A third inheritance from the Abahai period, closely related to his
governmental structure and his development of the Chinese banners,
was his concept of a Manchu historical mission. As early as 1631 Abahai began to break away from his father's notion of a Later Chin dynasty.
During the siege of Ta-ling-ho in that year, Abahai sent a message to
the Ming commander, Tsu Ta-shou, urging him to surrender:

> I truly wish to enter peace negotiations. . . . The officials of your
> country take the Sung dynasty's collapse as their mirror and thus
> will not give a word in response to my entreaties. But your Ming
> lords are not the descendants of the Sung, nor am I a descendant
> of the Chin. That was one era, and this is another. The heavenly
> times and the people's feelings are totally dissimilar.[50]

On 15 May 1636 Abahai dropped the dynastic name, Later Chin, and
adopted the new name Ch'ing ("clear and pure") parodying both in sound
and implication the Ming ("brilliant") dynasty. Having already established several institutions which were sinified in appearance, Abahai
recognized the propaganda value of posing not as a new version of earlier Jürched conquerors, but as one who would cleanse and purify China
of its Ming corruption. In fact, at the same time he began calling his
people the Manchus (Man-chou), thereby cutting ties in nomenclature
to their Jürched past.[51] Whether or not Abahai took this purification
mission seriously is a moot point, for he died before the conquest was
complete and never had the opportunity to develop policies from the
throne in Peking. But the regents of the 1660s, and many of the Manchu conquest elite, were fervently committed to this mission and would
often justify their actions as efforts to "eradicate the vile legacies of
the Ming."

---

50. T'ai-tsung shih-lu, ch. 9, pp. 31b-32a. For Abahai's many encounters
with Tsu Ta-shou, see Hummel, p. 769-70; Chin-liang, Man-chou lao-tang pi-
lu, vol. 2, passim. Abahai frequently sent messages to the Ming court in which
he endeavored to produce peace negotiations and usually implied his own equality
to the Ming sovereign. See T'ai-tsung shih-lu, ch. 6. pp. 21a-22b, 23b-24a; CS,
1 (pen-chi): 29-30.

51. T'ai-tsung shih-lu, ch. 28, pp. 17a-35b. The possibility that Chinese
were attracted by Manchu propaganda is discussed in Wakeman, "High Ch'ing,"
pp. 3-4.

In spite of his proclamations for Chinese audiences, Abahai had
not forgotten his Jürched past. He was, in fact, a close student of Chin
history and often lectured his officials about the lessons of the Chin dynasty. A few exerpts from one of these lectures may help illustrate the
Manchu side of his legacy to the conquest elite, and offer a logical conclusion to this chapter. On 29 November 1636 Abahai called together
his princes and other officials and ordered a reading from the Manchu
translation of the Basic Records of the Chin Emperor Shih-tsung (Ta-
Chin Shih-tsung pen-chi; Shih-tsung was the fifth Chin emperor, who had
reigned 1161-90). After the reading Abahai began his lecture:

> I have looked at this book and I know its general outline. . . . I
> feel that the laws and systems established by Chin T'ai-tsu and T'ai-
> tsung were carefully developed and clear, and they could have re-
> mained in effect for a long time. But as for Hsi-tsung, we see that
> he was addicted to drinking and sex and the costs of his pleasures
> cannot be measured. He imitated the vile customs of the Chinese.
> So when Shih-tsung succeeded to the throne, he was determined to
> establish the laws and regulations of his ancestors, and diligently
> sought to rule by reason. Fearing that his descendants would imi-
> tate Chinese customs, he prohibited this, and many times urged his
> people not to forget Tsu and Tsung. He ordered them to follow the
> old customs in clothing and language, to practice horsemanship and
> archery regularly so they would be ready for warfare. But in spite
> of these imperial admonitions, subsequent generations disregarded
> him and forgot their horsemanship and archery. Thus we come to
> Ai-tsung, where the gods of grain were threatened, and subsequently
> the dynasty was wiped out. Now from this we all know that if the
> princes become addicted to alcohol and obsessed with sex, all will
> be lost. [52]

Abahai went on to explain that he had refused to adopt Chinese court cos-
tumes, providing a conclusive illustration for his decision: "If those of
us at this great gathering were to wear loose-fitting garments with wide
sleeves, arrows at our left waist and bows under the right arm, and
were to encounter this eminent old man, Koro Baturu Loosa, who suddenly straightened up and rushed forward, how could we be able to re-
sist him?"[53] Abahai then closed his lecture on a more somber note:

> I say all this because I want my words to be a guide for the descen-
> dants over the ten thousand generations. While I rule, there can

---

52. T'ai-tsung shih-lu, ch. 32, pp. 8a-b. Similar pronouncements by Abahai
are found in ibid., ch. 34, pp. 26b-27b. Abahai was also strongly opposed to the
use of tobacco (ibid., ch. 54, pp. 22a-b).
53. Ibid., ch. 32, p. 9a.

be no alteration of these principles. But I fear the future generations will forget the old system, will dispense with archery and
horsemanship, and come to practice the customs of the Chinese.
So I often feel a sense of anxiety. We had few troops at the beginning, but they were experts at horsemanship and archery; when
they entered a savage battle they won, and when they attacked a
city they took it. The people of the world say of our soldiers:
when they stand they do not waver, and when they advance they do
not look back. Their awesome reputation brings fear and trem-
bling, there are none who dare raise spears to fight with us. Now
we are going to break through the Wall and attack Peking.[54]

54. Ibid., ch. 32, pp. 9a-b.

3   The Genesis of the
Regency, II: 1643–1661

Abahai's death on 21 September 1643 marked the end of one phase in the lives of Soni, Suksaha, Ebilun, and Oboi. They had achieved some distinction among the Manchu conquest elite for their military exploits and administrative talents. But they had always operated on the periphery of Manchu politics, close enough to observe Abahai's strategies, but too far away to have influence over major policies. Like many other banner officers, they had taken orders obediently and had occasionally made clever tactical maneuvers on their own. With Abahai's death, however, another succession battle ensued, and these four officers were suddenly in the midst of Manchu factionalism. Over the next seventeen years they struggled for recognition and power in the factional wars that raged in Mukden and, after 1644, in Peking. Here they discovered that victory in factional warfare was more elusive than on the battlefield. During Dorgon's regime (1643–50), Soni, Ebilun, and Oboi lived dangerously in the political opposition, while Suksaha was a minor figure in the Dorgon faction. Under Jirgalang (1651–53) all four enjoyed a brief moment of glory as key figures supporting the Shun-chih Emperor. But when the emperor began to rule on his own (1653–61), they found themselves with attractive titles but minimal power. The Joint Regents' faction of 1661, therefore, was born of the political adversity experienced by these men in the years 1643–61.

POLITICAL EDUCATION IN ADVERSITY, 1643–1650
From the Dorgon era the future regents drew some basic lessons about Manchu politics. They learned, often painfully, that factional success was based on a secure military foundation buttressed by a small group of loyal backers and by statements of authority. Dorgon established the first Manchu regency by skillfully using these tools, and thus he offered a political education for his adversaries and supporters alike. But Dorgon was much more than an adept factional leader; he was the Manchu ruler who realized the dream of Nurhaci and Abahai by conquering China and placing the Ch'ing dynasty in Peking. Dorgon relied on many of the institutions and personnel established by his half-brother, Abahai, while evolving new strategies to extend and consolidate Ch'ing control in China proper. Even his political enemies had to acknowledge that Dorgon was a tough general and a strong proponent of Manchu rule. The regents of the K'ang-hsi Emperor would hold Dorgon up for obloquy, but they would perpetuate his factional methods and Manchu-oriented policies.

The 1643 succession crisis in Mukden began as a clash among the imperial princes, but rapidly expanded until only a last-minute compromise averted internecine warfare among the banner troops. When Abahai died he had named no successor, and the issue polarized into two factions: those who supported Dorgon as emperor, and those who supported Haoge, the eldest son of Abahai. Dorgon, a fine military commander in the pre-conquest period, had resented the fact that his own mother had been forced to commit suicide in the 1620s to satisfy the ambitions of the older princes, particularly those of Abahai. Dorgon probably felt that he had been the rightful heir after Nurhaci died in 1626, and thus firmly pressed his case in 1643.[1] To back his claims, Dorgon relied on the support of his own Plain White Banner and of the Bordered White Banner controlled by his younger brother, Dodo (1614-49). Opposing Dorgon was the thirty-four-year-old Haoge, who had been a capable military leader under the reign of his father, Abahai, and who had been entrusted with managing the Board of Revenue. Since the rest of Abahai's sons were less than sixteen years of age, Haoge was the only one with the maturity and experience to rule on his own.[2] Supporting Haoge were the officers of the two Yellow Banners which had formerly been under the direct control of the emperor himself. The struggle between the two leading princes, therefore, was also a contest between the White and Yellow Banners for the prestige of serving as the new emperor's troops. When officers of the Yellow Banners rallied around Haoge with the slogan "support the emperor's son," they were endeavoring to maintain the status they had held as imperial bannermen since the late 1620s.

Soni, Ebilun, and Oboi, all members of the Yellow Banners, were strong advocates for Haoge. Five days after the death of Abahai, Dorgon called a conference of Manchu leaders to discuss the succession matter. When asked for his opinion, Soni replied, "The former Emperor had a son, and I have never heard of placing someone other than the Emperor's son on the throne." When it seemed that the Dorgon group would succeed in spite of such opposition, Soni resorted to a more forceful tactic. At dawn he led several troops of the Yellow Banners, including Ebilun and Oboi among other officers, and surrounded the imperial palace at Mukden. Confronting the Manchu princes who were seated at court, Soni demanded, "Place the imperial son on the throne."[3]

Under the threat of warfare between the Yellow and White Banners,

---

1. For Dorgon's career and the possibility that he was Nurhaci's choice as heir, see: Ch'en Chieh-hsien, Man-chou ts'ung-k'ao, pp. 86-88; Hummel, pp. 215-19.

2. Biography of Haoge in Hummel, pp. 280-81. For further information about the prominent figures in the 1643 succession crisis, the relevant biographies in Hummel provide a good starting point.

3. CSK, ch. 255, p. 1b. For Ebilun and Oboi in the 1643 crisis, see their biographies as cited in chapter 2, notes 32 and 34.

the aging prince Daišan, commander of the Plain Red Banner, broke
the deadlock by working out a compromise. According to the compromise, neither Haoge nor Dorgon would succeed. Instead, Abahai's
five-year-old son, Fu-lin, was placed on the throne under the reign
title Shun-chih (r. 1643-61). Dorgon and Jirgalang, both sons of Nurhaci, would administer the Ch'ing government until Shun-chih reached
maturity.[4] It was a pale victory for Soni and his cohorts: an "imperial
son" was on the throne and the Yellow Banners were nominally under
the new emperor's control. But the real power lay in Dorgon's hands.
As a result of the compromise Dorgon commanded not only the Plain
White Banner, but also the Plain Blue Banner which had formerly been
under Abahai's jurisdiction. Then when his brother Dodo died in 1649,
Dorgon assumed control of Dodo's Bordered White Banner, thus holding three of the eight banners and making his faction impregnable to
Manchu opponents in Peking.

With the succession crisis settled by October 1643, the new regent
Dorgon turned his attention to the final operations against the Ming.
Later he would move against Haoge and his supporters, including Soni,
Ebilun, and Oboi. But for now, he was preparing to strike the fatal
blow against Ming China and he wanted all of his officers ready for combat. To the great surprise of the Manchus, they were able to take Peking without a major battle. In April 1644 the city had fallen to rebels.
The rebel Li Tzu-ch'eng, who called himself the "Dashing General,"
entered Peking on 25 April, and the Ming emperor hanged himself on
Coal Hill, overlooking the Forbidden City. At this point the Manchus
were just outside the city of Shanhaikwan, where the brigade-general
Wu San-kuei was commanding the Ming forces. Wu was ready to make
a last desperate effort to hold the Manchus outside the Great Wall when,
according to a well-known legend, he was outraged by the news that his
favorite concubine was in the hands of Li Tzu-ch'eng. Also learning
that the rebel was marching towards Shanhaikwan, Wu San-kuei decided
to cast his lot with the Manchus. On 27 May Wu opened the gates of the
Wall to the Manchu troops, welcomed Dorgon in person, and together
they led their troops towards Peking. Li Tzu-ch'eng retreated rapidly
to Peking, where he looted and burned part of the city. Then, after
executing Wu San-kuei's family, Li left the capital on 4 June. Led by
Dorgon and Wu, the joint Sino-Manchu army marched into Peking on
6 June 1644.[5]

Once he had taken Peking, Dorgon confronted the enormous respon-

4. The best versions of this episode are found in the Hummel biographies,
particularly those of Dorgon and Daišan, and also Ch'en Chieh-hsien, Man-chou
ts'ung-k'ao, pp. 89-91.
5. For a detailed description of Li's brief reign in Peking and of Wu San-
kuei's decision to join the Manchus, see Parsons, Peasant Rebellions, pp. 132-
42. Parsons provides convincing evidence that the capture of Wu's concubine
was not a major factor influencing Wu's decision (ibid., pp. 138-39).

sibility of consolidating Ch'ing rule over the spacious and hostile Chinese empire. His success in meeting this responsibility over the short span of six years is a story in itself, but one outside the scope of our present investigation. We are concerned with the narrower question of the relationship between the Dorgon regime and the later emergence of the Joint Regents' faction in the 1660s. Two aspects of the Dorgon Regency had the greatest impact on Soni, Suksaha, Ebilun, and Oboi: the application of Abahai's political systems and methods to Ch'ing China and the sources of authority and power under the Dorgon faction.

From the moment Dorgon entered Peking, he began to display his ability to conceal Manchu rule behind a Chinese facade. On 6 June, shortly after leading his troops through the gates, Dorgon performed the kowtow to Heaven, ordered his soldiers to treat the residents of Peking with kindness and respect, and informed the Ming officialdom that they would be welcome to serve in the Ch'ing bureaucracy. He announced that he had come to rescue the city from the rebels and expressed the hope that those officials and commoners who had fled from Li Tzu-ch'eng would return to Peking.[6] On 18 June he ordered a mourning service and burial of the Ming emperor who had committed suicide.[7] Later in the summer Dorgon honored Ming T'ai-tsu, founder of the former dynasty, with a tablet in the Imperial Temple and a tomb surrounded by two thousand mou of sacrificial land.[8] Beginning in 1644 and continuing throughout the Shun-shih period, the exorbitant taxes of the late Ming were reduced; in areas ravaged by war and natural disaster, the taxes were remitted until economic recovery had taken place.[9]

But these actions, designed to gain popular support for the new dynasty, were paralleled by several moves for Manchu dominance over Peking and north China. The queue requirement, formerly applied to the Chinese of the Liaotung region, was extended to all residents of the Chinese empire as a symbol of subordination to the conquerors.[10] Much of the rich farmland in the metropolitan province of Chihli was confiscated and granted to Manchu troops, officers, and princes. Dorgon thus perpetuated the Manchu agrarian economy, while providing firm martial control over the metropolitan area.[11] The practice of Chinese enslavement to Manchu masters was continued in order to provide agrarian and household labor.[12] And lest the Chinese conclude that Manchus were infatuated with Ming emperors, Dorgon ordered several "barbarian"

6. SC Shih-lu, ch. 5, pp. 1a-3b.

7. Ibid., ch. 5, pp. 3b-4a.

8. Ibid., ch. 5, p. 25b; CS, 1 (pen-chi): 38.

9. For tax reductions and remissions in the Shun-chih reign, see CS, 1 (pen-chi): 34-64, passim.

10. SC Shih-lu, ch. 5, pp. 3a-b.

11. See chapter 8 under "The Banner Relocation Affair, 1666-67."

12. See chapter 5 under "Ch'ung-ming hsien: The Regents' Model for the Empire."

emperors added to the Imperial Temple, including Liao T'ai-tsu, Chin T'ai-tsu and Shih-tsung, and Yüan T'ai-tsu. [13]

The clearest indication of Dorgon's commitment to Manchu rule, however, was the political system he developed after taking Peking. On 10 June 1644 he issued his famous "dyarchy" order: all Ming metropolitan officials were invited to remain in their posts and rule along with Manchu appointees; ranks and privileges were to be granted "according to a single system." [14] But Dorgon failed to mention the fact that, for the first five years of his regime, the top metropolitan positions (presidencies of the Boards, Li-fan yüan, and the Censorate) would be held exclusively by Manchus, and that Manchus and Chinese bannermen would dominate the posts of vice-president. Although former Ming officials received appointments to subordinate posts, the top of the new Ch'ing bureaucracy in Peking was largely imported from Mukden. [15] The only exception was the Inner Three Departments where Chinese bannermen and regular Chinese officials held most of the posts of Grand Secretary under the Dorgon regency. Under Dorgon, however, the Inner Three Departments was an institution of minor importance, clearly subordinate to the Boards in terms of prestige and influence. [16]

---

13. SC Shih-lu, ch. 15, pp. 1b-2a; ch. 136, pp. 11a-12b. In 1645 Hife announced the completion of the translations of the Liao, Chin, and Yüan histories. He was heavily rewarded for this project which had begun under the auspices of Abahai (ibid., ch. 3, pp. 22b-24a).

14. Ibid., ch. 5, p. 5a.

15. For appointments to presidencies and vice-presidencies in the 1644-48 period, see CS, 4: 2513-17. By cross-checking these listings with biographical collections, several conclusions are evident. From June 1644 to September 1648 there were only Manchu presidents in the Six Boards; four of the initial appointments were imperial clansmen. During the same period there was only one president of the Censorate, a Manchu named Mandahai. The Li-fan yüan, as usual, had but one president, Bolo, who was to be a prominent figure in Dorgon's faction in the late 1640s. All of these Manchus, with the exception of Mandahai, are cited as "having been transferred to continue the previous government" in Mukden.

In the vice-presidencies of the Six Boards, the following division is found in the initial appointments made in 1644: seven Manchus, nine Chinese bannermen, one Mongol, one regular Chinese official, four uncertain as to ethnic background, and two posts left unfilled. Eleven of these officials, including six of the Manchus and three of the Chinese bannermen, are listed as transfers from the Mukden government.

There was only one vice-president of the Li-fan yüan appointed until 1648: a Manchu named Nikan (not to be confused with the Nikan who later held high status in the Dorgon faction). In the Censorate only one vice-president was appointed in 1644: a regular Chinese official who had formerly served under the Ming. By 1646, however, all four of the Censorial vice-presidencies were filled, divided equally between Manchus and Chinese.

The development of dyarchy in board presidencies in 1648 and after will be discussed later in chapters 4 and 8.

16. For appointments to the Inner Three Departments under Dorgon, see CS, 4: 2446-49. Three of the Grand Secretaries were transferred from Mukden. One

Capping Dorgon's bureaucracy was the Council of Deliberative Officials which was inherited from Abahai's governmental structure. In 1644 Dorgon expanded the Council to give it the upper hand over military and civil organizations. Consequently the post-conquest Council of Deliberative Officials included all lieutenant-generals and deputy lieutenant-generals of the Manchu and Mongol banners and all Manchus and Mongols holding positions of board president or Grand Secretary.[17]   For his provincial bureaucracy, Dorgon relied primarily on Chinese bannermen to fill the top posts of governor-general and governor; while regular Chinese officials were generally appointed to middle and lower ranks (prefects and magistrates) as the Manchus extended their control over the former Ming provinces.[18] In short, Ch'ing rule in China began with a loyal bureaucracy, governed by Manchus, Mongols, and Chinese bannermen, while preserving many Chinese institutional names and making room for regular Chinese officials in subordinate posts.

Just as Dorgon applied many of Abahai's governmental techniques to the Ch'ing state, he also sought to guarantee his own political position in Peking as Abahai had done a decade earlier in Mukden. This time, however, the four future regents were not just interested onlookers; they were personally affected by Dorgon's ascension to power. Shortly after becoming a regent, Dorgon struck a major blow against his fellow princes by abolishing the practice of assigning princes to manage the Six Boards. Instead, Dorgon explained, he and Jirgalang would work directly with the Boards themselves in order to avoid confusion and disorder.[19] One of the victims of this new policy was the prince Haoge, who had formerly been entrusted with the management of the Board of Revenue, and who had served as the main hope for the ambitions of those in the Yellow Banners. Haoge was left politically impotent and, after a few years of additional military service, was imprisoned by Dorgon in 1648 along with some of his followers. Haoge died in prison in the following year.[20]

---

of these was Soni's brother, Hife, who was shortly dismissed from the Grand Secretariat in an episode discussed later in this chapter. By the end of 1644 there were six Grand Secretaries: one Manchu (Ganglin), two Chinese bannermen (Hung Ch'eng-ch'ou and Ning Wan-wo, the latter now reinstated after having been removed by Abahai for gambling in 1635), one Chinese who had served under Abahai (Fan Wen-ch'eng), and two Ming officials (Feng Ch'üan and Hsieh Sheng).

On the relatively minimal influence of the Grand Secretaries under the Dorgon regency, see Silas Wu, Communication and Imperial Control, p. 14.

17. On the expansion and role of the Council of Deliberative Officials in the Dorgon period, see Silas Wu, Communication and Imperial Control, p. 12; Fu Tsung-mao, Ch'ing-tai Chün-chi ch'u, pp. 52-58, passim.

18. See Spence, Ts'ao Yin, pp. 4-5, 70-77. The use of Chinese bannermen in high provincial posts is a major topic of chapter 5 of this volume.

19. SC Shih-lu, ch. 2, pp. 17b-19a.

20. See Haoge biography in Hummel, pp. 280-81.

In November 1644, a few months after the conquest of Peking, Dorgon took another bold step to bolster his authority, a step that was to have enduring importance for the Joint Regents' faction of the 1660s. Dorgon issued an edict, written in the first person on behalf of the six-year-old Shun-chih Emperor, which named Dorgon as "Uncle Regent" (shu-fu she-cheng wang) and thus elevated him above his co-regent, Jirgalang. The edict then authorized some rich gifts for the "Uncle Regent," including a black fox cap with a button inlaid with pearls, a black fox robe, ten thousand taels of gold, one hundred taels of silver, and several horses and camels. But most important, the edict went on to cite Dorgon's virtues and his services to the Manchu cause. In the military campaigns under Abahai, it was "the Uncle Regent who devised the plans and thus each city was overcome, each battle brought a victory." The edict then made a favorable comparison between Dorgon and the famous Duke of Chou, who had been regent for King Ch'eng in the founding of the Chou dynasty over two and a half millenia earlier. "The deceased emperor [Abahai] held him in special affection and esteem. He granted him ranks and gifts, giving him the title of Prince Jui. He also assisted in my succession to the throne and has helped me personally. I consider his merits and virtues to exceed those of the Duke of Chou." The edict concluded with the Shun-chih Emperor urging support for Dorgon's rule: "Give close attention to the regulations which my Uncle establishes for pacification. He will assist my small self, exhausting himself with loyalty and sincerity."[21] This edict, raising Dorgon's status in the 1640s, was an apparent prototype for the second great forgery of the early Ch'ing period: the Shun-chih Will of 1661. In both cases, the forged words of the Shun-chih Emperor were used to justify the power of a regency. Dorgon's ingenuity in putting words in the mouth of a child emperor was to be matched by the future regents' putting words in the mouth of an imperial corpse.

While giving all of the future regents a useful lesson in forging statements of authority, Dorgon also provided a model for factional politics which was of special interest to Oboi. When the Joint Regents' faction fractured in the mid-1660s, the Oboi faction (1667-69) sought to duplicate most of Dorgon's achievements of two decades earlier. As mentioned earlier, Dorgon first established a firm foundation for his faction within the banner system. Then in 1647 he deposed his co-regent Jirgalang and appointed his own brother, Dodo, as the new co-regent.

21. Quotations are from SC Shih-lu, ch. 9, pp. 22a-23a; entire edict is on pp. 9b-23b. Dorgon, frustrated in his attempt to become emperor in 1643, had a passion for titles which would approximate those of an emperor. In 1645, for instance, he named himself "Imperial Uncle Regent" (huang shu-fu she-cheng wang) and in 1648 raised this to "Imperial Father Regent" (huang-fu she-cheng wang). On the matter of these titles, and on Dorgon's efforts to become emperor in all but name, see: Cheng, "Tuo-er-kang ch'eng huang-fu chih i-ts'e," pp. 1-14; Ch'en Chieh-hsien, "Tuo-er-kang ch'eng 'Huang-fu she-cheng wang' yen-chiu," pp. 1-19; Hsiao I-shan, 1:377-83.

Dodo, weakened by smallpox, presented no threat to Dorgon's leadership and at the same time added a third banner to Dorgon's military base. Meanwhile, Dorgon began to expand his control over military and civil affairs by relying on a select group of loyal subordinates. The leading figures in Dorgon's clique were three grandsons of Nurhaci: Bolo, Nikan, and Mandahai. How these men developed their loyal attachment to the regent is uncertain, but the bond was well established by November 1644, when all of them were granted high princely titles. Throughout the regency these three accompanied every major military expedition undertaken by Dorgon in order to keep a close watch over the princes and other commanders. In 1650, toward the end of the regency, Dorgon also used them to oversee the civil bureaucracy. In March of that year, Nikan, Bolo, and Mandahai were appointed supervisors of the daily activities of the Six Boards. Specifically, they were to handle all affairs which did not require a memorial to the throne.[22] To assure his personal control, therefore, Dorgon had cut through the usual chain of command in both the banner system and the metropolitan bureaucracy, and relied on the support of close associates.

For the time being, however, Soni, Ebilun, and Oboi were unable to apply Dorgon's valuable lessons in the art of Manchu governance and factionalism. Only Suksaha, who had the fortune of being enrolled in Dorgon's own Plain White Banner, made it through the 1640s unscathed. One biographer has even indicated that Suksaha may have been a minor figure within the Dorgon faction, and has called him "one of Dorgon's subordinates."[23] The other three suffered for their support of Haoge in 1643. Twice during the Dorgon regency, members of Dorgon's faction brought charges against Soni and his brother Hife for having opposed the regent. Both were removed from their offices (Soni had been a clerk in the Board of Civil Office and Hife a Grand Secretary) and stripped of their ranks. In 1648, when Haoge was convicted and imprisoned, Ebilun and Oboi were accused of having promoted his claims to the throne in 1643. Ebilun was sentenced to death, but an imperial edict reduced the punishment to withdrawal of his titles and captaincy, and confiscation of half his property. Similarly, Oboi was declared guilty and sentenced to death by beheading, but an edict lightened his penalty to loss of rank.[24] Dorgon maintained the pressure against these opponents to

---

22. Biographies of all of these figures are found in Hummel. Another relative of Nurhaci, Lekedehun, played a military and civil surveillance role similar to those of Bolo, Nikan, and Mandahai. See Hummel, pp. 443-44. The titles which Dorgon bestowed on Bolo, Nikan, and Mandahai are mentioned in CS, 1 (pen-chi): 39-46, passim. The edict appointing these three to oversee the Six Boards is found in SC Shih-lu, ch. 47, p. 15a-b. Parallels between the Dorgon faction and the Oboi faction will be discussed in chapter 8.

23. CSLC, ch. 6, p. 5a.

24. The best source for these charges against the future regents is ibid., ch. 6, pp. 10b-11a, 15b-16a, 17b. Other relatives of the future regents who suffered in Dorgon's purge of his opposition were Oboi's cousin, Tulai (see Hummel, p. 247), and Oboi's brother, Baha (see CSLC, ch. 6, pp. 12b-13a).

the very end of his reign. In August 1650, less than four months before his death, Dorgon brought several Manchu officials to an audience and asked each of them "whether or not they were on good terms with Soni and Oboi." The responses varied and one official even tried to dodge the question by saying that he was "too stubborn to be concerned with such matters." But Dorgon suspected conspiracy against his rule and punished all of them by loss of ranks.[25]

Soni's humiliation at the hands of the Dorgon faction meant that he was left without any political or military duties. He spent the 1640s in Peking, waiting for Dorgon's demise while struggling to preserve his life against his many accusers. Oboi and Ebilun were somewhat more fortunate. Sharing Soni's anxieties about their political futures, Oboi and Ebilun still managed to continue their military careers during the Dorgon regency. Over the years 1644-45 both of them assisted in chasing Li Tzu-ch'eng and his rebel army across north China. After Li died in 1645, Oboi was attached to the troops pursuing the other late Ming rebel, Chang Hsien-chung. Chang was finally captured and beheaded in Szechwan in 1647, but Oboi kept up the attack against Chang's subordinates into the year 1648. Then in 1648-49 Oboi was transferred to Shansi, where he successfully commanded some crack Manchu troops against a Ming loyalist general.[26] These military activities must have offered some consolation to Oboi and Ebilun for their political troubles. At least they were part of the massive military operations which resulted in Ch'ing domination over most of the former Ming provinces by the end of the 1640s. With able assistance from Chinese banner commanders, particularly from Hung Ch'eng-ch'ou and Wu San-kuei, Manchu rule covered all of the provinces with the exception of those in the extreme south and southwest (Kwangtung, Kwangsi, Yunnan, and Kweichow). The only remaining Ming loyalist movement was that of Chu Yu-lang (Ming Prince of Kuei), whose forces were restricted to this southern belt of provinces. Through the formidable victories of the Manchu conquest elite and their Chinese allies, the Ch'ing house appeared relatively secure by the end of the Dorgon regency in 1650.[27] Other military threats were to emerge in the late Shun-chih and K'ang-hsi reigns: the rise of Cheng Ch'eng-kung (Coxinga), Russian incursions into Manchuria, and the

---

25. SC Shih-lu, ch. 49, p. 16a-b.

26. Soni's biographers record no military activities or bureaucratic posts during the period of the Dorgon regency. The military ventures of Oboi and Ebilun during the 1640s are recorded in CSLC, ch. 6, pp. 10b-11a, 17a-b. None of Suksaha's biographies indicate important military assignments after the Sung-shan and Chin-chou campaigns until the 1650s.

Oboi lost his decorations for the battles against Chang Hsien-chung when it was reported that he had failed to rescue another commander who had been surrounded by the rebel forces (SC Shih-lu, ch. 36, pp. 12a-13b).

27. A history of the battles under the Dorgon regency is found in Hsiao I-shan, 1: 272-334. The battles against Chu Yu-lang were to continue through the 1650s into the Oboi regency; see chapter 4 of this volume.

growing independence of the feudatory princes. But these threats were only dimly perceived from the vantage point of 1650 when it seemed that the conquest was close to completion.

Dorgon died on a hunting trip in Jehol on 31 December 1650. His death gave new hope to the political aspirations of numerous senior Manchus, including Soni, Oboi, Ebilun, and Suksaha. Under his regency they had seen Manchu rule spread across the Chinese empire and had watched Dorgon apply Abahai's governmental systems to the Chinese state and society. As persecuted figures in the political opposition, three of them had learned much about the dangers and techniques of Manchu factionalism. One, Suksaha, seems to have learned his lessons from a safer position within the Dorgon clique. But all of them yearned for greater political influence. Moving quickly after Dorgon's death, the four Manchus began to apply their lessons by working together.

A GLORIOUS INTERLUDE, 1651-1653

Dorgon's death opened a period of intense factional rivalry. With most of the princes and Manchu officers stationed in Chihli after the successful campaigns of the 1640s, Peking became the new battleground. The factional conflict of 1651-53 was among the fiercest and most complex in the early Ch'ing. Joining the fray were princes, banner commanders, Chinese statesmen, eunuchs, the Empress Dowager, and the emperor himself. The struggle went through two phases, each phase directly involving or affecting Soni, Suksaha, Ebilun, and Oboi. In phase one, early 1651 to mid-1652, the Shun-chih Emperor was given nominal control over the government with prince Jirgalang as the dominant influence at court. Jirgalang moved against various remnants of the Dorgon faction and other contenders who might have weakened imperial rule. Then in phase two, late 1652 and 1653, a new faction coalesced around the emperor. This Shun-chih faction, a loose coalition of advisers and confidants assisting the young emperor, reigned for the remainder of the 1650s. We shall look only at the highlights of this factional history, concentrating on the involvement of the future members of the Joint Regents' faction.

In early Ch'ing history, funerals and factionalism are closely associated, and 1651 was no exception. In mid-January Dorgon was given imperial funerary rites and canonized as the "Righteous Emperor" (I huang-ti). During the ceremonies, however, several officers in the White Banners, led by a former Dorgon associate named Ubai, arrested Dorgon's only surviving brother, Ajige. Ajige, who might have established himself as a new regent, was tried, convicted on charges of usurping imperial authority, and placed in prison, where he was eventually forced to commit suicide. With Ajige out of the way, Ubai and several followers appointed themselves to board presidencies and prepared to assume the functions of imperial leadership.[28] A counterattack soon

28. A fine summary of these events is Fang Chao-ying's biography of Dorgon

materialized under the leadership of Jirgalang, the former co-regent who had suffered disgrace under Dorgon. Jirgalang moved slowly, rallying military support around himself, while acting under the ostensible motive of bringing the Shun-chih Emperor to personal rule.

Jirgalang began by approaching officers in three of the eight banners: the Plain Yellow, the Bordered Yellow, and the Plain White. The former two (in which Soni, Ebilun, and Oboi were enrolled) had been imperial banners under Abahai; the latter (in which Suksaha was enrolled) had been under Dorgon's own command. Jirgalang intended, therefore, to win allegiance from the Yellow Banner officers who had been disappointed under the Dorgon regency, while endeavoring to subvert the strength of the Dorgon faction in the Plain White Banner. To offer further incentive, these banners were given a new collective title, the Three Imperial Banners (shang-san-ch'i). Suksaha, an opportunist by nature, was among the first to turn on his former allies and join the Jirgalang faction. He and Oboi, another convert to the Jirgalang group, were rewarded for their loyalty by appointments to the Council of Deliberative Officials. Then on 1 February 1651 it was formally announced that the Shun-chih Emperor had taken personal control of the government. This announcement, of course, symbolized the growing power of Jirgalang and provided additional authority for those in his faction. But through most of February Jirgalang continued to proceed with caution and even entered Dorgon's name into the Imperial Ancestral Temple while honoring some of the followers of the deceased regent. Finally, in late February and March, Jirgalang initiated the attack. With Suksaha as the leading witness, Dorgon was posthumously accused of coveting imperial powers, wearing imperial garments, and plotting to construct a new capital for himself. The dead regent was judged guilty on all counts and was denied his posthumous honors. Now that Dorgon had been vilified, the Jirgalang faction began its purge of many leading figures in the Dorgon camp. Over the following months, Ubai was removed from his posts and lost his property, and several of Dorgon's associates were executed.[29] But the purge was still incomplete. The

---

in Hummel, pp. 217-18. Dorgon's posthumous elevation to imperial status, engineered by his factional associates to enhance their chances for political power, is mentioned in CS, 1 (pen-chi): 47; Hummel, p. 217. On Ajige and Ubai, see Hummel, pp. 4-5, 798. Trial of Ajige and rise of Ubai and his cohorts is covered in SC Shih-lu, ch. 51, pp. 11b-12b; ch. 52, pp. 2a-9a; ch. 61, pp. 3a-4a.

29. For the appointment of Suksaha and Oboi to the Council, see SC Shih-lu, ch. 52, pp. 9b, 24a. The imperial proclamation which announces Shun-chih's personal control of the government is in ibid., ch. 52, pp. 12b-15b. Suksaha's testimony is recorded in ibid., ch. 53, 18a-20a. The posthumous conviction of Dorgon is in ibid., ch. 53, pp. 21b-24a. Among those punished or executed for serving Dorgon were several figures who had formerly brought accusations against Soni, Oboi, and Ebilun. Tantai (1594-1651) was the most prominent of these, and he suffered execution in late 1651 (Hummel, pp. 898-99; CSLC, ch. 4, pp. 29b-31b). For a list of those removed in the purge of the Dorgon faction, see Hsiao I-shan, 1: 379-84.

three major figures in the regent's faction, Mandahai, Bolo, and Nikan, retained considerable military power and had rescued their political reputations by assisting in the testimony against Dorgon. On 25 April 1651 it was announced that these three princes would "manage" (kuan) the Boards of Civil Office, Revenue, and Rites according to the practice established under Abahai.[30]

During the remainder of 1651 and in early 1652, Jirgalang pursued his strategy of finding allies in the Three Imperial Banners and bestowing high ranks and titles on these followers. All four of the future regents joined Jirgalang's movement and shared in these rewards. Oboi, Soni, and Ebilun were exonerated of the accusations brought against them in the late 1640s. Their previous honors were restored to them. Furthermore, Soni and Ebilun were soon appointed to the Council of Deliberative Officials, thus joining Suksaha and Oboi in this most prestigious Manchu policy-making organization. All four were promoted to the post of chamberlain of the Imperial Bodyguard. As chamberlains they governed the elite banner troops within the Forbidden City and could provide strong military aid for Jirgalang and the Shun-chih Emperor. They were also admitted to the highest levels of the Manchu nobility as further compensation for their loyalty. Ebilun and Oboi received the rank of duke, the highest for anyone outside the imperial family. Soni was named an earl, while Suksaha became a viscount.[31] Relying on his expanded factional base, Jirgalang finally dealt the coup de grace to the Dorgon clique. On 22 April 1652 the system of having princes "manage" the boards was abolished. And, perhaps not coincidentally, Mandahai, Bolo, and Nikan all died in that same year (Nikan reportedly died in battle; causes of death for the other two are not reported).[32]

With Jirgalang as their patron, the four future regents had quickly reached the pinnacle of success. As Council members, chamberlains, noblemen, they were the envy of the Manchu conquest elite. They also enjoyed the special status of leading officers in the Three Imperial Banners. From their vantage point in 1652, Soni, Suksaha, Ebilun, and Oboi seemed to have glorious careers ahead. But they failed to foresee two developments which would cast shadows over their achievements. The first was the loss of their patron. Jirgalang's health began to fail, and he died in June 1655. As Jirgalang weakened, control of the Ch'ing government gradually passed to a new faction around the Shun-chih Emperor. This second development brought an end to our four Manchus' visions of glory. They were left with their military commands, but their political influence was minimal. Angry over their loss of power, they were further embittered as they observed the policies and personalities of the Shun-chih faction.

30. SC Shih-lu, ch. 55, pp. 5a-b.

31. For these honors and appointments, see the biographies of the regents cited in footnotes 32, 34, and 36 of chapter 3.

32. SC Shih-lu, ch. 63, p. 13b. Nikan was reduced in rank on April 22, and Bolo's death was announced the following day (ibid., ch. 63, pp. 13b-14a).

A MANCHU LEGACY FROM A SINOPHILE, 1653-1661

The central figure in the Shun-chih faction was the young emperor himself. Unfortunately for the historian, it is difficult to move beyond the
varying interpretations of the controversial Shun-chih to the real personality of this early Ch'ing monarch. Jesuit accounts have portrayed
Shun-chih as a man of wisdom and sensitivity, who almost converted to
Christianity. Some have stressed his Buddhist orientation, which is
symbolized by a mummy-statue of Shun-chih at the Buddhist shrine at
Mount T'ien-t'ai in Chekiang. Here we see him, a man of soft and gentle
features with a faint smile on his lips, dressed in imperial robes with a
Buddhist crown. Chinese biographies portray him as a man of extremes,
alternating between fits of rage and quieter times of reading and contem-
plation. Some have even speculated that Shun-chih may have been the
prototype for Pao-yu, the volatile hero in the famous eighteenth-century
novel, Dream of the Red Chamber (Hung-lou meng). But the least com-
plimentary portrait is provided in the Shun-chih Will, forged in substantial part by the four regents and the Grand Empress Dowager in 1661.
In the Will he is a remorseful ruler who regrets his rejection of the
Manchu heritage, his unfilial conduct towards his mother, and his fascination with things Chinese.[33]

Perhaps some day a biographer will sift through these interpretations and discover the real Shun-chih Emperor. But that is not the task
of this study. Instead, since the young emperor became many legends
in his own time, we are interested in those legends which were to moti-
vate the activities of the Joint Regents' faction in the 1660s. The Shun-
chih Will, therefore, is an invaluable document because it was forged
to suit the needs of a new regime. It tells us much about the attitudes
of the four regents and probably reflects the sentiments of most of the
Manchu conquest elite. By relating the key points in the Shun-chih Will
to the events and personalities of the 1650s, one can better understand
the political history of the following decade.

One difficulty must be mentioned at the outset. It is known that the
draft of the Will, taken by two subchancellors at the bedside of the dying
monarch, was intercepted by an imperial bodyguard and submitted to
the Grand Empress Dowager. Before the Will was made public on the
evening of 5 February 1661, it was altered by the Grand Empress Dowager and by Soni, Suksaha, Ebilun, and Oboi. But it is uncertain how
much of the final Will was forged.[34] The difficulty arises because the

33. A biography of the Shun-chih Emperor, based heavily on Jesuit and other
Western accounts, is Reid, "Peking's First Manchu Emperor," pp. 130-46.
Other Jesuit accounts will be cited later in this chapter and in chapter 7. A pho-
tograph of the statue-mummy of the Shun-chih Emperor is found in Backhouse and
Bland, Annals and Memoirs, frontispiece. A good composite of Chinese biographies of the emperor is provided in Hummel, pp. 255-59. The question of Shun-
chih as the prototype for Pao-yu is discussed in footnote 71 of this chapter.

34. The emperor's death and the forgery of the Imperial Will are discussed
at length in Appendix 1.

Shun-chih Emperor frequently issued proclamations during his reign in which he publicly degraded himself. Perhaps this tendency toward self-deprecation was fostered by his ill health. He had been a sickly and retiring man and may have contracted tuberculosis, for he was thin and spat blood. He also may have had a masochistic side to his personality which pushed him to punish himself. According to one account, the emperor became so angry on learning that the Ming loyalist Cheng Ch'eng-kung (Coxinga) was attacking Nanking in 1659 that he hacked up one of his thrones with a sword.[35] Because of these personality traits it is possible that some of the "sins" in the Will are genuine expressions of his own regrets.

One example of self-deprecation in the Shun-chih Will that may be genuine is the following: "It has been my nature to devote myself to pleasure, idleness, and quiet. I have always attempted to find leisure and to stay deeply in the palace. I have been negligent in attendance at court and have had but limited contact with officials."[36] This surely could have been uttered by the same man who announced during the rainy August of 1653: "Now we have had heavy rains for a whole moon and the harvest prospects are bleak. Water has filled the gutters, firewood is extremely expensive, and the commoners find it difficult to survive. Wives and children are wailing, and in some extreme conditions people have been pushed close to death. This elicits my deepest sorrow and it has all been caused by my lack of virtue."[37] Again and again Shun-chih issued his mea culpas. His final self-denunciation, before the Imperial Will itself, was issued in March 1660: "For the past seventeen years the people have not been brought to fulfillment. Greedy officials still have not been removed from office. . . . All of this comes from my lack of virtue. I have neglected Heaven's commands, brought shame to the trust of Tsu and Tsung, disregarded the merciful instructions of the Empress Dowager, and ignored my paternal duties to the hopes of the commoners."[38]

In his Will as in his reign, therefore, the emperor's public image reflected a moody, morose, even petulant man. He appeared as a ruler obsessed with the traditional Chinese belief that the emperor's character was the source of good or evil in the realm. But if these portions of the Imperial Will are genuine, the important point is that the future regents and the Grand Empress Dowager deliberately chose to leave them in the final version. Such remarks not only enhanced the credibility of the Will, but they also portrayed the emperor as the Manchus wanted him seen. The regents and the Grand Empress Dowager hoped

35. For Shun-chih's ill health and the throne destruction story, see Hummel, pp. 257-58. For other indications of Shun-chih's violence, see Hsiao I-shan, 1: 405.

36. SC Shih-lu, ch. 144, p. 5a.

37. Ibid., ch. 76, pp. 24b-25a.

38. Ibid., ch. 131, p. 13a. Other examples are ibid., ch. 88, pp. 4b-5a; ch. 111, pp. 23a-b; ch. 87, pp. 4b-5b.

that the Manchu conquest elite would turn away from such a figure in
disgust and enthusiastically support the new leadership.

Much of the Imperial Will, however, consists of "sins" which had
never been raised in the earlier "unvirtuous" proclamations of the Shun-
chih Emperor. In these sections, the emperor stops speaking in gene-
ralities about his personal inadequacies and specifically denounces close
associates and major policies. It is likely that these items were added
after the draft Will was intercepted. Four main themes emerge from
these parts of the Will: (1) Shun-chih's reliance on eunuchs; (2) his emphasis on Chinese officials and Ming institutions; (3) his disregard for
Manchu officers and traditions; and (4) his devotion to his empress rather
than to his mother. By exploring these themes in the context of the later
years of the Shun-chih reign, one can perceive the basis for many policies of the Joint Regents' faction. What follows is a political history of
the late Shun-chih period as perceived by our four Manchus and probably
by much of the Manchu conquest elite.

The Imperial Will was particularly firm on the emperor's employment of eunuchs in his retinue and his dependence on them for counsel:

> Tsu and Tsung founded the dynasty and they never used eunuchs.
> One reason that the Ming lost the empire was that they made the
> error of relying on eunuchs. I was clearly aware of their corrup-
> tion, but I was unable to heed this warning. I established the Thir-
> teen Offices and committed errors in choosing officials. This was
> no different than under the Ming.[39]

Under the Dorgon regency stern measures had been taken to diminish
the political influence of eunuchs. Aware of the rampant factionalism
caused by eunuchs in the late Ming period, Dorgon did not use them as
personal attendants and abolished many eunuch offices and posts.[40]
Shun-chih reversed this policy in 1653, when he began to assign eunuchs
as imperial aides. Then in July 1653 he established a personal bureaucracy, composed of eunuchs and other informal advisers, known as the
Thirteen Offices (shih-san ya-men). During the late 1650s the Thirteen
Offices handled key administrative and financial matters, offered advice
on political problems and appointments, and served to isolate the emperor from his regular civil and military officials.[41] The most notable
figures associated with the Thirteen Offices were Wu Liang-fu, the emperor's favorite eunuch, and Tung-i, a Manchu who served as an imperial confidant.[42] To the dismay of most of the Manchu conquest elite,

39. Ibid., ch. 144, p. 3b.

40. Spence, Ts'ao Yin, pp. 11-12; Cheng, Ch'ing-shih t'an-wei, pp. 64-67.

41. On the appointment of eunuchs and the establishment of the Thirteen Offices, see SC Shih-lu, ch. 76, pp. 16a-18a, and ch. 92, p. 12a-b. A brief description of the Thirteen Offices and their functions is provided in Hsiao I-shan,
1: 390-92.

42. Hummel, pp. 256-57.

Shun-chih had thus created an institution which in function, personnel, and even in name, bore a frightening resemblance to the infamous Twenty-four Offices (er-shih-ssu ya-men) of the late Ming. Instead of selecting Chinese bondservants to staff an Imperial Household as later emperors would do, Shun-chih had turned to eunuchs and other opportunists whose dependability was suspect.[43] Wu Liang-fu quickly confirmed Manchu fears about eunuchs by accepting bribes from metropolitan and provincial officials. In 1658 the emperor gave a reprimand to Wu Liang-fu for such corrupt activities, but he left Wu in office and only promised penalties for future indiscretions. Shun-chih's affection for Wu Liang-fu remained strong throughout his reign; only five days before his death, Shun-chih rose from his sickbed and attended Wu's tonsuring ceremony as the eunuch accepted the Buddhist faith.[44]

Although Manchus interpreted the creation of the Thirteen Offices as proof of the emperor's return to Chinese modes of imperial corruption, Shun-chih may have had other motives in mind. He was not oblivious to the dangers of eunuchs. In 1653 and again in 1655 he issued proclamations which listed the multitude of crimes committed by the late Ming eunuchs and specifically cited Wei Chung-hsien, the eunuch-dictator of the 1620s, as an example. Shun-chih promised to control his eunuchs, to limit their numbers, and to punish by the lingering death any who interfered with governmental activities.[45] But cognizant of the perils in his decision, Shun-chih may have concluded that the Thirteen Offices were his only hope in reasserting his own authority against Manchu factional opponents. The immediate threat was the Jirgalang group which had risen to power in the name of the Shun-chih Emperor but which had ignored him as a serious political factor in the early 1650s. Another threat, as we shall see later, was the emperor's mother, who sought to interfere with his personal life. Given these problems, Shun-chih may have been convinced by Wu Liang-fu and others that they could overcome his opponents while restraining themselves from the excesses of the late Ming era. The Thirteen Offices, therefore, gave Shun-chih his own factional power base, isolated the Jirgalang faction and the emperor's mother,

43. On the role of eunuchs during the Ming dynasty, see Hucker, "Governmental Organization," pp. 10-11; Hucker, Traditional Chinese State, p. 12; Ming Shih, ch. 74, pp. 778-82. On bondservants in the Imperial Household see Spence, Ts'ao Yin, pp. 33-36. On the organization and evolution of the Imperial Household, see Cheng, Ch'ing-shih t'an-wei, pp. 72-77; Hsiao I-shan, 1: 389-90; BH, pp. 13-35; Chang Te-ch'ang, "Economic Role of the Imperial Household," pp. 243-73. For the early organization of the Imperial Household, see Meng, "Pa-ch'i chih-tu k'ao-shih," p. 57; PCTC (1795), ch. 317, passim. Both bannermen and bondservants, as well as eunuchs, were eligible for positions in the Thirteen Offices (Hummel, p. 14).

44. The bribery cases involving Wu Liang-fu are recorded in SC Shih-lu, ch. 115, pp. 13b-14a; Hsiao I-shan, 1: 387. Shun-chih's attendance at Wu's tonsuring is covered in Appendix 1.

45. SC Shih-lu, ch. 76, pp. 16a-18a; ch. 92, pp. 12a-b; Hsiao I-shan, 1: 390-92.

and permitted the emperor to control his government by the mid-1650s.

In addition to the eunuchs, the Shun-chih Emperor surrounded himself with other non-Manchu associates, most of whom offered intellectual and religious companionship rather than political support. Ch'an
Buddhist monks were prominent in the emperor's retinue towards the
end of his reign. The emperor, with a bent for the supernatural, became convinced that in an earlier incarnation he had been a Buddhist
monk. He spent a great deal of time in meditation and discussion with
his two closest monks, Hsing-ts'ung and Tao-min. He also persuaded
the Empress Hsiao-hsien, the Grand Empress Dowager, and several
eunuchs to adopt the Ch'an Buddhist faith.[46] According to contemporary
Western accounts, the famous German Jesuit, Adam Schall, was also
one of the close associates of the Shun-chih Emperor. Under Dorgon,
Adam Schall had been elevated to the position of director of the Imperial
Bureau of Astronomy as a reward for his translation of Western works
on mathematics and for his preparation of a calendar based on Western
calculations. After the young emperor came to power, Adam Schall remained in the good graces of the Ch'ing court. Shun-chih not only granted Schall some of the highest honors in the empire, but he even excused
him from performing the kowtow. The emperor's fascination with the
Jesuit probably stemmed from Schall's knowledge of Western scientific
wonders rather than from a conversion to Christianity. Schall nevertheless believed that he could have converted the Shun-chih Emperor had it
not been for the obstacle of the Sixth Commandment. According to Schall,
the emperor "could not overcome the lusts of the flesh."[47]

From a Manchu perspective, the emperor's association with Adam
Schall, as well as with Wu Liang-fu, Tung-i, Hsing-ts'ung, and Tao-
min, was symptomatic of the decline of the Manchu state. New and corrupt institutions, symbolized by the Thirteen Offices, had replaced the
"pure and honest old system." Eunuchs, Buddhists, and even a Christian had replaced the Manchu advisers and Chinese bondservants who
waited on Nurhaci, Abahai, and Dorgon.

Another theme in the forged sections of the Shun-chih Will was the
emperor's emphasis on Chinese officials and Ming institutions. The
forgers believed that Shun-chih was afflicted with sinophilia: "The fact
that the Ming lost the empire was mainly due to their bias toward civil
officials. I have not taken this as a lesson. I have appointed Chinese
officials. Occasionally I have even ordered the Chinese to have control of the seals of office of the boards and departments."[48] To illustrate this point, the authors of the Shun-chih Will pointed to Liu Cheng-

46. Hummel, p. 257.
47. Dunne, Generation of Giants, pp. 347-53. Further information about
Schall's relationship with Shun-chih may be found in Spence, To Change China,
pp. 19-21.
48. SC Shih-lu, ch. 144, p. 3b.

tsung, an exceptionally powerful and corrupt favorite of the Shun-chih Emperor.[49] Liu, a <u>chin-shih</u> from Shantung, was promoted to Grand Secretary in 1652 and president of the Board of Civil Office in the following year.[50] From this vantage point Liu Cheng-tsung was able to bring wealth and prestige to his family and friends. His brother, Liu Cheng-hsüeh, was appointed to a military post in spite of the fact that he had formerly served the famous Ming loyalist and pirate, Cheng Ch'eng-kung (Coxinga). Another brother, Liu Fang-ming, became a brigade-general and received many favors from Liu Cheng-tsung. Several of Liu's friends and subordinates who gained offices through his recommendation used their positions for corrupt financial ends. A Chinese censor who impeached Liu Cheng-tsung in 1660 observed, "If Cheng-tsung's friends are men of this sort, what kind of man can he be?" Liu was also accused of making slanderous statements, submitting false testimony at trials, failing to memorialize about a rebellion, and committing various fiscal irregularities.[51]

To the Manchu conquest elite Liu Cheng-tsung symbolized the worst in Chinese malpractices.[52] His family was tainted by his brother's association with the Ming loyalist movement under Cheng Ch'eng-kung. Liu had been sheltered by the Shun-chih Emperor and thus represented another case of the emperor's "bias towards civil officials" and his "inability to dismiss the degenerate." Liu's case was a classic instance of corruption and factionalism and, to Manchu observers, was yet an-

---

49. The Will cited Liu Cheng-tsung as a man who was "biased, selfish, impatient, and envious." He was said to have retained his positions only because the emperor was "overly generous and indulgent" (ibid., ch. 144, p. 4a).

50. CSLC, ch. 79, pp. 31b-32b.

51. SC Shih-lu, ch. 136, p. 14b. The enumeration of Liu Cheng-tsung's intrigues is found in ibid., ch. 136, pp. 13b-15b, 17b-20a; ch. 142, pp. 5b-13b.

52. For other examples of factionalism under the Shun-chih reign, see Hsieh Kuo-chen, Ming-Ch'ing chih chi tang-she yun-tung k'ao, pp. 119-22. It is Hsieh's belief that the conflict between the Wei Chung-hsien clique and the Tung-lin party continued long after the passing of the original combattants. Hsieh claims that the main protagonists in the Shuh-chih period were Feng Ch'üan representing the Wei Chung-hsien remnants, and Ch'en Ming-hsia of the Tung-lin group. Hsieh has observed that the men recommended by Feng and Ch'en were generally supporters of the eunuchs or of the Tung-lin movement.

Ch'en Ming-hsia was accused of forming a faction in 1653 and was put to death by strangulation in the following year. Ch'en's case adds a new light to the matter of factionalism under Shun-chih. His accuser was the famous Chinese bannerman Ning Wan-wo. Among the accusations was the crime of having favored a return to Ming customs and having disapproved of the Manchu queue requirement. By approving the execution, Shun-chih seems to have taken a forthright Manchu stance on these matters and also to have proved that he was not tolerant of all factions under his reign. See Hummel, p. 95; SC Shih-lu, ch. 57, pp. 11b-12a; ch. 62, pp. 3b-5b; ch. 82, pp. 1b-9a. For Shun-chih's insistence on Manchu dress regulations, see Hsiao I-shan, 1: 388.

other reminder of similarities to the late Ming period. Since the opposition to Liu Cheng-tsung was widespread, the Shun-chih Emperor eventually decided to punish him. In December 1660 the emperor denounced
Liu, ordered that he be dismissed from his offices, and that one half of
his property be confiscated and given to bannermen. Liu Cheng-tsung,
however, was excused from suffering the death penalty. [53]

Other episodes in the emperor's reign may have reinforced the Manchus' conclusion that Shun-chih was strongly attracted to Ming precedents. In February 1653 the fifteen-year-old monarch paid a visit to
his Grand Secretaries and asked them who had been China's best emperor. Although several candidates were mentioned, T'ang T'ai-tsung
was singled out as the best of all by one of the Chinese Grand Secretaries. Shun-chih retorted, "How can you pick T'ang T'ai-tsung? I
feel that among all the emperors of history, none was as good as Ming
Hung-wu." The emperor went on to explain that Hung-wu had been the
most effective in promulgating regulations which were comprehensive
and detailed.[54] As we shall see in the next chapter, Shun-chih followed
this judgement by giving special attention to several Chinese institutions
including the Grand Secretariat, the Hanlin Academy, the Censorate,
and the civil service examination system. He also lavished honors on
several late Ming statesmen and performed special rituals for the last
Ming emperor.[55] While the Shun-chih Emperor may have taken these
public stands solely to appeal to dissident Chinese scholars and officials,
many Manchus concluded that their sovereign had contracted a bad case
of creeping Ming-ism.

The Will also criticized the Shun-chih Emperor for disregarding his
Manchu officials and his Manchu traditions. The Will was explicit on
this point: "Some of the Manchu officials have exhibited their loyalty
through successive generations, while others have devoted their efforts
year after year. They have continued to work even though they are exhausted, but I have not trusted them and appointed them. . . . Thus I
have caused the Manchu statesmen to have no desire to serve and their
zeal has been dissipated."[56] Here was a major complaint of Soni, Suksaha, Ebilun, and Oboi spliced into the Will. The advent of the Shun-
chih faction had brought the demise of their new-found power. Their
biographers have recorded few noteworthy events in the lives of the
four Manchus for the period of 1653-61. In 1657 Ebilun received the
honorary titles of Junior Guardian and Grand Guardian of the Heir Apparent, but these titulary rewards were not accompanied by increased
political influence. Suksaha fought several battles against rebels in

53. SC Shih-lu, ch. 142, pp. 12a-13b.
54. Ibid., ch. 61, pp. 24a-25a.
55. Ibid., ch. 76, pp. 5b-6a, and ch. 130, pp. 6b-7a, 10b; Hsiao I-shan, 1:
386.
56. SC Shih-lu, ch. 144, p. 3b.

Hukuang and Kiangnan provinces: in the latter instance he commanded
armed junks in the river areas of Kiangnan and gained the emperor's
praise for winning six battles in succession.[57] But Suksaha too was
without political power.

Soni and Oboi, sharing the frustration of the other two, endeavored
to while away the Shun-chih reign by making helpful suggestions to the
throne. In August 1660, for example, Soni submitted a sensible and
balanced memorial about several problems confronting the Manchu government. He argued that the commoners were oppressed and that officials who failed to report on local conditions should be investigated and
punished. He criticized the practice of showing favoritism to higher-
ranking military officers. He suggested that only those military officers
who had achieved merit in battle should be allowed to pass their ranks
on to their descendants. He requested that the dynasty be lenient in its
treatment of people living on the frontiers because they were not fully
cognizant of imperial regulations. He deplored certain excesses committed by Manchu princes and bannermen, such as forcing peddlars
to sell their goods at reduced prices and stealing lumber from merchants.[58] Oboi's concerns, on the other hand, focused exclusively on
military affairs. In 1656 he memorialized requesting that a general
military review be held triennially in the presence of the emperor in
order to evaluate the Manchu officer corps. He wanted the military
review to include an archery contest in which even the highest military
officials and imperial bodyguards would participate. Oboi continued to
insist on the need for fine military conditioning and, in fact, trained
several young soldiers himself. In an edict to the Board of War in 1660,
the emperor praised several military chin-shih who had been trained
by Oboi for their abilities in archery and horseback riding. All of these
young officers were appointed as imperial bodyguards.[59]

But receiving praise and honors was slight compensation for the future regents' political impotence under the Shun-chih Emperor. And
their anger must have intensified as they observed other developments.
The Council of Deliberative Officials, formerly an elite Manchu cabinet,
was greatly expanded with new appointments, a few of whom were selected from the Chinese banner officers.[60] The non-Chinese emperors
who had been admitted to the Imperial Ancestral Temple under Dorgon
were removed by Shun-chih on the grounds that they "had not stabilized
and perfected the empire."[61] In March 1653 the emperor called together
his officials and, holding up a Manchu bow, explained that the Ch'ing

57. See regents' biographies as cited in footnotes 32, 34, and 36 of chapter 2.
58. SC Shih-lu, ch. 137, pp. 19a-23b.
59. Ibid., ch. 136, p. 1b.
60. Shun-chih's handling of the Council of Deliberative Officials, as with all
other Manchu and Chinese metropolitan institutions, is discussed in chapter 4.
61. SC Shih-lu, ch. 136, pp. 11a-12b.

success depended on its military readiness and especially on the hunts
that used to be held two or three times a year. But Shun-chih explained
that he was too busy for such activities: "Now that I have personally
taken over the government, the empire has become very large and the
myriad things have become very troublesome. I have to endorse all
memorials and make decisions by myself without a minute of rest."[62]
Two weeks later, apparently feeling guilty about his earlier comment,
Shun-chih embarked on a mini-hunt that must have left his Manchu officers both amused and annoyed. According to a court chronicler:

> The Emperor was at the Southern Park. He called together all of
> the Chinese officials of the second rank and above and all of the
> literary officials. Then he ordered the bodyguards and members
> of the Guards Division to put on their armor, blow their horns, and
> shout the battle cries through the ranks, all in accordance with the
> military regulations. When the review was completed, he gave them
> a feast. Then in a self-satisfied manner, he left the Southern Park
> and hunted for three days, and netted fish within the Southern Park
> for one day. [63]

Uppermost in the forgers' minds concerning the question of Shun-
chih's relations with his Manchu officials was an episode which occurred
a few months before the advent of the Oboi regency. This was the Lu
Kuang-hsü affair. Lu Kuang-hsü was a Chinese civil official who had
received his chin-shih degree in 1651 and had been appointed to the post
of provincial censor on the Shensi circuit. On 16 September 1660 the
court received a scathing memorial from Lu Kuang-hsü which cited
rampant corruption and favoritism within the imperial bureaucracy and
bemoaned Manchu efforts to curtail the activities of censors. Lu observed that "this is not what we need to bring prosperity on this generation." Then he went on to criticize Manchu military activities: "Now
there is chaos and unrest, there is famine in the streets. Yet the military forces are increasing in number and the need for military supplies
is very great. Military officials occupy the heart of the provinces on
their own authority."[64]
     Lu Kuang-hsü's memorial was sent to a joint meeting of the Council
of Deliberative Officials and the Nine Ministers, the latter composed
of the top-ranking Chinese and Manchu officials in the regular metropolitan bureaucracy. The memorial precipitated an argument over procedure in the joint meeting. Chinese sentiment was expressed by Liang
Ch'ing-piao, president of the Board of War, who had received his chin-
shih in the waning years of the Ming dynasty. Liang felt that the Chinese
and Manchu representatives should draw up two draft proposals and then

62. Ibid., ch. 73, pp. 1b-2a.
63. Ibid., ch. 73, p. 7a.
64. Ibid., ch. 139, pp. 11a-b.

meet to work out the differences.[65] Manchu officials disagreed: "Previously in all meetings concerning military matters, Chinese officials have not been allowed to deliberate. If Chinese officials were permitted to offer their opinions, and if we dismissed their words as if they had not been spoken, they would soon usurp power and we would have to accept the consequences."[66]

The divided result of the meeting was submitted to the emperor and his advisers. The emperor not only reaffirmed Lu Kuang-hsü's right to memorialize, but also sanctioned Chinese involvement in decision-making: "At all meetings on government affairs, we should have both Manchus and Chinese meet together to discuss the facts. In the consideration of facts and principles, we are searching for what is right. No matter whether one is Manchu or Chinese, all may prepare drafts. . . . Lu Kuang-hsü is an official permitted to memorialize. The merits and demerits of the dynasty must be clearly pointed out by factual evidence."[67] Thus ended the Lu Kuang-hsü affair, with the Shun-chih Emperor refusing to support the Manchu's claim to exclusive jurisdiction in military affairs. To the future regents, this must have seemed clear evidence of the emperor's bias towards his Chinese officials and his rejection of Manchu prerogatives.

A final theme in the Shun-chih Will concerned the emperor's financial extravagances on behalf of his empress, and insults to his own mother, the Grand Empress Dowager. The Will stated: "Our dynasty's expenditures are great and the soldiers' pay and rations are not sufficient. The revenue from taxes has been wasted on expenditures in the palace."[68] Elsewhere in the Will the emperor was accused of disobeying the "way of the filial son" (tzu-tao) and of deviating from the "path of sincerity."[69] Probably both the Grand Empress Dowager and the regents had a hand in drafting these "sins." The Grand Empress Dowager had been frustrated by her late son's occasional refusal to heed maternal advice. The regents may have been delighted at the inclusion of these crimes against filiality for that added to the Will's credibility by striking a note of Confucian outrage in an otherwise Manchu-oriented document.

65. Liang Ch'ing-piao had served briefly under Li Tzu-ch'eng before surrendering to the Manchus in 1644. He worked his way up through a readership in the Grand Secretariat and vice-presidencies in the Boards of Rites and Civil Office. In 1669, in his capacity as president of the Board of Rites, he drafted the imperial edict which restored those who had been unjustly removed from office during the Oboi regime. Liang, therefore, seems to have been able to combine his commitment to joint Manchu-Chinese authority with enough political acumen to endure the Oboi period. See biography of Liang Ch'ing-piao in CSLC, ch. 79, pp. 39a-40b.

66. SC Shih-lu, ch. 141, pp. 9b-10a.

67. Ibid., ch. 141, pp. 10a-b.

68. Ibid., ch. 144, p. 4a.

69. Ibid., ch. 144, p. 2b.

Tension between the Grand Empress Dowager and her young son had built up through the 1650s. In 1651 the Grand Empress Dowager arranged a marriage between Shun-chih and her own niece. Whether because he disliked his cousin or because he resented his mother's interference, the emperor boldly deposed his new empress in 1653. Not deterred by this initial failure, the Grand Empress Dowager tried again to engineer an imperial marriage, this time to her twelve-year-old grandniece, the Empress Hsiao-hui. Although Hsiao-hui was not deposed as her predecessor was, the Grand Empress Dowager's continued matchmaking alienated the emperor from his mother. As noted earlier, Shun-chih may have increased the power of the eunuchs and instituted the Thirteen Offices partly to counteract the growing power of his mother.[70]

The major source of tension between the Shun-chih Emperor and the Grand Empress Dowager, however, was the emperor's favorite consort, the Empress Hsiao-hsien. Hsiao-hsien was the daughter of a Manchu named Osi and the sister of the famous commander, Fiyanggū, who was to be largely responsible for the defeat of Galdan in 1696.[71] She came to the palace in 1656 at the age of eighteen sui and quickly became the favorite of the emperor, gaining the title of Imperial Consort of the First Class (Huang Kuei-fei). The emperor was so enamoured of Hsiao-hsien that he wanted to depose his second empress, Hsiao-hui, in order to give Hsiao-hsien this title. But the Grand Empress Dowager and several other officials adamantly opposed this maneuver. In spite of this opposition,

70. The Grand Empress Dowager, formerly known as Empress Hsiao-chuang, was the daughter of the Mongol Prince Jaisang who was himself a descendant of Chinggis Khan. She became one of Abahai's concubines in 1625 and during the next decade she gave birth to three of his several daughters. In 1636 Hsiao-chuang's aunt, Hsiao-tuan, was given the title of Empress, and Hsiao-chuang herself received the title of secondary consort (chuang-fei). Two years later Hsiao-chuang gave birth to Fu-lin, the future Shun-chih Emperor. After the succession occurred and the Ch'ing court had moved from Mukden to Peking, Hsiao-chuang was made Empress Dowager. When the Empress Hsiao-tuan died in 1649, Hsiao-chuang emerged as the dominant force in the inner chambers of the palace. At Shun-chih's death, she became the Grand Empress Dowager.

Biographical information about the Grand Empress Dowager is available in Hummel, pp. 300-301; CSK, ch. 219, pp. 4b-5b; T'ang, Ch'ing huang-shih ssu-p'u, ch. 2, pp. 5a-6a; and Chang Ts'ai-t'ien, Ch'ing lieh-ch'ao hou-fei, ch. shang, pp. 27b-42b.

71. The romance between Fu-lin and Hsiao-hsien has been the theme of many mythical tales. Some writers have claimed that Hsiao-hsien was the concubine of a Chinese scholar who was abducted by Manchu soldiers and brought to the Emperor because of her exceptional beauty. Others have argued that the hero and heroine of the famous Ch'ing novel, The Dream of the Red Chamber [Hung-lou meng] were really the Shun-chih Emperor and the Empress Hsiao-hsien. Both of these speculations are probably false. See Johnston, "Romance of an Emperor," pp. 1-12; Meng, "Ch'ing-ch'u san ta i-an," pp. 449-76. For biographies of the Empress Hsiao-hsien, see CSK, ch. 220, pp. 8a-9a; Chang Ts'ai-t'ien, Ch'ing lieh-ch'ao hou-fei, ch. shang, p. 65a; T'ang, Ch'ing huang-shih ssu-p'u, ch. 2, p. 9a.

Shun-chih lavished favors on his beloved companion. A general amnesty was declared after she became Imperial Consort and her father, Osi, was made an earl. When an infant son born to the emperor and Hsiao-hsien died in 1658, the child was posthumously awarded the rank of prince of the first class—contrary to accepted practice. Together with the emperor, Hsiao-hsien studied the Chinese language and calligraphy. She was also converted to Ch'an Buddhism through the urgings of the emperor.[72]

When Hsiao-hsien died on 23 September 1660, the emperor was overwhelmed by grief. He wrote a long eulogy in which he cited the many virtues of his consort. He gave her the posthumous title of empress with the elaborate designation, "The Empress who has been Filial, who has evidenced her Correctness in Conduct, who has lived Peacefully to the point that she had been Virtuous, Proper, Humane, Kind, Gracious, Upright, and Reverent." Lavish ceremonies were conducted in her memory. Her casket was carried in a huge procession of the entire court to Ching-shan Hill in northern Peking. Every time the procession went under a gate or crossed a bridge, libations of wine were poured and paper money was distributed. Arriving at Ching-shan Hill, the mourning was carried out according to elaborate Buddhist ceremonies and then her body was cremated. Several of her maids and some of the emperor's eunuchs committed suicide so that their spirits might accompany her—a practice of the Manchus, known as hsün-tsang, which had been long abandoned by the Chinese.[73]

The Shun-chih Will obviously reflects the resentment of the Grand Empress Dowager over the emperor's devotion to Hsiao-hsien and his aloofness from his own mother. And to the future Manchu regents the extravagance of Hsiao-hsien's funeral was additional proof of the emperor's financial irresponsibility. According to the Shun-chih Will: "I exceeded the usual funeral ceremony and was overly generous. I was unable to restrain myself and unable to keep to the proper ceremony. In all matters I was excessive without limits. This was one of my sins."[74]

After helping to forge the Imperial Will, the Grand Empress Dowager avoided direct political interference during the early 1660s. Instead she chose to work behind the scenes exerting private influence in the imperial apartments. She undertook the responsibility of raising the K'ang-hsi Emperor, and she directed his early education. Because of her political inactivity in the early stages of the Oboi regency, we shall have little occasion to refer to the Grand Empress Dowager again until the end of this study. As the new emperor matured in the 1660s,

72. Hummel, p. 301.

73. On the death of the Empress Hsiao-hsien, see SC Shih-lu, ch. 139, pp. 17b-18a, 18a-20a; Hummel, pp. 301-2. For mourning ceremonies carried on at a later date, see SC Shih-lu, ch. 143, pp. 8b-9b.

74. SC Shih-lu, ch. 144, p. 4b.

it was the Grand Empress Dowager who eventually made the crucial decisions about his choice of an empress in 1665 and about his assumption
of personal control of the government in 1667. The K'ang-hsi Emperor,
unlike his father, was devoted to the Grand Empress Dowager and followed her advice carefully. The Grand Empress Dowager must be credited with helping to formulate the K'ang-hsi Emperor's forceful and sensitive personality and with engineering his accession to the throne in the
late 1660s. A failure as a mother, she became one of the most influential grandmothers in Ch'ing history.

THE REGENCY ESTABLISHED: FEBRUARY 1661

The last paragraph of the Shun-chih Will carried the news which the court
awaited with anticipation. It named the imperial successor and established the regency (the last section of the paragraph is almost certainly
a forgery):

> My son, Hsüan-yeh, was born of the imperial concubine of the third
> rank of the Tung clan. His age is now eight sui. He is exceptional
> and clever, and he is capable of inheriting the ancestral traditions.
> Now I designate him as Heir Apparent. On the twenty-seventh day
> of mourning, he is to shed his mourning garments and be estab-
> lished as Emperor. I give a special order to the chamberlains of
> the Imperial Bodyguard, Soni, Suksaha, Ebilun, and Oboi, to serve
> as Regents. These are influential officers with long records of ser-
> vice. I place my sincere trust in them. They have exerted them-
> selves and displayed their loyalty. They are to protect and assist
> the young Emperor, and to aid in the affairs of state.[75]

Then, to introduce an element of legality to the proceedings following
the death of the Shun-chih Emperor, the regents announced that they had
received the unanimous approval of the Ch'ing court in a dramatic scene
following the reading of the Will on the eve of February 5:

> The high princes, dukes, high officials, bodyguards, and others
> cried painfully until voiceless. Soni and the others knelt and an-
> nounced to all the princes and the rest: "In the present Imperial
> Will there is an order for four of us to serve as Regents for the
> Emperor in his minority. Previously the affairs of the dynasty
> have been managed by those in the Imperial Clan. We are sons of
> officials from non-imperial clans. How can we manage affairs?
> Now we ought to undertake the responsibility together with all the
> high princes and others."
> But the high princes and others said: "The deceased Emperor
> knew you four men very well. It was for that reason that he en-

75. Ibid., ch. 144, pp. 5b-6a.

trusted you with managing the affairs of state. The Imperial Will is quite clear. Who can disobey it?"[76]

Finally, the regents then took an oath of fidelity and honesty. In the light of events which transpired later in the regency, particularly the emergence of self-seeking factionalism under Oboi, the regents' oath of 1661 assumes almost ludicrous proportions:

> We promise to provide assistance with loyalty and honesty. We will work together until death. In offering assistance in the affairs of state, we will not act selfishly and will not show favor to our relatives. We will not harbor resentments. We will not be swayed by those at our sides and we will not listen to the provocations of our brothers, sons, clansmen, and teachers. We will not seek unrightful riches. We will not have private dealings with the princes and others, and will not accept their gifts. We will not form cliques and will not take bribes. It is with loyalty in our hearts that we respectfully try to repay the enormous favor shown by the former Emperor. If we should act for private ends and disobey this oath, may heaven strike us down and let us suffer cruel deaths.[77]

The Imperial Will of the Shun-chih Emperor served several purposes. First, it named the K'ang-hsi Emperor as heir to the Manchu throne, thus establishing the man who was to be one of the most dynamic and long-lived of all the Chinese emperors. Secondly, the Will appointed the four powerful Manchu regents whose policies would dominate the decade of the 1660s. Thirdly, the Shun-chih Will and the events which surrounded its promulgation assured the regents the mantle of imperial authority; they were men whom the Shun-chih Emperor "knew well" and had "entrusted with managing the affairs of state." Finally, the Will set the framework and the mood for many of the developments which were to occur in the 1660s.

76. KH Shih-lu, ch. 1, p. 5a.
77. Ibid., ch. 1, pp. 5b-6a.

4   The Regency and the Metropolitan Bureaucracy

By the spring of 1661, after the feverish activities of the successsion had taken place, the regents found themselves entrusted with the governance of a gigantic empire having an immense population and complex intellectual and social traditions stretching back for millennia. What thoughts ran through their minds as they sat in the lavish imperial palaces in Peking? They probably were amused at the contrast between their present status and their earlier lives: four rugged Manchus considered "barbarian" by the Chinese were now living in this splendid city and giving orders to the most eminent officials of the "civilized" Middle Kingdom. But they also had to ponder the awesome responsibilities of overseeing the Chinese empire. They had not fought their way to the conquest of China and connived their way to the regency simply to languish in material and sensual pleasures. They were men with a strong sense of mission.

The establishment of the Joint Regents' faction in February 1661 was both an individual and a group accomplishment. On the one hand, the regents were men with distinct backgrounds and personalities. Soni was the senior statesman among the four. His unusual combination of linguistic, diplomatic, administrative, and military abilities made him the most experienced and most versatile. By contrast, Oboi had a narrower outlook which stemmed from his preoccupation with battlefield command and military training. Like others in his family, Oboi was a man conditioned and toughened by the rigors of war so that militarism permeated his entire being. He was a proud, aggressive, and stubborn individual. One biographer has called him a "domineering man" and observed that "most people despised him."[1] Suksaha, though his military record rivaled that of Oboi, is best characterized as a political opportunist. He had made an abrupt and advantageous break with the Dorgon faction in 1651, and was to try a similar maneuver against the Joint Regents' faction in the late 1660s. Ebilun appears to have been the least assertive of the four. His military career was confined to the few years around 1644; most of his early honors were due to the inheritance of the ranks and reputation of his father rather than to his own achievements. During the Oboi regency, and especially in the factional conflicts at the end of the 1660s, Ebilun would remain a passive figure, acquiescing to the decisions of others while making few moves on his own.

1. CSLC, ch. 6, p. 5a.

On the other hand, the creation of the regency was a cooperative venture, born of shared frustrations in the 1643-61 period and of shared aspirations for the Ch'ing dynasty. As the regents indicated in the ceremonies after Shun-chih's death, they were men from "non-imperial clans" and thus recognized that their authority depended on support from the Manchu conquest elite. The regents knew their position was tenuous and realized their policies would be scrutinized by Manchu colleagues in Peking. The regents had created a Manchu mandate for themselves and were thus committed to a more authoritarian, more disciplined, and more Manchu-dominated government than under the Shun-chih period. Although they accepted certain Chinese governmental forms and felt that Chinese should participate in the political processes, they believed that Manchus should have the dominant voice. The regents wanted an efficient and functional administration and were intolerant of Chinese institutions which seemed silly or dangerous. Their self-appointed task was the purification of the Ch'ing dynasty by cleansing it of tainted resemblances to the late Ming era, of bureaucratic corruption, and of a weakened role for the Manchu conquerors.

A MANCHU REIGN OF VIRTUE: EARLY 1661
Shortly after the reading of the Imperial Will and the performance of the proper funerary and succession ceremonies, the regents addressed themselves to the task of running the Ch'ing state. The first order of business was to eradicate the legacies of the Shun-chih reign, starting with the Thirteen Offices and the eunuchs and imperial servants who staffed it. On 15 March 1661 the regents issued an edict in which they referred to the Shun-chih Will as a justification for the abolition of the Thirteen Offices and the execution of Wu Liang-fu and Tung-i:

> Our T'ai-tsu [Nurhaci] and T'ai-tsung [Abahai] carefully examined precedents and did not appoint eunuchs. By appointing eunuchs previous emperors brought on their own depravity.
>
> It was written in the Imperial Will: "Tsu and Tsung founded the dynasty and they never used eunuchs. One reason that the Ming lost the empire was that they made the error of relying on eunuchs."
>
> With fear and awe we have received the former emperor's intentions. We must distinguish fraud from justice. Thus we have made a detailed investigation. We know that the Manchu Tung-i and the eunuch Wu Liang-fu have been secretive and deceptive. They have been clever in spreading licentiousness and devious in taking advantages and in concealing the truth. A change was brought about in the old system of Tsu and Tsung and the Thirteen Offices were brought in as a substitute. Factionalism has been rampant. Revenues were borrowed and wasted. . . .
>
> Wu Liang-fu has already been executed, but Tung-i is still alive. Under the law it is impossible to forgive him and thus he has been

sentenced to death. Let his descendants be executed as well. As
for the Thirteen Offices, they must be abolished and all must be
according to the regulations established under T'ai-tsu and T'ai-
tsung. Eunuchs must never again be employed. [2]

While the eunuchs and the Thirteen Offices were the major concerns
of the Manchu regents, they also turned their attention to the Buddhists
and even to Father Adam Schall. Soon after the imperial funeral, the
Shun-chih Emperor's Buddhist advisers were expelled from the palace.
Then the regents brought Schall before them and demanded that he swear
his allegiance to the new regime in the presence of what the Jesuit considered an idol. Schall firmly refused, but the regents apparently decided to overlook his obstinacy and waited until later in the 1660s to
punish Schall and his Jesuit colleagues. [3]

Having purged the court of what they saw as the worst remnants of
the Shun-chih period, the regents looked to more positive actions in the
future. They sought to put the empire on a new footing and to establish
a framework for the Manchu-oriented policies which they anticipated.
On 15 April 1661, the regents announced a complete review of the dynasty's government and regulations:

> Now we must take all departments and examine their activities and
> duties as to methods of selection, the military system, currency,
> fiscal administration, punishments and laws. . . . Let all the
> high princes, the high officials, the Nine Ministers, and the cen-
> sors meet together and carefully examine the systems established
> by T'ai-tsu and T'ai-tsung. Let them consider what should be
> changed and what preserved. Let them collect and collate the en-
> tire body of laws. Let these be engraved as the rules and regula-
> tions for the entire dynasty, always to be respected and obeyed. [4]

The regents evidently wanted to purify the Ch'ing state in spirit and substance. Pointing back to the Ch'ing founders, Nurhaci and Abahai, they
intended to rectify the damage done by the Shun-chih Emperor. They
promised a reign of virtue which emphasized both Manchu supremacy
and governmental efficiency.

METROPOLITAN GOVERNMENTAL INSTITUTIONS (1661-1666):
MANCHU INSTITUTIONS

In their policies towards the metropolitan bureaucracy during 1661-66,
the regents sought diligently to realize these twin goals. To guarantee
authority and discipline, they stressed the importance of Manchu insti-

2. KH Shih-lu, ch. 1, pp. 21a-22b.
3. On the removal of the Buddhists in 1661 and the pressures brought against
Schall, see Greslon, Histoire de la Chine, pp. 60-61.
4. KH Shih-lu, ch. 3, pp. 9a-b.

tutions such as the Council of Deliberative Officials at the expense of
Chinese institutions like the Grand Secretariat, the Hanlin Academy,
and the Censorate. To select more capable and reliable administrators
the regents reorganized the civil service examination and evaluation
systems. To establish more effective administrative structures, they
refined certain organizations, such as the Imperial Household and the
Li-fan yüan. Quite clearly, the regents looked to a metropolitan government directed by Manchu officials and Manchu-oriented institutions,
but one which could also cope with the problems of managing the vast
empire.

The Imperial Household (nei-wu-fu)

By abolishing the Thirteen Offices and deposing the eunuchs in early 1661,
the regents made a sharp departure from the policies of the 1650s. But
these acts left a vacuum in the structure and personnel of the Imperial
Household. Had the regents left the Imperial Household in disarray,
with few attendants and little organization, we might conclude that the
regents were just conquerors who could not cope with the more complex
difficulties of post-conquest administration. On the contrary, they created a new and more streamlined Imperial Household staffed by Manchu
personnel and trusted Chinese bondservants.

   The regents developed an Imperial Household consisting of six main
departments under the supervision of department directors, assistant
department directors, and clerks. At the head of the new Imperial
Household were two or three Ministers of the Household (nei-wu-fu tsung-
kuan ta-ch'en) who oversaw the operation of this growing imperial bureaucracy. In the 1670s the K'ang-hsi Emperor accepted the basic system created by his regents and, making modifications and additions,
brought the Imperial Household to its final Ch'ing form by the end of
his reign.[5]

   5. For the development of the Imperial Household in the Shun-chih and K'ang-
hsi reigns, see HTSL, ch. 21, pp. 1a-4b (pp. 5325-26); ch. 1170, pp. 1a-b (p.
18749); Cheng, Ch'ing-shih t'an-wei, pp. 72-80; Ch'ing-ch'ao wen-hsien t'ung-
k'ao, ch. 77, p. 5572; Chang Te-ch'ang, "Economic Role of the Imperial Household," pp. 243-73. Jonathan Spence has observed that "the time of greatest administrative change [in the Imperial Household] was between 1661 and 1677, from
the death of the Shun-chih Emperor to the attainment of a successful working system" (Spence, Ts'ao Yin, p. 33). The Imperial Household system developed under
the Oboi regency was quite different in structure from that of the Ming period.
First of all, the Ming Twenty-four Offices (er-shih-ssu ya-men) were all separate
organizations and there was no overall supervision like the Ministers of the Household. Each of the Twenty-four Offices was headed by a eunuch apparently responsible directly to the emperor himself. Secondly, the Ch'ing Imperial Household
seems to have been a much simpler and more functional organization than the Ming
arrangement. The division of the Imperial Household into six departments, rather
than twenty-four, provided for a more coherent and efficient administration. See
Ming-shih, ch. 74, pp. 778-80.

The changes wrought in the 1660s are best illustrated by examining the development of the Department of the Privy Purse (kuang-ch'u ssu), one of the departments of the Imperial Household. By the late seventeenth century this department oversaw the imperial wardrobe and all of the great imperial storehouses of bullion, fur, porcelain, silk, and tea. The predecessor of the Department of the Privy Purse was the Supervisorate of Imperial Supplies (yü-yung chien), which had been established as one of the Thirteen Offices in 1655. During the Shun-chih reign, however, there was no subdivision of this organization and no regulations about its personnel. In 1661, therefore, while the regents preserved the name of the Supervisorate of Imperial Supplies, they also divided the organization into four storehouses: the Bullion Vaults (yin-k'u), the Fur Store (pi-k'u), the Silk Store (tuan-k'u), and the Imperial Wardrobe (i-k'u). At the same time the regents assigned new officials to administer this organization: three department directors, eight assistant department directors, eight clerks, and seventy-two superintendents of the vaults. During the 1670s and 1680s the K'ang-hsi Emperor built upon this system established by the regents. He changed the name to the Department of the Privy Purse, added the Porcelain Store (tz'u-k'u) and the Tea Store (ch'a-k'u), and appointed three more department directors and many new subordinate personnel. [6]

The regents also altered the personnel of the Imperial Household. To replace the ousted eunuchs, the regents used Chinese bondservants (pao-i) of the Upper Three Banners at the lower levels, and imperial princes and members of the Imperial Bodyguard at the higher levels. As described by Jonathan Spence, the reliance on bondservants during the K'ang-hsi reign was a major step towards Manchu centralization of power. In a period during which both the Chinese official elite and the Manchu elite could not be fully trusted, the bondservants "filled the vacancy left by the eunuchs, and they were used accordingly by the K'ang-hsi Emperor both as checks on the bureaucracy and as 'instruments for the implementation of autocracy.'"[7]

During the 1660s and after, the position of Minister of the Household became one of the most prestigious Manchu posts in the empire. The Minister of the Household not only oversaw the emperor's personal bureaucracy, but he also enjoyed close contact with the emperor himself. The most famous of the Ministers of the Household during the Oboi

---

6. HTSL, ch. 1170, pp. 2b-3b (pp. 18749-50). For a description of the Department of the Privy Purse in its final Ch'ing form, see BH, p. 14.

7. Spence, Ts'ao Yin, p. 17; also see pp. 11-18. Spence has noted, for example, that the edict of 1663 which appointed Ts'ao Yin's father, Ts'ao Hsi, as textile commissioner, marked an important administrative change. Previously textile commissioners had been Board of Works personnel, but after 1663 they were selected from the bondservants of the Imperial Household. Thus control of these positions shifted from the regular bureaucracy to the imperial bureaucracy (Ts'ao Yin, p. 87).

regency was Mingju (1635-1708). Mingju was a member of the Manchu
Plain Yellow Banner and began his service under the Ch'ing as an imperial bodyguard in the 1650s. From this post he was elevated to Minister of the Household in 1664 and emerged as an extraordinarily powerful official in the late 1660s and 1670s. During these years he held the
presidencies of three of the Six Boards, the presidency of the Censorate,
and the post of Grand Secretary. At the time of the Rebellion of the
Three Feudatories, Mingju was one of the emperor's closest confidants
and one of the few who advised the emperor to move decisively against
the uprising.[8] Mingju's influence was made possible at least in part by
his position as Minister of the Household in the 1660s. Here he was one
of the select Manchu leaders who had regular access to the K'ang-hsi
Emperor in the critical period at the end of the Oboi regency.

The Li-fan yüan (Court of Colonial Affairs)

Like the Imperial Household, the Li-fan yüan was another Manchu institution which received special attention from the regents. As indicated
previously, the Li-fan yüan had been established by Abahai in 1638 to
handle relations with Mongols. Under Dorgon the Li-fan yüan continued
to perform this function, while traditional tributary relations with the
countries of East and Southeast Asia were left under the Board of Rites.
In 1658, however, the Shun-chih Emperor abolished this dual approach
to foreign affairs and ordered the presidents and vice-presidents of the
Board of Rites to manage the affairs of the Li-fan yüan.[9] Although the
Li-fan yüan remained in existence, its independence was lost and Abahai's new system of foreign policy was severely compromised.

The regents, exasperated by what they perceived as another instance
of sinification, reversed Shun-chih's policy and elevated the position of
the Li-fan yüan in the metropolitan bureaucracy. In an edict of 24 September 1661 which observed that the responsibilities of the Court of
Colonial Affairs were "extremely important and not comparable to the
Ming dynasty," the Li-fan yüan was given a status equal to the Six Boards
and its president was admitted to the Council of Deliberative Officials.
The regents ordered that the name of the Li-fan yüan be listed immediately after the Board of Works and before that of the Censorate, thus
establishing the institutional hierarchy until the reorganization in the
first decade of the twentieth century. [10]

The Manchu regents also refined the organization of the Li-fan yüan.
Its staff, officially established in 1644, consisted of one president, two
vice-presidents, and several clerks and other functionaries who pro-

8. There were four Ministers of the Household in the 1661-66 period: Tuba,
Mingju, Baka, and Hairasun (PCTC [1795], ch. 317, pp. 17a-24a). Biographies
of Mingju in Hummel, pp. 577-78; CSK, ch. 275, pp. 2b-5a; PCTC (1795), ch. 151,
pp. 4b-16b.
9. Ch'ing-ch'ao wen-hsien t'ung-k'ao, ch. 77, pp. 5571-72.
10. KH Shih-lu, ch. 4, pp. 7b-8a.

cessed and recorded documents in Manchu, Mongol, and Chinese languages. Unlike the Six Boards and the Censorate, the Li-fan yüan was the only one of these basic metropolitan institutions whose leadership consisted solely of Manchu and Mongol officials. While keeping this personnel policy, the regents expanded the organization of the Li-fan yüan by dividing its functions into four departments. Two of these departments (lu-hsün and pin-k'o) supervised relations with Mongol tribes which had fully submitted to Ch'ing rule. These tribes of Inner Mongolia were organized into forty-nine banners by the Ch'ing and were kept under close supervision. A third department (jou-yüan) was entrusted with tribute relations with Mongols who had not formally submitted to the Manchus, such as the Khalkhas and the Oirats. A fourth department (li-hsing) oversaw the Ch'ing regulations which had been developed to deal with these Inner Asian peoples, and imposed punishments for infractions. [11]

The Council of Deliberative Officials (i-cheng ta-ch'en)

Although the regents emphasized both the Imperial Household and the Li-fan yüan as important Manchu organizations, the most prominent Manchu institution under the Oboi regency was the Council of Deliberative Officials. In chapters 2 and 3 we saw the emergence of the Council from its roots in Nurhaci's reign, its formal establishment under Abahai, and its expansion under Dorgon. The Council had been created as a Manchu cabinet to reinforce imperial authority over possible opponents among the princes, and to discuss major military decisions and civil policies during the Ch'ing period. After 1644 the Council included the highest-ranking military and civil officials from the Manchu and Mongol ethnic groups. The Council of Deliberative Officials was the central institution in what the regents called "the pure and honest old system of the Manchus." Their affection for this institution was enhanced by the fact that all four of the regents had been appointed to the Council under Jirgalang.

During the 1650s, however, the membership of the Council greatly increased, and the Council probably lost some of its prestige and effectiveness. In the Dorgon regency, one will recall, Council members were appointed on an ex officio basis: lieutenant-generals and deputy lieutenant-generals of the Manchu and Mongol banners, and all Manchus and Mongols with positions of board president or Grand Secretary. Jirgalang, however, made a large number of special appointments to the

---

11. Ibid., ch. 4, pp. 7b-8a. The functions of the four departments created by the regents are treated in HT (1690), ch. 142-44, passim. There were four presidents of the Li-fan yüan in the first six years of the Oboi regency: two were Manchus and two were Mongols. One of the Mongols, Minggadari, pursued an interesting career as a specialist in Mongol affairs. Biographies of Minggadari are available in Hummel, p. 576; CSK, ch. 234, pp. 9b-10a; CSLC, ch. 5, pp. 7b-8b; KCCH, ch. 43, pp. 1a-2b.

Council in return for factional loyalty. In the years of 1651-53 thirty
new Council members were added, many of whom (like the future regents) did not possess ex officio qualifications. Among these new appointments were two Chinese bannermen, Fan Wen-ch'eng and Ning
Wan-wo, thus reversing the former policy of naming only Manchus and
Mongols.[12] The only effort to restrict the burgeoning growth of the
Council was a regulation in 1656 which abolished the automatic appointment of Manchu and Mongol Grand Secretaries.[13]

When the regents came to power, they made a severe cut in the size
of the Council of Deliberative Officials. In 1662 they limited its membership to the lieutenant-generals of the Manchu and Mongol banners
and to Manchu and Mongol presidents of the Six Boards. At the same
time it was decided that the president of the Li-fan yüan would also be
included.[14] By 1662, therefore, the members of the Council by virtue
of their appointed positions totalled thirty-one. In addition the regents
kept their own membership and permitted some of the previous special
appointments to remain in force. During the 1661-66 period the total
number of Council members was at least thirty-nine, and may have exceeded that number (see table 1). But it was substantially smaller than
the Council during the late Shun-chih period, when the ex officio membership alone exceeded fifty.

During the later K'ang-hsi reign modifications were made in the
membership of the Council of Deliberative Officials. The president of
the Censorate was added to the list. In 1683 it was decided that since
the conquest of Taiwan marked the end of the major Ch'ing consolidation campaigns, the lieutenant-generals of the banners would no longer
be ex officio members. Thereafter the Council became much more
civil-administrative in character and was dominated by the most prominent Manchu statesmen of the period. The influence of the Council of
Deliberative Officials began to dwindle after the formation of the Grand
Council (chün-chi ch'u) in 1729. The Grand Council soon took over many
of the responsibilities formerly carried out by the Council. Finally,
on 18 January 1792, in the fifty-sixth year of the Ch'ien-lung reign, the
Council of Deliberative Officials was abolished.[15]

Even during its most potent stage in the seventeenth century, the
Council of Deliberative Officials was never permitted to live a separate

12. Appointments to the Council during the 1650s are covered well in Kanda,
"Shinsho no gisei daijin ni tsuite," pp. 177-81. Altogether there were only three
Chinese appointed to the Council in its entire history (ibid., p. 181).

13. Ibid., p. 181.

14. KH Shih-lu, ch. 4, pp. 7b-8a; ch. 6, pp. 4b-5a.

15. This later history of the Council is treated in Silas Wu, Communication
and Imperial Control, p. 12; Kanda, "Shinsho no gisei daijin ni tsuite," pp. 182–
84; Fu Tsung-mao, Ch'ing-tai Chün-chi ch'u, pp. 51-84, passim. Recent evidence uncovered by Silas Wu has indicated that the Grand Council performed only
secretarial functions until the T'ung-chih period (Silas Wu, "Memorial Systems
of the Ch'ing Dynasty," pp. 48-49, 54-55).

institutional life. As in the rest of the Ch'ing government, the appointment and dismissal of Council members were always the ultimate responsibility of the emperor. In all cases the meetings of the Council
were held by imperial request and the Council did not have the right to
initiate policy on its own. Depending on the inclination of the emperor,
moreover, the Council could easily be by-passed in the policy-advising
function in favor of the Grand Secretariat or later the Grand Council.
Such was often the case during the later K'ang-hsi, Yung-cheng, and
Ch'ien-lung reigns.

Nevertheless, during much of the seventeenth century and particularly in the Oboi decade, the jurisdictions of the Council of Deliberative
Officials were broad. After an investigation of the "Veritable Records"
of the early Ch'ing period, Fu Tsung-mao has concluded that the jurisdiction of the Council included a variety of military matters: major
military expeditions (cheng-fa), military regulations (chün-chih), awards
for military bravery (chün-kung hsü-hsü), deliberations over punishments for military crimes (chün-pei i-fa), meetings on promotions
and punishments (hui-t'ui), and management of border garrisons (pien-
fang). In addition the Council often considered civil matters including
the following: functions of officials (kuan-chih), deliberations on promotions and appointments (hui-t'ui), decisions on punishments (i-fa),
noble titles and hereditary honors (feng-hsi), tax levies (k'o-shui), and
judicial investigations (ch'a-hsing).[16]

According to the "Veritable Records," those issues sent to the Council of Deliberative Officials during the early 1660s were largely concerned with major problems of civil administration. Among the most
important of these questions were: privileges for Manchu and Chinese
officials (1661); review of the severe revenue deficit (1664); illegal taxation by local officials (1665); and the trial and sentencing of the Jesuit
missionaries (1665).[17] All of these issues, which will be discussed elsewhere in this book, were too complex and in some cases too delicate to
be resolved through the regular administrative channels. Accordingly

16. These functions of the Council are taken from the chart in Fu Tsung-mao,
"Ch'ing-ch'u i-cheng," p. 282. It should be noted that this list of jurisdictions
does not mean that the Council of Deliberative Officials was consulted every time
these matters were discussed. These were matters which at one time or another
were recorded in the "Veritable Records" as having been referred to the Council
for deliberation.

Generally the Council met by itself and then reported its findings to the emperor, but on rare occasions the Council met personally with the emperor to discuss important military matters. The decisions of the Council were usually followed by the emperor, but there were a few instances where the K'ang-hsi Emperor rejected the advice of the Council. Deliberations of the Council were kept
secret (see below at end of section on the Council). There may have been a separate office for the Council called the i-cheng wang ta-ch'en ya-men. For further
information on these aspects of the Council, see ibid., pp. 257-62.

17. Ibid., pp. 262-64.

TABLE 1. Members of the Council of Deliberative Officials, 1661-66

	Manchu	Mongol
Members by virtue of		
Board president	13	0
Lieutenant-general	18	3
Special appointment	5	0
Banner allegiances		
Plain Yellow	6	...
Bordered Yellow	6	...
Plain White	3	2
Bordered White	3	1
Plain Red	2	...
Bordered Red	2	...
Plain Blue	3	...
Bordered Blue	...	...
Imperial Clan	2	...
Unknown	9	...
Previous experience*		
Grand Secretariat		
Sub-chancellor	4	...
Other	4	...
Six Boards		
Vice-president	9	...
Other	5	...
Censorate		
Vice-president	2	...
Other	1	...
Li-fan yüan		
Vice-president	...	...
Other	...	...
Imperial Bodyguard	3	2
Military Service		
Deputy lieutenant-general	4	...
Captain or above	12	2

	Manchu	Mongol
Role in conquest or consolidation		
1620s	3	1
1630s	6	1
1640s	10	2
1650s	5	1
Unknown	13	...
Oboi faction		
Opponent	6	...
Adherent	7	...
No information	23	3
Later service as high official**		
None after 1660s	24	3
1669-75	2	...
1676-80	4	...
1680s	1	...
1690s	1	...
Unknown	4	...
Date of death		
1660s	20	2
1670s	2	1
1680s	2	...
1690s	1	...
Unknown	11	...

SOURCES: Pa-ch'i t'ung-chih (1795); Ch'ing-shih kao; Ch'ing-shih lieh-chuan; Hummel; Ch'ing-shih; Kuo-ch'ao ch'i-hsien lei-cheng.

* Every time that a Council member held one of these posts, his name was entered. There are, therefore, a number of cases in which a man has several entries in this section.

** Entries were made next to the latest date that a Council member held high positions under the later K'ang-hsi period. High officials include only board presidents, Grand Secretaries, and lieutenant-generals.

the regents entrusted them to the Manchu Council over which they had
considerable control.

The "Veritable Records" list no instance of military matters being
considered by the Council of Deliberative Officials during the Oboi period.
The probable explanation is that Council deliberations on military affairs
were kept in strict secrecy. As already seen in the case of Lu Kuang-
hsü, the over-zealous censor who criticized Manchu military developments, and in the Shun-chih Will, the regents jealously guarded the exclusive Manchu privilege of discussing military policy. Exposing such
affairs to court scrutiny would have compromised that privilege. Furthermore, the military questions that were considered in the Oboi period
concerned touchy issues: defense against the Russians in Manchuria,
fortification of the southeastern coastal region, and possibly the ouster
of the feudatory princes and Wu San-kuei in particular. To have revealed Council discussions on these questions might have reduced the
effectiveness of the proposed strategies and, in the case of the feudatory princes, might well have provoked immediate rebellion.

The Council of Deliberative Officials during the early Oboi period
was composed of older, predominantly Manchu, leaders who had considerable experience in both military and civil administration. The
membership was weighted heavily in favor of the Three Imperial Banners, but no single banner was dominant. Most of the members remained
aloof from the factionalism which grew around the regent Oboi in the
last few years of the 1660s (see table 1). Instead of becoming a tool in
the hands of the Oboi group and other Manchu factions in the early Ch'ing
period, the Council of Deliberative Officials served to express the general sentiments of the Manchu conquest elite. Its membership was almost entirely Manchu and represented a diversity of backgrounds and
banner allegiances. Most of the policies which emanated from the Council were generated by Manchu concerns for administrative experimentation, centralization of power, and military consolidation. Considering the wide range of civil and military jurisdictions of the Council during
the seventeenth century, one may conclude that it was the key Manchu
institution in metropolitan policymaking. According to a censor of the
K'ang-hsi period, "The influence of the Manchu officials is very great,
[while] the Chinese officials of the Six Boards and the Nine Ministers
merely process documents. When a Manchu makes a statement or
coughs, none of those below dares disobey."[18]

18. Turtei quoted in ibid., p. 283. The biographical backgrounds of the members of the Council of Deliberative Officials in the years 1661-66 are explained
in table 1. Those examined totaled thirty-nine men who qualified for membership
because of their functional positions or because of special imperial appointment.
Of the thirty-nine, thirty-six were Manchus and three were Mongols. A majority
of twenty-one achieved membership by becoming a lieutenant-general of a Manchu
or Mongol banner, thirteen by becoming board presidents, and only five through
special imperial favor. Although a sizable percentage belonged to the Upper

The regents, by limiting the membership and emphasizing the function of the Council, had provided a major institutional legacy for the early Ch'ing period. The K'ang-hsi Emperor shared their commitment to the role of the Council of Deliberative Officials. Perhaps the best indication of K'ang-hsi's attitude about the Council is an edict he promulgated in November 1669 after learning of some security problems in Council deliberations:

> The matters sent to the Council of Deliberative Officials for discussion are of the highest top-secret nature. When there are deliberations, there must be absolute secrecy. Now I have learned that those outside the Council quickly learn about matters under discussion before decisions have been reached. This has occurred because of insufficient security around the Council chamber, and because of insufficient discipline over those idling about. Such individuals, having overheard the special discussions, have the

---

Three Banners (70 percent of the thirty whose banner affiliations are known), seven of the eight banners were represented with two or more members.

It is evident from table 1 that in the 1661-66 period the Council included men with impressive records in military service and in civil administration prior to their appointment as members of the i-cheng ta-ch'en. But this depth of military experience is to be expected from the Manchu elite only two decades after the conquest. More surprising is the high number of Manchu members of the Council who had substantial backgrounds in the regular bureaucracy. Of the twenty-six for whom biographical information is available, nine had previously served as vice-presidents in the Six Boards, two as vice-presidents of the Censorate, and four as sub-chancellors of the Inner Three Departments (the Manchu substitute for the Grand Secretariat). The Council of Deliberative Officials in the 1660s, therefore, was not just a Manchu military oligarchy, but represented a wide range of Manchu administrative experience in both the civil and military realms. Table 1 also indicates that most of the members of the Council were elderly statesmen. The great majority, twenty-two of twenty-eight known, died prior to the year 1670.

For our purposes, however, the outstanding general characteristic of the i-cheng ta-ch'en is that neither the Oboi faction nor the opponents of the Oboi group held an upper hand in the Council. As the Oboi faction grew in both numbers and strength in the last years of the 1660s, the Council of Deliberative Officials still remained beyond Oboi's total control. The majority of the members did not become embroiled in the factionalism which was rampant in 1667-69. Of those who eventually took sides over the question of Oboi's quest for personal power, the membership was almost evenly divided before 1667 (seven adherents, including Oboi and Ebilun, and six opponents). Among the members of the Oboi faction who were admitted to the Council in the early 1660s were Oboi's brother, Murma (lieutenant-general of the Manchu Bordered Yellow Banner), Asha (president of the Board of Revenue and later president of the Board of Civil Office), Ka-ch'u-ha (lieutenant-general of the Mongol Plain Red Banner), and Ch'i-shih (lieutenant-general of the Manchu Plain Blue Banner). But also among the members were several critics of the ambitious regent, including Oboi's arch-enemy, Prince Giyešu, who became the spokesman for the Council in the late 1660s and eventually directed the purge of the Oboi faction in 1669.

greatest matters of state in their hands. These leaks are intolerable. . . . Henceforth all princes and high officials must
maintain absolute secrecy. There will be no leaks.[19]

METROPOLITAN GOVERNMENTAL INSTITUTIONS (1661-1666):
THE TRADITIONAL BUREAUCRACY

The regents' emphasis on Manchu institutions was accompanied by a
corresponding decline in the potency of traditional Chinese institutions.
Of the vital organs in the Ming polity, including the Grand Secretariat,
the Hanlin Academy, the Censorate, and the Six Boards, only the latter
retained a semblance of their previous strength under the regency. In
all instances, the regents endeavored to redress what they saw as sinified policies of the Shun-chih Emperor.

The Inner Three Departments (nei-san-yüan)

In the reigns of Abahai and Dorgon, the Inner Three Departments had
performed clerical functions and had never been involved in governmental deliberations like those of the Ming Grand Secretariat. When
the Shun-chih Emperor came to power, however, the Inner Three Departments were gradually elevated until their resemblance to the Ming
system was unmistakable. In December 1653 the Grand Secretaries
were permitted to express opinions to the emperor about his responses
to memorials. If the Grand Secretaries detected errors or improper
endorsements, they were ordered to inform the emperor of possible
corrections.[20] Then in 1658 the emperor discarded the name and organization of the Inner Three Departments and reinstituted the Grand
Secretariat and the Hanlin Academy. Shun-chih justified this return to
the Ming format by invoking a famous Confucian phrase, "The name and
the purpose must correspond." In addition to this change in nomenclature, the emperor also ordered each Grand Secretary to "manage"
(kuan) the president of a certain board. It is possible that the Grand
Secretaries were expected to perform some sort of supervisory functions with respect to the board presidents.[21] Finally, in 1660, the

19. KH Shih-lu, ch. 31, pp. 1a-2a.
20. Silas Wu, Communication and Imperial Control, pp. 15-16. In July 1653,
when three new Chinese Grand Secretaries were appointed, each title was prefaced with the phrase "Inner Hanlin." Liu Cheng-tsung, for instance, became Nei
Han-lin Hung-wen yüan ta-hsüeh-shih (KH Shih-lu, ch. 76, p. 18a).
21. For this return to the Ming system, see KH Shih-lu, ch. 119, pp. 6b-
10a; Silas Wu, Communication and Imperial Control, pp. 16-17; CS, 4: 2450-51.
With the exception of the three years of 1658-60 the Hanlin Academy did not exist
as a separate institution from 1644 to 1670. When the Manchus conquered China,
they incorporated the Academy into the Inner Three Departments. The probable
reason for this move was that two of the Inner Three Departments--the Department of Dynastic History and the Department of Literature and Conduct--per-
formed many of the functions formerly carried out by the Ming Hanlin Academy.
In 1658, when the Shun-chih Emperor reinstituted the Grand Secretariat, he also

Grand Secretaries were permitted to write draft rescripts to memorials.
The power to write such draft rescripts meant that the Grand Secretariat had once again become a deliberative agency with considerable
influence over the throne. [22]

On 15 July 1661, a few months after they had assumed office, the regents declared a return to the Manchu system, both in name and function:

> In the Imperial Will of the Shun-chih Emperor it is written that:
> "I have been unable to imitate the majestic examples of T'ai-tsu
> and T'ai-tsung in making laws and regulations and in choosing men
> for administrative posts. I have gradually come to practice the
> customs of the Chinese. The pure and honest old systems [of the
> Manchus] have been changed daily."
>
> Now in all aspects of government, we intend to follow the sys-
> tems of our ancestors and will restore the old regulations in order
> to fulfill the former Emperor's Will.
>
> The Inner Three Departments were established under the reign
> of T'ai-tsung. Now we must restore the old system and re-estab-
> lish the Department of Dynastic History, the Department of the
> Secretariat, and the Department of Literature and Conduct. The
> name and structure of the Grand Secretariat and Hanlin Academy
> must be abolished. [23]

The regents also rejected the dyarchic system of appointments to

---

established the Academy as a separate institution with Wang Hsi as its first
Ch'ing Chancellor. With the return to the Inner Three Departments in 1661, the
Academy once again lost its independent status until 1670. During the 1660s the
top-ranking chin-shih were appointed as compilers in the Inner Three Depart-
ments rather than in the Academy (HTSL, ch. 11, pp. 1a-32 [pp. 5205-6]; KH
Shih-lu, ch. 6, pp. 7b-8a; Hsieh Pao-chao, Government of China, pp. 275-76;
Hummel, p. 819).

Another change wrought by the regents was the abolition of the chin-shih "ob-
server" system (kuan-cheng) in 1661. Under the Ming and during the Shun-chih
reign, new recipients of the chin-shih were sometimes assigned as "observers"
and attached to the Hanlin Academy in that capacity (KH Shih-lu, ch. 3, p. 11a;
HTSL, ch. 72, p. 1b [p. 6019]; Hucker, "Governmental Organization," p. 15).

A. L. Y. Chung has observed that in 1662 "a number of Hanlins" were ordered to become "Recorders of the Emperor's Deeds." Chung claims that they
were to provide records of the emperor's actions written in both Manchu and
Chinese and that these records were to be sealed away so that even the emperor
himself was not permitted to see them. Chung explains this institution as a Confucian effort on the part of the emperor "to impress the people with his adherence
to enlightened ideas" (Chung, "Hanlin Academy," pp. 108-9). I feel that Chung
has misinterpreted the reasons for the development of this institution. The regents, desirous of keeping track of the young emperor and his advisers, probably
appointed the "Recorders" to spy on his actions. I doubt that the regents were
interested in the Confucian overtones that such an institution might have indicated.

22. Silas Wu, Communication and Imperial Control, p. 17.

23. KH Shih-lu, ch. 3, pp. 9a-b.

the Inner Three Departments which had been prevalent in the Shun-chih
period. In the 1650s the Manchu-Chinese balance had been maintained
and in fact was slightly in favor of the Chinese during the last few years
of the Shun-chih reign. The regents, however, established a decidedly
Manchu-oriented ratio, and in 1665-68, for example, there were six
Manchu Grand Secretaries and only three Chinese. During the Oboi
period eight new Grand Secretaries were appointed and only two of these,
Sun T'ing-ch'üan and Wei I-chieh, were Chinese.[24] In spite of the fact
that the Inner Three Departments acquired a distinctly Manchu bent in
the 1660s, however, none of the appointees in the 1661-66 period were
associated with the Oboi faction of the later years of the decade. This
policy of racial imbalance, therefore, was spawned by the general Manchu bias shared by all of the regents rather than by Oboi's special brand
of factionalism.

Although these changes in structure and personnel were clear-cut
gestures of Manchu superiority, the Inner Three Departments were di-
vorced from the decision-making process during the Oboi regency. In
the "Veritable Records" of the 1660s there is not a single entry recording deliberations of the Inner Three Departments. The only entries
which mention the Grand Secretaries at all are a few edicts discussing
questions of membership in the Inner Three Departments. The locus
of Manchu political power at the metropolitan level remained in the hands
of the regents themselves and the Council of Deliberative Officials, while
the Inner Three Departments gained little more than symbolic importance.

The Six Boards (liu-pu)

The Six Boards, which had been the functional nucleus of the traditional
Chinese state since the T'ang dynasty, seemed to retain most of their
former power under the regents. When memorials were received from
provincial and metropolitan officials, the regents usually transmitted
them to one or more of the Six Boards for consideration. When the regents drafted edicts, they generally submitted them to the appropriate
boards for implementation.

From a Chinese viewpoint, however, the malady of Manchu dominance did affect the Six Boards in three respects. First, the presence
of the Council of Deliberative Officials considerably reduced the policymaking role which the Chinese board presidents had played under the
Ming system. Secondly, the dyarchic system was not preserved per-

----

24. CS, 4: 2446-54. Most of those who relinquished the title of Grand Secretary in the early 1660s seem to have done so because of either genuine retirement or death. Of the six Grand Secretaries who left in 1661, two died in 1663,
and two in 1665--thus their retirement was probably genuine. One of the others
died in 1661 while still holding the post of Grand Secretary. The sixth was a Manchu, Tuhai, who was temporarily stripped of his ranks because of his involvement
in a miscarriage of justice. In short, it was a Manchu-oriented policy of appointment rather than a purge which characterized the regents' approach to the Inner
Three Departments in the early 1660s.

fectly during the 1660s. In 1668, when there was already one Chinese
and one Manchu president of the Board of Revenue, the regent Oboi appointed one of his closest followers, Marsai, as the third president of
that powerful board. Oboi thus augmented the strength of his own faction and enraged the Chinese officialdom in Peking.[25] Thirdly, the
regents decreed that the ranks of the Manchu department directors
(lang-chung) and assistant department directors (yuan-wai-lang) be
raised to 4a and 5a, while Chinese holding these posts kept the ranks
of 5a and 5b. The rationale for this decision was that while the Chinese
could achieve higher ranks later on, the Manchus generally were not
promoted beyond these positions.[26]

The regents also kept a strict watch over their Chinese underlings
in the Six Boards, fearing that factions might develop. In 1664 they
prohibited persons of close family connection from holding concurrent
posts in the Six Boards.[27] And in the third year of the Oboi regency a
case of alleged factionalism involving three of the highest officials on
the Six Boards was revealed. The three officials were the president of
the Board of Civil Office, Sun T'ing-ch'üan; the president of the Board
of Revenue, Tu Li-te; and a vice-president of the Board of Civil Office,
Feng P'u. The regents demanded memorials from all of these officials.
Apparently satisfied with their explanatory memorials, the regents
dropped the case and the officials were exonerated.[28] This case, however, along with the Liu Cheng-tsung factionalism case of 1660, indicated the regents' acute fear of Chinese cliques.

As with the Inner Three Departments, Oboi had little factional leverage in the Six Boards during the early years of the regency. Prior
to 1667 only one of the board presidents, Asha, was affiliated with the
Oboi faction which forced its way into the metropolitan arena in the late
1660s. Nevertheless, Asha held an impressive array of positions: senior president of the Censorate (1660-61), president of the Board of
Revenue (1661-62), president of the Board of Civil Office (1662-66, 1667-
69), president of the Board of War (1667), and lieutenant-general of the
Manchu Bordered White Banner (1667-69).[29]

25. See chapter 8 under "Marsai and the Oboi Faction."
26. KH Shih-lu, ch. 2, pp. 19b-20a.
27. HTSL, ch. 35, p. 1a [p. 5509]; ch. 47, p. 7b [p. 5666].
28. The official account of this episode is in KH Shih-lu, ch. 9, p. 3b. Biographies of Feng P'u in Hummel, p. 243; CSLC, ch. 7, pp. 38a-40b. Biographies
of Tu Li-te in Hummel, p. 778; CSK, ch. 256, pp. 2b-4a. Biographies of Sun
T'ing-ch'üan in CSK, ch. 256, pp. 1b-2b; CSLC, ch. 5, pp. 43b-44b.
29. There are no biographies of Asha in the standard sources. The information on his positions in the 1660s is taken from CS, 4: 2534-46, passim; PCTC
(1795), ch. 320, pp. 17b-19a, passim. For further information on Asha, see KH
Shih-lu, ch. 29, pp. 3b-28b, passim.
    The rate of turnover (transfer, retirement, dismissal, or death) of board
presidents and vice-presidents during the 1650s and 1660s was exceptionally high.
Turnover was particularly intense in the years of 1651-52, 1660-61, and 1667-69
—those years which marked a change of administration. In the year of 1661, for

The Censorate

Of all the traditional metropolitan agencies of government, the censorial establishment received the most ruthless treatment from the regents. They not only downgraded the functional role of the censors but also made substantial reductions in the numbers of censorial officials. Under the Ming the various metropolitan and provincial censors had performed a broad scope of duties including reviewing major government documents, overseeing and impeaching officials, and memorializing the throne on administrative policies and the conduct of officials.[30] During the early Ch'ing period, however, censors found themselves in an awkward position. The censors, most of whom were Chinese, were reluctant to criticize the policies and appointments of their Manchu conquerors who did not share the Chinese concept of loyalty.[31]

Censorial inactivity was particularly noticeable during the Oboi regency. In the second year of the K'ang-hsi reign (8 February 1663 – 27 January 1664), for example, the "Veritable Records" cite only the following documents involving the Censorate: six memorials from metropolitan censors, four memorials from provincial censors, one issue sent to the censorate for deliberation, one edict on the numbers of censorial officials, and four orders making new censorial appointments.[32]

---

example, there were changes in nine of the twelve board presidents, the president of the Li-fan yüan, and the two senior presidents of the Censorate. In the case of 1661, however, these changes do not seem to have constituted a purge, but rather an administrative readjustment; of the fifteen men involved, two retired, two died, and the remaining eleven were reappointed as board presidents or Grand Secretaries at various times during 1661-66 (CS, 4:2536). Further information about the appointment policy during 1661-66 may be found in appendix 2.

30. The Ch'ing followed the Ming censorial system very closely. During most of the Ch'ing period there were two censorial institutions at the metropolitan level, the Censorate (tu-ch'a yüan) and the Office for Scrutiny of Metropolitan Officials (chi-shih-chung ya-men). The Censorate itself was manned by two senior presidents, two senior vice-presidents, and four junior vice-presidents. The Office for Scrutiny of Metropolitan Officials was divided into six sections (one for each of the six boards) and in each section there were two senior metropolitan censors and two junior metropolitan censors. In addition to these metropolitan censorial officials there were also provincial censors (yü-shih), numbering two to each province and four in the Metropolitan and Manchurian circuits (Hucker, Censorial System of Ming China, pp. 28-30; Hsieh Pao-chao, Government of China, p. 89; BH, pp. 75-79).

31. On censorial quiescence in the early Ch'ing, see Huang, "Study of the Yung-cheng Period," pp. 189-200, passim. Silas Wu attributes the censorial reluctance in the early Ch'ing period to causes other than Sino-Manchu tensions: the low rank of censorial officials, the circumstantial nature of their evidence in impeachments, and so forth (Silas Wu, "Memorial Systems of the Ch'ing Dynasty," p. 39).

32. KH Shih-lu, ch. 8-19, passim. I have selected the second year of the K'ang-hsi reign because the "Veritable Records" are fuller for that year than any other during the Oboi regime.

A daring metropolitan censor, Li T'ang-i, criticized the reluctance of his colleagues to speak out and noted that "there are actually censors who complete their tours of duty without submitting a single memorial." After enumerating a variety of crimes which went unpunished because of the negligence of the censors, Li asked that irresponsible censors be punished. The regents, obviously displeased with Li T'ang-i's criticisms, took no action on the memorial and merely added the noncommittal imperial response, "Let it be made known."[33] Oboi himself treated the censors harshly. When Oboi was finally removed in June 1669, he was specifically accused of intolerance towards critics: "He prohibited words of judgment and impeachment from lower-ranking officials. He feared that they would reveal and make public his corruption. He closed up the avenue of words."[34]

Another way in which the regents downgraded the Censorate was by reducing the numbers of high censorial officials. In 1661 and again in 1668 there were wholesale reductions in the size of the censorial establishment in fourteen provinces.[35] In 1665 the number of senior metropolitan censors and junior metropolitan censors was cut in half so that there were only twelve of these officials instead of the usual twenty-four.[36] The regents also showed their disrespect for the Censorate by lowering its official status in the metropolitan hierarchy of institutions. One will recall that in 1661 the regents ordered that the Censorate be listed in a position inferior to that of the Li-fan yüan, reestablishing Abahai's system of listing institutions.

Thus the Censorate, like the Grand Secretariat and the Hanlin Academy, fell victim to the regents' efforts to restrict traditional Chinese institutions. But such acts were only small indications of what was to ensue when the regents turned to the civil service evaluation and examination systems.

CHINESE INSTITUTIONS FOR MANCHU ENDS: EVALUATION AND EXAMINATIONS

The regents of the K'ang-hsi Emperor devoted considerable attention to reforming the existing civil service evaluation and examination systems. These systems were draped in tradition that extended back almost a mil-

---

33. Ibid., ch. 12, pp. 6a-b. On the inactivity of the Three High Courts of Judicature and Revision during the 1660s, see ibid., ch. 11, pp. 24a-b. In 1661 the regents prohibited censors from making impeachments on unverified hearsay (ibid., ch. 1, p. 12b; ch. 2, pp. 20a-b; Huang, "Study of the Yung-cheng Period," p. 196).

34. KH Shih-lu, ch. 29, p. 8b.

35. HTSL, ch. 20, pp. 15a-b (p. 5322).

36. KH Shih-lu, ch. 14, pp. 5a-b, 6b; HTSL, ch. 20, pp. 19a-b (p. 5324). The number of metropolitan censors was again restored to twenty-four in 1667 (HTSL, ch. 20, p. 19b [p. 5324]). For further information on this matter, see Huang, "Study of the Yung-cheng Period," pp. 193, 196.

lennium, and they not only prescribed the criteria for entrance into and
advancement within the bureaucracy, but they also determined the lifestyle of the entire Chinese elite who aspired to political office. The regents made drastic revisions in both the examinations and the evaluations
and thus made a substantial impact on the size and nature of Chinese officialdom in the early Ch'ing period.

Reform of the Evaluation System

As Manchus and conquerors, the regents dispensed with the Confucian
veneer of benevolence traditionally expected from Chinese emperors,
and were primarily concerned with tax receipts and police control in
dealing with provincial China. They sought to establish an evaluation
system which would measure officials on the basis of tax collection and
the preservation of local order and which would provide for maximum
central control over the assessment of bureaucrats at all levels of government.

From the Ming the Ch'ing inherited a complex official evaluation
system designed to provide regular assessments of the honesty and competence of metropolitan and provincial bureaucrats. For evaluation of
provincial officials, the Ming relied on two basic systems, the k'ao-man
("the fulfillment of ratings") and the ta-chi ("the great reckoning"). The
k'ao-man was a triennial evaluation of general administrative capability
whereby superiors rated their subordinates as excellent (ch'en-chih or
tsui), adequate (p'ing or p'ing-ch'ang), or inadequate (tien or pu ch'en-
chih). After nine years those rated as excellent were promoted, those
rated as adequate were retained in rank, and those rated inferior were
degraded or dismissed. The ta-chi evaluations, conducted at the same
time as the k'ao-man, provided a rigorous assessment of personal character based on ratings in eight categories, including attentiveness to
duty, personal stability, tendency to greed or cruelty, age, and health.
The ta-chi and k'ao-man reports were first drawn up by officials at all
levels of the provincial bureaucracy and then sent on to Peking, where
they were processed in what was called the "outer evaluation" (wai-ch'a).
A similar system called the "capital evaluation" (ching-ch'a) was adopted
for the metropolitan bureaucrats whose rank was 4a and below. Those
of the rank of 3b and above were exempted from the "capital evaluations"
but were required to submit self-examinations (tzu-ch'en).[37]

During the Shun-chih period this Ming evaluation system was preserved with little alteration, but the regents felt that it was inadequate
in two respects. First, the provincial evaluations rested in the hands
of local Chinese officials and left ample opportunity for bribery and favoritism. The regents, who did not personally know the local situations
and were not acquainted with the local officials, were loath to trust the

37. On the Ming and early Ch'ing evaluation systems, see Watt, District
Magistrate, pp. 170-84; HTSL, ch. 78, pp. 1a-6a (pp. 6095-97); Hucker, "Governmental Organization," pp. 15-16.

Chinese assessments. The metropolitan evaluations, on the other hand, reviewed officials under the direct surveillance of the regents and thus the ching-ch'a was of less concern under the Oboi regency than the k'ao-man and the ta-chi.[38] A second problem that the regents found in the inherited evaluation system was its failure to measure administrative performance in terms of tax collection and the preservation of local order. Tax revenues and local peace were paramount concerns of the Manchu regents who faced a severe treasury deficit and who still feared anti-Manchu uprisings (see appendix 4).

The first stage in the regents' reforms occurred in 1662 when they abolished the ta-chi and restructured the k'ao-man. Under the new k'ao-man system only those provincial officials who had fulfilled their tax quotas and who had cleared up all outstanding criminal cases were to be considered in the triennial evaluations. Officials who had not completed these matters were to be singled out for punishment and not accorded the privilege of inclusion in the k'ao-man evaluations.[39] The regents, however, were not fully satisfied with the revised k'ao-man system. Most of the provincial bureaucracy was still evaluated by lower-ranking provincial officials outside the immediate control of the regents. Furthermore, the regents wanted an evaluation system on a graduated scale of rewards and punishments for performance in tax collection and police work. In early 1665, therefore, following the advice of the Council of Deliberative Officials, the regents abolished the k'ao-man system altogether.[40]

To replace the k'ao-man, the regents resorted to two techniques. First of all, they placed heavy emphasis on the recommendations made by governors and governors-general in the evaluation of provincial officials. Since many of the governors and governors-general had been appointed by the regents themselves, and since the regents knew most of them personally, their evaluations were considered more trustworthy than those of local Chinese officials. Moreover, the majority of the governors and governors-general during these years were Chinese bannermen. Since, as bannermen, their success was largely dependent on the Manchu military structure, they represented the will of the Manchus more closely than members of the Chinese official elite.[41]

As a second alternative to the abolished k'ao-man system, the regents

---

38. Several edicts in the early Oboi period criticized the existing evaluation system for its bureaucratic complexity and its tendency towards favoritism. See KH Shih-lu, ch. 6, p. 23a; ch. 12, pp. 7a-8a; ch. 13, pp. 9b-10a; ch. 13, pp. 12a-b.

39. HTSL, ch. 80, pp. 4b-6b (pp. 6124-25).

40. KH Shih-lu, ch. 14, pp. 6b-7a, 8a; HTSL, ch. 78, pp. 5a-6a (p. 6907). When the regents abolished the k'ao-man, they reinstituted the ta-chi and retained the existing systems for metropolitan evaluations (ching-ch'a and tzu-ch'en).

41. On the appointment of governors-general and governors during the Oboi period, see chapter 5 under "The Oboi Regency and the Provincial Bureaucracy."

reestablished the k'ao-ch'eng evaluation system, which had been developed in the Sung and revived again in the late Ming period. Unlike the
k'ao-man, the k'ao-ch'eng established a sliding scale of rewards and
punishments solely on the basis of tax collection and prosecution of
criminals. In 1665 the regents declared that those who fulfilled the tax
quotas would be raised one rank, and those who fulfilled their quotas for
three years in succession would be raised an additional rank (or four
ranks in all). Those who failed to meet the quotas were to be degraded
and fined in accordance with the percentage of the tax received. Thus
an official who remitted 90 percent of his tax quota was fined a year's
salary and demoted one degree in rank.[42] With respect to the appre-
hension of criminals, local officials were allowed two months to submit
their preliminary reports and one year for the completion of the matter
(capture, trial, and sentencing). If these time limits were exceeded, the
official responsible was to be punished by fines and demerits in rank.[43]

The re-institution of the k'ao-ch'eng system and the reliance on recommendations from governors-general and governors were major steps
towards administrative centralization. In this respect the regents seemed
to anticipate the tougher and more authoritarian side of their successors,
the K'ang-hsi and Yung-cheng Emperors. The new evaluation system
reflected three general characteristics of administrative policy in the
late seventeenth and early eighteenth centuries: centralization of power,
heavy reliance on trusted imperial appointees, and experimentation in
governmental institutions.

Reform of the Examination System

Unlike the evaluation system whose roots could be traced only to the
Sung period, the examination system was the oldest and most revered of
all the traditional institutions inherited by the Manchu conquerors. The
examinations had been at the heart of Chinese elitism since the T'ang
dynasty. They guaranteed the perpetuation of the Classics as the corpus of literary orthodoxy, they provided the prime route to official appointment, and they were a major factor in determining the prestige of
the Chinese upper class. Any tampering with the examination system,
therefore, was bound to elicit a reaction from the Chinese elite. During
the Oboi regency, however, the anger of the Chinese scholar-official
class was ignored as the regents altered the content of the examinations
and the size of the examination quotas.[44]

42. On punishments and rewards for tax receipts in the k'ao-ch'eng system,
see Watt, "Theory and Practice in Chinese Administration," pp. 335-37; Silas
Wu, "Memorial Systems of the Ch'ing Dynasty," pp. 19-20; HTSL, ch. 173,
pp. 1a-4b (pp. 7363-64), and ch. 173, pp. 21a-22a (p. 7373).
43. KH Shih-lu, ch. 13, pp. 20b-21b; ch. 17, pp. 6b-8b. The k'ao-ch'eng
system was retained and developed by the K'ang-hsi Emperor, and the k'ao-man
system was not reintroduced until 1736 (Watt, "Theory and Practice in Chinese
Administration," p. 335).
44. The least controversial aspect of the regents' reforms was their effort

A controversial reform initiated by the regents was the abolition of the "eight-legged essay" (pa-ku wen-chang). The "eight-legged essay" was a very formalized style of literary essay adopted in 1487 as the only accepted form for examination papers. The "eight-legged essay" system might be compared to a Western civil service examination in which the candidates would be required to comment on certain quotations from the works of Milton and Shakespeare and be forced to couch their comments in the form of an Italian sonnet. [45]

To the regents in the Oboi period this examination essay requirement seemed a blatant example of Chinese intellectual snobbery. The regents sought officials, both Manchu and Chinese, who were competent administrators, not experts in pedantic rhyme schemes. In one of the boldest moves of the regency, therefore, the "eight-legged essay" was scrapped at all levels of the examination system in September 1663. The examination format was completely revamped to include five dissertations (ts'e) on problems in contemporary affairs, two discussions (lun) on topics from the Four Books and the Five Classics, one address to the emperor (piao), and five judgments in judicial cases (p'an). [46] No

---

to eliminate corruption in the examinations. To both Manchus and enlightened elements in the Chinese elite community, cheating destroyed the effectiveness and integrity of the civil service examinations. (For examples of Chinese reactions to examination corruption, see Franke, Chinese Examination System, pp. 19-23.) From the regents' perspective, moreover, the examination system had become a Manchu institution and Chinese disobedience of Manchu injunctions was intolerable. During the Shun-chih reign there were several cases of corruption in the metropolitan and provincial examinations. On at least four occasions between 1644 and 1661 officials involved in these corruption cases were executed or removed from office (Chang Chung-li, Chinese Gentry, p. 189).

During the 1660s, therefore, the regents issued several orders prohibiting bribery of examining officials, use of crib notes, employment of substitute candidates, exchanging information, and so forth (HTSL, ch. 358, pp. 6b-7b [p. 9813]). On 5 March 1664 the regents outlined in detail a new system for administering the metropolitan examinations which was designed to circumvent all types of possible corruption. The emperor (in this case, the regents) was to meet personally with the examining officials prior to the examination to assure their honesty and to warn them of severe penalties for dishonesty. Examining officials were prohibited from contact of any sort with the candidates before the examinations. Examination topics were not to be revealed to anyone before the start of the examinations and all officials involved in administering the examinations were to submit memorials immediately after the conclusion of the testing (KH Shih-lu, ch. 11, pp, 10a-b).

45. Some of the most famous Chinese thinkers in the seventeenth century, such as Ku Yen-wu and Huang Tsung-hsi, expressed their scorn for the pa-ku essay. Huang, for example, commented that "insincere and thoughtless people, without any [proper] learning, can all write such essays" (Franke, Chinese Examination System, p. 21). But these Ming loyalist critics of the pa-ku essay were exceptions among the Chinese elite, most of whom had studied it and were committed to its perpetuation.

46. KH Shih-lu, ch. 9, pp. 24a-b. Unfortunately, the major compilation on

effort was made to explain the reasoning behind this decision, and, in fact, the official records indicate that the Board of Rites recommended the abolition of the pa-ku while the regents merely offered the neutral endorsement, "Let it be followed."[47] In all probability, however, the regents collaborated with the Manchu officials on the Board of Rites to force the issue in spite of Chinese protests.

Adverse reactions from conservative officials were soon forthcoming. Most of the key Chinese officials had been trained in the pa-ku essay style and had devoted their early careers to a study of the Chinese Classics. Examinations written in free prose form and not solely devoted to the Classics were incomprehensible to many of them. In 1665, for example, Huang Chi, a vice-president in the Board of Rites, protested in a memorial:

> If the Classics are not made the subjects of the essays, then the
> people will disregard the teachings of the sages. I fear that this
> is not what the court really intends when it sets up the examina-
> tions to select scholars. I request that henceforth the old regu-
> lations . . . be reestablished. Then the candidates will know
> their duties and have a solid education. And the examining offi-
> cials can discriminate and select true Confucian scholars who will
> fulfill [the expectations] of this dynasty which has chosen them.[48]

The regents chose to overrule their Chinese critics, and the examinations of 1664 and 1667 were held under the new system. When the K'ang-hsi Emperor began to assert his influence towards the end of the decade, however, he proved more sensitive to Chinese complaints. In 1668 he discarded the examination reforms of his regents and reinstituted the "eight-legged essay." This was the first of many acts of the young emperor designed to alleviate the Manchu-Chinese tensions which had developed during the Oboi period.[49]

---

examination officials, examination candidates, and examination topics does not include any more than the discussion (lun) topics for the examination of 1664 and 1667. The discussion topics for these years, as always, were taken from the Confucian Classics. The 1664 topic was from the Analects (Lun Yü, bk. 14, chap. 45: "The cultivation of one's self with reverence and care"); the 1667 topic was from the Doctrine of the Mean (Chung Yung, chap. 22: "Only those who have complete sincerity can exist under Heaven and can give full development to their nature"). So the topics are no different than the earlier topics, but of course the candidates' answers, which are not available, would not be in the pa-ku style (Fa-shih-shan, Ch'ing-pi shu-wen, ch. 1-2, passim).

47. KH Shih-lu, ch. 9, pp. 4a-b. On the regents' reforms in the examination system, see HTSL, ch. 331, p. 2a (p. 9505); Franke, Chinese Examination System, p. 28; Zi, "Pratique des examens littéraires," p. 178.

48. KH Shih-lu, ch. 14, pp. 29a-b.

49. Ibid., ch. 26, p. 15b; Franke, Chinese Examination System, pp. 28-29; HTSL, ch. 331, p. 2a (p. 9505). Although there is no definite proof that the restoration of the pa-ku was the work of the K'ang-hsi Emperor, logic seems to in-

In addition to their changes in the content of the examinations, the regents also slighted the Chinese elite by making severe reductions in the quotas for successful examination candidates. In the chin-shih examinations, the most prestigious degree of all, the restricted quotas of the Oboi period marked a departure from the liberal quotas established under the Shun-chih Emperor. Over the years of 1652-61, for example, there was an average of 380 successful candidates per examination and 190 per year.[50] These generous quotas followed a late Ming trend and were calculated to win the support of the Chinese official class for the Manchu conquerors.[51] The regents of the K'ang-hsi Emperor, however, seemed much less concerned with appeasement and more interested in reducing the size of the body of chin-shih degree-holders. From the figures presented in table 2, one can see that in the examinations of 1664 and 1667 the quotas were cut almost in half (to 200 in 1664, and 155 in 1667).[52] In the examinations held under the Oboi regency, excluding the examination of 1661, there was an average of 59 per year for the 1664–69 period. These sharp cutbacks in chin-shih quotas set a pattern for

TABLE 2. Chin-shih Granduates, 1659-70

Year	Number of Graduates
1655	399
1658	343
1659	376
1661	383
1664	200
1667	155
1670	299
1673	166
1676	109

SOURCE: Fang and Tu, p. xv.

the remainder of the K'ang-hsi reign, in which the number of successful candidates never exceeded three hundred (except in the examination of 1700, when the total was 305). Throughout most of the Ch'ing dynasty, in fact, the chin-shih quotas remained substantially lower than in the

---

dicate that this was the case. First of all, it is doubtful that the regents would have changed their minds simply because of adverse reactions from the Chinese elite. Secondly, as we shall see later, the K'ang-hsi Emperor and his imperial faction began to assert their influence during the years of 1667-68, and the restoration of the pa-ku was but one of many acts designed to mollify the Chinese elite.

50. These figures are taken from Fang and Tu, p. xv.

51. Ho, Ladder of Success, pp. 172-90, passim.

52. In discussing the social backgrounds of successful candidates, Ping-ti Ho unfortunately does not include the examinations of 1664, 1667, and 1670. Thus it is impossible on the basis of Ho's information to say whether or not the drop in Category A (those from humble backgrounds) began in the 1660s. See Ho, Ladder of Success, pp. 112-13.

late Ming and in the Shun-chih period.[53]

Another method by which the regents diminished the number of Chinese candidates for official office was their abolition of the "additional candidate list" (fu-pang) in 1664. The "additional candidate list," established in 1406, named several hundred metropolitan candidates who had not obtained the chin-shih degree, but whose competent performance on the examination permitted them to be considered for minor metropolitan posts. Thus the regents not only cut the number of regular chin-shih almost in half, but they also eliminated the possibility of appointment to official position for those who might well have obtained the chin-shih under the more generous Shun-chih quotas.[54]

The regents' reforms in the content of the examinations and their effort to eradicate corruption in the examinations must be viewed as positive acts in the interest of efficiency. The policy of restricting examination quotas, however, points up the harsh and haughty attitude which the regents displayed towards the Chinese elite. It is easy to imagine the enormous hostility which the regents' new quota system elicited from the Chinese scholar-official class.

As one looks over the regents' policies towards the metropolitan bureaucracy in general, certain characteristics seem apparent. The

53. Ibid., pp. 111-14, 185-86, 190, 262. This pattern of restricted entry into the highest ranks of the Ch'ing officialdom was exacerbated by two other factors--the growth of population and the appointment of Chinese and Manchu bannermen to key provincial posts. It was thus much more difficult for a successful degree-holder to gain office under the K'ang-hsi reign and after than under the late Ming and early Ch'ing up to 1661 (ibid., pp. 119-20).

54. HTSL, ch. 350, p. 2b (p. 9717); Shang, p. 105. Substantial reforms in the chü-jen and sheng-yüan examinations were also made in the late 1650s and early 1660s. In 1660 the quotas for the provincial examinations were cut approximately in half so that the total number of successful candidates was 799. This total may be compared with the quotas of 1645, for example, which allowed for 1,865 chü-jen degrees (HTSL, ch. 348, pp. 1a-b [p. 9689], and ch. 348, p. 5a [p. 9691]; Shang, p. 76). These quotas were raised once again in 1668, but remained far below the levels of the Shun-chih period (HTSL, ch. 348, p. 5b [p. 9691]). As in the case of the metropolitan examinations, the regents abolished the "additional candidate list" for the chü-jen in 1662 (HTSL, ch. 348, p. 5a [p. 9691]; Shang, p. 77). The regents also adopted a policy of prohibiting chü-jen from holding substantial official positions. By order of 1664 chü-jen were forbidden to serve as district magistrates and to serve as examiners in the sheng-yüan examinations. Under the Shun-chih reign both of these posts had been open to men with the chü-jen degree (HTSL, ch. 73, pp. 1a-b [p. 6031]).

During the early years of the Shun-chih period sheng-yüan quotas had been quite high, but in 1658 it was ordered that a large prefecture would have a quota of 20, a large county a quota of 15, and a small county a quota of four or five. Also in 1658 it was decided to limit the sheng-yüan examinations to one in every three years instead of the previous policy of two examinations in every three years (HTSL, ch. 370, pp. 1a-b [p. 9963]; Chang Chung-li, Chinese Gentry, pp. 74-75, 77-78). Ping-ti Ho claims that the date for the restrictive sheng-yüan quotas was 1661 rather than 1658 (Ho, Ladder of Success, pp. 179-81).

regents deliberately sought to elevate the prestige of Manchu officials and the influence of Manchu institutions. The Manchu-oriented appointment policy to the Inner Three Departments and the elevated status of the Li-fan yüan point to this conclusion. Heavy reliance on the Council of Deliberative Officials, especially for crucial policy decisions, also supports this interpretation, since the Council membership was predominantly Manchu and included the regents themselves. Correspondingly, the regents endeavored to degrade Chinese institutions, reduce the power of Chinese officials, and decrease the size of the Chinese elite. The censorial establishment dwindled in size and censorial officials were berated for their activities. The Grand Secretariat and the Hanlin Academy were both abolished and the regents returned to the earlier Manchu system of the Inner Three Departments. The policy of generous examination quotas under the Shun-chih reign was abandoned as the quotas were cut back by half. The 1660s were frustrating years for the Chinese elite, from the promising examination candidate to the Grand Secretary.

But another characteristic of the regents' activities in the metropolitan bureaucracy was their commitment to advancing the cause of administrative efficiency. In both the Imperial Household and the Li-fan yüan substantial structural and personnel changes were made to meet the complex needs of imperial administration. The regents' civil service evaluation system laid the foundations for a more reliable scrutiny of candidates for appointment and promotion. The "eight-legged essay" was abolished and replaced by an examination system designed to measure administrative capability rather than pedantic literary skills. In these developments and others the regents aimed to create an effective bureaucratic structure staffed by responsible personnel.

5 The Oboi Regency and Provincial China

Peking and the metropolitan province of Chihli were the Manchu stronghold in the early Ch'ing period. In this area, the regents pursued their goals of Manchu dominance and administrative efficiency with confidence. Supported by the Manchu conquest elite and the banner troops, the regents made sweeping changes in the structure, personnel, and procedures of the metropolitan bureaucracy. In the provinces, however, the situation was different. On the surface Ch'ing rule seemed established by the 1650s with the conquest of all of the Ming provinces and the appointment of Chinese bannermen as high provincial officials. But these measures were only the beginning steps in a long process of consolidating Ch'ing control. The banner forces were effective in taking provinces from rebels and Ming loyalists, but they were too small in number to garrison all of provincial China. Banner troops could respond to dissidence and insurrection, but they could not exert day-to-day control over the entire Chinese empire. The provincial officialdom theoretically answered this problem by providing regular surveillance of provincial China and by keeping Peking informed of developments. Realizing the importance of this officialdom, the regents endeavored to appoint loyal officials who would maintain open lines of communication and who would obey orders without question. Nevertheless the regents' search for loyal officials proved to be a frustrating endeavor. They tried Chinese bannermen, regular Chinese officials, and even Manchus in various combinations, but never found a satisfying answer.

The regents' insecurity over their provincial officials was exacerbated by their fears about Chinese activities. Although the last Ming loyalist movement was crushed in 1662 (see chapter 6), the regents knew that hostility to the Manchu rulers remained high among many members of the Chinese elite. The regents feared that loyalists, rebels, and pirates were to be found almost everywhere, threatening their regime with covert expressions of disloyalty and criticism as well as with armed uprisings. Such fears reinforced the regents' natural inclination to resort to martial means when dealing with problems throughout the empire. Their policies with respect to provincial administration and to the native Chinese population reflected their military background. They tried tough measures to bring the provincial bureaucracy into line. When confronted with more subtle forms of defiance, such as the publication of anti-Manchu literary works or the refusal to pay taxes, Oboi and his fellow Manchus responded with force which sometimes reached the intensity of a military campaign.

There was, however, another dimension to the regents' provincial policies, a dimension which clearly underscored their Manchu heritage. They realized that the Ch'ing dynasty could not continue to rule the Chinese provinces by force alone. Rule by coercion produced short-lived results and was frightfully expensive (see appendix 4 for the costs related to Manchu military ventures). But they also knew that the Manchu conquest elite would not countenance a return to sinified measures in provincial policies. The regents, therefore, tried one experiment in rule by example rather than by force. They selected what they felt was a model district in exemplifying Manchu values of discipline, self-reliance, and courage. By publicly praising the model district and honoring its officials and subjects, the regents seemed to say to both Manchus and Chinese, "look here, this is what we fought for."

But the model district approach, like the coercive methods, ultimately failed because the Chinese populace was unreceptive. Manchu dominance was very effective in metropolitan policy and, as we shall see later, in military and foreign policies. In the provinces, however, Manchu-oriented techniques elicited either apathy or further hostility. It was in the provinces that the regents ran directly into the insurmountable obstacle of Chinese society and tradition. The Chinese people could tolerate the new barbarian dynasty, but they would not accept a Manchu way of life.

THE OBOI REGENCY AND THE PROVINCIAL BUREAUCRACY: THE SEARCH FOR LOYAL OFFICIALS

The regents' insistence on loyal and effective provincial officials was clearly expressed in an edict issued in 1665: "The peace or unrest of the common peoples' lives is dependent upon the purity or corruption of the officials. And the purity or corruption of the officials is entirely based on the example of the tu-fu [governors-general and governors]. If the tu-fu are pure and just, and sincerely care for the people, who then among their subordinates will not cleanse himself and maintain justice?"[1] In their search for loyal officials the regents exhibited an enduring dilemma in Chinese history: no matter how refined the governmental institutions the sine qua non of successful administration was the appointment of obedient and competent officials.

The political tension between the centralizing force exerted by the imperial capital and the regional interests of powerful individuals in the provinces has been a major theme in the history of China. The crucial problem for a dynasty was to achieve a balance between the centralization of power and the division of power. Without a strong exercise of the imperial institutions, China would fragment into several regional satrapies as it had at the end of the Han and the T'ang dynasties. But without delegating responsibility to provincial officials, the emperor would remain isolated from the towns and villages of China, unable to implement his edicts and deaf to conditions outside the capital.

1. KH Shih-lu, ch. 14, p. 19a.

In the early Ch'ing period, and especially during the Oboi regency,
the dilemma of centralization and regionalism reached crisis proportions. On the one hand, most Manchu leaders, including Dorgon and the
K'ang-hsi Emperor as well as the regents, were deeply concerned about
strengthening the power and authority of the Ch'ing throne. At the expense of over-centralization, therefore, they deliberately concentrated
power in their own hands. The regents, as we have seen earlier, contributed to this process by relying on bodies over which they had considerable influence, such as the Council of Deliberative Officials, while
diminishing the roles of such traditional metropolitan institutions as the
Grand Secretariat and the Censorate. On the other hand, during most
of the seventeenth century the Manchu ruling house encountered regional-
ist threats in the extreme. Wu San-kuei and the feudatory princes, for
example, were capable of ruling gigantic portions of China while ignoring
directives from Peking. In brief, conditions of over-centralization and
over-regionalism were twin ills for the young Ch'ing dynasty.

In most of Chinese history the creation and maintenance of a balance
between these centripetal and centrifugal forces was the primary responsibility of the high provincial officials. During the Ch'ing the most important provincial officials were the governors-general, the governors,
the financial commissioners, the judicial commissioners, the circuit
intendants, and the provincial censors. These officials undertook activities essential to the smooth and unified operation of the empire: tax
collection and grain transportation, preservation of local order and prosecution of criminal cases, evaluation and recommendation of officials,
and the transmission of information concerning local events. The health
of the empire depended on the proper performance of these functions. A
weak, corrupt, and disloyal provincial officialdom might allow the empire to polarize into enemy camps: the imperial forces in the capital
and their opponents in the provinces.

When the early Manchu emperors and regents considered these high
provincial posts, however, they faced a problem in the selection of personnel. Whom could they trust? To have left the provincial administration solely in the hands of the Chinese official elite would have fractured China into a Manchu-dominated metropolitan bureaucracy and a
Chinese provincial bureaucracy. On the surface one might have assumed that Manchu appointments would be the logical alternative. For
several reasons, however, provincial posts were not granted to Manchus during the first twenty-five years of the Ch'ing dynasty. There
were relatively few Manchus with experience in non-military governmental affairs and certainly not enough to have filled the entire provincial administration. Most Manchus lacked sufficient proficiency in the
Chinese language to deal with complicated legal documents or to com-
municate with local Chinese groups. Furthermore there was no assur-
ance that Manchu provincial officials would be obedient to the orders of
their superiors in Peking. Manchu factionalism was ever present in
the early Ch'ing period, and to have introduced Manchu banner cliques

and clan cliques into the provincial structure would have exacerbated such tensions. The regents of the K'ang-hsi Emperor were well acquainted with this phenomenon. Having been personally involved in the political clashes of the 1640s and 1650s, and having themselves formed a faction at the end of the Shun-chih reign, they were as wary of Manchu opposition as they were of Chinese loyalism.

For the greater part of the 1660s, therefore, the four regents followed a compromise solution which had been developed by Dorgon during the first years of his administration. Unable to trust regular Chinese officials or Manchus, Dorgon had relied heavily on Chinese bannermen to fill the posts of governors-general, governors, financial commissioners, and judicial commissioners.[2] Even at the lower levels of provincial government, in the posts of prefects and magistrates, Dorgon appointed a few Chinese bannermen in addition to the predominance of regular Chinese officials.[3] In theoretical terms, the use of Chinese bannermen was a superb compromise. These bannermen had originally been soldiers in the Ming army but had surrendered to the Manchus prior to the conquest. They were then enrolled in the Manchu military structure as members of the Chinese banners established during the reign of Abahai. Recognizing that many of them had performed as brilliant and loyal subordinates of the Manchus during the conquest, Dorgon held high expectations for them as civil officials after the conquest. Moreover, Dorgon felt that, being Chinese, they would be more adept in dealing with provincial China than would their Manchu counterparts, whose knowledge

2. During the first two years of the Dorgon regency (1644-45) a total of nine men were appointed to the post of governor-general; of these three were regular Chinese officials and six were Chinese bannermen. In 1644 Dorgon appointed eight governors, of whom three were regular Chinese officials and five were Chinese bannermen (Yen, Ch'ing-tai cheng-hsien lei-pien, tsung-tu, ch. 1, p. 1a; ibid., hsün-fu, ch. 1, p. 1a).
Using the province of Shantung as an example, one can see that Dorgon also relied heavily on Chinese bannermen to fill the posts of financial commissioner and judicial commissioner. During 1644-49 there were fourteen men appointed to these two positions in Shantung; of these nine were Chinese bannermen and only five were regular Chinese officials (Shan-tung t'ung-chih, ch. 51, p. 1777). All those listed from Liao-tung or Liao-yang are presumed to be Chinese bannermen. For the general practice of listing Chinese bannermen in local gazetteers, see Spence, Ts'ao Yin, pp. 71-72, n 119; Kessler, "Ethnic Composition of Provincial Leadership," p. 495. Kessler's article indicates very clearly the predominance of Chinese bannermen in the posts of tu-fu during the early Ch'ing period and explains the rationale for the Manchu's reliance upon these bannermen (Kessler, "Ethnic Composition of Provincial Leadership," pp. 496-99).
3. In Chi-nan prefecture in Shantung province there were five prefects between 1644 and 1648; three were Chinese bannermen and two were regular Chinese officials (Shan-tung t'ung-chih, ch. 55, p. 1865). In the six hsien under the jurisdiction of Chi-nan prefecture there were twenty-four magistrates appointed during the same years. Seventeen were regular Chinese officials, six were Chinese bannermen, and one was listed without any additional information (ibid., ch. 56, p. 1893). All those listed as from Feng-t'ien are presumed to be Chinese bannermen.

of Chinese government and of the Chinese people was often superficial. [4]
As we shall see later, however, the Manchus' expectations of obedience
on the part of these civil officials from the Chinese banners proved to be
an unfortunate miscalculation.

During the first seven years of the Oboi regency, the Dorgon compromise in official appointments was followed without deviation. An
analysis of fifty-two of those who held the posts of governor-general or
governor (collectively called tu-fu) during the period of 1661-66 indicates
the continued predominance of the Chinese bannermen (see appendix 3).
Of these fifty-two tu-fu, forty-five were Chinese bannermen and only
seven were regular Chinese officials. Only half of the governors-general and governors were recorded as holding any Chinese examination
degree, and only five held the prestigious chin-shih degree. Lacking
degrees and being primarily military officials in the service of foreign
conquerors, the Chinese bannermen were a far cry from the traditional
image of the Chinese scholar-official.

For the subordinates of the tu-fu, those holding the posts of financial
commissioner and judicial commissioner, the regents of the K'ang-hsi
Emperor divided their appointments fairly equitably between Chinese
bannermen and regular Chinese officials. As one looks to the lower
echelons of the provincial bureaucracy in the Oboi period, the incidence
of regular Chinese officials increases, while that of the Chinese bannermen decreases. Nevertheless, a small but significant number of the
prefects and magistrates appointed in the 1660s were Chinese bannermen (see appendix 3).

By adhering to the Dorgon compromise, the four Manchu regents
were perpetuating a pattern that would predominate throughout the K'ang-
hsi reign.[5] The combination of Chinese bannermen and Chinese officials
was instituted in an effort to assure a provincial officialdom that was
competent, loyal, and acceptable to both Manchus and Chinese. Nevertheless, there is considerable evidence that the provincial officials, particularly the highest provincial officials, were far from obedient and
diligent servants of the Manchu throne in the 1660s. In a constant flow
of edicts and rescripts throughout the decade, the high provincial officials, often the governors and governors-general themselves, were
sharply chastised for their failures.

    4. On the appointment of bannermen to provincial posts during the early Ch'ing
period, see Spence, Ts'ao Yin, pp. 4-5, 70-77; and Kessler, "Ethnic Composition
of Provincial Leadership," pp. 498-99.
    5. Jonathan Spence has made a study of the provincial officialdom in the prov-
ince of Kiangnan throughout the K'ang-hsi period in which he concluded: "Such
groupings show that the appointments were carefully regulated, with the Banner
elite holding most of the senior positions (though not to the exclusion of the ordinary Chinese); the Banner elite and the Chinese official elite having virtual parity
in the middle positions; and the Chinese elite holding most of the junior positions
(though not to the exclusion of the Banner elite)" (Spence, Ts'ao Yin, p. 72). My
investigation, therefore, confirms Spence's assessment.

Like Dorgon before them, the regents had erred in their assumption
that the Chinese bannermen, fine officers during the conquest, would remain obedient after the Manchus had taken China. After the conquest,
when the Chinese bannermen were appointed to provincial posts, their
loyalty to the Manchus diminished. They were now in direct contact with
Chinese officials and the Chinese elite and were no longer under the day-
to-day supervision of Manchu commanders. The Chinese bannermen
had slipped away from the status of military officers to a vague position
between the Manchus in Peking and the Chinese in the provinces. The
Chinese bannermen, moreover, lacked the self-image of the Chinese
scholar-official. They had been trained as military personnel during
the declining years of the Ming dynasty, and they did not accept the traditional notion of the virtuous and obedient official.

The regents' criticisms of their provincial subordinates fell into
three categories: failure to transmit reliable information, failure to
make proper evaluations of officials, and failure to act honestly in financial matters. The four Manchu rulers in Peking feared they would lose
touch with actual events in the provinces. They were annoyed when
memorials from provincial officials failed to describe events correctly
and in detail. They were particularly adamant about military reports.
On one occasion they reprimanded the governor-general of Fukien, Li
Shuai-t'ai, for inadequate information in a memorial which described
his victory over pirates. In his memorial Li stated that his troops had
killed over 170 pirates, taken fourteen of them alive, and captured many
of their arms. Li also noted that he had burned the pirates' boats, since
he had lacked the sailors to man them. Under ordinary circumstances
Li Shuai-t'ai's memorial would have been considered quite satisfactory,
but the regents made it clear that they expected more:

> You have said that "we have killed many of the pirates, captured
> their arms, and burned their boats because we had no sailors, and
> so forth." Where did the pirates come from? Who was the pirate
> leader? Moreover, why did you burn the boats which were cap-
> tured near the shore? . . . How is it that there was not one among
> our officers who was wounded? . . . Let the said governor-general
> make a careful investigation and memorialize. [6]

Li Shuai-t'ai apparently learned his lesson, for his next memorial describing a victory gave a much fuller account including the place of the
attack, the names of the Ch'ing commanders, the date of the encounter,
and the exact number of enemy losses and captured. [7]

On another occasion the regents complained that memorials citing
the death of bandits were often fallacious:

6. KH Shih-lu, ch. 13, pp. 11a-12a.
7. Ibid., ch. 14, pp. 7a-b.

Recently in reviewing the reports from all provinces on the question of bandits, the majority announce "death in prison," "death by drowning," "death from sickness," "death caused by resisting capture," and so forth. It is feared that there are numerous instances where officials keep their offices [by gaining merit] for having apprehended bandits, but have actually accused innocent persons of being bandits. [8]

Oboi and his fellow regents were accustomed to the terse and factual language of battle reports, and they were dismayed by the stylized and often vague memorials which they received from provincial officials. At one point they issued an edict deploring improper memorials:

Recently we have observed that the memorials of the officials permitted to speak [yen-kuan], in addition to discussing facts and administration, also make comparisons which are largely just wasted talk. There are many which merely discuss matters already completed and other which are simply plagiarism. There are still others which are reckless and try to weaken good laws which have already been established. Moreover, memorials were originally limited to no more than three hundred characters, but now there are many which exceed that limit with frivolous chatter. [9]

The regents of the K'ang-hsi Emperor sought open lines of communication between the imperial capital and the provinces. When there were cases of local disorders, military campaigns, and financial irregularities, they expected an immediate memorial to Peking. But the great number of imperial orders issued on the matter of careful investigations and accurate memorials during the 1660s testifies to the fact that capital-provincial communications were irregular at best. [10] The regents, like so many Chinese emperors before and after them, were often forced to make momentous decisions on the basis of distorted and scanty information.

A second major type of criticism leveled against the provincial bureaucracy during the Oboi regency concerned the failure to make proper recommendations and impeachments of officials. As observed in the previous chapter, the alterations made in the evaluation system placed a premium on reliable testimony about subordinate provincial officials by the governors-general and the governors. The revamped system was designed to promote an officialdom highly adept in the areas most prized by the regents: tax collection and the preservation of local order.

---

8. Ibid., ch. 24, pp. 7a-b.
9. Ibid., ch. 24, p. 27a.
10. For references to the problem of inadequate investigations and improper memorials during the 1660s, see ibid., ch. 11, p. 27a; ch. 12, p. 21a; ch. 17, pp. 5b-6a; ch. 21, pp. 18b-19b; ch. 26, pp. 12b-13b, 17a-b.

But the efficient operation of the evaluation system rested entirely on the assessments sent on by upper provincial officials, and once again the Manchus in Peking were disappointed in their subordinates. In an edict of April 1665 the regents displayed their anger:

Recently in looking at impeachment memorials from all of the tu-fu of the provinces, we have found impeachments of only one or two decrepit or obscure officials who have evaded their responsibilities. How can we avoid situations whereby the subordinates [of the tu-fu] are greedy and bring harm to the people? All of this arises from excessive toleration of corruption. . . . Those tu-fu who are completely worthless, let them be impeached and punished.[11]

The third area in which the regents found fault was that of corruption on the part of the highest officials in the provinces. There were several cases of such corruption revealed in the "Veritable Records" during the first eight years of the K'ang-hsi reign. In 1667, for example, the Shansi financial commissioner, Wang Hsien-tso, was dismissed from his post and forever stripped of his honors for heavy embezzlement from the public granaries. The governor of the province, a Chinese bannerman named Yang Hsi, was also implicated in the case and thus received a stern reprimand from the regents.[12] In the same year it was revealed that several of the top provincial officials, including governors-general and governors, in the provinces of Fukien, Kwangtung, Kiangsi, and Hukuang, were engaging in commercial ventures for their own profit. Because of their prestige and power they were able to sell goods at a higher price to the detriment of both consumers and other merchants.[13]

Such cases were undoubtedly only the surface indications of corruption during the Oboi regency. In an edict of 1668, which was probably composed by the K'ang-hsi Emperor's advisers rather than by the regents, the prevalence of corrupt local officials during the regency was clearly pointed out:

Formerly because the local officials were excessive in tax collections and sent their own private functionaries to collect the taxes, they brought suffering and hardship to the people. There was frequently oppression and famine. . . . In addition to the regular taxes, there was added the meltage fee; or the public tax lists were seized and not made known to the people. In order to establish their

---

11. Ibid., ch. 14, pp. 19a-b. Imperial admonishments to the tu-fu about their recommendations and memorials were common during the Shun-chih reign as well. See CS, 1 (pen-chi): 48-56, passim.

12. KH Shih-lu, ch. 22, pp. 5a-b. A former Shansi governor, Chang Tzu-te, was impeached on similar charges in 1660 (SC Shih-lu, ch. 133, p. 18a; ch. 134, p. 3a).

13. KH Shih-lu, ch. 22, pp. 7a-b; ch. 23, pp. 2a-b.

reputations, the local officials did as they liked in the collection of taxes, or they bribed the higher officials, All of this has reached the point where the commoners' wealth is exhausted and their suffering is extreme. I am terribly grieved about this.[14]

The foregoing survey indicates that there were severe flaws in the relations between Peking and the provinces under the Oboi regency. Although it would be a gross overstatement to conclude that corruption and incompetence pervaded the entire provincial establishment, it is safe to say that on many occasions provincial officials failed to perform in a fashion acceptable to the regents.

The four Manchu oligarchs in Peking, acting in characteristic fashion, experimented with a variety of techniques to improve the situation in provincial administration. First of all, they conducted several full-scale evaluations of the upper provincial officialdom. During the year of 1661, for example, there were very heavy turnovers in the positions of governors-general and governors. Of the twenty-four incumbent governors in that year, two were dismissed outright and ten were recorded as having retired (probably many of these retired under pressure). Eight of the remaining fourteen retained their offices, while six were transferred to governor-generalships.[15] Among the governors-general, a more complex development occurred. Although all of the nine governors-general (including the director-general of River Conservancy) who held the posts in 1660 were kept, the regents expanded the number of governors-general to twenty. Consequently, eleven new appointments were made, and the regents were thus able to choose men to their liking.[16] In all, then, the regents introduced twenty-one tu-fu during the first year of their regime while eliminating twelve others. Through such extensive maneuvers the regents endeavored to remold the nature of the provincial officialdom.

Another method which the regents used to improve the conduct of provincial administration was the reduction in numbers or the complete elimination of certain provincial posts. The censors, traditionally considered guardians of morality, were among the victims of this policy.

---

14. Ibid., ch. 26, p. 12b. After the K'ang-hsi Emperor began to assert influence over the court in 1667, there were a number of edicts which were obviously drafted under the orders of his own personal advisers rather than by the regents. The general tone of these imperial pronouncements is far more sympathetic to the problems of the common people than those of the regents. In addition, the use of such terminology as "I am terribly grieved about this" (chen shen min chih) tends to indicate the sanction of the emperor rather than his regents. The imperial pronoun (chen) was seldom employed by the regents in the early years of their regime except in their forgery of the Shun-chih Will, where they used the imperial pronoun to give the document veracity. For further information on this matter, see chapter 8 of this book under "The Emergence of the Imperial Faction."

15. CS, 4:3014-15.

16. Ibid., 4:2856-57. See also appendix 3 of this book.

The regents seem to have mistrusted the censors as potential critics
of Ch'ing policies and as possibly corrupt figures in the imperial bureaucracy. In mid-1661, therefore, they completely abolished the post of
hsün-an censor (hsün-an yü-shih, the "censor who tours and pacifies")
in response to reports that these officials, numbering one to a province,
had neglected their responsibilities and had committed financial irregularities.[17] Furthermore, as was mentioned in a previous chapter, there
were considerable cuts in the numbers of regular provincial censors in
the years 1661 and 1668. The regents followed a similar pattern in dealing with financial commissioners. In August 1667 the number of financial commissioners, formerly two to a province, was reduced to one for
each province in almost every case.[18] The post of financial commissioner, charged with overseeing the provincial budget and the taxation
system, was one with almost unlimited opportunities for fraud, and the
regents were evidently trying to alleviate some of their problems by
eliminating officials.

The third and most drastic step taken by the regents to resolve their
problems with the provincial officialdom, in addition to conducting evaluations and eliminating certain provincial posts, was that of altering the
Dorgon compromise itself. During the months of July and August of 1667,
following the advice of joint sessions of the Council of Deliberative Officials, the Nine Ministers, and the Censorate, a major departure from
the earlier policy on provincial appointments was announced. It was determined that the posts of tu-fu, as well as those of financial commisioner
and judicial commissioner, ought to be open to "the able and virtuous, no
matter whether he is Manchu, Chinese bannerman, or Chinese."[19]

17. The position of hsün-an censor had been created under the Ming, and
throughout most of the Shun-chih reign one hsün-an censor was appointed to each
province. These censors were given several responsibilities, including impeaching incompetent or corrupt provincial officials, touring the province to gain information on local conditions, and supervising the chü-jen examinations. See Fu-
chien t'ung-chih, ch. 107, p. 3b; Shang, p. 74; Kessler, "Ethnic Composition of
Provincial Leadership," p. 491. Concern about corruption among the hsün-an
censors had been expressed as early as 1651 (SC Shih-lu, ch. 55, pp. 13a-15b).
The post had been temporarily abolished in June 1653 (ibid., ch. 75, pp. 7b-8a).

In 1660 the hsün-an censor of Chekiang, Mou Yün-lung, was convicted of em-
bezzling 40,000 taels worth of grain and was sentenced to execution by beheading
(SC Shih-lu, ch. 133, p. 11a). In early 1661 the Manchu president of the Board
of War, Asha, memorialized that the hsün-an censors were often corrupt and that
they had failed to make thorough investigations and unbiased evaluations of officials
(KH Shih-lu, ch. 1, pp. 12a-14b). On the abolition of the post of hsün-an censor,
see KH Shih-lu, ch. 3, pp. 5a-7a, 9b; Shang, p. 74; HTSL, ch. 335, p. 1b (p.
9542). Both the HTSL and Shang set the date for the abolition of the hsün-an cen-
sorship as 1663 rather than 1661.

18. KH Shih-lu, ch. 23, pp. 5b-6a; HTSL, ch. 24, pp. 20a-21a (pp. 5366-67);
Fu, Ch'ing-tai tu-fu chih-tu, p. 3.

19. KH Shih-lu, ch. 22, pp. 17b, 18b, 20a; ch. 24, pp. 27a-28a. Manchus
had been appointed as provincial censors as early as 1665 in Chekiang, Shansi,
Shantung, and Shensi (ibid., ch. 14, p. 16a).

The decision to admit Manchus to the top echelons of the provincial bureaucracy must be interpreted at least in part as a desperate attempt to resolve the loyalty dilemma. This departure from the Dorgon compromise indicates disgust with the performance of the Chinese bannermen. In spite of the regents' effort to foster a loyal officialdom at the provincial level, the failures of the Chinese bannermen were obvious. The regents probably reasoned that the appointment of a few, carefully selected, Manchus to top provincial spots might help tip the balance in favor of greater loyalty.

The use of Manchus at the provincial level, however, was also an act of factionalism on the part of Oboi. Although the Oboi faction will be treated in a later chapter, Oboi's exploitation of the provincial bureaucracy must be mentioned at this point. By late 1667 two of the regents, Suksaha and Soni, were dead, and Ebilun failed to stand in Oboi's path. In that year Oboi appointed many of his closest associates to key positions in the metropolitan and banner hierarchies. Only the provincial officialdom was free from Oboi's direct grasp. The announcement of the new appointment policy by mid-1667, however, promised that Oboi would soon disrupt the provincial bureaucracy as well. In the first three months of 1668 Oboi made his first Manchu appointments to key provincial posts. Virtually all of them were members of his faction. In February he named Moro, a member of the Plain Red Banner and vice-president of the Censorate, to the post of governor-general of Shansi-Shensi. In March he appointed Ata (former director of the Court of Judicature and Revision) as governor of Shansi, and he designated Becingge (former director of the Banqueting Court) as governor of Shensi.[20]

Oboi's experiment in Manchu appointments at the provincial level, however, was short-lived. When Oboi was arrested and imprisoned in June 1669, his Manchu appointees were removed from their posts in both

20. Ibid., ch. 25, pp. 12a, 13a. Although biographical data is lacking on these tu-fu, they are designated as members of the Oboi faction because they were cited as such by the K'ang-hsi Emperor in an edict of 24 June 1669, in ibid., ch. 29, pp. 5b-6a. In March 1668 Oboi also appointed Manchus as financial commissioners of Shansi and Shensi (ibid., ch. 25, p. 13a). While it is probable that they were also affiliated with Oboi, there are no biographies available for these officials. Their names were Darbu, A-hsi-hsi, Se-t'e, and Mucengge.

Oboi's choice of Shansi and Shensi to inaugurate his experiment in Manchu appointments was probably determined by two considerations. First, as mentioned earlier in this chapter, in 1667 there was a case of embezzlement which involved the financial commissioner of Shansi and implicated the governor of the province. Surely there was no province which might have been a better choice for experimenting in the eradication of corruption. Secondly, Shansi and Shensi were in close proximity to Peking. Oboi, therefore, could keep a close watch on the actions of his Manchu appointees. Lawrence Kessler has noted that the practice of appointing Manchus as tu-fu of Shensi-Shansi continued over the years of 1668-1723. According to his evidence, these were the only tu-fu posts specifically reserved for Manchus during the entire history of the Ch'ing period (Kessler, "Ethnic Composition of Provincial Leadership," p. 494).

the metropolitan and provincial bureaucracies. But the K'ang-hsi Emperor did continue to follow Oboi's example of using Manchus as well as Chinese bannermen in the upper provincial bureaucracy. By the year of 1673, for example, three of the ten governors-general and five of the eighteen governors were Manchus.[21] Oboi himself was surely a villain in the eyes of the young K'ang-hsi Emperor, but many of Oboi's policies were quite acceptable.

In spite of the careful attention which the regents paid to the provincial officialdom, it must be concluded that they failed to resolve their problems. Corruption and inadequate provincial-metropolitan communications persisted throughout the decade. The appointment of Manchus to high provincial posts was an innovative step, but, for reasons mentioned earlier, Manchus were not the ultimate answer. Although the K'ang-hsi Emperor did continue Oboi's policy in this respect, he also looked to new and more successful solutions to problems on the provincial level. The K'ang-hsi Emperor's famous Southern Tours and his increased reliance on bondservants as informants were far more creative moves than anything attempted under the Oboi regency.[22] In general, the regents had remained trapped in Peking, deaf to much of what transpired in provincial China.

THE OBOI REGENCY AND THE PROVINCIAL ELITE: AUTHORITARIANISM AT ITS EXTREME

The two most famous incidents which occurred outside Peking during the Oboi period were the Kiangnan Tax Case of 1661 and the Ming History Case of 1661-63. Both of these events are worthy of close attention not only as instances of Manchu-Chinese conflicts, but also as case studies of the regents' problems in provincial administration.

The provinces of Kiangnan and Chekiang, in which these incidents occurred, were the center of Chinese elitism during the seventeenth century. In the commercial centers along the Grand Canal, such as Yangchow, Soochow, and Hangchow, lived many of the most opulent merchants, officials, scholars, and artists. In education as well, Chekiang and Kiangnan far surpassed any of the other provinces. Over one-third of all the chin-shih degrees granted in the K'ang-hsi reign were to residents of these two provinces.[23]

21. CS, 4:2865-66, 3022. In the case of the governors in 1673, all those Manchus who held this post during the year are included even if their appointments were only temporary.

22. On the K'ang-hsi Emperor's Southern Tours, see Spence, Ts'ao Yin, pp. 124-57; on his use of bondservants and the palace memorial system, see ibid., pp. 213-54.

23. Ho, Ladder of Success, p. 228. Computing from the figures Ho gives here, 1375 of 4088 chin-shih under the K'ang-hsi reign were from Chekiang, Kiangsu, and Anhwei; thus 34 percent of the total came from these provinces.

The central coastal region was also the heart of the Ming-loyalist movement in the early Ch'ing period. The people of this area had many reasons for resentment of their Manchu conquerors. In the 1640s vicious Manchu massacres were carried out against the Chinese living in these provinces. The brutal executions and rapes which occurred in the city of Yangchow, for example, were long remembered by the Chinese (such memories were revived in the early twentieth century by Chinese revolutionaries eager to overthrow the Manchu throne).[24] Although actual fighting between Chinese loyalists and Manchu troops in this region subsided by the end of the 1640s, a residue of hatred remained. Many loyalists, rejecting the alternative of direct military action, turned to more indirect forms of protest, such as refusing to serve the Manchu court while devoting themselves to scholarship.[25]

To the four Manchu regents, who had little sympathy for the refined life of the Chinese scholar-official, the provinces of Chekiang and Kiangnan were the most troublesome. In addition to the pervasiveness of Chinese elitism and Ming loyalism, the regents had yet another cause for distrust of this area. Cheng Ch'eng-kung (Coxinga) had almost conquered the province of Kiangnan by moving his troops up the Yangtze to within reach of Nanking in late 1659. Although the Manchus were able to drive Cheng back to sea and eventually to Taiwan (see chapter 6), the Manchu court suspected collusion between Chinese residents of the central coastal region and the pirate forces.[26]

The incidents which took place in Kiangnan and Chekiang in the early 1660s, therefore, constituted a basic clash of attitudes and life-styles between Manchu and Chinese. While the Chinese clung to their elite society and loyalism, the Manchus sought absolute obedience and recognition of their superiority. The provincial officialdom was caught between this crossfire.[27]

The Kiangnan Tax Case

The Kiangnan Tax Case of 1661 occurred in four prefectures located on the wide peninsula between Chinkiang and Hangchow (prefectures of Soochow, Ch'ang-chou, Chen-chiang, and Sung-chiang). The center of the incident was the city of Soochow on the Grand Canal (just to the northwest of Lake T'ai-hu). If the award of chin-shih degrees is used as a

---

24. On the Yangchow massacre, see Wang Hsiu-ch'u, "Memoir of a Ten Days' Massacre," pp. 515-37.

25. On loyalism in the early Ch'ing period, see Willhelm, "The Po-hsüeh Hung-ju Examination," pp. 60-66.

26. For cases of surrender in the face of Cheng Ch'eng-kung, see SC Shih-lu, ch. 133, pp. 16a-17a, 21b-22a; and KH Shih-lu, ch. 7, p. 18a.

27. Lawrence Kessler has made the convincing suggestion that several Chinese officials from the north (Chihli, Shantung, Honan, Shansi) may have been active supporters of the regents' actions against the scholars and officials of Kiangnan and Chekiang (Kessler, "Chinese Scholars," pp. 181-82).

measure, this area of Kiangnan (in particular the prefectures of Soochow and Ch'ang-chou) was one of the most outstanding centers of the
Chinese literati in the Ch'ing dynasty. Soochow and Ch'ang-chou ranked
among the four highest prefectures for chin-shih recipients during the
entire dynasty. [28]

In spite of the academic success and prosperity of this region, its
residents had ample cause to detest the Manchu dynasty. The taxes imposed on these four prefectures were exceptionally high, and, in addition
to the regular taxes on property and commuted corvée payments (ting),
a variety of miscellaneous taxes and surcharges was collected.[29] The
people of this area had also suffered in terms of official appointments.
It was not until June 1660 that an order prohibiting persons of these four
prefectures from holding high metropolitan posts was rescinded. The
probable reason for this discrimination in appointments was that loyalist
resistance in these areas had been very strong during the 1640s.[30]

The issue which provoked the Kiangnan Tax Case was the existence
of a tax deficit in the province of Kiangnan when the regents took over in
early 1661. On 21 February 1661 Chang Feng-ch'i, a censor appointed
to Kiangnan, reported that there were serious deficits in the taxes of the
four prefectures of Su, Sung, Ch'ang, and Chen.[31] Six days later the
regents issued an edict which made clear their intention to punish officials for failure to fulfill their tax quotas:

> Tax revenues are urgently needed by the army and the dynasty. In
> the supervision of all officials there must be special attention de-
> voted to the collection of taxes. Only when one has filled his tax
> quota by the proper time has he fulfilled the responsibilities of his
> post. Recently in reviewing memorials, it has been observed that

28. Ho, Ladder of Success, p. 247, table 36. During the Shun-chih reign the
province of Kiangnan received no fewer than 564 chin-shih (ibid., p. 228, table 28).

29. Meng Sen uncovered information which indicates that the taxes of Kiangnan in general, and those of Soochow and Sung-chiang in particular, were many
times those of other provinces and prefectures during this period (Meng, "Tsou-
hsiao an," p. 436; Hsü, Ch'ing-pai lui-ch'ao, ts'e 8, p. 29).

30. SC Shih-lu, ch. 135, pp. 8a-b. In addition to the four prefectures mentioned, this order also applied to those in Hangchow, Chia-hsing, Hu-chou (all
in Chekiang). The order specifically applied to the posts of ssu-kuan; Brunnert
and Hagelstrom define this term as a "common designation of all officials of the
Ministries below the rank of Secretary" (BH, p. 104). The entry in the "Veritable
Records" does not indicate when the order first went into effect; it may date from
the early years of the dynasty when the fighting in Chekiang and Kiangnan against
the Manchus was fierce.

31. KH Shih-lu, ch. 1, p. 15b. Tax delinquency in Kiangnan had been a central concern of the early Ch'ing state since the mid-1650s. Several regulations
were established in the late Shun-chih period to provide penalties for officials
and local elites who were involved in tax evasion (Kessler, "Chinese Scholars,"
p. 184).

statements of tax deficits in Chihli and other provinces have been
most numerous. . . . We must wait until the quotas are completely
filled without any deficits before memorials requesting transfer or
promotion will be permitted.[32]

Through this edict the regents placed the onus for tax deficits on the officials rather than on those who had evaded taxation. The provincial officials, therefore, were under sharp pressure from the new Oboi regime.[33]
One local official in Kiangnan who felt this pressure more intensely
than most was Jen Wei-ch'u, the newly appointed magistrate of Wu-hsien
(which encompassed the city of Soochow). Jen Wei-ch'u, a kung-sheng
degree holder from Shansi, was a self-impressed individual whose pom-
posity eventually brought him to disaster. On the day that he took office,
Jen paid a visit to the prefect of Soochow, Hou Yü-kung. When he arrived
at the gate of the prefectural yamen, the gate-keepers requested that he
descend from his palanquin and walk in. Jen was enraged and responded,
"He [the prefect] is an official. I too am an official. How is it that I
should walk in?" Although the gate attendants were greatly disturbed,
they allowed him to be carried into the yamen courtyard while cautioning
Jen that "it is better when one is just assuming responsibility not to be
carried in." Hou Yü-kung, the prefect, overheard this incident and remarked, "the newly appointed magistrate is a fool. To pay a visit to his
superior and act like this antagonizes his superior. I will not see him."
Hou then returned to his yamen reception hall and announced that "governmental regulations are very strict, and tax revenues are the most
important. In the evaluations of merit and demerit, all will depend on
this."[34]
Jen Wei-ch'u apparently decided to take the prefect at his word and
embarked on a ruthless tax collection campaign. Trying to fill his quota
as rapidly as possible, Jen flogged commoners who did not pay immediately. He even confiscated grain from the public storehouses and sold
this to merchants in order to enrich the revenue receipts.[35] The people
of Kiangnan were irate about Jen's activities, and many of those in the
upper class decided to protest the matter. Their protests took two forms,
which have come to be called the "laments in the temple" (k'u-miao) incident and the "taxation case reported to the Board of Revenue" (tsou-
hsiao an).
The "laments in the temple" incident occurred during the first few
days of March 1661, when a number of important dignitaries had gathered at the Confucian Temple in Soochow to conduct mourning ceremonies

32. KH Shih-lu, ch. 1, pp. 17a-b.
33. In late March 1661 regulations were issued calling for the punishment of
all provincial officials of the rank of tu-fu and below for tax deficits (KH Shih-lu,
ch. 2, p. 1b).
34. This episode is recorded in K'u-miao chi-lüeh, 2: 1a.
35. Hummel, p. 165; K'u-miao chi-lüeh, 2: 1a-b.

in memory of the Shun-chih Emperor. Among those present was the
governor of the province, Chu Kuo-chih. On March 4 over one hundred
scholars gathered in front of the temple. They were led by the well-
known writer Chin Jen-jui and by the prefectural director of schools,
Ch'eng I-tsang. These scholars, crying and shouting in anger, presented
to the governor a written denunciation of Jen Wei-ch'u which asked that
Jen be removed from his post. Eleven of these scholars, including Ch'eng
I-tsang, were immediately arrested and imprisoned for their outspoken-
ness.[36]

Following these preliminary actions over the temple incident, Governor Chu Kuo-chih engineered an extensive campaign against tax evaders
in Kiangnan. The governor ordered prefectural and district officials to
make careful investigations of the tax registers and to report the names
of the delinquent individuals. In some areas—Ch'ang-chou prefecture
and Lien-ch'uan district, for instance—local officials and elites realized
the danger they faced and paid their outstanding tax debts quickly to avoid
reprisals.[37] But in many sections of Kiangnan, tax evasion continued.
In a memorial to Peking Governor Chu claimed that 13,517 local elites
and 254 yamen clerks were still guilty of unpaid taxes. Chu also observed
that the scholars had rioted just to avoid the payment of taxes and that

36. For descriptions of the k'u-miao incident, see Hummel, p. 165; K'u-miao
chi-lüeh, pp. 1a-b; Hsü, ts'e 8, p. 67; and Kessler, "Chinese Scholars," p. 185.
Biographies of Chin Jen-jui in Hummel, pp. 164–66, and Ch'en Teng-yüan, Chin
Sheng-t'an chuan. Although he possessed no traditional examination degree, Chin
Jen-jui was one of the most successful novelists and playwrights of his day. According to Fang Chao-ying, "Chin Jen-jui attacked the oppressive measures of
the government and even advocated rebellion on the part of the people who were
pressed beyond their endurance. For him the novel and the drama portrayed best
the hollowness of obsolete conventions and taboos" (Hummel, p. 164). The Shun-
chih Emperor had read some of Chin's works and observed that Chin was "highly
talented but with unconventional ideas" (Hummel, p. 256).

Ch'eng I-tsang was from Chiang-ning, Kiangnan, and was a chin-shih of
1652. After serving for a time in the Hanlin Academy, Ch'eng was transferred
to the post of prefectural director of schools in Soochow in 1656 (K'u-miao chi-
lüeh, pp. 2a-b).

37. Kessler, "Chinese Scholars," pp. 186–87. For further information on
the tsou-hsiao an, see Hsiao Kung-chuan, Rural China, p. 599; Ch'ü T'ung-tsu,
Local Government in China, pp. 185, 331–32; Hsiao I-shan, 1:390; and Su-chou
fu-chih, ch. 88, pp. 9b-10b. Chu Kuo-chih was a member of the Chinese Plain
Yellow Banner and had received the kung-sheng degree. During the years of
1649-57 he held the post of magistrate of Ku-an, Chihli, and later prefect in
Shun-te, Chihli. In 1659 he was made director of the Court of Judicature and
Revision and was then transferred to governor of Chiang-ning. In 1659-61 Chu
was actively involved in the defense against Cheng Ch'eng-kung and submitted
several memorials concerning military matters (CSLC, ch. 6, pp. 25a-26a).

A preliminary hearing of those involved in the k'u-miao episode was held in
March 1661, at which Jen Wei-ch'u justified his actions by declaring that Chu
Kuo-chih had demanded the rapid collection of taxes. According to several ac-
counts, Chu Kuo-chih responded by producing a falsified order (with a fictitious

Chin Jen-jui in particular had not only "offended the spirit of the deceased emperor" but had also been a traitor in league with the pirate
Cheng Ch'eng-kung. [38]

The four Manchu regents in Peking responded to Chu's memorial by
ordering a massive criminal investigation in the province of Kiangnan.
While in February 1661 they had placed the burden for tax deficits on the
local officials, by April they had changed their tactics and now blamed
the local elite (shen-chin). [39] Accordingly, the regents sent Manchu commissioners to Kiangnan to arrest and try all of those involved in the evasion affair and the temple protest as well as those who had been charged
earlier with surrender to Cheng Ch'eng-kung in 1659. Evidently the regents saw the scholars' demonstration, tax evasion, and surrender to
Cheng Ch'eng-kung as events related to one another—all comprising treason against the Manchu regime.

The Manchu commissioners arrived in May 1661 and established a
tribunal at Nanking (outside of the four prefectures in question to avoid
further demonstrations). [41] The main event of the summer was the trial
of twenty-two of those involved in the temple protest, including the writer
Chin Jen-jui, who became the symbolic figure in the affair because of
his prominence within the elite class in Kiangnan. [42] Chin and the others
were repeatedly interrogated and beaten. At one point in a flogging, Chin

---

date many days before the actual events) which announced that military problems
forced the immediate collection of taxes (Hummel, p. 165; Hsiao I-shan, 1:390;
K'u-miao chi-ltieh, p. 2a; Su-chou fu-chih, ch. 88, pp. 9b-10b). Kessler has
argued, with considerable justification, that Chu Kuo-chih may have been acting
within the guidelines of the regents' edict of February 27. See Kessler, "Chinese
Scholars," p. 185, n 17.

38. KH Shih-lu, ch. 3, p. 3a.

39. KH Shih-lu, ch. 2, pp. 3b-4a. On the precise meaning of the term shen-
chin and related terms in the early Ch'ing period, see Spence, Ts'ao Yin, pp. 77-
81.

40. On the regents' decision for a mass trial, see Ch'en Teng-ytian, Chin
Sheng-t'an chuan, p. 65; Hummel, p. 165.

41. On the choice of Nanking rather than Soochow for the location of the trial,
see Ch'en Teng-ytian, Chin Sheng-t'an chuan, p. 65.

42. Ch'eng I-tsang, the prefectural director of schools in Soochow, was originally arrested and then later released through an unusual series of events. Ch'eng
was imprisoned after the March hearing because he had enraged Chu Kuo-chih by
declaring that Jen Wei-ch'u's excesses were prompted by the demands of his superiors and that Jen "had no way of avoiding the problem." When the full-scale
trial opened in May, however, Lang T'ing-tso, the governor-general of Kiangnan
and a former pupil of Ch'eng I-tsang, ordered that Ch'eng be released. For some
reason, perhaps because of orders from Chu Kuo-chih, Ch'eng was not freed from
his cell. A few days later Ch'eng was called before the governor-general in the
presence of the Manchu commissioners sent to Nanking. When asked why he had
remained, Ch'eng feigned stupidity and indicated that he thought that Lang T'ing-
tso had only meant for him to leave the room and not the prison. Lang laughed
and said to the Manchus, "In all of heaven, can there be another fool such as
this?" The Manchus, taken in by the ploy of Ch'eng and Lang, responded, "Let
this fool be released" (K'u-miao chi-ltieh, pp. 2a-4a).

Jen-jui called out to the spirits of former emperors to help him. The Manchu commissioners lept on this as an admission of Chin's guilt and declared: "The Emperor has just been crowned. Why do you call out to the former emperors? It must be to curse the Emperor himself."[43] Eventually the Manchu commissioners and Chu Kuo-chih felt that they had sufficient evidence, and they memorialized Peking that Chin Jen-jui and seventeen others were guilty not only of tax resistance but also of plotting rebellion. On 7 August 1661 a mass execution took place in Nanking as Chin and the other seventeen were beheaded. One account provides a graphic description of the event:

At the time of the execution the place was encircled by armed sol-diers and the Governor himself presided. During the seventh and ninth hours hours, the criminals were taken from the prison. Their hands were tied behind them, small flags were placed on their backs, and their mouths were stuffed with pieces of chestnut wood. Hus-tled [by soldiers on both sides] they were rushed through the street. Relatives and other spectators who tried to stand close were driven back by the handles of spears and the flat sides of swords. In a short while, the cannon roared, and the heads of the criminals fell to the ground. Armed soldiers ran in all directions, and the offi-cials dispersed in fear. On the execution ground, there remained only the reek of blood and severed heads. [44]

The repercussions of the Kiangnan Tax Case were loud and many. Many in the province suffered loss of examination degrees and property confiscations. According to one estimate, a total of 11,346 individuals were deprived of their sheng-yüan degrees in the prefectures of Soochow, Sung-chiang, Ch'ang-chou, and Chenkiang, and in the district of Li-yang.[45] Some well-known scholars and officials from Kiangnan lost ranks and government posts as a result of the Tax Case.[46] One prefect in Chekiang described the conditions in the neighboring province:

43. Ibid., p. 5b.
44. Ibid., p. 9a. Translation is in John Ching-yu Wang, Chin Sheng-t'an, p. 36. Chin's property was confiscated along with that of seven other unfortunate scholars, and their families were banished to Ninguta in Manchuria (ibid., pp. 5b-10a). A complete list of the eighteen executed is found in ibid., pp. 10b-11b.
45. Kessler, "Chinese Scholars," p. 187. An excellent account of the per-secutions of the Chinese elite in Kiangnan during the Tax Case of 1661 is Meng, "Tsou-hsiao an," pp. 438-51. Meng lists several cases of persons arrested, beaten, deprived of property, and so forth. One man, Shu Yüan, became a fugi-tive for sixteen years before he was granted a pardon by the K'ang-hsi Emperor and given a post in the metropolitan prefecture (ibid., pp. 441-42). Wei Hsiao was removed from his local posts and stripped of all ranks and degrees but was later forgiven by the K'ang-hsi Emperor and permitted to take the po-hsüeh exam-ination of 1679 (ibid., p. 443).
46. Kessler, "Chinese Scholars," pp. 187-89.

In addition to local officials demoted or dismissed, local gentry and
sheng-yüan who have their ranks or titles taken away from them
amount to about one hundred in small districts and almost one thousand in large ones. Since the occurrence of the Clearance Case,
not only does the number of persons with gentry status dwindle to
to no more than a handful and the tracks of their carriages no longer
mark the entrances to the yamen but the number of scholars dimin-
ishes to such an extent that when the educational authorities arrive
to conduct the examinations, no more than a few appear to take them. [47]

The residents of Kiangnan did gain some small satisfaction, however, from
the removal of the key officials involved in the events of 1661. Jen Wei-
ch'u was ousted from his post in late 1661 and executed in Nanking in 1662.
Chu Kuo-chih was punished in 1662 when, after requesting temporary retirement to mourn his father's death, Chu failed to wait in his post until
a replacement arrived. Eventually Chu was killed in 1673 during the Rebellion of the Three Feudatories.

But the resentment of the people of Kiangnan against the Manchu dynasty did not abate quickly. Continued hostility prompted the K'ang-hsi
Emperor to take special measures in dealing with Kiangnan. In 1679,
when the emperor instituted the famous po-hsüeh hung-ju examination to
woo the support of Ming loyalists and Chinese dissidents, he paid particular attention to the Kiangnan area. Twenty-six of the fifty who passed
were from this province. Four of the successful candidates had been directly involved in the Kiangnan Tax Case. [48] When the emperor visited
Kiangnan in his Southern Tour of 1684, he was polite and yet careful in
his dealings with local residents. He carried out a sacrifice at the tomb
of a Ming emperor; he praised the local administration of Nanking; and he
even stressed the fact that he had been reading the Classic of History
every night. But the emperor was fearful of the native population and
spent his time with the Tartar general within the walls of the Manchu section of Nanking. [49]

Ming History Case (1661–1663)

The second major confrontation between the regents and the Chinese elite
occurred in the area of Hangchow, Chekiang, only one hundred miles to
the south of Soochow. In the Ming History Case the provocation was less
obvious than in the Kiangnan Tax Case, but the response of the Manchus
was equally brutal. As mentioned earlier, by the 1660s the loyalists of
the China coast had abandoned the hope of military success against the
Manchus and had turned to more subtle alternatives. One such alternative was dedication of one's life to scholarship and refusal to serve the

47. Wu Chai, prefect of Chin-hua prefecture in Chekiang, quoted in Hsiao
Kung-chuan, Rural China, p. 127.
48. Kessler, "Chinese Scholars," pp. 194–95.
49. Spence, Ts'ao Yin, pp. 127–28.

Manchu court in an official capacity. Scholarship not only provided a
useful occupation for upper-class Chinese, but it sometimes offered opportunities for venting one's loyalist sentiments through anti-Manchu
and pro-Ming references in prose and poetry. In general this sort of
loyalism remained beyond the reach of the Manchu court, but in the Ming
History Case of 1661-63 the Manchus in Peking were able to strike back
at covert criticism from these loyalist scholars.

The story of the Ming History Case begins in the 1620s with the writing of a work entitled Huang Ming shih-kai [Draft History of the Ming Dy-
nasty] by Chu Kuo-chen (1557-1632), a prominent official and historian
of the late Ming period.[50] During the 1640s some unpublished sections
of this work were purchased by Chuang T'ing-lung, the eldest son of
Chuang Yün-ch'eng, a wealthy merchant living in the town of Nan-hsün,
Chekiang. Chuang T'ing-lung, a sheng-yüan degree-holder, had become
blind after receiving his degree, but continued his scholarly efforts in
spite of his misfortune.[51] Consequently he decided to revise Chu Kuo-
chen's work and to complete the history through 1644, the final work to
be given the new title of Ming-shih chi-lüeh [Compilation and Summary
of Ming History].

Chuang T'ing-lung requested that a number of scholars assist him in
the revising and editing of the Ming-shih chi-lüeh. One such scholar, indicating the despair of the loyalists, responded to Chuang's invitation by
lamenting, "today the fortunate are those who are not dead; what else
is there for those who remain other than scholarship?"[52] Eventually
some seventeen or eighteen scholars were gathered to carry out the project, but there were few prominent names among them.[53] Only two—Wu
Yen and P'an Ch'eng-chang—have become well known, and their fame is
due largely to the fact that Ku Yen-wu wrote a short biography about them
entitled the Shu Wu P'an er-tzu shih. In this work Ku Yen-wu pointed out
the rather poor quality of the Ming-shih chi-lüeh by recounting his own

50. Chu Kuo-chen was a chin-shih of 1589 who rose to the posts of president
of the Board of Rites and Grand Secretary in the early 1620s. In 1625, however,
because Chu refused to cooperate with the Wei Chung-hsien clique, he retired to
his home in Nan-hsün, Chekiang. During the last few years of his life he composed the Huang Ming shih-kai, and it was published in the year of his death (1632)
(Hummel, p. 187; Goodrich, Literary Inquisition of Ch'ien-lung, pp. 75-76 n;
Nan-hsün chih, ch. 42, p. 1a; Meng, "Shu Ming-shih ch'ao-lüeh," p. 141; Hsieh
Kuo-chen, "Chuang-shih shih-an," p. 423.

51. Biography of Chuang T'ing-lung (and Chuang Yün-ch'eng) in Hummel,
pp. 205-6. Meng Sen has recorded that Chuang Yün-ch'eng was a chin-shih of
1658 and served in the Hanlin Academy (Meng, "Shu Ming-shih ch'ao-lüeh,"
p. 143).

52. Biography of Lu Ch'i in CSLC, ch. 70, p. 8b. Lu Ch'i and two other
scholars, Cha Chi-tso and Fan Hsiang, later disclaimed any part in the compilation and were thus spared the fates of those who had participated (Hummel, pp. 18-
19, 206; Nan-hsün chih, ch. 42, p. 1b).

53. For a list of those who participated in the project, see Nan-hsün chih,
ch. 42, p. 1a.

refusal to offer his services: "When Chuang compiled his work, he invited me to come to his house. I felt that he was incompetent as a scholar
and finally left. Thus my name was not listed and I averted disaster."[54]
The fact that Ku Yen-wu even considered contributing to the work and
that so many scholars of lesser caliber did contribute, however, indicates the relaxed atmosphere of the late Shun-chih reign which permitted
the compilation of a private history of the Ming period.

Chuang T'ing-lung died early in 1660 and the history was completed
by his father, Yün-ch'eng. In spite of the mediocre nature of the finished
product, the Ming-shih chi-lüeh was published in late 1660 and sold in
bookstores around Hangchow. On the whole, the work was a factual account of the history of the Ming, but there were certain details which
were forthright attacks against the Manchus. First, the early Manchu
emperors were called by their personal names rather than by their posthumous titles; thus T'ai-tsu was called Nurhaci. Such references would
seem to imply that the Manchus were still barbarians rather than emperors. Secondly, references to seventeenth-century events before the
conquest were dated according to the Ming reign-titles rather than by the
Ch'ing reign-titles; thus an event which occurred in 1621 was dated T'ien-
pi first year rather than T'ien-ming sixth year (the Manchu reign title).
Thirdly, such outstanding Chinese bannermen as K'ung Yu-te and Keng
Ching-chung were described as rebels in the Ming History.[55]

These details apparently went unnoticed when a copy of the history
was sent to Peking in January 1661. The Board of Rites and the Censorate reviewed the Ming-shih chi-lüeh, perhaps in cursory fashion, and
deemed it "harmless."[56] The work would probably have been circulated
without complications if certain local officials had not taken advantage of
the indiscretions in the history and threatened exposure to the regency if
heavy bribes were not paid. The main extortionists were Ch'en Yung-
ming, a Chinese bannerman and prefect in Chekiang; Li T'ing-shu, a former circuit intendant in Kiangnan; and Wu Chih-jung, former magistrate
of Kuei-an, Chekiang. These three, and particularly Wu Chih-jung, tried
to blackmail Chuang Yün-ch'eng for several thousand taels. When Chuang
refused to pay the bribe, Wu Chih-jung sent a memorial to Peking, where
it was handed on to the Board of Punishments.[57] Wu Chih-jung had thus
tried to capitalize on the suspiciousness of the Manchu regents and, failing this, brought about a vicious reprisal from the regents.

54. Ku, "Shu Wu P'an er-tzu shih," ch. 35, pp. 25a-b. Biographies of Wu
and P'an in Hummel, pp. 606, 883. Another commentator said that the Ming-
shih chi-lüeh was "basically not worth looking at" (Meng, "Shu Ming-shih ch'ao-
lüeh," p. 142).

55. Meng, "Shu Ming-shih ch'ao-lüeh," pp. 143-46, passim; Hsü, Ch'ing-pai
lui-ch'ao, ts'e 8, p. 37; Kessler, "Chinese Scholars," pp. 182-84.

56. The history was sent to Peking under the orders of Wang Yüan-tso, an
official in the Office of Transmission (Nan-hsün chih, ch. 42, p. 1b).

57. Ibid., ch. 42, pp. 1b-2a, and ch. 43, pp. 8b-9a; Hummel, p. 206.

In the early months of 1661 a Manchu commissioner, Lodo, was sent
to Hangchow, where he confiscated and burned all of the copies of the
Ming-shih chi-lüeh. Chuang Yün-ch'eng was imprisoned and soon died
in confinement. Both Chuang and his son, T'ing-lung, were disinterred
and burned. In early 1662 two Manchu commissioners were sent to Chekiang to prosecute the case. Arriving in Hangchow on 9 March 1662,
these Manchus brought along several hundred bannermen and provincial
garrison troops. They interrogated all of the civil and military officials
of Wu-ch'eng (the district where the Chuangs had lived) and then arrested
all persons in the area bearing the surnames of Chuang or Chu (recalling
that Chu Kuo-chen had written the original history). After lengthy judicial proceedings, the verdicts were announced in 1663. Virtually every-
one connected with the Ming History was executed. This included not
only the compilers but also the publishers and even many of the purchas-
ers of the Ming-shih chi-lüeh. The total number of executions amounted
to seventy persons; their families were exiled to Manchuria and their
properties were confiscated by the government. One contemporary, while
probably exaggerating the numbers involved, expressed the dismay that
must have been universal in Chekiang and Kiangnan: "I have heard that
in the case of Chuang's arrest, over two hundred others were executed
on the same day. Their wives, children, and servants were all banished
to the frontiers never to return; these numbered many times the others
[who were executed]. Alas, this is the greatest catastrophe since the
change of the dynasty."[58]

Although the Ming History Case and Kiangnan Tax Case were the
most famous persecutions against the Chinese elite during the Oboi regency, there were several other less publicized confrontations. In 1661
Sung Wan, a writer and calligrapher, was falsely accused of fomenting
a rebellion in his native province of Shantung. Sung remained in prison
until 1664, when he was cleared of the charges and released.[59] In 1664
Sun Ch'i-feng, an outstanding scholar from Chihli, published a work entitled Chia-shen ta-nan lu which included biographies of men who died
defending China against the Manchus in 1644. A magistrate who had
sponsored the publication of the work was arrested briefly and then released when it was decided that Sung's work was not treasonous.[60] Three
years later, in 1667, several persons in Kiangnan were arrested for hav-

58. Ku, "Shu Wu P'an er-tzu shih," p. 27a. For information on the trial and
execution of those in the Ming History Case, see Nan-hsün chih, ch. 42, pp. 2b-
3a; Hummel, p. 206. The Manchu commissioner at the Ming History trials, Lodo,
was lieutenant-general of the Manchu Bordered Blue Banner (1659-64). In 1667
he was made a vice-president in the Board of Works, and in 1669 he became the
director-general of River Conservancy. In 1671 he was made governor-general
of Shensi-Shansi (PCTC [1795], ch. 320, passim; CS, 4:2543, 2863). In 1669 he
was cited as a member of the Oboi faction, but was exonerated and allowed to remain in his official posts (KH Shih-lu, ch. 29, p. 16b).
59. Hummel, p. 690.
60. Ibid., pp. 671-72.

ing contributed to a poetry collection which was deemed traitorous by the
Manchu court. One of the chief figures in the poetry collection was Shen
T'ien-fu, who was banished for his participation. [61]

The regents' reprisals against the Chinese elite were thus concentrated primarily in a triangle from Nanking to Shanghai to Hangchow—the
wealthiest and best-educated area in seventeenth-century China. While
the ostensible issues were tax evasion and Ming loyalism, the ruthless-
ness of the Manchu court greatly exceeded the provocations. These were
acts which reflected the Manchu's deep suspicions about the Chinese
elite. To be sure, tax evasion was a threat to the Manchu dynasty, as
was possible collusion with Cheng Ch'eng-kung, but the regents' violent
reaction was more an emotional than a rational effort to defend the Manchu regime.

MANCHU VALUES IN THE PROVINCIAL POLICIES
OF THE OBOI REGENCY

The Kiangnan Tax Case and the Ming History Affair were undoubtedly
expressions of the regents' distrust of the Chinese upper class. To the
regents every educated Chinese was a loyalist, not necessarily to the
Ming dynasty, but inevitably to the scholarly and sophisticated Confucian tradition. Even without such explicit evidence as the Ming-shih chi-
lüeh, the regents knew full well that many Chinese considered them and
their Manchu associates to be "barbarians." How could the regents create the conditions for obedience in the tense atmosphere of the culturally
and ethnically mixed early Ch'ing society? One answer, of course, was
continuous surveillance and suppression through heavy military force.
Such was the response of the regents in the tax evasion and Ming history
affairs. But the regents realized that military pressure was a thin foundation on which to maintain the empire; if the Manchu military weakened,
or if a Chinese renegade was able to create a strong army of opposition,
the Manchu dynasty might well crumble.

The regents, therefore, looked to other means to reinforce their superiority. They envisioned a society in which Chinese obeyed the Manchus not simply out of fear, but also out of respect for their talents which
had led to the conquest of China. The regents hoped to inculcate this respect by a system of rewards for proper behavior, rather than always
using stern punishments. To do this they chose a model town on the China
coast and urged their subjects to follow its example.

Ch'ung-ming hsien: The Regents' Model for the Empire
Only fifty miles from the city of Soochow, the opulent symbol of the re-

---

61. KH Shih-lu, ch. 21, p. 22a; Hstl, ts'e 8, pp. 37-38. There was another
famous Ming History incident which occurred later in the K'ang-hsi reign. The
incident centered on the scholar Tai Ming-shih. As in the earlier Ming History
episode, the major charge was the use of Ming reign titles for the period prior to
1644. For his part in the compilation of this work, Tai Ming-shih was arrested
and executed (Hummel, p. 701).

gents' hatreds, was located the district of Ch'ung-ming, the symbol of
their martial ideals. Ch'ung-ming is an island which fits like a cork
in the mouth of the Yangtze just to the north of Shanghai. Because of its
unusual location Ch'ung-ming was of crucial strategic importance to the
security of the Yangtze River and consequently to the security of much
of central China.

In the late 1650s Ch'ung-ming was fiercely defended by Ch'ing forces
against the invasions from Cheng Ch'eng-kung. Although Cheng was able
to push up the Yangtze to within reach of Nanking before his defeat in
1659, the island of Ch'ung-ming remained secure and Ch'ing troops were
able to hamper the pirates' communications and supply lines. Several
civil and military officials distinguished themselves in the defense of
Ch'ung-ming in the late Shun-chih period. Among them were Lang T'ing-
tso, the governor-general of Kiangnan; Chiang Kuo-chu, the governor of
Kiangsu; and especially Liang Hua-feng, the brigade-general of Soochow
and Sung-chiang prefectures. These officials were ably assisted by the
magistrate of Ch'ung-ming hsien, Ch'en Shen, and by valiant support
from the townspeople. The campaigns against Cheng Ch'eng-kung were
costly in terms of the lives of the people of Ch'ung-ming: the census of
1647 recorded 73,000 households in the district, but by the end of the
Shun-chih reign there were only 27,000 households. While suffering
these losses, the people of Ch'ung-ming hsien bravely cooperated with
officials as well as military forces in order to defend their city. Such
civilian sacrifice and military success earned the admiration of Oboi
and the other regents. [62]

In order to establish Ch'ung-ming as an example for the empire, the
regents rewarded officials and residents of the district regularly during
the early 1660s. Liang Hua-feng was made provincial commander-in-
chief of Soochow and Sung-chiang and was given the title of Grand Guardian of the Heir Apparent. [63] In 1661 the regents reinstated Ch'en Shen
as a department magistrate after he had been removed for a failure to
remit full tax receipts. An imperial rescript announced: "When the
pirates surrounded and attacked Ch'ung-ming, the magistrate Ch'en
Shen devoted himself to a strong defense and the entire city exhibited
exceptional military valor. On account of this, let the official who has
been removed for a failure to fulfill his tax quotas be reinstated in office.
And also let him be raised one degree in rank." [64] When Ch'en died in
April 1661, he was given a posthumous post in the provincial financial

---

62. For the census figures on Ch'ung-ming hsien, see Ch'ung-ming hsien-
chih, ch. 4, p. 34a. On the defense of Ch'ung-ming against Cheng Ch'eng-kung,
see ibid., ch. 8, pp. 27b-28a: ch. 7, pp. 5a-6b, 8b-11a; ch. 14, pp. 5b-6a; ch.
12, pp. 35b-36a; Chiang Jih-Sheng, T'ai-wan wai-chi, ch. 10, pp. 11a-b, 18b-
19a, 19b. Also see biographies of Chiang Kuo-chen and Liang Hua-feng in CSLC,
ch. 5, pp. 20a-b, 23a-24a; SC Shih-lu, ch. 83, p. 6a, and ch. 112, p. 15a.
63. CSLC, ch. 5, pp. 23b-24a; KH Shih-lu, ch. 4, pp. 4a-b.
64. KH Shih-lu, ch. 1, pp. 18a-b.

commissioner's office.[65] When Ch'en Shen's successor, Kung Pang, failed to collect his salt tax quota, once again the regents forgave the matter on the grounds that Kung had been an industrious official in the defense of the district.[66] For other officials as well, rewards were granted in an order of September 1661: "As for all of the civil and military officials who defended the city of Ch'ung-ming, they exerted themselves energetically and they kept the entire city protected from the pirates. These achievements are very admirable and all must receive hereditary titles in order to encourage [others]."[67]

Another means by which the regents exalted Ch'ung-ming hsien was the liberal granting of tax remissions. In every year from 1661 to 1665 the taxes of Ch'ung-ming were remitted on the grounds that its people had suffered greatly and had shown exceptional military prowess.[68] Evidently officials of other areas were impressed by these rewards; on one occasion a censor in Szechwan tried to persuade the court to grant tax exemptions to certain areas under his jurisdiction "in accordance with the gracious precedent of Ch'ung-ming hsien."[69] As if the rewards given to Ch'ung-ming did not make the regents' intentions clear, the following regulations were promulgated in 1664: "Henceforth when bandits overthrow and plunder a city, all of the officials of that city are to be removed from office and investigated."[70] Ch'ung-ming was the regents' model for the empire; failure to live up to that model meant punishment.

The enshrinement of Ch'ung-ming through remuneration to its officials and inhabitants was an imaginative step in the direction of establishing new norms for Chinese society under the Ch'ing. Unfortunately the Ch'ung-ming experiment was an isolated adventure during the regency period. Ch'ung-ming remained a solitary positive note in the discordant relations between Manchus and Chinese in the 1660s. To most Chinese the tax evasion and Ming History episodes were more in line with the dominant theme of Manchu authoritarianism which had begun with the massacres of the Dorgon era. Heavy garrisons of Ch'ing troops, stationed at campaign strength in many provinces, often tyrannized local residents.[71] In Chihli and along the southeastern coast, large numbers

65. Ibid., ch. 2, pp. 4a-b.
66. Ibid., ch. 5, pp. 15b-16b.
67. Ibid., ch. 4, pp. 4a-b.
68. Ch'ung-ming hsien-chih, ch. 6, pp. 11a-b. KH Shih-lu, ch. 1, pp. 20a-b; ch. 5, pp. 16a-b; ch. 8, p. 6b; ch. 9, p. 11a; ch. 14, p. 11b.
69. KH Shih-lu, ch. 2, p. 15b.
70. Ibid., ch. 12, p. 12a.
71. In the province of Kwangtung, for example, the feudatory prince, Shang K'o-hsi, commanded huge numbers of unruly troops which often stole property and even killed local residents without provocation. Such conditions had begun with Shang's conquest of Kwangtung in the 1650s and continued into the Oboi regency. See Hummel, p. 415; Bowra, "Manchu Conquest of Canton," pp. 86-96, passim; KH Shih-lu, ch. 7, pp. 23b-24a; ch. 14, pp. 23a-b; ch. 19, pp. 11b-13a, passim; ch. 26, p. 1b.

of Chinese were forced to evacuate their homes in accordance with Manchu military plans.[72] The regents continued to enforce rigidly the institution of Chinese enslavement to Manchu masters.[73] With such heavy
evidence for oppression, one doubts that many Chinese gained a more
favorable impression of the Manchus during the Oboi regency.

The Rejection of Ideological Controls

The use of Ch'ung-ming as a model district. therefore, was the regents'
only attempt to develop a noncoercive alternative in their provincial policies. Interestingly enough, the regents even failed to rely on the traditional Chinese techniques of ideological control. By celebrating officially
acceptable norms of behavior, earlier emperors had placed a premium
on conformity throughout Chinese society. The examination system had
forced the intelligentsia into a rigid life of studying and memorizing the
classics in preparation for entrance into the bureaucracy. At the level
of the commoner as well there were well-developed techniques of ideological control. One method was the local lecture (hsiang-yüeh) whereby
prominant figures were chosen to read from "moral maxims" in the
presence of the common people. "Local worthies" (hsiang-hsien) were
also honored by the imperial government for outstanding demonstrations
of filiality and other traditional virtues.

In the Oboi regency, however, there was a striking absence of reliance on such propaganda devices. The regents failed to promote or develop the hsiang-yüeh system.[74] Their failure in this respect was particularly noticeable since the content of the moral maxims was set forth
in the Shun-chih Emperor's Liu Yü (The Six Edicts) of 1652 and revised

72. The coastal evacuation policy will be considered in chapter 6, and the
banner relocation affair in Chihli in chapter 8.

73. The enslavement of Chinese to Manchu masters began long before the conquest and continued well after the Manchus were established in Peking. Slavery
was a basic ingredient in the Manchu social and economic order, and it symbolized
Manchu superiority over the Chinese. See Ma, "Manchu-Chinese Social and Economic Conflicts," pp. 340–47. The regents in the 1660s promulgated a considerable number of regulations dealing with the legal conditions for the sale and purchase of slaves and with penalties for concealing fugitive slaves (HTSL, ch. 129,
pp. 6a-7a [pp. 6807-8]; ch. 156, p. 7a [p. 7126]; ch. 1116, p. 3a [p. 18214]; and
KH Shih-lu, ch. 129, pp. 6a-7a). In some cases Chinese formed a conspiracy to
falsely accuse commoners of being runaway slaves in order to gain their property
as promised by the regents' regulations (KH Shih-lu, ch. 8, pp. 2a-b; ch. 13, pp.
22a-23a; ch. 14, pp. 2a-b). Another discussion of the use and misuse of the fugi-
tive laws in the early Ch'ing period is Ross, The Manchus, pp. 703-7.

74. In the HTSL there is a striking gap on this matter from 1659 to 1670
(HTSL, ch. 397, pp. 1b-2b [p. 10332]). Background information on the hsiang-
yüeh and hsiang-hsien techniques may be found in Hsiao Kung-chuan, Rural China,
pp. 184–220. Hsiao clearly documents the fact that these techniques were relatively ineffective as propaganda devices for the dynasty. But, as indicated, the
regents' aversion to relying on these techniques was probably determined more
by considerations of values than of efficacy.

in the K'ang-hsi Emperor's famous <u>Sheng Yü</u> (The Sacred Edict of K'ang-hsi) in 1670. The regents also neglected the institution of the "local worthies."[75] As will be recalled, moreover, the regents made drastic reductions in the examination quotas and thus weakened the examination system as a means of controlling the Chinese elite. In short, almost all of the traditionally effective institutions of ideological control were bypassed in the Oboi decade.

The explanation for this seeming anomaly in the regents' policies is found in their values. Oboi and his fellow regents were caught between the martial values of their own backgrounds and the problem of ruling a Chinese people who prized the pacific values of the Confucian tradition. The regents' distrust of the Chinese elite blinded them to the possibility of using Chinese norms as a means of imperial control. Unlike the K'ang-hsi Emperor, who patronized the Chinese elite while maintaining his commitment to the Manchu heritage, the regents lashed out against symbols of Chinese elitism. By rejecting most of the Confucian ethical system, the regents also rejected certain authoritarian aspects of the imperial tradition.

Having bypassed the use of Chinese beliefs as ideological tools, why did the regents fail to go beyond the Ch'ung-ming experiment and develop a concrete ideology? Why not take some of the main points in the Shun-chih Will and create a Manchu-oriented Sacred Edict to be read to the Chinese elite and commoners in the provinces? One reason is that the regents were predominantly militarists who lacked the philosophical bent of mind necessary to articulate their beliefs into a coherent ideological statement. Instead they were guided by a set of attitudes which emerged primarily in reaction to the military and political exigencies of the day. But this cannot be the entire explanation, for at least one of the regents, Soni, had the requisite linguistic expertise to compose such a statement and was well acquainted with the ideological pronouncements of Nurhaci and Abahai. The second reason, therefore, is that the regents realized, consciously or subconsciously, that it was futile to expect the Chinese populace to adopt a Manchu outlook on life. Unlike Nurhaci and Abahai, who could deliver their long lectures to receptive audiences north of the Great Wall, the regents' position was accepted only by the small minority of subjects enrolled in the banner system. At the provincial level, the Chinese population was too large and the Chinese cultural tradition too

---

75. As in the case of the <u>hsiang-yüeh</u>, the <u>HTSL</u> is silent on the <u>hsiang-hsien</u> in the Oboi period. The first regulation was dated 1644 and the second regulation was 1668, but this latter was certainly the work of the K'ang-hsi Emperor rather than his regents. In this order, the emperor observed that the institution of the <u>hsiang-hsien</u> was so corrupt that in one area no fewer than 658 persons were cited as local worthies. The emperor went on to demand that local officials grant this status sparingly (<u>HTSL</u>, ch. 402, pp. 1a-b [p. 10404]; Hsiao Kung-chuan, <u>Rural China</u>, p. 227).

strong for the regents to bring about a conversion to a Manchu ideology.
The regents thus faced a stalemate in their provincial policies. Their
aversion to sinification carried to the point of their dismissing sinified
forms of authoritarianism. But their commitment to Manchu dominance
left them no real alternative to the use of force in controlling the Chinese
populace.

6 The Military Policies of the Oboi Regency

In their policymaking, as should be apparent by now, the regents were inventive, forceful, occasionally ruthless, and always eager to protect Manchu interests and Manchu values. In some respects these traits characterized their military policy as well as their metropolitan and provincial policies. They concluded several of the campaigns which had been inaugurated during the Shun-chih period, most notably those against Chu Yu-lang (Ming Prince of Kuei) and against Cheng Ch'eng-kung (Coxinga). In the operations against Cheng Ch'eng-kung in particular the regents were clever tacticians: first by evacuating the coastline to prevent Cheng's troops from obtaining supplies and secondly by allying with Dutch merchants and building a fleet to overcome the Ch'ing weakness in naval power.

In spite of such tactical breakthroughs, however, the four regents were relatively conservative in their overall military strategies. They were content to continue the programs of their predecessors with respect to the size and structure of the military forces. Furthermore, they failed to initiate any massive new campaigns. Although it was recognized in the 1660s that Wu San-kuei and the feudatory princes were becoming economic and military threats to the dynasty, the regents tried to restrain them by nonmilitary means. The great military operations against the Ölöd Mongols, the Russians in northern Manchuria, the successors of Cheng Ch'eng-kung on Taiwan, and against the Three Feudatories were left to the K'ang-hsi Emperor.

At first it may seem paradoxical that the four regents, rugged military leaders themselves and obstinate proponents of military values, should leave so much of the military burden to their successor. There are, however, several reasons why they exhibited restraint in military matters. One is that the regents took power at a point when the Manchu dynasty was exhausted both economically and militarily. The battles of the conquest had been very expensive ventures and had severely strained the imperial treasury (see appendix 4). The banner forces had been fighting almost constantly since their inception in the early seventeenth century, and the invasion of China had consumed an enormous amount of military energy. Considering these problems, the regents may have thought it reckless to embark on new campaigns of expansion.

A second explanation is that the regents saw themselves as perpetuators of a great Manchu tradition, not founders of a new order. When the Joint Regents' faction was in power, they refrained from modifying the size or the structure of the banner system because they felt that it was a sacred inheritance of pre-conquest days. Similarly, the regents

thought that it was their role to act along military guidelines established
by earlier Manchu leaders, carrying on previous campaigns to fruition
but not embarking on new military enterprises.

A third reason for the regents' military conservatism is found in
their backgrounds in the Manchu army. Before taking over in 1661, they
had all served as commanders, but never as commanders-in-chief.
Their military achievements were in the realm of exceptional personal
exploits and tactical decisions on the battlefield. The strategic framework for the conquest, however, had been outlined by Nurhaci, Abahai,
and Dorgon. Without the deeds of such Manchu military officers as Oboi,
Ebilun, Suksaha, and Soni, the conquest might well have never succeeded;
but the effectiveness of the overall planning must be attributed to their
superiors. When they became regents, therefore, the four Manchus were
capable of considerable prowess on the field of battle, but they lacked the
military vision of their predecessors.

MILITARY STRUCTURE AND THE MILITARY OFFICIALDOM

In the banner system, the regents diligently followed precedents of the
Shun-chih period. They maintained the numerical strength of the Ch'ing
army at approximately the same level as in the 1650s. They relied upon
the same types of commanders to lead major military expeditions. And
they followed long-established procedures for appointing military personnel who would be loyal to the dynasty as a whole and to the occupants of
the Manchu throne in particular.

The banner system was the heart of the "pure and honest old system"
to which the regents had pointed in the Shun-chih Will.[1] Whereas the regents had felt free to experiment with the Chinese metropolitan and provincial institutions, they refrained from tampering with either the size
or the structure of the banner system. The only important deviation
from this pattern occurred in 1666-67 when Oboi tried to move the troops
of his own banner, the Bordered Yellow, to the most favored locations
in northern Chihli. But since the banner relocation affair was an offshoot
of Oboi's factionalism rather than a product of the regents' collective
policies, it is appropriate to postpone consideration of this matter until
our discussion of the Oboi faction in a subsequent chapter.

Structure and Size of the Banner Forces

The basic structure of the banner system had been formulated long before
the regents came to power in 1661. The eight Manchu banners of Nurhaci's time had been complemented by eight Chinese and eight Mongol

---

1. Franz Michael has argued that the origins of the Manchu banner system
created under Nurhaci may be traced primarily to the Ming military system on
the frontiers (Michael, Origin of Manchu Rule, pp. 64-67). A study by David
Farquhar, however, has indicated that the banner system arose from the tribal
structure common to both the Manchus and the Mongols (Farquhar, "Origins of
the Manchus' Mongolian Policy," pp. 204-5).

banners during Abahai's reign. The fundamental organizational unit of
these twenty-four banners was the company (Chinese: tso-ling; Manchu:
niru). During the early Ch'ing period there were three major types of
companies differentiated on the basis of their location and function. The
companies which provided most of the combat troops were called "external companies" (wai tso-ling). The external companies were stationed
in the metropolitan province of Chihli and were granted both regular
wages and land grants to support themselves and their families. In wartime certain of these companies were mobilized and transported to the
battle areas under special commanders. A second type of company was
the "garrison company" (chu-fang tso-ling). The garrison companies
were located in various garrison cities in China and Manchuria and were
entrusted with the task of guarding major cities, important border areas,
and strategic transportation routes. In addition the garrison companies
were occasionally involved in major military campaigns. The third type
of company, the "company of the household" (pao-i tso-ling), was attached to the households of the emperor and the imperial clan. Companies of the household performed administrative duties in Peking and also
served as bodyguards for the emperor and his family. This latter type
of company was seldom commissioned as a combat force, and most of
the military operations were left in the hands of the external companies
and the garrison companies.[2]

In the early years of the regency not only was this basic structure
perpetuated, but the regents also kept the number of combat troops (external companies) at the level established in the late Shun-chih period.
Although the total number of companies increased dramatically during
the seventeenth century, large increases occurred only in certain periods
when the banner forces were being readied for major combat operations:
1601-14, 1634, 1642, 1667-74, 1683-84, and 1695. The early years of
the Oboi period constituted one of those interim periods when the total
number of companies remained relatively stable. In 1661 there was a
total of 617 Manchu, Mongol, and Chinese external companies. During
the years of 1661-66, only six new companies were added, to make a
new total of 623 external companies (an addition of from 600 to 1200 bannermen). During the last two full years of the regency (1667-68), however, twenty-six new companies were formed, bringing the total to 649
companies. This trend toward increasing the size of the banner forces
continued into the 1670s, and by 1675 there were some 799 external companies (176 more companies than in 1666).[3]

How can we explain the sudden rise in the number of combat troops
over the years of 1667-75 after the minimal increments during the period

2. On these subdivisions in the company structure, see Fang Chao-ying,
"Early Manchu Military Forces," pp. 203-4; BH, pp. 323-26; Spence, Ts'ao Yin,
pp. 2-18.
    3. These figures are taken from Fang Chao-ying, "Early Manchu Military
Forces," pp. 208-9, table II. Fang's source for his information is PCTC (1739),
ch. 3-16, passim.

of 1661–66? The probable explanation is that the decision to expand the
banner forces was made by the K'ang-hsi Emperor himself, assisted
by some of his advisers such as Mingju and Mishan, in preparation for
the campaigns against the Three Feudatories which began in 1673. The
first striking numerical increases occurred in 1667, which was the same
year that the young emperor began to take over personal control of the
Ch'ing state. Although it is possible that the regents themselves made
the monumental decision to use Manchu troops against Wu San-kuei and
the other feudatories, such a bold move would have marked an extraordinary departure from their generally conservative military policies. It
is likely, therefore, that the regents intended to maintain combat strength
at approximately the same level as in the 1650s, with the idea of preserving the gains made in the consolidation campaigns rather than undertaking
new military operations.

Military Command Structure during the 1660s

In the Shun-chih period and under the Oboi regency as well there were
three general categories of Ch'ing commanders in the military operations along the China coast and in southern China: (1) special campaign
commanders; (2) feudatory princes; and (3) provincial civil and military
officials.

Those in the first category were high-ranking officials who were commissioned to lead contingents of combat troops from Peking to the field
of battle. Usually this type of commander was chosen from the highest
banner officers (lieutenant-generals or deputy lieutenant-generals of the
twenty-four banners), imperial military aides (chamberlains of the Imperial Bodyguard, captains-general of the Guards Division, and so forth),
and occasionally from top metropolitan statesmen (presidents or vice-
presidents of the boards). They were commissioned only for the duration of a specific campaign and then returned with their troops as soon
as the expedition was concluded. These special commanders served to
counterbalance the regional interests of the feudatory princes and the
provincial officials during the actual fighting, but did not remain outside
Peking long enough to become regional threats to the dynasty themselves.

The second category, feudatory princes, was composed of Chinese
bannermen who had been appointed by the court to oversee all of the military operations in a given theatre of battle. During the Shun-chih period
such men as Wu San-kuei, Shang K'o-hsi, and Keng Chi-mao were given
princely titles (wang) and sent to various regions of southern China to
take up temporary residence and direct campaigns against loyalists and
insurgents. By the end of the 1650s these feudatory princes, and especially Wu San-kuei, had amassed large armies of their own and had
gained considerable control over the civil as well as military affairs in
the provinces under their jurisdiction.

The third category of commanders during the early Ch'ing period
consisted of various provincial civil and military officials. Governors-
general often assisted in making tactical decisions, providing supplies,

and sending military information to Peking. While governors-general
seldom took personal command of large armies, they were often highly
influential in determining the course of a campaign. As mentioned earlier, the banner garrisons, commanded by Manchu generals-in-chief
(Tartar generals) and Manchu brigade-generals, supplied additional military force to the wai tso-ling. While most of the crucial military action
was conducted by banner troops, sometimes the regular Chinese Army
of the Green Banner (lü-ying) offered reinforcements. These Chinese
regulars were led by provincial commanders-in-chief and provincial
brigade-generals who were usually ordinary Chinese military officers
rather than bannermen.

It may be wondered how coordinated military expeditions were possible when responsibility was delegated to several commanders and to
several bodies of troops. There were in fact enormous difficulties in
launching unified assaults against the enemies of the Ch'ing during the
1650s and 1660s. Rivalries between commanders, differing opinions on
tactics, and poor communications all hampered Manchu military efforts.
Besides, the profusion of commanders and armies proved very costly to
the Ch'ing; in 1660 the officials of the Board of Revenue complained:

> The reason that the dynastic revenues are insufficient and that
> the commoners are suffering is that the number of troops and
> horses increases daily. In the province of Kiangnan there have long
> been a governor and a governor-general, a provincial commander-
> in-chief, a naval commander-in-chief, and a garrison of Manchu
> troops in Chiang-ning. Recently at Chinkiang we have appointed a
> lieutenant-general and two brigade-generals, one for the left route
> and one for the right. Altogether this has amounted to an increase
> of 16,000 troops and an increase in the troops stationed in Feng-
> yang by 1,500 men. [4]

In spite of the cost and confusion, the multiple delegation of military
authority was intentional. The regents followed this procedure in an effort to prevent commanders from achieving total control over the troops
in a given area. Although Wu San-kuei and the feudatory princes were
the most obvious examples of the potential for regionalism, any Chinese
or Manchu commander with sufficient military strength might have challenged the Manchu regime. Consequently, the regents willingly sacri-
ficed military coordination in an effort to diminish the threat of regional
fragmentation.

Civil Service Examination Degrees for Bannermen
Considering the bias which the regents felt in favor of military officials,
one might assume that their policy of granting the chin-shih to banner-

4. SC Shih-lu, ch. 136, p. 21a.

men would have been extremely liberal. During the Shun-chih reign a
sizeable number of Manchu, Mongol, and Chinese bannermen had received the chin-shih degree by participating in the regular civil service
examinations.[5] In 1652 and 1655, moreover, there were special Manchu
chin-shih examinations, held in the Manchu language and restricted solely
to Manchu bannermen. In the 1650s ninety-eight Manchus and Mongols
and fifty-eight Chinese bannermen had received the regular chin-shih degree—thus totaling one more than all of the chin-shih degree recipients
in the examination held in 1667.[6]

Yet in a somewhat enigmatic move the regents completely abolished
the practice of granting regular chin-shih to any bannermen. Throughout the nine years of the regency not a single bannerman received the
chin-shih and there were no special chin-shih examinations for bannermen.[7] There are two possible explanations for this policy which seems
to reflect an atypical attitude on the part of the regents. First, the appointment of Manchu, Mongol, and Chinese bannermen during the early
Ch'ing period was based largely on their personal ability and loyalty and
not on their possession of Chinese examination degrees. There is no evidence to suggest that the bannermen who held degrees during the early
Ch'ing were preferred for official positions to those without degrees.[8]
Secondly, study for any Chinese examination degree, and particularly for

5. There was also a special translators examination which offered degrees
for those who could translate Mongol and Manchu, or Manchu and Chinese. This
examination was abolished in the early 1660s (HTSL, ch. 363, p. 2a [p. 9876];
Zi, "Pratique des examens littéraires," p. 213).

6. On bannermen receiving the chin-shih in the 1650s, see Spence, Ts'ao
Yin, pp. 75-76; Shang, pp. 119-20; Fang and Tu, pp. 10-21, passim.

7. Fang and Tu, pp. 24-30.

8. From the information presented in table A (appendix 3) of this book, it is
evident that very few of the Chinese bannermen chosen as governors-general or
governors were degree holders. Of the fifty-two studied, only five held the chin-
shih, and none of these were Chinese bannermen. Of the fifty-two, only twenty
held any degree at all.

A great deal of emphasis was placed on military training and on the military
examinations in the 1660s. The military examinations paralleled the system of
regular civil service examinations and were held at the same time as the regular
examinations. In the Oboi regency there were generally about two military chin-
shih recipients for every three who received the civil chin-shih (Chang Chung-li,
Chinese Gentry, p. 124; Shang, p. 189). As mentioned in a previous chapter,
Oboi helped to train the military chin-shih candidates in martial skills during the
1660s (Shang, p. 201; SC Shih-lu, ch. 136, p. 1a).

The regents also established new regulations concerning the government
schools for bannermen (pa-ch'i kuan-hsüeh) in 1661. They decreed that one student would be admitted for every officer holding the rank of captain or above and
for every graduating student. The admissions were to be restricted to the sons
of officials in purely military positions and not to sons of civil officials. By the
same order the curriculum of the government schools for bannermen consisted
of study in the Manchu and Chinese languages and training in archery and horsemanship (HTSL, ch. 394, pp. 2a-b [p. 10302]).

the chin-shih degree, meant the devotion of several years to memoriza-
tion of the Chinese classics and to the perfection of one's calligraphy.
The examination life was an intellectually arduous, but physically passive, existence. Oboi and his fellow regents evidently refused to submit some of their best officer material to the soft and delicate life of
the Chinese scholar-official class.

Military Appointments in the Oboi Regency

Throughout the seventeenth and early eighteenth centuries, including the
Oboi decade, the Manchu emperors and regents sought military personnel who were both loyal and competent. The regents of the K'ang-hsi
Emperor insisted on these qualifications. During the conquest these
four Manchus had distinguished themselves by performing extraordinary
personal exploits on the battlefields. One will recall that Oboi himself
had led the attack against the Ming forces on P'i-tao Island in the Gulf
of Liaotung, achieving a spectacular victory against heavy odds. During
their regime the regents expected similar devotion and personal leadership from high military officials. In an edict to the Board of War the
regents made their expectations clear:

> Recently in reviewing the memorials from all of the provinces
> [it is observed] that in all cases where there are bandits and rob-
> bers, those who lead the troops forth to exterminate them are mere
> lieutenants and sub-lieutenants [of low rank]. There have been very
> few cases where provincial commanders-in-chief, brigade-generals,
> colonels, lieutenant-colonels, and majors have led the troops. In
> the old days when our dynasty conducted a military campaign, the
> commander himself always personally led the troops and gave or-
> ders. Everywhere we went we were victorious. But now when ban-
> dits are discovered, the commanders-in-chief and brigade-generals
> throughout the empire refrain from commanding the troops them-
> selves and instead they send out low-ranking military officers. This
> is similar to the vile practices of the Ming.[9]

In order to assure both loyalty and competence the regents resorted
to several devices. First of all, appointments to the highest positions
in the regular banner hierarchy were kept under rigorous review. During
the Oboi period those appointed to the posts of lieutenant-general, deputy
lieutenant-general, Manchu general-in-chief, and Manchu brigade-general
lived in constant jeopardy of losing their positions. Turnovers were particularly high in the first few years after the regents came to power.[10]
When making new appointments to military posts, the regents insisted
that several candidates be considered and that the final choice be based

9. KH Shih-lu, ch. 17, pp. 15a-b.
10. For a list of appointments to these posts in the Oboi period, see PCTC
(1795), ch. 320, 323, 326, 329, passim. With respect to the turnover in high
military posts in the early Ch'ing period, Ping-ti Ho has noted that social mobil-

on military experience and military achievements.[11] Moreover, the regents depended heavily on Manchus to staff the upper echelons of the regular banner hierarchy. Although Chinese bannermen were generally used to bridge the gap between Manchu and Chinese in the provincial bureaucracy, the regents felt that the top posts in the banner system could be most efficiently filled by Manchu officers. The majority of those appointed as lieutenant-generals in the Manchu and Mongol Banners, and as Manchu generals-in-chief, were Manchu bannermen. Some Manchus were even chosen for the posts of lieutenant-generals in the Chinese Banners.[12]

As an ultimate effort to secure the loyalty of the banner forces, Oboi appointed several members of his own following to important military positions. Indeed it was in the banner hierarchy that Oboi built the nucleus of his clique during the early years of the regency. During 1661-66, before Oboi was able to place significant numbers of his followers in key metropolitan and provincial posts, at least ten members of the Oboi clique held high banner offices and several held more than one key military position. Seven were lieutenant-generals, four were deputy lieutenant-generals, two were chamberlains of the Imperial Bodyguard, and four served as Manchu generals-in-chief.

One of Oboi's brothers, Murma, was appointed lieutenant-general of the Manchu Bordered Yellow Banner and successfully commanded a large Manchu army against the Li Lai-heng rebellion in 1663. Another brother, Baha, was made a chamberlain of the Imperial Bodyguard.

---

ity was very high in the military as opposed to the civil officialdom. Ho has observed that there were many key military officials who originated from obscure backgrounds during the late seventeenth century and again during the Taiping rebellion (Ho, Ladder of Success, pp. 217-18).

11. KH Shih-lu, ch. 11, pp. 9b-10a. In 1662 the regents approved a memorial which asked that provincial military officials be evaluated every two years (ibid., ch. 6, p. 31a).

12. PCTC (1795), ch. 320, 323, 326, 329, passim. It is difficult to gain accurate figures on the ethnic origins of the high military officials during the Oboi period. The standard biographical sources do not provide information on all of the incumbents in high military posts during these years. Although the nature of the names listed often indicates the origins of the officials (e. g., T'u-er-pai-shan is obviously a Manchu or Mongol, while Li Hsien-kuei is probably a Chinese bannerman), one cannot venture to make numerical assessments on this basis.

Relying on the available biographical data, let us look at the lieutenant-generals in the Manchu banners seem to have been Manchus (only one of these, Mu-ch'en, lacks biographical information). Similarly, in the posts of lieutenant-generals of the Mongol banners, seven of the eight were Manchus and the eighth, Kuo-er-ching, may have been either a Manchu or a Mongol. In the Chinese banners, four of the lieutenant-generals were Chinese bannermen, and one was a Manchu. The remaining three, Li Hsien-kuei, K'o Yung-chen, and Tung Chuang-nien, were probably Chinese bannermen, but I have been unable to find biographical information concerning them.

Oboi's own son, Namfe, held the post of chamberlain of the Imperial
Bodyguard from 1663 until he was removed from office by order of the
K'ang-hsi Emperor in 1669. Marsai, Ka-ch'u-ha, and Ch'i-shih, all of
whom held board presidencies during the last years of the regency,
served as lieutenant-generals in the early 1660s. Lodo and Hife (the
latter not to be confused with Soni's brother of the same name), although
less prominent than the above-mentioned disciples of Oboi, were re-
spectively appointed to the posts of lieutenant-general and deputy lieutenant-general. Lodo had been sent to Chekiang in early 1661 as an imperial commissioner to oversee the confiscation and burning of the controversial Ming History discussed in the previous chapter.[13] Two other
members of the early Oboi faction, Liu Chih-yüan and his son, Liu
Kuang, were the only Chinese bannermen among the followers of the ambitious regent. Liu Chih-yüan served as lieutenant-general of the Chinese
Bordered Yellow Banner and as Manchu general-in-chief in charge of
the garrison at Chinkiang. When Chih-yüan retired in 1665, Liu Kuang
took over both of his father's positions.[14]

The leading members of the Oboi clique prior to 1667, therefore,
consisted of eight Manchus and two Chinese bannermen. Although the
clique expanded significantly during 1667 and 1668, the basis of Oboi's
quest for personal power had been established in the banner hierarchy
during the early years of the regency. His appointments gave him considerable leverage in the Manchu military establishment. The five Manchu lieutenant-generals, who were ex-officio members of the Council of
Deliberative Officials, probably gave Oboi a powerful, though not dominant, voice in the meetings of the council. Furthermore, Oboi was able
to select certain of these high-ranking followers as special commanders
to oversee banner troops sent to southern China. In short, the appointment of members of his clique to key military offices not only increased
Oboi's personal power, but it also helped to circumvent the potential for
disloyalty and regionalism.

The growth of Oboi's banner clique, however, was not an unprece-
dented phenomenon in the early Ch'ing period. As we have seen, Abahai,
Dorgon, and the Shun-chih Emperor each had endeavored to protect themselves by appointing loyal subordinates to key military posts.[15] In an
era when military power was the dominant cohesive force in a China frag-
mented by regional interests, racial tensions, loyalist movements, and
personal rivalries, the control of the banner system was an essential
condition for the security of both the Manchu dynasty and any particular
regime.

13. These men are designated as members of the Oboi faction because they
were cited as such in KH Shih-lu, ch. 29, pp. 6b-18b, passim. Biographical information about these men is taken from the lists of officials in the PCTC and CS
and from the biographical sections of the PCTC, CSK, CSLC, and KCCH.
14. An extensive biography of Liu Chih-yüan, with a short section of Liu
Kuang, is found in CSLC, ch. 5, pp. 14a-16a.
15. Hummel, pp. 1, 216-17, 256; Corradini, "Civil Administration," p. 135.

CAMPAIGNS OF CONSOLIDATION IN THE OBOI REGENCY

Although all of Ming China was nominally under Ch'ing control by the end of the Shun-chih reign, the effort to eradicate internal military threats continued into the 1660s. The major campaigns in these post-conquest consolidation drives were those against Cheng Ch'eng-kung and his successors on the southeastern coast and Taiwan, those against Chu Yu-lang in the southwest and Burma, and those against smaller rebel groups in central and southern China.

In all of these military ventures, which had begun during the Shun-chih period, the regents relied upon many of the same personnel and upon the same basic Manchu strategy that had been employed in the 1640s and 1650s. The feudatory princes, in conjunction with regular banner officers, provincial officials, and special military leaders sent from Peking, served as commanders in these campaigns. The regents also followed a strategy which had been adopted in the Dorgon period: occupation and consolidation of major cities, control of key transportation routes, control of the basic supply sources, and slow and safe movement of large bodies of troops. The only striking innovations in military strategy during the Oboi regency were the coastal evacuation policy and the brief alliance with the Dutch fleet in 1663. On the whole, therefore, the Oboi period did not introduce a new, more aggressive military effort, but rather a continuation of military operations along the guidelines set in the Shun-chih reign.

Consolidation of the Southeastern Coast: Fukien

The effort to bring the entire coastal region of China under complete Ch'ing control was the most difficult military venture of the late Shun-chih and early K'ang-hsi periods. Cheng Ch'eng-kung, his family, and his subordinates were clever and persistent opponents. The Chengs, unlike any of the other major military opponents of the Manchu dynasty, possessed a large fleet capable of moving their army from one coastal base to another very rapidly. The mobility of the Cheng fleet, coupled with the bravery of their troops, placed the entire coastal region from Kwangtung to Shantung in danger. The Manchus, of course, were highly skilled in land-based warfare but had very little experience in maritime conflicts. Realizing the Manchu deficiency in naval strength, the regents devoted their efforts to driving the Chengs away from the China coast and the offshore islands. The regents tried to induce the Chengs to surrender their position on Taiwan through negotiotions and, with the exception of one abortive expedition in 1664, refrained from military efforts to take Taiwan.

Before discussing the Ch'ing–Cheng encounters in the Oboi period we must briefly review the fortunes of the Cheng clan during the preceding years. Cheng Ch'eng-kung's power reached its high point during the years 1654–59. In this period Cheng established his base on the island of Amoy just off the Chinese mainland in southern Fukien. Cheng raised a large army (perhaps well over 100,000 men), established seventy-two military stations (chen) in the coastal areas of Fukien, and set up his own civil administration consisting of six boards on the model of the imperial government in Peking. In 1658 Cheng began a massive assault against the Ch'ing with Chang Huang-yen, another armed loyalist, as his ally and chief commander. The combined fleets of Cheng and Chang moved quickly up the coast, taking several towns in Fukien, Chekiang, and Kiangnan, and by the late summer of 1659 they had moved up the Yangtze within reach of Nanking. The Shun-chih Emperor, one may remember, was so angry about Cheng's advance that he is reported to have hacked up one of his thrones with a sword. The battle of Nanking, however, resulted in a disastrous defeat of the loyalist forces, and Cheng was forced to withdraw to his base at Amoy. [16]

Entrenched at Amoy, protected by his fleet and thousands of troops, Cheng continued to present an immediate threat to the Manchus. In June 1660 Ch'ing troops attacked Cheng's positions on Amoy, but the loyalist commander, relying on his well-trained soldiers and his long-established defenses on Amoy, was able to repulse the Ch'ing advance. When the regents came to power in February 1661, the memory of the late Shun-chih campaign was still fresh and the defeat of Cheng Ch'eng-kung was a matter of very high priority. The regents were determined to drive Cheng off the China coast, and they seemed willing to try almost any tactic to achieve that end.

The first and most famous measure adopted by the regents was the coastal evacuation policy enacted in the initial year of the regency in order to prevent the Chinese coastal population from trading with loyalists and pirates under the Cheng family. By this policy persons living in coastal areas of the provinces of Kwangtung, Fukien, Chekiang, and to some extent in Kiangnan and Shantung, were forced to move inland, and thus the coastal areas were evacuated for several miles into the interior. At the same time strict orders were issued which prohibited any trade with the Cheng pirates. Those commoners, merchants, and officials who violated the prohibitions on coastal residency and trade were to be punished according to the laws of treason. [17]

The origins of the coastal evacuation policy can be traced to the mid-1650s when the threat from Cheng Ch'eng-kung became intense along the China coast. Cheng's primary source of economic support was com-

16. On the life and military achievements of Cheng Ch'eng-kung, see Hummel, pp. 108-10; Chiang, ch. 11, pp. 1a-24a; Wills, pp. 48-57. For studies of the Cheng campaign against the Dutch on Taiwan, see Boxer, "Seige of Fort Zeelandia," pp. 16-47; Campbell, Formosa under the Dutch, pp. 383-492, passim; Keene, Battles of Coxinga, pp. 53-75; Wills, pp. 82-89.

17. MCSL, vol. 4, ch. 3, p. 257a. Also see Fu Lo-shu, Documentary Chronicle, pp. 28-30. The actual edict ordering the coastal evacuation has not been included in any of the standard sources (KH Shih-lu, HTSL, MCSL, etc.). The date of 1662 is given in Ponsby-Fane, "Koxinga," p. 121.

merce with Chinese merchants and commoners.[18] In August 1656, therefore, the court prohibited all maritime commerce in the provinces of
Shantung, Kiangnan, Chekiang, Fukien, and Kwangtung. An imperial
edict proclaimed: "If anyone dares to trade food and goods with the
treacherous pirates, whether he is an official or a commoner, he will
be reported to the throne and beheaded."[19] The plan for evacuating the
coastline, however, was suggested a few years later by Huang Wu, a
former general under Cheng Ch'eng-kung who had been defeated by the
Manchus in 1656 and who had offered his services to the Ch'ing.[20] Toward the end of the Shun-chih reign Huang Wu memorialized that the
military potency of Cheng's forces would be reduced if the residents of
the Chinese coast were moved inland, thus eliminating the possibility of
any maritime trade.[21] In 1660 a Manchu commission, headed by Sunahai,
the president of the Board of War, was sent to the southeastern coastal
region to inspect the defenses. On its return the commission suggested
that Huang Wu's plan of evacuating the coastal population be implemented.[22]

Following the advice of the commissioners, the regents adopted the
policy at some point in 1661 or early 1662. High Manchu officials were
sent to work along with provincial officials to carry out the evacuation
of the coastal inhabitants.[23] The most extensive evacuations were carried out in Fukien, where Cheng Ch'eng-kung had based his regime during the 1650s. Large numbers were also evacuated from the coastal sec-

18. On Cheng Ch'eng-kung's reliance on maritime trade for supplies, see
Wills, pp. 55-56.

19. MCSL, vol. 4, ch. 2, pp. 155a-b; SC Shih-lu, ch. 102, pp. 10a-12a.
Prohibitions on maritime trade had been enacted in the late fourteenth century
and revived in the mid-fifteenth century in order to counter threats from Japa-
nese pirates (Wills, pp. 13-15).

20. Biographies of Huang Wu in Hsieh Kuo-chen, p. 584; Hummel, p. 355.

21. This famous memorial is found in Chiang, ch. 11, pp. 17b-18b. Also
see Hsieh Kuo-chen, pp. 565-67.

22. On the Manchu commission, see Hsieh Kuo-chen, "Removal of the Coastal Population," pp. 567-68. Biography of Sunahai in CSLC, ch. 6, p. 6b; biography of Ilibu in CSK, ch. 265, p. 1a, and Chiang, ch. 11, p. 18b. Hsieh Kuo-
chen suggests that Oboi himself was sent to check defenses and to implement a
coastal evacuation in the 1640s: "When the present Dynasty was founded, the Emperor sent two Manchu Grand Secretaries of the Cabinet [sic], Su Nai Hai and
Nao Pe to establish mounds along the coast so that when invaders came in, tor-
ches should be lighted as a warning and to move people to the interior so as to
stop supplies from being sent to Formosa" (Hsieh Kuo-chen, pp. 591-92). I
have been unable to verify this point. If it is true, the coastal evacuation policy
must be dated much earlier and Oboi himself must be considered one of the in-
augurators of the policy.

23. The commissioners sent to the China coast in 1662-63 included Sunahai,
Ilibu, Situ (vice-president of the Board of War), Korkon (vice-president of the
Board of Civil Office), and several others (Hsieh Kuo-chen, pp. 591-92). Among
the key Chinese bannermen involved in the implementation of this order were Li
Shuai-t'ai, governor-general of Fukien, and Shang K'o-hsi, prince of the feudatory

tions of Kwangtung and Chekiang. In only a few areas of Shantung and Kiangnan was the policy of coastal evacuation fully implemented. As if to show that the policy was being enacted justly, however, the regents moved much of the population of Ch'ung-ming island into the interior of Kiangnan.[24] The suffering among those forced to evacuate their homes was severe, particularly in the province of Fukien. In 1663, after the policy had been in effect only a short while, it was observed that over 8,500 of those evacuated in Fukien had already died.[25] One resident of Fukien, after recounting the hardships endured by the evacuated persons, exclaimed, "how can the people possibly survive?"[26]

In spite of the misery inflicted upon the commoners, the coastal evacuation policy remained in force throughout most of the regency. It was not until late 1668 that the governor-general of Kwangtung-Kwangsi, Chou Yu-te, reported that since adequate military garrisons had been established, the displaced persons should be resettled in their former homes.[27] The emperor, in a characteristic gesture of concern both for the well-being of the common people and for the maintenance of military strength, responded:

Let the Lieutenant-General Tejin meet along with the governor-

---

in Kwangtung. Almost every high provincial official on the China coast was involved in the execution of this order in some fashion. See, for example, the biographies of Chou Yu-te (governor of Shantung, 1664-68; governor-general of Kwangtung-Kwangsi, 1668-70) in CSLC, ch. 7, pp. 9a-10b; Hsü Shih-ch'ang (governor of Fukien, 1661-66) in Fu-chien t'ung-chih, ch. 140, p. 15b; Lu Ch'ung-chün (governor-general of Kwangtung, 1661-65) in KCCH, ch. 190, p. 42b; Liu Ping-ch'üan (governor of Kwangtung, 1667-75) in KCCH, ch. 151, pp. 1a-4b.

24. On the regional variations in the application of the coastal evacuation policy, see Hsieh Kuo-chen, "Removal of the Coastal Population," pp. 582-93; KH Shih-lu, ch. 9, pp. 8a-b; Fu-chien t'ung-chih, ch. 86, pp. 10b-20a, 38a-b; Che-chiang t'ung-chih, ch. 96, p. 1723. On the application of the policy to Ch'ung-ming hsien, see Ch'ung-ming hsien-chih, ch. 14, pp. 4b-5a. On Governor Hsü Shih-ch'ang's efforts to care for the evacuated persons from Ch'ung-ming hsien, see Su-chou fu-chih, ch. 68, p. 35a.

25. KH Shih-lu, ch. 7, p. 19b.

26. Fu-chien t'ung-chih, ch. 87, p. 15b. A Dutch envoy, Constantine Nobel, who was in Fukien during these years observed that those caught returning to their homes were sent on to Foochow. Here the men were executed and the women and children were enslaved (Wills, p. 154). The Manchu court did make some efforts to compensate for the suffering caused by the coastal evacuation policy. In 1661 the governors and governors-general of the provinces affected were ordered to make personal investigations and to find land and housing for the homeless (KH Shih-lu, ch. 4, p. 10b). Evacuated persons were exempted from both the land tax and the ting assessments (KH Shih-lu, ch. 6, pp. 17a-b; ch. 12, p. 10b; ch. 14, pp. 23b-24a; HTSL, ch. 268, pp. 1b-2a [pp. 8631-32]). Chiang Jih-sheng has observed, however, that in spite of court orders, most of those evacuated from their homes were left without either land or homes and became wanderers (Chiang, ch. 11, p. 19b).

27. On the relaxation of the coastal evacuation policy and the trade prohibitions, see Wills, p. 351, and Chiang, ch. 13, pp. 4b-6b.

general, governor, and provincial commander-in-chief to discuss,
on the one hand, the establishment of military garrisons, and, on
the other, the return of the evacuated population. Let there be no
delay past the time of the agricultural season so as not to cause the
people to lose their homes.[28]

But once again, as in the case of his appointing Manchus to high provincial posts, the K'ang-hsi Emperor did not wholly reject the policies of
his regents. In 1678, when the pirates under Cheng Ching (son of Cheng
Ch'eng-kung) threatened the China coast, the coastal residents of Fukien
were again evacuated and the prohibition on trade reinforced.[29]

It remains a question whether or not the coastal evacuation policy
was actually an effective weapon against the Cheng family. One historian,
Hsieh Kuo-chen, has observed that since the Chengs relied on the economic resources of Taiwan and since their power lasted for twenty years
after the first evacuations, the policy "was not greatly detrimental to
Cheng but was very burdensome to the people along the Southeastern
coast."[30] Although the endurance of the Chengs on Taiwan is an established fact, Hsieh has not considered that the regents may not have intended the coastal evacuation policy to bring about the starvation or submission of the Chengs. The policy was probably designed to guarantee
the prohibition on maritime trade and to prevent the Cheng pirates from
establishing permanent bases on the Chinese mainland. Considered in
this light, the coastal evacuation policy was relatively effective. In 1661
Cheng Ch'eng-kung decided to take a large portion of his fleet and retreat to Taiwan because the evacuation of the coastline had curtailed
much of his former supply from maritime trade. In making this decision, Cheng sought the advice of his loyalist ally, Chang Huang-yen, who
concluded that "henceforth we cannot maintain control over the two islands of Amoy and Quemoy."[31] For nine months between April 1661 and
February 1662 Cheng's army besieged the Dutch garrison at Fort Zeelandia on Taiwan. During this siege against the Dutch, the troops under
Cheng Ch'eng-kung almost starved for lack of supplies from the mainland.[32] But eventually the Dutch capitulated and withdrew to Batavia,
and the Chengs became the masters of Taiwan for two decades.

Cheng Ch'eng-kung's death in mid-1662 seriously weakened the military unity of the Ch'eng clan. Fratricidal war ensued and the eldest son,
Cheng Ching, emerged victorious; but another son and two of Cheng Ch'eng-
kung's brothers surrendered to the Manchus and took many of their troops
with them.[33] These defections, however, did not completely eradicate

28. KH Shih-lu, ch. 27, p. 16a.
29. Ibid., ch. 72, pp. 19b-20a; ch. 77, pp. 12b-13a.
30. Hsieh Kuo-chen, p. 596.
31. Wei, Ta-Ch'ing sheng-wu chi, ch. 8, pp. 6a-b. See also Wills, pp. 96-97.
32. Keene, Battles of Coxinga, pp. 59, 172; Yang Ying, Ts'ung-cheng shih-lu,
pp. 185-87; Shen, T'ai-wan Cheng-shih shih-mo, p. 52.
33. On the succession crisis after Cheng Ch'eng-kung's death, see Hummel,
p. 111, and Wills, pp. 99-101, 128-29. Cheng Ch'eng-kung's retreat also brought

the Cheng threat to the China coast. Cheng Ching kept the old bases on the islands of Amoy and Quemoy, and occasionally Cheng's troops occupied towns along the Fukien coast such as Ting-hai and Hsiao-ch'eng.[34]

The fact that the Chengs continued to endanger Fukien even after the defections of 1662-63 and after the implementation of the coastal evacuation policy may be attributed to three causes. First, the Manchus lacked sufficient troops to occupy all of the towns in Fukien much less the entire China coast. Consequently Cheng forces were able to return to coastal towns after the Ch'ing armies had withdrawn. Second, the absence of a strong Ch'ing fleet made it difficult to destroy the Chengs' bases on the offshore islands. Third, the coastal evacuation policy and the prohibition on maritime trade were never implemented completely. Dutch traders reported that some coastal areas in Fukien were reinhabited with the approval of provincial officials such as Hsü Shih-ch'eng, the governor of Fukien. Not only did these officials profit from the sale of licenses for fishing and commerce, but they even engaged in clandestine maritime trade themselves.[35] Once again the conflict between the Manchu interests in Peking and the self-interest of the provincial officials obstructed the implementation of policy in the Oboi period.

The Manchu court, although probably ignorant of the violations of the coastal evacuation policy and the maritime trade regulations, realized the necessity for increasing military strength in Fukien and for securing naval power to deal with the continuing Cheng threat. During the last years of the Shun-chih period, therefore, Ch'ing military pressure along the China coast was focused on the province of Fukien. Military leadership was characteristically delegated to a number of commanders. In almost every case, the regents continued to depend on those commanders who had been appointed in the years of 1655-60 to carry out the campaign in Fukien. The most important provincial official involved in this campaign was the governor-general of Fukien, Li Shuai-t'ai. An exceptional Chinese bannerman with a record of thirty years' service as a Ch'ing officer and provincial official, Li Shuai-t'ai had been a prominent figure in the campaigns against Cheng Ch'eng-kung in the 1650s.

---

about another unfortunate result: the execution of his father, Cheng Chih-lung, and other members of his family who had been imprisoned in Peking during the 1650s (Hummel, pp. 110-111; Keene, pp. 63-66). For an account of the life and death of Cheng Chih-lung, see Boxer, "Rise and Fall of Nicholas Iquan (Cheng Chih-lung)," pp. 401-39, passim.

34. During late 1662 and early 1663 the main commanders on Amoy and Quemoy were Cheng Ching's uncles, Cheng T'ai and Cheng Ming-chün. After the defection of the latter two in early 1663, however, Cheng Ching himself took over command of these troops (Hummel, p. 111; Wills, pp. 154-58).

35. On the inability of the Ch'ing to patrol the Fukien coast and on the reinhabitation of the coast, see Wills, pp. 121-23. Keng Chi-mao, Li Shuai-t'ai, Hsü Shih-ch'ang, Huang Wu, and Shang K'o-hsi engaged in clandestine maritime trade and operated through special merchants (ibid., pp. 201-2, 228-29, 277-82, 295-98, 307-10, 328, 398-99).

Although Li was not explicitly commissioned to command Ch'ing troops, he was responsible for much of the planning behind the coastal operations of the early 1660s.[36]

In addition to Li Shuai-t'ai, two other figures played a major role at the provincial level in Fukien. These two, Keng Chi-mao and Huang Wu, both had received special noble ranks and exercised a considerable degree of independent power in southeastern China. Keng Chi-mao, along with Shang K'o-hsi, led the ruthless campaign against Chu Yu-lang in Kwangtung during the 1650s. In 1660 Keng, who had been given the title of the "Prince who Subdues the South" (Ching-nan Wang), was transferred to Fukien to devote his energies to the battles against the Cheng clan. Under Keng's command were approximately 10,000 troops--3,000 of his own soldiers and 7,000 from the Chinese Green Banner forces.[37] Huang Wu, on the other hand, was a former general under Cheng Ch'eng-kung. After surrendering to the Manchus in 1656, Huang Wu was rewarded with the title of "Duke of Hai-ch'eng" (Hai-ch'eng kung). As mentioned earlier, Huang Wu invented the idea of the coastal evacuation policy as a strategic weapon against the Chengs. During the Oboi period Huang remained in Fukien, offering military advice and leadership in the campaigns to secure the coast and the offshore islands.[38]

Not desiring to leave the conduct of the operations against the Chengs totally in the hands of provincial officials, the court commissioned several high military officers to command a large army of bannermen sent from Peking to Fukien. The commander of this combat force of "external companies" was the lieutenant-general and Imperial clansman, Loto; he was assisted by the president of the Board of Revenue, Ceke, the chamberlain of the Imperial Bodyguard, Daso, and the lieutenant-general of the Manchu Bordered White Banner, Sohon. The sending of this special army under metropolitan civil and military officials is an excellent example of the regents' effort to overcome the danger of regionalism. They ordered the leaders of this expeditionary force to work along with the provincial officials and to make a careful inspection of the garrisons and defenses along the coast.[39] The commanders probably received private instructions to keep a close watch on the activities of the provincial officials and over such persons as Keng Chi-mao and Huang Wu.

Beyond the problem of increasing military strength in Fukien and selecting suitable commanders, the court also had to secure a fleet to confront the Chengs' island bases on Amoy and Quemoy. The Manchus

36. Biography of Li Shuai-t'ai in Hummel, pp. 484-85. For an account of Li's activities in Fukien during the late 1650s, see CSLC, ch. 5, pp. 27b-28b.

37. Biographies of Keng Chi-mao in Hummel, p. 415, and CSK, ch. 240, pp. 7a-b. See also Tsao, Rebellion of the Three Feudatories, pp. 66-67.

38. Biographies of Huang Wu in Hummel, p. 355, and Hsieh Kuo-chen, p. 584.

39. The imperial order commissioning this expeditionary force is in SC Shih-lu, ch. 138, pp. 22a-23a.

overcame their deficiency in naval strength in two ways: the formation
of a small Ch'ing fleet and the development of a temporary alliance with
a Dutch fleet. The Ch'ing fleet was created during the early 1660s primarily from boats captured when Cheng leaders surrendered. Although
there are no accurate figures available on the total size of this fleet, it
was reported that one-hundred eighty boats were turned over to the
Ch'ing when Cheng Ching's uncles surrendered in early 1663.[40] To direct the Ch'ing fleet the regents selected Shih Lang, a former naval
commander under the Chengs who had defected to the Manchus in 1646.
Shih Lang had gained a great deal of knowledge about maritime warfare
both from his service under the Chengs and from his own studies of
naval strategy. Shih Lang served as the chief admiral during the campaigns of the 1660s and played a major role in the successful expedition
against Taiwan in the early 1680s.[41]

The Manchu expedition to retake Amoy and Quemoy in late 1663 was
also facilitated by the assistance of an armed Dutch merchant fleet.
When the Dutch traders were forced from Taiwan by Cheng Ch'eng-kung
in early 1662, they lost their trading base near China and felt an intense desire to gain revenge against the Cheng family. By allying with
the Ch'ing, the Dutch sought their revenge and also expected that the
Manchus would permit free trade on the China coast. In addition, the
Dutch hoped that an alliance with the Ch'ing might lead to the eventual
restoration of Taiwan as a Dutch commercial center.[42]

The Manchu court under the regents, on the other hand, wanted the
alliance with the Dutch purely for tactical reasons and intended to make
only limited concessions to satiate the Dutch hunger for trade. In early
1663 a Dutch fleet of seventeen vessels (with 440 guns and over 2500
sailors and soldiers) was sent from Batavia under the command of Balthasar Bort. While in Batavia, Bort had been instructed to secure free
trade with China and to try to retake Taiwan. When the fleet arrived at
Foochow in September 1663, two months of negotiations ensued between
Balthasar Bort and Keng Chi-mao and Li Shuai-t'ai. Keng and Li conceded vaguely worded trading rights to the Dutch in return for an alliance with the fleet but were unwilling to offer Ch'ing help in the recon-
quest of Taiwan. The issue of trading privileges, moreover, was further confused by the fact that both Keng and Li knew that they could not
make formal concessions on this matter since that was the exclusive
prerogative of the regents and the court. The Dutch, not realizing that
the Fukienese officials were acting without imperial sanction, agreed to
the alliance in October 1663.[43]

40. KH Shih-lu, ch. 9, p. 25b.
41. Biography of Shih Lang in Hummel, p. 653. John Wills, Jr., has noted
that Shih Lang was a protégé of Huang Wu (Wills, pp. 245-46).
42. On Sino-Dutch relations in the seventeenth century and the background to
the alliance of 1663, see Wills, pp. 58-187, passim.
43. On the Dutch mission of 1663 and the negotiations which led to the alliance, see Wills, pp. 163-68, 181-87. In 1662 and early 1663 the Dutch had tried

After all of these preparations, increasing troop strength, choosing appropriate commanders, assembling a Ch'ing navy, and concluding an alliance with the Dutch, the actual confrontation with the Cheng forces in November 1663 was almost an anticlimax. The banner forces under Keng Chi-mao, Huang Wu, and the imperial commanders were transported by Shih Lang's Ch'ing fleet to the shores of Amoy and Quemoy. While the Dutch ships bombarded the island fortresses with cannon fire, the Ch'ing armies landed and massacred both the Cheng troops and the inhabitants of the islands. According to reports, some 18,000 Cheng soldiers surrendered to the invading army. By the end of the month, the Chengs had retreated with the remnants of their defeated forces and sailed to Taiwan. [44]

Throughout the remainder of the 1660s and into the early 1670s Cheng Ching and his armies remained on Taiwan, not venturing to harrass the China coast. In mid-1664 Shih Lang commanded a joint Sino-Dutch expedition to conquer Taiwan. Shih Lang was given the special title of the "Admiral who Pacifies the Seas" (ching-hai chiang-chün) and set sail for Taiwan. But the fleet was forced to turn back because of foul weather. [45] After this abortive expedition the regents remained content to conserve the gains they had achieved and endeavored to bring about Cheng Ching's surrender through diplomatic channels. On three different occasions during the latter years of the regency, Ch'ing envoys traveled to Taiwan to negotiate with Cheng Ching. But Cheng Ching insisted that he would submit to the Manchus only under three conditions: (1) that he be permitted to remain on Taiwan; (2) that the Ch'ing recognize Taiwan as a tributary state; and (3) that his subjects not be forced to wear the queue. Since these conditions amounted to recognizing Cheng Ching's Taiwan as a kingdom equal to those of Korea and Annam, the regents and the Manchu court refused his proposals. [46]

As part of their legacy to the K'ang-hsi Emperor, therefore, the regents left a relatively secure southeastern coast. But the regents failed

---

to seal a similar alliance. The regents had sanctioned the alliance and granted the Dutch the right to trade either every year or every other year and to establish a trading station at Foochow. But this imperial order arrived after the Dutch fleet had departed for Batavia and apparently regulations required another imperial order to sanction such concessions (Wills, pp. 161-62; KH Shih-lu, ch. 8, p. 21a).

44. Wei, Ta-Ch'ing sheng-wu chi, ch. 8, pp. 9a-b. For descriptions of the campaign to take Amoy and Quemoy in November 1663, see Wills, pp. 188-202; Chiang, ch. 13, p. 13b; Fu-chien t'ung-chih, ch. 119, pp. 1a-b.

45. Hummel, p. 653; Wills, pp. 188-202; KH Shih-lu, ch. 12, 26b-27a; Ross, Manchus, pp. 406-7. The court reconsidered the question of a Taiwan expedition in 1666-68, but the regents never again ordered a fleet to set sail for Taiwan. Shih Lang himself submitted a memorial calling for an expedition to be sent in 1668, but the regents took no action on the matter (Hummel, p. 653; Wills, p. 301).

46. Wills, pp. 350-51. For diplomatic efforts to bring about the surrender of Cheng Ching in 1662, see Wills, pp. 129-30.

to carry out the campaign to its logical conclusion: the conquest of Taiwan and the obliteration of the Cheng family. With the Chengs severely weakened by internal feuds and desertions, the Oboi period provided an opportune moment to crush the armies of Cheng Ching. Considering the fact that by the mid-1660s all of the major campaigns elsewhere in China had been successfully completed, the regents could have directed formidable military strength to a Taiwan expedition.

Consolidation of the Southeastern Coast: Kwangtung

Although military operations along the Fukien coast tended to overshadow other military events in southeastern China during the 1660s, the struggle to bring the province of Kwangtung under complete Ch'ing control also continued into the Oboi period. After the Ming loyalist prince, Chu Yu-lang, retreated from Kwangtung in the early 1650s, the major threat to the consolidation of the province came from a group of aborigines called the Tanka (Mandarin: Tan-k'ou; the "Tan pirates"). The Tanka lived on junks which they sailed along the rivers and streams of the Canton delta. At several points during the 1660s the Tanka rallied around certain of their leaders and pillaged villages and towns in the delta region.[47] Although the Kwangtungese authorities tried to enforce the prohibitions on trade and navigation against the Tanka, such efforts generally failed for lack of sufficient troops to patrol all of the waterways of Kwangtung.[48]

While the Tanka posed no threat to the dynasty itself, their constant uprisings jeopardized the exercise of Ch'ing authority in Kwangtung. The prime figure in the eradication of the Tanka menace was the feudatory prince in Kwangtung, Shang K'o-hsi. By the advent of the Oboi regency, Shang K'o-hsi had gained considerable control over the civil and military affairs of Kwangtung and ruled under the title, "Prince who Pacifies the South" (P'ing-nan Wang). During 1663-69 Shang led several expeditions against the Tanka rebels. In some of the ensuing battles, thousands of the aborigines were massacred and many more surrendered. Eventually, by the end of the Oboi decade, the Tanka people were pacified.[49] Shang K'o-hsi, like Keng Chi-mao to the north and Wu San-kuei to the west, had proved once again his military value to the dynasty.

Suppression of Chu Yu-lang (Ming Prince of Kuei)

While the conflicts with the Cheng clan and with the Tanka pirates raged to the east, Chu Yu-lang and his supporters in southwestern China persevered in their struggles against the relentless onslaught of Ch'ing

---

47. According to some accounts, the Tanka made an alliance with Cheng Ch'eng-kung and claimed to support the restoration of the Ming dynasty. On this matter and on the Tanka in general, see Hsiao I-shan, 1:406-7; Hummel, p. 635; Fu Lo-shu, "Two Portuguese Embassies," p. 78n.

48. Fu Lo-shu, "Two Portuguese Embassies," p. 78n.

49. Hsiao I-shan, 1:406-7; KH Shih-lu, ch. 15, p. 6b, and ch. 16, pp. 11a-b.

troops. The campaigns against Chu Yu-lang, by contrast to the unusual operations against the Chengs, followed the classic Manchu pattern of land warfare. For sixteen years (1646-61) Ch'ing forces pursued Chu Yu-lang through the mountains and valleys of southern China. At each stage in the campaign, the Ch'ing commanders consolidated the areas which they had occupied by bringing the cities, transportation routes, and sources of supply under their control. In this manner, the Ch'ing troops slowly advanced westward across the provinces of Kwangtung, Kwangsi, Hukuang, Kweichow, and Yunnan, while Chu Yu-lang was prevented from escaping to the east or north. By 1659 Chu could not maintain a poisition within the boundaries of China and retreated southward to Burma.

Chu Yu-lang was the grandson of the Ming Wan-li Emperor (reigned 1573-1620) and was the last major Ming challenge to the Manchu dynasty. In 1646 he had received the title Prince of Kuei (Kuei Wang) and established a Ming dynasty in Kwangtung with himself as emperor (under the reign-title Yung-li). In the following years of military engagements with the Ch'ing, Chu Yu-lang moved headquarters several times as he suffered defeat after defeat. Chu, however, had one source of strength which allowed him to survive and defy the Manchus for so many years: he was the last important claimant to the Ming throne and thus attracted the support of various pro-Ming militarists. Loyalist leaders on the China coast, including Cheng Ch'eng-kung and Chang Huang-yen, were closely associated with Chu's movement, kept in regular contact with him, and received ranks and titles from the Ming prince.[50] Other independent military leaders, particularly Li Ting-kuo, a former supporter of the rebel Chang Hsien-chung, rallied to the prince's cause during the Shun-chih period. By the late 1650s, however, Chu's strength had been largely eroded as he was forced away from the loyalist military leaders in the east and as his own coalition of armies disintegrated under Ch'ing pressure. When he retreated to Burma in 1659, Chu Yu-lang was left with his personal entourage of about 1500 persons and with the military support of Li Ting-kuo's army.[51]

Although the final episode in the Chu Yu-lang campaign occurred in the first year of the Oboi regency, the credit for the eventual victory belongs to the personnel appointed and to the strategies adopted during the Shun-chih geign. Wu San-kuei, who had been invested with the title of "Prince who Pacifies the West" (P'ing-hsi Wang), served as the primary Ch'ing commander in the battles against Chu Yu-lang throughout the years 1657-62. During 1657-59 Wu, with the support of various provincial officials, led his troops from Szechwan down through Kweichow

50. Hummel, pp. 41, 108-9.
51. On Chu Yu-lang's life and his military campaigns, see Hummel, pp. 193-95; Ross, Manchus, pp. 360-79; Harvey, History of Burma, pp. 196-201; Wu Wei-yeh, Lu-ch'iao chi-wen, ch. hsia, pp. 93-103. On Li Ting-kuo, see Parsons, Peasant Rebellions, pp. 168-207, passim; Hummel, pp. 489-90.

and finally pushed Chu Yu-lang southward to Burma after having captured the last Ming stronghold in China at Yunnanfu. The final drive
against the Ming Prince of Kuei bagan in early 1661 as Wu San-kuei
marched his troops into northwestern Burma, where they encountered
the army of Li Ting-kuo. After defeating Li Ting-kuo at the city of Hsi-
paw, the Ch'ing army advanced towards Ava (near Mandalay), where
the Burmese had kept Chu Yu-lang and his followers under house arrest
since their arrival in May 1659. Wu San-kuei finally encamped near
Ava in early 1662, and the Burmese surrendered Chu Yu-lang, his family, and his followers to Wu on 22 January 1662. After being transported
back to Yunnanfu, Chu Yu-lang and his fourteen-year-old son were executed by strangulation with a bowstring.[52] Throughout this campaign
against the Ming Prince of Kuei, Wu San-kuei not only provided competent leadership over his armies and laid out the basic tactics for the
movement of troops, but he also kept the Manchu court informed about
his proceedings through frequent and often secret memorials.[53]

In the final battles against Chu Yu-lang, Wu San-kuei was assisted
by a special imperial army sent from Peking under Aisingga in 1660.
Aisingga, who held the hereditary title of duke and was a chamberlain
of the Imperial Bodyguard, was sent to the southwest with orders to co-
ordinate his movements with those of Wu San-kuei and to help supervise
the entire operation against Chu Yu-lang. Aisingga represents another
of that category of special commanders commissioned to lead troops
for the duration of a specific military campaign and to act as a moderat-
ing influence over the regional ambitions of the feudatory princes.[54]

When the news of the capture and death of Chu Yu-lang reached Peking in the spring of 1662, the regents issued jubilant imperial decrees
and ordered sacrifices to Nurhaci and Abahai to celebrate the event.
Both Wu San-kuei and Aisingga were rewarded with ranks and titles in
recognition of their achievement. To the regents the victory over the
Ming Prince of Kuei marked the last of the great battles of the Manchu
conquest, and their pronouncements indicated a sense of completeness:

---

52. For accounts of the final campaign against Chu Yu-lang in 1659-62, see
Hummel, pp. 194-95, 878-79, 490; Chiang, ch. 12, pp. 2b-3b; Shen, T'ai-wan
Cheng-shih shih-mo, p. 53; MCSL, vol. 3, ch. 10, p. 994a.

53. SC Shih-lu, ch. 134, pp. 18b-20a; KH Shih-lu, ch. 3, pp. 7b-8a. For
an example of a "secret memorial" (mi tsou-pen) sent from Wu San-kuei to Peking concerning the battle against Li Ting-kuo, see MCSL, vol. 3, ch. 10, p.
997a.

54. Biographies of Aisingga in CSLC, ch. 4, pp. 48b-49b; Hummel, p. 898.
The imperial orders commissioning Aisingga to lead an army to the southwest
are found in SC Shih-lu, ch. 139, pp. 16a-17a. Several other provincial officials
and subordinate military officers made major contributions to this campaign. For
example, the governor-general of Szechwan, Li Kuo-ying, was highly influential
in offering military advice, leading troops, and transmitting military information
both to the commanders in the field and to the court at Peking (CSLC, ch. 78, p.
30a).

Truly this conquest has been accomplished under the extensive
blessings of heaven and earth and of our ancestors. Our great joy
extends across the seas as well as to the interior and the frontiers.
. . . By this victory the borders have been pacified and the villages
may peacefully return to their business. Relate all of this in an imperial proclamation to the empire so as to soothe the common people. Our military might has been displayed and now our joy is complete. [55]

Compared to the monumental struggles against Chu Yu-lang and a-
gainst Cheng Ch'eng-kung, the other battles during the Oboi period were
of lesser magnitude. Even the campaign against Li Lai-heng in 1663,
which will be discussed below, was a relatively short operation against
scattered bandit armies who posed little danger to the security of the
Ch'ing dynasty. In the eyes of the regents, therefore, the death of the
Ming Prince of Kuei marked an important turning point from the period
of conquest to the period of peaceful Ch'ing rule. The regents evidently
did not share the K'ang-hsi Emperor's belief that the Manchu conquest
could not be considered complete until the Ch'ing had triumphed over the
feudatory princes, the western Mongols, the Russian cossacks, and the
Cheng loyalists on Taiwan.

Suppression of the Li Lai-heng Rebellion

This rebellion, named after Li Lai-heng because he was the most famous
of several leaders, began in the early 1650s and spread through central
and southwestern China. Because of the location of this widespread uprising, it has also been called the rebellion of the "bandits of the western mountains" (hsi-shan k'ou).

The origins of this movement may be traced to two very different
sources: the rebellion of Li Tzu-ch'eng and the loyalist resistance of
Chu Yu-lang. The Li Lai-heng rebellion was a strange extension of
these earlier insurrections. Li Lai-heng himself was reported to have
been a descendant of Li Tzu-ch'eng, and others among his following,
such as Shih Tao-ch'i, had been former subordinates of Li Tzu-ch'eng.
After the defeat of Li Tzu-ch'eng, Li Lai-heng mustered a large army
(estimated at several tens of thousands) and allied himself with the Ming
Prince of Kuei. While fighting for the Ming prince, Li Lai-heng served
as one of the chief commanders under the loyalist general, Sun K'o-wang.
When Sun K'o-wang split with the Ming Prince of Kuei and surrendered
to the Manchus in 1657, Li Lai-heng also severed his ties with the loyalist movement and struck off on his own towards Szechwan. During the
late 1650s and early 1660s several independent militarists aligned themselves with Li as the uprising spread through the provinces of Hukuang
and Szechwan and as far north as Shensi. The rebels, acting as a loosely

---

55. KH Shih-lu, ch. 6, pp. 14b-15a.

scattered coalition, raided town after town in these provinces and then
retired to mountain bases.[56]

Before 1663 resistance against the "bandits of the western mountains"
consisted primarily of sporadic attacks by high provincial officials leading small contingents of garrison troops. The governor-general of Szechwan, Li Kuo-ying, courageously tried to crush the rebellion in his province, and his example was emulated by others in Hukuang and Shensi.[57]
But, realizing that his efforts were inadequate, Li Kuo-ying sent a memorial to Peking in 1662 in which he suggested a massive assault against
the rebels.[58] The regents responded to Li's request on 20 September
1663 by commissioning a large army of banner troops to "go forth, attack, and annihilate them." To command this army the regents selected
the brother of Oboi, Lieutenant-General Murma.[59]

The drive against the Li Lai-heng rebels began in late 1663 and continued throughout most of the following year. Murma's expeditionary
force cooperated with provincial troops under civil and military officials
from the four provinces involved. As in the confrontations with Li Tzu-
ch'eng and Chang Hsien-chung two decades earlier, the Ch'ing troops
slowly drove the rebels back to their mountain refuges. By the summer
of 1664 the "bandits of the western mountains" had suffered a series of
defeats in which thousands were killed or forced to surrender. Manchu
troops ruthlessly slaughtered many of the captured rebels. Li Lai-heng's
chief subordinate, Shih Tao-ch'i, was killed in battle, and Li himself
was forced to retreat to the mountains of western Hukuang. In the late
summer of 1664 Murma's army surrounded Li Lai-heng and his remaining followers on one of these mountains. Unable to escape, Li gave orders to build a fire and then threw himself into the flames. Li Lai-heng's
family and, according to one exaggerated report, thirty thousand of his
troops followed Li's example and leapt into the fire.[60] When the Ch'ing
troops finally reached the rebel's camp, there was little left but ashes
and the rebellion had been extinguished.[61]

Tribal Rebellions in the Southwest

In one respect the campaign against the "bandits of the western mountains" was an unusual military operation, since none of the feudatory
princes was directly involved. In the southern provinces of Yunnan

56. Biography of Li Lai-heng in Wang Fu-chih, Yung-li shih-lu, vol. 12, ch.
15, pp. 1a-2b. Biography of Shih Tao-ch'i in ibid., ch. 15, 2b-3a.
57. CSLC, ch. 78, pp. 30a-b; Hu-pei t'ung-chih, ch. 69, pp. 1788-89; Hsiao
I-shan, 1: 403-4. On the efforts of other provincial officials to deal with Li Lai-
heng in the early 1660s, see Hu-pei t'ung-chih, ch. 121, pp. 2917-18; KH Shih-lu,
ch. 8, pp. 7b-8a, 9a, and ch. 9, pp. 1b, 22a, 25a.
58. CSLC, ch. 78, p. 30a.
59. KH Shih-lu, ch. 9, p. 26a.
60. Wang Fu-chih, Yung-li shih-lu, ch. 15, pp. 1a-2b.
61. On the final campaign against the Li Lai-heng rebellion, see ibid., ch.
15. pp. 1a-2b, 2b-3a; Hsiao I-shan, 1: 403-4; Ssu-ch'uan t'ung-chih, ch. 82, pp.
7a-8a; KH Shih-lu, ch. 11, pp. 4b-5a, and ch. 13, pp. 4a-b.

and Kweichow, however, Wu San-kuei found himself occupied with a number of tribal uprisings among the Miao and other non-Chinese minority groups. Many of these local rebellions were led by tribal leaders who had been invested with the title of "local administrator" (t'u-ssu) by the Manchu dynasty and who ruled a specific geographical area in a semi-feudal relationship to the Ch'ing state. In 1664 a local administrator named An-k'un rose up against the provincial authorities in Yunnan, and the uprising spread to other native tribes in both Yunnan and Kweichow. Troops subordinate to Wu San-kuei and to the provincial authorities of both provinces struggled against An-k'un and his followers for almost a year before the rebellion was suppressed. Although An-k'un's was the most troublesome uprising, Wu San-kuei was plagued by similar rebellions throughout the 1660s. By the end of the Oboi regency, however, Wu's persistent efforts and the able assistance of provincial leaders had brought the tribal leaders to submission across most of southern and southwestern China. [62]

The military successes of Wu San-kuei gradually brought segments of Szechwan, Yunnan, and Kweichow into the sphere of his personal control. In these conquered regions, however, Wu followed the regular system of Chinese provincial administration. Through a process called "transformation" (kai-t'u kuei-liu), areas which formerly had been governed through the local administrator system were designated as prefectures, departments, and districts. Regular Chinese officials were appointed to serve as prefects and magistrates.[63] Although the local administrators continued to operate in several areas, Wu San-kuei's application of the transformation process paved the way for the extension of Ch'ing authority in the southwest. In fact, by the end of the Oboi decade the only major obstacle to Ch'ing control in southwestern China was Wu San-kuei himself.

WU SAN-KUEI AND THE THREE FEUDATORIES IN THE 1660s

Throughout the preceding section we have seen the crucial importance of the feudatory princes in the military campaigns of the 1660s. All three major feudatory princes—Keng Chi-mao, Shang K'o-hsi, and Wu San-kuei—had been exceptional military officers, and they offered considerable aid in the Ch'ing conquest of the southern coastal area and the

---

62. For a general description of the An-k'un uprising and other tribal disturbances in Yunnan and Kweichow during the 1660s, see Hsiao I-shan, 1: 404-6. Other accounts are Yün-nan t'ung-chih-kao, ch. 103, pp. 36b-39b; Kuei-chou t'ung-chih, ch. 21, pp. 38a-b, and ch. 24, pp. 5a-6b. Wu San-kuei submitted several memorials to Peking during the 1660s about his military operations against the tribal rebels (KH Shih-lu, ch. 10, p. 7b; ch. 11, pp. 6b, 16b-17a; ch. 18, pp. 2a-b, 7a).

On the role of the t'u-ssu system in Ch'ing China, see Wiens, China's March towards the Tropics, pp. 226-40.

63. HTSL, ch. 32, pp. 16b-17a (pp. 5476-77); KH Shih-lu, ch. 18, p. 7b. For a memorial from Wu San-kuei suggesting the application of the transformation process, see KH Shih-lu, ch. 15, pp. 15a-b.

wide belt of provinces stretching south from the Yangtze. With most of
the fighting successfully concluded in these areas by the mid-1660s, however, the feudatories were increasingly recognized as military and economic liabilities rather than assets. During the late Shun-chih and early
K'ang-hsi periods the feudatories became almost independent regional
strongholds as these court-appointed princes achieved a large measure
of civil and military control. The Manchu regents in Peking recognized
the growing danger posed by the feudatories and tried to weaken the
princes' power through various nonmilitary means.

The most powerful and most famous of the feudatory princes was Wu
San-kuei. By the late 1650s Wu had gained the dominant voice in the affairs of Yunnan and Kweichow. During the Oboi period, moreover, Wu
began to appoint the major civil and military officials not only in these
two provinces but also in Szechwan, Hukuang, Shensi, and Kansu. This
power of appointment, reluctantly recognized by the Manchu court,
brought almost half of the geographical extent of China into Wu's grasp.
By 1660 Wu San-kuei commanded an army of about 70,000, composed
of 10,000 of his own combat forces, 48,000 troops of the Green Banner,
and 12,000 men and officers from surrendered armies. Economically
Wu had established a financial empire in the southwest. In addition to
the imperial revenues which he received (some twenty million _taels_ annually by the late 1660s), Wu also levied his own taxes and set up mo-
nopolies over salt production and over gold and copper mining. Like
Shang K'o-hsi and Keng Chi-mao, who secretly traded with the Dutch
and Southeast Asians, Wu San-kuei made fruitful commercial transactions with Tibetan merchants. Well before the rebellion of the feudatories broke out in 1673, then, the feudatory princes, and especially Wu
San-kuei, had become virtual emperors in their respective domains.[64]

Although the increasing menace of the feudatories to the prosperity
and security of the dynasty was an obvious fact, there were only a few
public statements of protest. In July 1660 the Board of Revenue memorialized the throne about the financial burden of supporting Wu San-kuei:

> In Yunnan the Prince who Pacifies the West has ten thousand
> troops directly subordinate to him. The Green Banner troops and
> the surrendered troops altogether amount to sixty thousand sol-
> diers. There are also Manchu troops of the Eight Banners. The
> needs [of these armies] in terms of supplies are very great. In
> order to supply them the people of all provinces must be taxed,

64. For information about the size of Wu San-kuei's military forces, see SC
Shih-lu, ch. 136, pp. 21b-22b, and ch. 138, p. 3b; Tsao, Rebellion of the Three
Feudatories, p. 65. On Wu San-kuei's power to appoint provincial officials, see
KH Shih-lu, ch. 6, p. 29a; ch. 7, pp. 24b-25a; and ch. 12, p. 21a. Wu San-kuei
seems to have held a much superior position with respect to provincial officials
than either Keng Chi-mao or Shang K'o-hsi. John Wills, Jr., has noted that Keng
Chi-mao and Li Shuai-t'ai, for example, were equals in many respects and their
relationship was like that of governor-general to governor (Wills, p. 187).

and their hardships and suffering are severe.

The income from the taxes for the entire empire is only 8,750,000 taels while the needs of Yunnan alone are more than 9,000,000 taels. Thus the revenue from the entire empire is not sufficient to meet the needs of a single province. [65]

A few months later a Szechwan censor, Yang Su-yün, courageously submitted a memorial criticizing the court for permitting Wu San-kuei to appoint officials on his own authority:

> I have carefully examined the Peking Gazette [Ti-pao], and I have seen the respectful requests of the Prince who Pacifies the West for the promotion and transfer [of officials]. . . . He has received the approval of the metropolitan officials. On this matter I cannot overcome my horror. The appointment of officials is a great responsibility of the dynasty wherein the court has the ultimate power. [66]

In spite of these warnings, the regents and the court were reluctant to restrain the power of Wu San-kuei in the early 1660s. The only significant move in this direction occurred in 1665 when about 9,000 of Wu's troops were disbanded by order of the Board of War and the regents. Throughout the later years of the Oboi period, therefore, Wu's troops comprised an army of approximately 60,000 (only ten thousand less than during the heat of the Chu Yu-lang campaign). [67] The regents seem to have ignored the matter of Wu's making official appointments on his own authority during the years 1661-66. [68]

As the K'ang-hsi Emperor gradually asserted his power in 1667-68, however, a hard line began to emerge against the feudatories. As mentioned earlier, the emperor ordered a sharp increase in the numbers of combat troops (wai tso-ling). By the end of the 1660s it was apparent that the K'ang-hsi Emperor was mobilizing for a major assault and the feudatory princes were the likely targets. Perhaps because he feared that the newly formed companies were to be used against him, Wu San-kuei offered his resignation to test the emperor's response. In a memorial received in Peking on 8 July 1667, Wu requested "that he be re-

65. SC Shih-lu, ch. 136, p. 22a.

66. Ibid., ch. 142, pp. 18b-19a. For his audacity Yang Su-yün was dismissed from his post. In 1673, when Wu San-kuei rebelled, Yang was reinstated as an official in recognition of his former warning and he eventually became a provincial governor (Hummel, pp. 893-94).

67. KH Shih-lu, ch. 15, pp. 12b-13a.

68. In 1660, a year before the Oboi regency took power, however, the president of the Board of Civil Office suggested that appointments in the provinces of Szechwan, Hukuang, Kwangsi, Yunnan, and Kweichow be made temporary. Such appointments, presumably made by Wu San-kuei, were to be reviewed after two years. This suggestion was approved by the Shun-chih Emperor (SC Shih-lu, ch. 134, pp. 2a-b).

lieved of the responsibility of managing the affairs of the provinces of Yunnan and Kweichow because of weakening eyesight."[69] On 20 July the emperor approved the suggestion by the Board of Civil Office that Wu's resignation be accepted:

> We must take the affairs of those border areas and, in accordance with the precedents for all provinces, entrust them to the management of the tu-fu of those provinces. All civil officials, again in accordance with the precedents for all provinces, will be recommended and appointed by this Board.
>
> Imperial Endorsement: "Agreed."[70]

Although Wu San-kuei was eventually reinstated to his various posts in late 1667, the temporary acceptance of Wu's resignation indicated a new toughness towards the feudatory princes. Just as Wu's memorial was an experiment to test the reaction of the court, the acceptance of his resignation was an imperial probe to determine whether or not Wu could be induced to retire peacefully. In November 1667 Wu San-kuei clearly indicated that he was not really interested in retirement, as he permitted several of his subordinates, including Governor-general Pien San-yüan, to request that he remain in office. In effect this request by Wu San-kuei's followers amounted to an ultimatum from Wu: either continue to tolerate my influence in the southwest, or meet me on the field of battle. The young emperor and his advisers apparently felt that they lacked sufficient military and economic strength to wage an immediate campaign against the feudatories, and thus they backed away from the ultimatum. But at the same time that the emperor granted the request of Pien San-yüan and others, he also issued the following statement which left open the option of requiring Wu's resignation on grounds of physical weakness: "By ordering the Prince to return to the management of affairs, it is feared that he will over-exert himself and thus bring great harm to his spirit. For if there are military problems in the border areas, the Prince must himself undertake the matter."[71]

The K'ang-hsi Emperor also sought to restrict Wu San-kuei's power to appoint high provincial officials. In early 1668, when the governor of Yunnan retired, Wu suggested that one of his own followers, Lin T'ien-ching, be appointed to the post. The Censorate and the Nine Ministers gave the customary approval of Wu San-kuei's recommendation. The emperor, however, boldly rejected Wu's appointee and instead appointed Commissioner of the Office of Transmission, Li T'ien-yü, to the governorship. The emperor announced in an imperial rescript: "Lin T'ien-ching is one of the personal subordinates of the Prince who Pacifies

69. KH Shih-lu, ch. 22, p. 10a.
70. Ibid., ch. 22, pp. 11a-b.
71. Ibid., ch. 24, pp. 8a-b. See Morgan, "Times and Manners," p. 25.

the West. It is now observed that the Prince will remain in Yunnan and [thus] Lin T'ien-ching ought not to fill the vacancy. Let Li T'ien-yü be the governor of Yunnan."[72]

By 1668, therefore, the K'ang-hsi Emperor had taken a much more forceful stance against Wu San-kuei than had his regents. There are two likely explanations for the regents' reluctance in this matter. First, they may have felt that the imperial treasuries were too depleted and the imperial armies too exhausted to challenge Wu San-kuei. Even when the emperor decided to send troops against the feudatories in 1673, there was considerable opposition in the Manchu court from those who felt the venture too risky. Secondly, the regents genuinely respected the feudatory princes as exceptional military leaders and thus were hesitant to fight against their former comrades-in-arms. The regents may have concluded that although the feudatory princes provided some annoying problems for the Ch'ing government in Peking, they were really no threat to the dynasty and thus a modus vivendi could be worked out without recourse to warfare. In any case, it is clear that the regents were cautious in their dealings with the feudatory princes in general and with Wu San-kuei in particular. In coping with the feudatory princes, as in most of their policies towards military strategy and military administration, the regents operated conservatively. The problems of the Ch'ing economy and the limitations of their own backgrounds had led them to act indecisively in many military matters.

---

72. KH Shih-lu, ch. 25, p. 3a. Li T'ien-yü served as governor of Yunnan for only three years (1668-71) and then retired because of the death of one of his parents. As governor, Li was known for his efforts to eliminate corruption. One biographer described Li's tenure as "a time when none dared commit a crime" (Chi-fu t'ung-chih, ch. 226, p. 7984).

Lin T'ien-ching was a chin-shih from Chihli who had formerly served as director-general of River Conservancy and then as governor of Nan-kan (Kiangsi) from 1662 to 1665 (Yen, Ch'ing-tai cheng-hsien lei-pien, hsün-fu, ch. 1, pp. 6a-b). Later in 1668 Lin became governor of Hukuang, a post which he held until 1670 when he retired on grounds of illness (CS, 4:3018-20; KH Shih-lu, ch. 25, p. 12a). Although the "Veritable Records" do not indicate that this appointment was made at Wu San-kuei's request, it is quite likely that Lin was made governor of Hukuang as a concession to Wu.

7   The Foreign Policies of
the Oboi Regency

In this final chapter on the collective policies of the Joint Regents' faction, three problems will be considered: the persecution of Jesuit missionaries during the 1660s, tributary relations under the regency, and Manchuria (including Sino-Russian relations) during the Oboi period. These problems are related both because they shed light on the regents' attitudes in dealing with foreigners and because they reinforce earlier conclusions we have reached about the policies of the Joint Regents' faction in general.

In their persecution of Jesuit missionaries, the regents remind us again of their terrorist campaigns against the Chinese elite in Kiangnan and Chekiang. The Jesuits, like the dissident students and loyalist scholars, bore the double stigma of having been favored by the Shun-chih Emperor and of seeming subversive to the Manchu regime. The regents' approach to the various tributary countries, on the other hand, seems a direct extension of their military policies. They were anxious to consolidate and defend the existing borders of the empire but were reluctant to venture into expansionist military operations beyond previously established frontiers. Similarly, the regents endeavored to preserve the upper reaches of Manchuria from Russian incursions while avoiding full-scale war against the forces of imperial Russia. But in their Manchurian policy the regents again displayed their willingness to make insitutional innovations in a quest for both governmental efficiency and for Manchu control.

PERSECUTION OF THE JESUITS UNDER THE OBOI REGENCY

The persecution of the Jesuit missionaries during the 1660s, including such famous Jesuit fathers as Adam Schall and Ferdinand Verbiest, is perhaps the best-known episode of the regency. In many of the contemporary accounts written by Jesuits, the regents are portrayed as narrow-minded bigots because of their campaign against the Jesuits, while the Shun-chih Emperor is seen as an enlightened ruler who almost converted to Christianity. In spite of their obvious bias, however, some of these accounts provide some reliable information about the background and nature of the persecutions under the regency.

The persecutions were caused by the latent anti-Jesuit hostility shared by both the Manchu and the Chinese elites. The Chinese feared the presence of alien elements which might undermine their social position and their traditional culture. The Manchus, on the other hand, feared the growth of subversive influences which could weaken their hold

on the Chinese empire. These fears were intensified by the variety of
Jesuit loyalties in the crucial years of the Manchu conquest. During the
Oboi period certain Chinese and Moslem elements in Peking were able
to play upon these latent fears and a full-scale anti-Jesuit campaign ensued.

The Chinese, rather than the Manchus, were the first to display ani-
mosity towards the Jesuits. The alien origins of the Jesuits, their growing influence among the scholar-official class, and the strangeness of
their religious beliefs brought a hostile reaction from certain segments
of the Chinese upper class as early as the 1610s and 1620s. During these
years Jesuit missionaries in China suffered persecutions similar to those
during the Oboi period. Many Jesuits were arrested, beaten, and then
exiled to Macao. Several of their missions were destroyed.[1]

Another factor which spawned suspicion among the Chinese elite was
the Jesuits' association with members of the reformist societies in the
last decades of the Ming. Several Chinese who befriended the Jesuits
and many of the Jesuits' most famous converts, including Hsü Kuang-
ch'i, Li Chih-tsao, and Yang T'ing-yün, were members of the Tung-lin
Party or other reformist groups.[2] The fact that the Jesuits were associated with late Ming factional struggles aroused skepticism. Factionalism of any sort, progressive or not, was traditionally considered a cardinal flaw in the political structure and a harbinger of the fall of a dynasty.

During the period of the Manchu conquest, moreover, the Jesuits
played roles which were certain to elicit suspicion from both Manchus
and Chinese. Uncertain of the future political situation, various Jesuits
offered their services to loyalists, rebels, and conquerors. In the 1630s
Adam Schall assisted the Ming military in the construction and use of
cannon to defend against the Manchu assaults. While Schall himself offered his allegiance to the Manchus in 1644 and was made director of
the Imperial Bureau of Astronomy under Dorgon, other Jesuits supported
Chinese rebels and Ming loyalists. Some Jesuit fathers attached themselves to the Kwangtungese regime of the Ming pretender, Chu Yu-lang.
Christian converts gained high civil posts in Chu's government and continued to fight for the Ming cause throughout the 1640s and 1650s. Other
Jesuits, such as Louis Buglio and Joseph de Magalhaens, served the ty-
rannical Chinese rebel, Chang Hsien-chung, in southwestern China. This
multiplicity of Christian allegiances during the dynastic transition left
doubts in the minds of both Chinese and Manchus.[3]

Hostility towards the Jesuits remained latent during the reign of the
Shun-chih Emperor. As we have already seen, the Shun-chih Emperor
developed an affection for the elderly Jesuit father, Adam Schall, and
was reputed to have spent many hours in informal conversations with

1. Dunne, Generation of Giants, pp. 109-61, passim.
2. On the Jesuit association with Ming factions, see ibid., pp. 43, 199-205.
3. On the role of the Jesuits in the 1630s and 1640s, see ibid., pp. 316-46,
passim; du Halde, Description de la Chine, 2:79-80.

Schall.[4] To the future Manchu regents, whose political power was eb-
bing in the late 1650s, the emperor's association with Adam Schall
seemed further evidence that he regarded aliens and civil officials more
highly than military officers of his own race. The regents saw the Jesuits in the same category with the eunuchs and Buddhists, as persons
who diverted the Shun-chih Emperor from his Manchu military advisers.

   Adrien Greslon, a French Jesuit in China during the years 1651-60,
has provided a brief contemporary account of the attitude of the regents
towards Schall and the other Jesuits. According to Greslon, the four
regents called Schall to appear before the full court immediately after
the death of the Shun-chih Emperor and ordered Schall to proclaim his
loyalty. But when Schall discovered that the ceremony was held before
what he considered an idol, he refused to compromise his religious beliefs by swearing allegiance in the presence of a pagan image. The regents, according to Greslon, were impressed by Schall's bravery and
resolve. For the time being, therefore, he was permitted to retain the
ranks and privileges which he had been given under the Shun-chih Emperor. Nevertheless Greslon also observed that the regents, and particularly Suksaha, remained suspicious of Schall and shared hostility
towards the Jesuits in general. Early in the Oboi regency an edict ordered special imperial commissioners to tour the provinces, investigate the Jesuit missionaries and their missions, and send the information back to Peking.[5]

   The regents' suspicion of the Jesuits, and the latent hostility among
the Chinese upper class, might never have come to actual persecutions
without the presence of a catalyst in the form of a professional anti-
Christian, Yang Kuang-hsien. Yang's personal career was built on the
foundation of mobilizing prejudice and championing the cause of purification. Because of Yang's recurrent fits of violent rage in his youth,
his father felt that he was unfit for civil office and thus prohibited him
from competing in the examinations. In spite of his father's efforts,
however, Yang retained an interest in politics and in 1637 submitted a
memorial criticizing some of the favorite officials of the last Ming emperor. Assuming that he would be executed, Yang went to Peking and
carried his coffin with him. Although Yang was not given the death penalty, he was flogged and exiled to Liaotung. Finally, when the Manchus
came to power in 1644, Yang was permitted to return to China, and
during most of the Shun-chih reign he lived in Nanking.

   Beginning in the late 1650s Yang Kuang-hsien sought prominence
through a new route, attacking the Jesuit missionaries in Peking. He
found allies in his anti-Jesuit venture among Moslem members of the
Bureau of Astronomy who were jealous of the superior positions given
to the Jesuits. The leader of the disgruntled Moslems, Wu Ming-hsüan,

4. Dunne, Generation of Giants, pp. 347-54.
5. Greslon, Histoire de la Chine, pp. 69-71, 111.

accused Schall of innacurate astronomical observations in 1657. Thereafter Yang and Wu cooperated in an effort to oust the Jesuit fathers. [6]

Their campaign against the Jesuits intensified during the early 1660s
and finally achieved results. In the first four years of the Oboi regency,
persecutions against Jesuits occurred in the provinces of Szechwan, Hukuang, Kiangsi, and Shantung. In all these cases local officials, often
abetted by Buddhist monks, accused the Jesuits of spreading pernicious
doctrines and offering sanctuary to rebels. During these provincial persecutions of 1661-64 many Jesuit fathers were arrested and interrogated,
churches and missionary establishments were destroyed, and hundreds
of Chinese converts were imprisoned, tortured, and, in some cases,
executed. [7]

Severe persecutions in the metropolitan area, however, did not occur
until 1664-65, when Yang Kuang-hsien, enjoying the more favorable cli-
mate of the regency, gained support in his anti-Jesuit campaign. In 1664
Yang published his famous anti-Jesuit tract entitled Pu te i ("I Could Not
Do Otherwise"). In this volume Yang explained that Adam Schall was a
"posthumous follower of Jesus, who had been the ringleader of the treacherous bandits of the Kingdom of Judea." Following this argument, Yang
contended that Schall and his followers had come to China as infiltrators
with the intention of fomenting rebellion.

Yang's Pu te i aroused the fears of the Manchu regents and the court.
Soon after its publication the Jesuit missionaries in Peking, including
Schall and Verbiest, and several of their Chinese associates on the Bureau of Astronomy were arrested and imprisoned. The trial of the Jesuits was a lengthy episode which occupied the fall, winter, and spring
of 1664-65. [9] During these months the Jesuits were repeatedly interrogated by members of the Board of Punishments and required to defend
themselves against accusations of heretical teachings and mathematical
inaccuracies. The trial was arduous for the missionaries and especially
for Schall, who had suffered a stroke. At one point in the proceedings
the Jesuits sought to prove their mathematical abilities by predicting the

6. Much of the information about Yang Kuang-hsien and the Jesuit persecutions is found in Hummel, pp. 889-92.

7. On the provincial persecutions during 1661-64, see Greslon, Histoire de
la Chine, pp. 61-84; Pfister, Notices biographiques, p. 253.

8. Yang Kuang-hsien, Pu te i, ch. 1, pp. 4a-7a. The translation is taken
from Fu Lo-shu, Documentary Chronicle, 1:35. The information about Yang's
Pu te i which follows is taken from the translation available in ibid., 1:35-36.

One source notes that the Jesuits were also accused of having deliberately
chosen an inauspicious day for the burial of the infant prince of the Shun-chih Emperor and the Empress Hsiao-hsien in 1658 (Hummel, p. 891).

9. For accounts of the 1664-65 trial, see Hummel, p. 891; Dunne, Generation of Giants, pp. 362-63; Pfister, Notices biographiques, pp. 173-76; Bosmans,
"Ferdinand Verbiest," pp. 224-30; Greslon, Histoire de la Chine, pp. 100-181;
d'Orleans, Histoire des deux conquerans tartares, pp. 59-69.

time of a solar eclipse. Both Wu Ming-hsüan and Ferdinand Verbiest made predictions, but when the eclipse arrived Wu's prediction was thirty minutes off and Verbiest's was correct. Nevertheless, the regents and other officials remained unconvinced, and the trial wore on.

Finally on 30 April 1665 the regents announced their verdict on the basis of a decision made by the Council of Deliberative Officials. They called for the execution of Schall and seven Chinese astronomers by the gruesome slicing process. Verbiest, Buglio, and de Magalhaens were to be flogged and exiled.[10] On the first of May, however, a series of earthquakes shook Peking. The regents and the frightened Grand Empress Dowager interpreted the earthquakes as a sign of heavenly disapproval and consequently lightened the punishments in the Jesuit case. The sentences against all of the Jesuit fathers and against most of the Chinese were retracted in an edict of 17 May 1665. But for five of the Chinese astronomers there was no reprieve, and they were executed by decapitation.[11] The regents permitted the Jesuits to remain in Peking, but the next four years (1665-69) marked a major setback for Jesuit ambitions in China. Missionary establishments throughout China were closed and all missionaries living on the mainland were required to accept exile in Macao. During these years Yang Kuang-hsien and Wu Ming-hsüan supervised the Imperial Bureau of Astronomy.

By the end of the decade of the 1660s, however, the K'ang-hsi Emperor began to doubt the accuracy of the calculations made by the Bureau of Astronomy. In late 1668 he sent to Ferdinand Verbiest for his inspection a copy of a calendar which Yang and Wu had drawn up. Verbiest reviewed the calendar and cited a number of errors. The issue was finally resolved in another eclipse prediction contest held at the end of January 1669. Once again Verbiest made the most accurate calculation, and on 17 April he was reinstated as an assistant director of the Imperial Bureau of Astronomy.[12] Later in 1669 both Yang Kuang-hsien and Wu Ming-hsüan were tried and sentenced for their inaccurate calculations and for having sided with the Oboi faction. Wu Ming-hsüan was flogged in punishment and Yang was spared from execution only because of his old age.[13] Yang died later in the same year.

After the K'ang-hsi Emperor took firm command of his government in 1669, he returned to the earlier policy of amicable relations with the Jesuit fathers in Peking. The story of his close contact with such Jesuits as Verbiest and Gerbillon is well known. But at the same time the K'ang-hsi Emperor continued to regard the Jesuit establishments in China with suspicion. One of the reasons for his famous Southern Tours,

10. KH Shih-lu, ch. 14, pp. 27a-29a.
11. Ibid., ch. 15, pp. 1b-2a.
12. On the reinstatement of Verbiest, see ibid., ch. 27, pp. 24a-b, and ch. 28, pp. 6a-b; Hummel, p. 891.
13. KH Shih-lu, ch. 31, pp. 4a-5a; Hummel, p. 891.

in fact, was to keep an informal surveillance over the Catholic missions outside the capital area. He was disturbed when, on his fourth Southern Tour in 1703, he discovered groups of missionaries that he had never known about.[14]

TRIBUTARY AND WESTERN RELATIONS IN THE 1660s

Because of the concentration of both military and diplomatic power in the hands of the four regents, there was considerable continuity between military and foreign policy in the 1660s. Certain characteristics of the regents' dealings with foreign countries are particularly noteworthy. First and foremost, the regents desired security against foreign threats to the dynasty. Essentially this amounted to a holding policy whereby the regents avoided military ventures beyond the borders established during the campaigns of the previous two decades but also endeavored to maintain those borders through close military surveillance. Secondly, the regents followed the classic Chinese pattern of permitting foreign trade only in conjunction with tributary missions to Peking. Foreign trade was a suasive tool in the hands of the regents and, unlike the K'ang-hsi Emperor, they did not look to commercial intercourse as a source of dynastic revenue. Finally, the regents insisted upon adherence to tributary regulations in all respects. The Manchus had adopted the tributary technique in their Mongol policies as early as the Nurhaci reign. Under Abahai, with the creation of the Li-fan yüan, tributary missions were required from both Mongols and Koreans. After the conquest, the Manchus developed their dual systems of foreign policy, administered separately by the Li-fan yüan and the Board of Rites (except in the years 1658-61), and both systems relied heavily on tributary embassies. Tribute, therefore, was a well-established practice in the Manchu approach to foreign relations and the regents dutifully preserved this practice.

Inner Mongolia in the 1660s

During the mid-seventeenth century Ch'ing-Mongol relations were largely confined to Mongolian tribes living in western Manchuria and Inner Mongolia. Most of the Mongolian peoples in this area had submitted to Ch'ing authority in the decade preceding the conquest in 1644. Under the aegis of the Li-fan yüan, these Mongols were organized into a subordinate relationship on the basis of banners.[15] By this system the Manchus established territorial boundaries for the various Mongol tribes and sanctioned the succession of tribal chieftains. Under the banner structure Mongols were required to pledge loyalty to the Ch'ing and were occasionally used

14. Spence, Ts'ao Yin, pp. 134-38.
15. On the application of the banner system to Mongolian tribes, see Michael, Origin of Manchu Rule, pp. 96-98; Farquhar, "Origins of the Manchus' Mongolian Policy," pp. 204-5.

as auxiliaries in Manchu campaigns. After 1644 most of the Mongol
tribes sent regular tributary envoys to Peking. [16]

The regents sought close ties with their Mongolian allies but were
also careful to prevent these tribes from endangering the security of the
dynasty. The tributary embassy was the primary vehicle of Ch'ing contact with and control over these Mongols during the regency. Each year,
for example, the Li-fan yüan supervised several tributary missions sent
by Chahar Mongols to the Ch'ing court at Peking. Such tributary missions reinforced Ch'ing superiority over the Mongol tribesmen and also
provided the Manchu court with information about political and military
developments beyond the Great Wall. At the same time, the regents promulgated regulations designed to prevent the Mongol embassies from becoming a threat to Manchu rule. All members of Mongol tributary missions were required to gain imperial permits before they were allowed
through the passes in the Great Wall. Mongols could not enter China to
trade unless they were accompanying tributary envoys. In addition, all
items designated for trade had to be inspected and registered at the borders. While in Peking, Mongols were kept under strict surveillance,
and their purchases in particular were closely monitored. And if a Mongol wished to purchase a large quantity of arms, he was required to submit a report to the Li-fan yüan. [17]

The regents also endeavored to maintain order among the Mongolian
tribes by sending forth imperial commissioners to conduct "meetings of
alliance" (meng-hui) with leaders of the various Mongolian banners. In
1666 the president and a vice-president of the Li-fan yüan, Karantu and
Cokto, both of whom were Mongols, were commissioned to meet with
the leaders of the Korchin Mongols and the other tribes of the forty-nine
banners in northwestern Manchuria. Two years later the two vice-presidents of the Li-fan yüan, Cokto and Ta-ha-t'a, were ordered to hold a
meeting of alliance with the Chahar Mongols. [18]

Relations with Central Asia: Chinese Turkestan and Tibet

Before the late seventeenth and early eighteenth centuries, Ch'ing relations with the Mongols of Central Asia and with the Tibetans were minimal. During the 1660s the regents preserved Ch'ing strength along the
borders to the east and southeast, but they did not embark on expansionist ventures into Chinese Turkestan and Tibet similar to those of the

16. On the major Mongolian tribal confederations in the early Ch'ing period,
see Howorth, History of the Mongols, 1:388-487, passim; Lattimore, Mongols of
Manchuria, pp. 57-59. The Mongol tribes and banners are discussed fully in Tayama, Shin-jidai ni okeru Mōko no shakai seido.

17. For Mongol regulations promulgated in the 1660s, see Pien-i tien, ts'e
209, pp. 26b-27a. See also HTSL, ch. 627, pp. 1a-b (p. 13329); KH Shih-lu,
ch. 5, pp. 22a-b.

18. KH Shih-lu, ch. 18, p. 13a, and ch. 25, p. 16b. A biography of Karantu
is available in CSK, ch. 235, p. 4a.

K'ang-hsi Emperor later in his reign. The only military encounters between the Ch'ing and the Mongols of the west during the 1660s were a
few skirmishes between troops under Wu San-kuei and some isolated
Mongol tribes who had penetrated into Li-chiang prefecture in northwestern Yunnan.[19] With respect to Tibet, relations with the Ch'ing were
strengthened by the visit of the fifth Dalai Lama to Peking in 1652, but
during the Oboi period interest in Tibet seems to have tapered off.

Under the regency, Manchu relations with the eastern Mongol tribes
and with the Tibetans were generally conducted by provincial civil and
military officials in the border provinces. These officials had the responsibility of protecting the borders of the dynasty, keeping a vigilant
watch over the activities of the various tribes, and sending information
to the Manchu court. In 1667, for example, the governor-general of
Shensi-Shansi, Lu Ch'ung-chün, sent a report to the regents in which he
described the precautionary measures he had taken after hearing rumors
of a Mongol uprising:

> Formerly because the Mergen and other aboriginal tribes wanted
> to use the lands within China for grazing and also because some de-
> serters from the barbarian tribes gave us warning, saying that they
> had seen all of the chieftains preparing to make war in the eighth
> month, I immediately went in person. In addition to easing my own
> mind, I subsequently received the report of the brigade-general,
> Sun Ssu-k'o, who said that all of the wandering barbarians had re-
> turned to their native places to raise their flocks. Moreover, last
> year I sent a commissioner to the Lama of Tibet and he returned
> praising the Dalai Lama.
>
> In accordance with an Imperial Rescript I have given orders to
> all of the Mongol taiji [lowest order of Mongol nobility] that they
> must not cause trouble. All of the taiji have complied with the Im-
> perial Orders and Edicts of the Court of our Dynasty. They have
> honestly changed their hearts and have sent representatives to ac-
> knowledge their faults and to present thousands of horses, cattle,
> and sheep. And now subsequently the Lama has presented tribute.
>
> On the basis of all this [we may conclude] that the restoration of
> obedience among the western barbarians is already a fact. Manchu
> and Chinese officials and soldiers must be requested to withdraw.[20]

This memorial is an interesting example of the general approach to frontier problems in the Oboi period: strong protection of the imperial bor-

---

19. Yün-nan t'ung-chih-kao, ch. 103, pp. 39b-41a. On the matter of the Central Asian Mongols not posing a major threat to the Ch'ing prior to the rise of Galdan, see Fletcher, "China and Central Asia," p. 192; Li Tieh-tseng, Historical
Status of Tibet, pp. 33-35.

20. KH Shih-lu, ch. 24, pp. 13b-14a.

ders but immediate withdrawal of Ch'ing troops as soon as threats were
eliminated.

Tributary Relations with Other Asian Nations

The other Asian countries, including Korea, the Ryukyu Islands, Annam,
and Siam, posed little military threat to the Manchus, and the regents
generally handled diplomatic contact with them through the tribute system. Under the supervision of the Board of Rites, all of these countries
sent regular tributary envoys during the 1660s (the Koreans presented
tribute annually on the Chinese New Year). During their tenure the regents enforced fairly strictly the tribute regulations, many of which
dated from Ming times. Tributary envoys were carefully limited as to
size, and their credentials were reviewed painstakingly to assure the au-
thenticity of the embassy.[21] Although the regents occasionally permitted
Asian nations to present items not approved in the Ch'ing Statutes as tribute, they generally enforced the prohibitions on nontributary trade.[22]

With most of these tributary nations to the south and the east, relations were relatively smooth during the regency. The one major exception was Annam. In 1666 the regents sent an edict to the king of Annam
which accused the Annamese of providing sanctuary and perhaps even
supplies to pirates who had raided the coast of Kwangtung. In their edict
the regents promised war if the pirates were not turned over to Ch'ing
authorities; the edict concluded:

> Today we issue this special Imperial Edict and you must obey it
> completely. Immediately search out Yang Er, Yang San, and Huang
> Ming-piao, along with their families, as well as Hsi Piao and his
> wife and children, and hand them all over to the governor-general
> of Kwangtung-Kwangsi. In addition you are to search out and punish
> all those who committed the crime of offering aid to the enemy. If
> you do not apprehend the pirates and hand them over, and if you do
> not punish your subordinate officials, we fear that this will be a
> cause for war and you should consider this.[23]

21. Wills, pp. 272-73.

22. KH Shih-lu, ch. 11, p. 3b. The most forceful statement of the "no tribute, no trade" rule in the Oboi period came in May 1668 (KH Shih-lu, ch. 25,
p. 22a). In this entry in the "Veritable Records" it was noted that both the Dutch
and the Siamese were allowed to trade once in 1664, but those were the only devi-
ations from the rule which were cited. See Fairbank and Teng, Ch'ing Administration, p. 140.

One of the reasons that the regents were firm on the "no tribute, no trade"
rule was that they wished to maintain the tactic of prohibiting maritime trade as
a weapon against the Chengs. The regents may not have shared the usual Chinese
bias against commercialism and might well have relaxed the commercial prohibitions had it not been for the Cheng threat along the coast. On this matter and on
early Ch'ing commercialism in general, see Wills, pp. 23-24; Mancall, "Ch'ing
Tribute System," pp. 85-89.

23. KH Shih-lu, ch. 19, pp. 4a-b.

The king of Annam apparently handed over the pirates, and afterwards the regents had little trouble with Annam or any other East or Southeast Asian tributary country.[24]

Relations with the Dutch and Portuguese

In contrast to the Asian tributary countries, the Dutch and Portuguese aroused considerable concern in Peking.[25] From the Manchu point of view these western merchants constituted a nuisance if not an actual threat to the Ch'ing regime. The Dutch and the Portuguese, untutored in the system of tributary relations, were the only foreigners who dared to seek unlimited commercial privileges. To have permitted regular nontributary trade with these two groups would not only have destroyed the superior-inferior relationship implied in the tributary arrangement, but it might also have opened the floodgates of commercialism to other Asian countries.

Various acts committed by these foreigners intensified the Manchu reluctance to permit such trade with the Dutch and the Portuguese. During the late Ming period, Portuguese merchants, like the Jesuit fathers, offered military assistance to Ming troops in their defense against the Manchu conquerors. Such military aid, particularly in the making and use of cannon, raised Manchu doubts about the peaceful intentions of the foreigners.[26] In the 1650s, moreover, the Dutch negotiated with the arch-enemy of the Manchu house, Cheng Ch'eng-kung, and actually obtained from Cheng a license to trade in return for payments of money and military supplies.[27] Furthermore, Dutch attacks on coastal towns in Chekiang and Fukien, particularly their sacking of P'u-t'o-shan in 1655, reminded the Manchus of previous western brutalities committed in the Ming period.[28]

24. There is no further reference to these pirates in the "Veritable Records," but the matter seems to have been resolved, since two years later Annam was permitted to send regular tributary missions (KH Shih-lu, ch. 26, p. 7b).

There were also minor difficulties with the Koreans during the 1660s. In 1663 a Korean embassy brought along some cloth which had not been registered before arriving in Peking. Although the embassy was permitted to remain in the capital city, its trading privileges were cancelled (KH Shih-lu, ch. 8, pp. 4b-5a). In 1664 a document was sent to the king of Korea prohibiting Koreans from digging ginseng in Manchuria (KH Shih-lu, ch. 11, pp. 13b-14a).

25. On the background to Sino-Portuguese relations in the early Ch'ing period, see Boxer, South China in the Sixteenth Century, pp. xix-xxxvii; Chang T'ien-tse, Sino-Portuguese Trade, pp. 32-141; Wills, pp. 16-21. For documents relating to Sino-Portuguese trade during the Shun-chih reign, see Fu Lo-shu, Documentary Chronicle, 1: 6-9. On the background to Sino-Dutch relations, see Wills, pp. 58-187.

26. Wills, pp. 21-22.

27. See Yang Ying quoted in Fu Lo-shu, Documentary Chronicle, 1: 21-22. John Wills, Jr., has noted that the Dutch fleet sent to China in 1663 received orders that if the alliance with the Ch'ing could not be effected, the Dutch might ally with the Cheng rebels on Quemoy and Amoy against both the Ch'ing and against Cheng Ching on Taiwan (Wills, pp. 163-67).

28. Wills, pp. 269-70, 305-7.

The regents' policies on the China coast and their anti-Jesuit campaign added new fervor to the Manchu mistrust of the Dutch and the Portuguese. In the first few years of the regency, the Portuguese found that they were subject to the prohibition against maritime trade. Although the Jesuit Adam Schall managed to convince the regents in 1662 that the Macao population need not be transported inland, the garrison guarding Macao was doubled and rice rations were brought into Macao only a few times a month.[29] The regents' campaign against the Jesuit missionaries, under the prodding of the fanatic Yang Kuang-hsien, strengthened Manchu measures against all Westerners in China. As the 1660s wore on, both the Portuguese and the Dutch merchants found their limited relations with Manchu China increasingly curtailed. Let us look separately at the Dutch and the Portuguese during the Oboi years.

The Dutch had entered into the previously mentioned military alliance with the Ch'ing in 1663 primarily for the purpose of gaining trading rights along the coast. Initially the regents were willing to reward the Dutch for their services, not as the fulfillment of a bargain between equals, but rather as an expression of imperial gratitude for barbarian aid. In early 1664 an imperial rescript permitted the Dutch to trade "once in every two years," and in July 1664 the Dutch were given presents of silver and satin in recognition of their military assistance in 1663.[30] These commercial concessions to the Dutch, however, applied only to tributary trade and did not sanction open trade along the coast. The Dutch merchants were irate. They became even more angry when in late 1664 the Ch'ing admiral Shih Lang failed to carry out the proposed Sino-Dutch expedition to retake Taiwan. Although during 1664-65 the Dutch continued to carry on clandestine trade with provincial authorities in Fukien, the Dutch dreams of free trade and the restitution of their position on Taiwan were shattered.[31]

In 1665 and 1666, as the anti-Jesuit movement gained momentum, the regents adopted harsh policies towards the Dutch. Inspectors were sent from Peking to assure that the prohibitions on maritime trade were enforced. Officials accompanied the Dutch boats when they traveled in Chinese waterways, and the Dutch were forced to obtain special passes every time they went up the Min River to Foochow.[32] Finally, in March 1666, the regents revoked the biennial trading privilege on the grounds that "if we permit them to come and go frequently, they will probably cause trouble."[33]

---

29. Fu Lo-shu, "Two Portuguese Embassies," pp. 75-79; Bowra, "Manchu Conquest of Canton," p. 230.

30. Fu Lo-shu, Documentary Chronicle, 1:33. On the background to the regents' decision to grant the Dutch trading rights in early 1664, see Wills, pp. 223-26. On the material rewards granted to the Dutch in July 1664, see KH Shih-lu, ch. 12, p. 15b.

31. Wills, pp. 238-61, 310-14.

32. Ibid., pp. 264-65.

33. KH Shih-lu, ch. 18, pp. 6a-b.

The Dutch were stunned by what they saw as a Manchu betrayal of the bargain transacted in 1663, but they resolved to negotiate with the Ch'ing once again. In 1667 the Dutch sent a diplomatic mission to Peking under the guidance of Pieter van Hoorn, a Batavia bureaucrat and councillor. Van Hoorn was instructed by the Batavia Council to seek free trade through negotiations in Peking and was given 10,000 taels in silver to bribe officials to grant commercial concessions. The van Hoorn embassy arrived in Peking in June 1667 and remained in the imperial capital for two months.[34]

With respect to the main intent of the van Hoorn embassy—the negotiation of free trade—the Dutch were completely disappointed. The Manchu court treated the embassy not as a special diplomatic mission, but rather as a tributary delegation. In the "Veritable Records" there is only the following short reference to the van Hoorn embassy, dated 7 July 1667: "The Dutch King of Batavia [Ka-lo-pa], John Maatzuiker [Yu-fan Ma-sui-chi] sent subordinate officials to present tributary goods. They were given feasts and gifts according to precedents."[35] Being categorized as a tribute mission, the Dutch were merely treated to the usual rituals and permitted to sell their excess gifts in Peking. They were admitted to one imperial audience but were not afforded an opportunity to speak privately with the emperor, his regents, or other high officials on the matter of trading rights.

After the abortive van Hoorn embassy, the Dutch East India Company waited seventeen years before the Ch'ing ban on maritime trade was finally lifted. During those years the only Dutch trade along the China coast was conducted by merchants independent of the Dutch East India Company, and even that trade was limited to infrequent visits to the port of Canton. When the K'ang-hsi Emperor finally lifted the prohibition on maritime trade in 1684 after the conquest of Taiwan, Dutch interest in the Chinese trade had begun to decline. In particular, the demand for Chinese silk in the Netherlands had dwindled, and the more efficient British East India Company was able to sell Chinese goods on the Continent at lower prices than the Dutch.[36]

The Portuguese experience during the Oboi period was even more

---

34. All the information which follows on the Van Hoorn embassy, unless otherwise cited, is from the excellent description in Wills, pp. 349-91. Wills has noted that the Dutch embassy aroused considerable interest in Peking. The two remaining regents, Oboi and Ebilun, and the K'ang-hsi Emperor himself inspected the goods and the animals which the Dutch had brought with them. The young emperor was particularly fascinated with the Dutch horses, while Oboi was more interested in the possibility of purchasing Dutch goods and sent a eunuch to inquire whether the Dutch wished to sell any cloth or coral. Van Hoorn, wanting to avoid illicit trade, said that the Batavian authorities had forbidden him to sell anything.

35. KH Shih-lu, ch. 22, p. 10a. The transliteration of names is taken from Fu Lo-shu, Documentary Chronicle, 1:40. See also HTSL, ch. 503, pp. 4a-5a (pp. 11763-64).

36. On Sino-Dutch relations in the 1670s and 1680s, see Wills, pp. 406-558.

painful than that of the Dutch. Unlike the Dutch, the Portuguese lacked
an armed merchant fleet to offer to the Manchus in return for trading
concessions. The Portuguese settlement at Macao, moreover, was a
base for many of the foreign missionaries in China and consequently '
came under attack during the Manchu persecutions of the Jesuits. In the
mid-1660s the Manchu court once again considered applying the coastal
evacuation policy to Macao. The Portuguese residents were able to remain at Macao only after bribing the governor-general of Kwangtung-
Kwangsi, Lu Hsing-tsu, with the sum of 20,000 ducats. After Lu Hsing-
tsu obtained permission for the Macao settlement to remain, the Portuguese enraged the governor-general by insisting that the bribe would
not be paid unless the trade restrictions were revoked. Lu responded
by locking the Kuan-cha gate, which controlled passage from Macao to
the rest of Kwangtung.[37] The governor of Kwangtung, Wang Lai-jen,
who was sympathetic to the Portuguese plight, drew up a memorial in
which he described the situation at Macao: "Every few days the gate
was opened to allow them to buy consumer goods. Extortionate prices
were charged. . . . The total population at Hsing-shan and Macao a-
mounted to tens of thousands and when their communications with the
Interior were severed, their means of making a living disappeared.
They were very miserable!"[38]

Conditions at Macao became so desperate that the Portuguese called
upon the authorities at Goa to send an ambassador to Peking to ask the
emperor for rights to navigation and open travel to the mainland. In
1667 Manuel de Saldanha was sent from Goa and arrived with his entourage of ninety persons at Canton in November of that year. Unfortunately de Saldanha was detained at Canton by Chinese bureaucratic procedures for three years; during this time he had to draw upon the limited
supplies at Macao to support himself and his aides. By the time the embassy reached Peking in 1670, the Oboi regime had been dismissed, the
campaign against the Jesuits discontinued, and the coastal prohibitions
relaxed. The Jesuit fathers, Buglio and Verbiest, thus advised de Saldanha not to make any complaint about former conditions at Macao since
most of the problems had been alleviated. The Portuguese ambassador,
therefore, spoke to the K'ang-hsi Emperor about the Portuguese depri-
vations only once, and the young emperor replied, "I had already known
this."[39]

37. Fu Lo-shu, "Two Portuguese Embassies," pp. 77-79.

38. Translation of Chiang Jih-sheng in Fu Lo-shu, Documentary Chronicle,
1: 40.

39. Fu Lo-shu, "Two Portuguese Embassies," p. 87. On the de Saldanha
embassy in general, see ibid., pp. 79-87.

Sino-Russian diplomatic relations have not been covered in this section because there were no Russian embassies in Peking during the Oboi period. The
Perfilieff and Albin mission left Peking in 1660, and the next Russian embassy
did not arrive until October 1669.

THE OBOI REGENCY AND MANCHURIA

In many respects the regents' Manchurian policies provide a fitting conclusion to our treatment of their policies as a whole. Manchuria was the
regents' homeland, and it received special attention in the 1660s. By
posing a wide array of political, economic, and military challenges, Manchuria was a tough test for the regents, and it revealed many of their
characteristics as statesmen.

The regents and the K'ang-hsi Emperor both viewed Manchuria as
two broadly defined segments differing in race, culture, and geographical nature. The southernmost area of Manchuria, comprising what is
now Liaoning Province (formerly called Fengtien Province or Liaotung
Province), was settled mainly by Chinese and constituted the northernmost zone of Chinese culture and Chinese agrarian economy. The symbolic delineation of southern Manchuria was the famous willow palisade
planted by the Ming and revived by the Ch'ing. The willow palisade extended from the mouth of the Yalu River in a semicircle north of Mukden
and then southward a few miles inland of the China coast to Shanhaikwan.
In this area Nurhaci and Abahai had staged their military operations
prior to the taking of Peking in 1644. The early Ch'ing rulers, including
the regents, thus realized the strategic importance of southern Manchuria and kept this area under strong military surveillance. But recognizing the fact that economically and culturally southern Manchuria was an
extension of the Chinese tradition, the regents also endeavored to bring
this region into the regular provincial administration.

Beyond the willow palisade to the north as far as the Amur River
was an immense geographical area sparsely populated by tribes of Tungusic and Mongol stock. Long before the Manchus conquered China,
they had extended their authority throughout much of northern Manchuria.
The K'ang-hsi Emperor and his regents were committed to maintaining
the Manchu hold over this large portion of Manchuria. In northern Manchuria the regents faced two major problems. First of all, some sort
of governmental apparatus had to be established in order to maintain
control over the tribal peoples. Since the ethnic composition of northern Manchuria was diverse and was further complicated by the advent
of Chinese settlements (fur trappers, ginseng diggers, and political
exiles), the regents were pressed to establish a viable governmental
system which would provide both control and unity. Secondly, the regents faced a military challenge in northern Manchuria from Russian
cossacks in search of trade and loot.

A Governmental System for Southern Manchuria

During the 1630s and 1640s southern Manchuria had been the staging
area for the conquest of China. From his capital at Mukden Abahai expanded the banner bureaucracy, developed the Council of Deliberative
Officials, and created new agencies of civil administration (including the
Manchu six boards, the Inner Three Departments, and the Li-fan yüan).

But with the conquest in 1644, the Mukden bureaucracy was transferred to Peking, leaving only a garrison commander to govern all of Manchuria. In 1653 an embryonic civil administration was created in southern Manchuria as the entire Liaotung region was designated Liao-yang prefecture (Feng-t'ien prefecture after 1657). In 1658-59 Mukden became a secondary capital for the Ch'ing dynasty, and three of the six boards were reestablished (the boards of Rites, Revenue, and Works). [40]

When the regents came to power in 1661, therefore, they inherited a skeletal administration in southern Manchuria composed of a few Manchu officials and lacking a clear definition of responsibilities. To rectify the situation, the regents expanded the governmental apparatus in this region. First of all, they established the post of military governor of Fengtien (Feng-t'ien chiang-chün). The new military governor, who replaced the former garrison commander was to have the ultimate responsibility for both civil and military affairs throughout southern Manchuria. The military governor was designated as commissioner in charge of Fengtien prefectural affairs (chien-kuan Feng-t'ien fu-yin shih-wu ta-ch'en), as the chief figure in the management of matters pertaining to the banner system in Fengtien, and as supervisor of the Mukden boards. [41] In the Oboi regency, and throughout the early Ch'ing period, all Fengtien military governors were Manchus. This new system was quite different from the tu-fu arrangement in the regular Chinese provinces. Under the tu-fu system civil and military authority was delegated to two individuals, a governor and a governor-general, who had overlapping powers and who served to check the actions of each other. In addition, one will recall that most of the tu-fu in the early Ch'ing period were Chinese bannermen and relatively few were Manchus. The military governorship of Fengtien, on the other hand, brought all responsibilities into

---

40. Information on the development of the civil and military administration of southern Manchuria in the early Ch'ing period is found in: Sheng-ching t'ung-chih, ch. 19-20, passim; Lee, Manchurian Frontier, pp. 59-77. Manchu captains of the Plain Yellow and Plain White Banners were also appointed in Mukden beginning in the reign of the reign of the Shun-chih Emperor. See Sheng-ching t'ung-chih, ch. 20, pp. 17a-18b.

41. See Lee, Manchurian Frontier, pp. 61-63. The Board of Punishments was added to the Mukden ministries in 1662 and the Board of War in 1691; the only board which was permanently omitted from the Mukden bureaucracy was that of Civil Office. See Sheng-ching t'ung-chih, ch. 19-20, passim; du Halde (trans. R. Brookes), 4: 89-90.

Robert Lee has argued that the existence of the five Mukden Boards tended to check the authority of the military governor because of the heavy overlap in their responsibilities and because the Mukden board vice-presidents were subordinate to the board presidents in Peking as well as to the military governor (Lee, Manchurian Frontier, pp. 61-63). While this was certainly the case in the latter part of the seventeenth century and throughout the eighteenth century, I have found no evidence to support this contention during the Oboi period. From all appearances, the military governor was the dominant figure in the 1660s with the Mukden boards playing a distinctly subordinate role.

the hands of one man who was a Manchu. By establishing this post, therefore, the regents had recognized the special strategic importance of southern Manchuria and had sought to preserve the security of this region by concentrating power in Manchu hands.[42]

As a second step to reform the government of southern Manchuria, the regents developed the regular system of Chinese local government beneath the military governor of Fengtien. As mentioned previously, the only semblance of traditional local government in Manchuria before the Oboi regency was in Fengtien prefecture. In the other major cities of southern Manchuria, including T'ieh-ling, Chin-chou, Ning-yüan, Kuangning, and Ho-hsi, the highest official was a military officer, usually a captain, who commanded a garrison and who was entrusted with preserving local order.[43] In January 1662 the Fengtien prefect, Chang Shanghsien, memorialized that this system was unsatisfactory. In particular Chang noted that the population registers were improperly kept and only a small percentage of the residents of southern Manchuria were taxpayers. As a remedy, Chang suggested that all of Chinese Manchuria be divided into prefectures, departments, and districts on the model of the regular provincial administration.[44] The regents, after deliberation with the Board of Civil Office, followed the suggestions in Chang Shang-hsien's memorial. The city of Mukden was designated as the capital district (hsien) of Fengtien prefecture. Other key cities in southern Manchuria became capitals of prefectures and districts. As in the rest of China, both regular Chinese and Chinese bannermen were appointed to the newly established posts of prefects and magistrates.[45]

This system of government established under the regency was perpet-

42. A list of the officials appointed as military governors and deputy military governors during the Oboi period is available in Sheng-ching t'ung-chih, ch. 20, passim. See also Yang Pin, Liu-pien chi-lüeh, ts'e 117, pp. 7a-b. In 1657 a deputy military governor had been appointed at Mukden. Three years later, Wuk'u-li, who was appointed the first military governor of Fengtien in 1662, was sent to Mukden with the title of ang-pang chang-ching. It is unclear whether or not Wu-k'u-li performed the same tasks as the military governor before he received the title in 1662. A careful analysis of the "powers and responsibilities of the military governor" is found in Lee, Manchurian Frontier, pp. 63-71.

43. For a list of Fengtien prefects in the Shun-chih and K'ang-hsi periods, see Sheng-ching t'ung-chih, ch. 20, pp. 19a-b. Two districts, Hai-ch'eng and Liao-yang, were established under the Fengtien prefecture in the 1650s. See ibid., ch. 20, passim.

Prior to 1644 the various cities of southern Manchuria were governed under the Ming commandery system. After 1644 the commandery system was abolished in most of these cities and replaced by a garrison of Manchu troops under captains. For an example of the evolution of local government in southern Manchuria, see T'ieh-ling hsien-chih, ch. 3, pp. 8a-10b.

44. KH Shih-lu, ch. 5, p. 17a.

45. Ibid., ch. 11, p. 23a, and ch. 12, p. 10b; HTSL, ch. 23, p. 1b (p. 5347), and ch. 30, pp. 2b-3b (pp. 5441-42); Sheng-ching t'ung-chih, ch. 20, passim, and ch. 35, pp. 1b-2a. For the application of these changes to various areas in south-

uated through the Manchu dynasty until 1907, when the post of military governor was scrapped in favor of the tu-fu arrangement.[46] By placing authority in the hands of a Manchu military governor, the regents underscored their concern for the security of southern Manchuria. But by bringing the local administration into the sphere of regular provincial government, the regents not only recognized the sinification of this region, but also increased central control over such operations as tax collection.

Governmental Control in Northern Manchuria

In contrast to the ethnic unity of southern Manchuria, northern Manchuria was populated by tribes of Tungusic, Mongol, or mixed origins.[47] During the first four decades of the seventeenth century the Manchus under Nurhaci and Abahai had gained the allegiance of most of these tribal peoples either through conquest or diplomacy. Those tribes which submitted to the Manchu conquerors were tied to the Ch'ing ruling house through a number of relationships: feudal military alliances, intermarriage of tribal and Manchu clans, inclusion in the banner system, and tributary missions.[48] In spite of these contacts, the early Ch'ing rulers were fearful that the tribes of northern Manchuria might stray from the Ch'ing fold and challenge the Manchu dynasty in China just as the Manchus had challenged the Ming. Some sort of permanent governmental apparatus had to be devised to assure the continuation of Ch'ing control.

Another incentive for increasing Ch'ing control over northern Manchuria was the advent of Russian cossacks in the region of the Amur and Sungari Rivers. The Russian military and commercial expansion toward the Siberian frontier began in the late sixteenth century and was accelerated by the establishment of the Romanov house in Moscow in 1613. As various Russian cossack groups moved towards the east, they established fortified posts (ostrogs) at such towns as Irkutsk, Okhotsk, and Nerchinsk. From these fortified posts the Russian military adventurers led expeditions into the wilderness in search of trade with the native tribes. During the 1640s and 1650s several Russian expeditions penetrated deep into northern Manchuria along the Amur and the Sungari. One expedition, led by a cossack named Yarka Pavlov Khabarof, plundered town after

---

ern Manchuria, see Liao-yang hsien-chih, ch. 18, p. 9b; K'ai-p'ing hsien-chih, ch. 1, p. 47a; Shen-yang hsien-chih, ch. 2, p. 2b.

As an example of the appointments to the newly established local posts, let us look at Chin-chou prefecture. There was one prefect in Chin-chou during the Oboi period; he was a regular Chinese official from Chihli. There were ten magistrates appointed to the three hsien under the jurisdiction of Chin-chou prefecture during these same years. Of these, five were regular Chinese officials and five were Chinese bannermen (Sheng-ching t'ung-chih, ch. 42, passim).

46. BH, pp. 384-86.

47. On the ethnic composition of Manchuria, see Lattimore, Manchuria, pp. 32-35.

48. Lee, Manchurian Frontier, pp. 24-58.

town along these rivers, stole grain and goods from the natives, and massacred tribesmen who offered resistance. Another expedition, sent from Siberia in 1654 under Stepanof, followed Khabarof's route and continued the Russian pillage of northern Manchuria. [49]

During the early part of the Shun-chih reign, Ch'ing military strength in northern Manchuria was weakened by the deployment of most of the banner forces in the Manchu conquest of China. Not until the early 1650s was there any significant Manchu effort to ward off the Russian encroachments and to increase military control in northern Manchuria. In the years between 1652 and 1656 small detachments of banner troops were sent to the Amur valley where they engaged in several encounters with the cossacks. Although these banner contingents impeded the Russian advance, they were unable to win decisive victories or to drive the cossacks back to their Siberian bases. In 1657, therefore, the Manchu court established a permanent Ch'ing garrison at the frontier city of Ninguta (now called Ning-an). The commander appointed to this post was Šarhūda, a Manchu of the Bordered Blue Banner. In 1658 Šarhūda led his garrison troops against the Russians. The cossacks suffered a major defeat and withdrew to the ostrog at Nerchinsk. [50]

When Šarhūda died in 1659, his son, Bahai, succeeded him as commander of the Ninguta garrison. Bahai soon proved a talented military leader. In 1660 Bahai's troops clashed with a Russian expedition at the juncture of the Sungari and Amur Rivers. According to the report submitted to Peking by Bahai:

> We concealed our warships along both banks of the river. When the enemy boats arrived, we came out of our hiding and the enemy immediately retreated. Our troops pursued them and the enemy deserted their ships and attempted to flee along the shore. We beheaded more than sixty of the enemy and a great number of them drowned. Forty-seven women were captured. We also took firearms, shields, armor, and other implements of war. [51]

After this Ch'ing victory in 1660 Russian incursions were curtailed for several years, and the regents turned their attention to the consolidation of Ch'ing control over northern Manchuria.

---

49. See Mancall, Russia and China, pp. 9-64; Chen, Sino-Russian Relations, pp. 1-45.

50. Chen, Sino-Russian Relations, pp. 41-45. On the development of the garrison at Ninguta, see Fu Lo-shu, Documentary Chronicle, 2: 426 n 40; Yang Pin, Liu-pien chi-ltteh, ch. 1, p. 2a; Golder, Russian Expansion, pp. 38-49. For official records of the development of Ninguta and of Sino-Russian encounters in the 1650s, see SC Shih-lu, ch. 68, p. 24a, and ch. 119, pp. 4b-5a.

51. SC Shih-lu, ch. 138, p. 16a. Biographies of Bahai in Hummel, pp. 14-15; CSK, ch. 249, pp. 2a-3a; KCCH, ch. 267, pp. 3b-5a. Apparently Bahai concealed some losses of garrison troops when writing the above-mentioned memorial and he was later deprived of his hereditary rank of baron in punishment (Hummel, p. 14).

In 1662 the regents appointed Bahai as military governor at Ninguta (Ning-ku-t'a chiang-chün) with the same powers as the military governor of Fengtien to the south. Under Bahai's tenure as military governor (1662-81) major steps were taken to bring northern Manchuria firmly under Ch'ing dominion. The new presence of a strong garrison at Ninguta increased Manchu surveillance of the various tribes in the area and permitted the Ch'ing to respond quickly to tribal rebellions and foreign invasions. Bahai, moreover, followed the Ch'ing pattern of dividing Mongolian tribes into banners and applied that system to several tribes in northern Manchuria. The tribes included in Bahai's banner system were organized into regular companies which were expected to provide military assistance for Ch'ing operations in Manchuria. These tribes received the name "New Manchus" (Hsin Man-chou), thus stressing their close relationship to the Ch'ing dynasty. The regents also designated Ninguta as the primary city for receiving tributary embassies from tribes in northern Manchuria. By requiring tribal envoys to travel to Ninguta, the regents not only assured regular contact with native leaders but also prevented the envoys from taking their tribute to Peking, where they might have posed a security problem. [52]

Another important step taken under the regency to augment Manchu control in northern Manchuria was the encouragement of Chinese immigration into this region. During the Shun-chih reign and the Oboi period, Chinese political criminals were regularly sent into northern Manchurian exile. In the 1660s, moreover, Chinese were given land, seeds, and oxen by the Manchu government if they chose to move to Manchuria. Other Chinese went to Manchuria for commercial reasons, to trade small goods, trap furs, or dig ginseng. Although there seem to be no accurate census figures to measure the movement of Chinese to Manchuria during the early Ch'ing period, the emigration seems to have been considerable, and large settlements of Chinese were established around the towns of Ninguta and Kirin.

The apparent reasons for the regents' desire to increase the Chinese population in Manchuria were both economic and military. They hoped to develop agricultural and commercial activity in northern Manchuria with an eye to expanding the revenues of the dynasty. Militarily the Chinese settlements in Manchuria were also an asset. When the Russians attacked in 1668, all Chinese exiles in Manchuria under the age of sixty sui were mobilized and all Chinese settlements were ordered to provide supplies. [53]

52. On the development of the New Manchus and on tributary relations with the Mongol tribes of northern Manchuria, see Lee, Manchurian Frontier, pp. 41-58; Hummel, p. 14; KH Shih-lu, ch. 11, p. 9a.

53. A translation of Wu Chen-ch'en's account of preparations of the Chinese for the Russian attack of 1668 is found in Fu Lo-shu, Documentary Chronicle, 1: 41-42. On the matter of Chinese being encouraged to settle in Manchuria during the early Ch'ing period, see Lee, Manchurian Frontier, pp. 78-79; Ho, Studies on the Population, p. 158. In 1668 the K'ang-hsi Emperor reversed this policy

In addition to all the above-mentioned techniques for increasing the Manchu hold over northern Manchuria, the regents continued the Shun-chih campaign to halt the Russian advance. Twice during the Oboi regency, in 1665 and again in 1668, Bahai led garrison troops from Ningu-ta up the Sungari and Amur rivers and defeated bands of Russian cos-sacks.[54] But while these Ch'ing victories helped to stave off Russian encroachments and to provide security for native tribes, the military operations in northern Manchuria during the 1660s amounted to a hold-ing action. The regents refrained from taking the offensive against the Russian cossacks. It was not until the late 1670s and the early 1680s that the Manchus embarked on a full-scale campaign to drive the Rus-sians completely out of the Amur area. In the years between 1676 and 1684 the K'ang-hsi Emperor sent large numbers of troops to Manchuria, trained a navy for river warfare, and moved the Manchurian headquar-ters to Kirin (closer to the Siberian border than Ninguta). Then in 1685–86 the Ch'ing troops moved up the Amur and forced the Russians to re-treat from their posts at Albazin and Nerchinsk. Eventually the Russian czar agreed to negotiate with the Chinese, and these negotiations resulted in the famous Treaty of Nerchinsk (1689).

The regents, in their Manchurian policies, had acted with vigor, but once again their record was overshadowed by the K'ang-hsi Emperor. To the historian, however, the regents' policies toward their homeland seem to summarize their general approach to policymaking. Suspicious in dealing with foreigners; aggressive in defending the borders; conser-vative in starting foreign wars; stubborn in defending Manchu interests; and inventive in reforming governmental institutions—all of these char-acteristics were apparent in their Manchurian policies.

---

and prohibited further Chinese emigrations to Manchuria (Lee, Manchurian Fron-tier, pp. 78-115; Ho, Studies on the Population, pp. 157-59).

54. Chen, Sino-Russian Relations, pp. 45-46; Golder, Russian Expansion, pp. 53-56; Fu Lo-shu, Documentary Chronicle, 1:39-43; Yang Pin, Liu-pien chi-lüeh, ch. 1, p. 12a.

8   Factionalism and the End of the Oboi Regency

In the preceding several chapters we have focused on the regents as a collective group, seeking to determine the characteristics of the Joint Regents' faction by examining their major policies over the years of 1661-66. The Joint Regents' faction, however, was but the first of three powerful factions which dominated Ch'ing politics in the 1660s. In our treatment of the matter of factionalism, the term faction will be used to denote a small political group whose distinguishing characteristic is an expression of similar attitudes and/or a commitment to similar goals. The term will be applied to all such groups whether their membership is Manchu, Chinese, or both. It will be applied whether their organization is formal or informal, legal or illegal. Above all, the term faction is not to connote good or evil, but rather to describe a particular political phenomenon.[1] Following this definition, then, the three major factions of the 1660s were the Joint Regents' faction, the Oboi faction, and the Songgotu-Mingju faction.

The Oboi faction emerged rapidly in the mid-1660s, and by 1667 Oboi himself was able to eliminate the influence of the other regents and to manipulate the metropolitan and military establishments by appointing his family and followers to important posts. The Oboi faction, unlike the Joint Regents' faction of which Oboi had been a significant member, did not attempt to represent the broader interests of the Manchu community but instead concentrated on the fulfillment of the bold and selfish aspirations of his small coterie of supporters.

One might well wonder just what Oboi and his associates expected to gain from their factional activities. The probable answer is that Oboi expected to run the Ch'ing state for a considerable period of time in place of the emperor himself. With the aid of his followers Oboi intended to fulfill what Mary Wright has called "the imperial role": "the Chinese Emperor was always more important as a function than as a personality. The concurrence of a ritually acceptable Emperor and a group of capable officials was enough."[2] Hoping that the young K'ang-hsi Emperor would be inactive for several years, perhaps even permanently, Oboi sought to have all of the prestige and power of an emperor while lacking only

---

1. For an excellent discussion of the traditional use of the term factionalism in Chinese history and of the development of factionalism in the early Ch'ing period, see Nivison, "Ho-shen and His Accusers," pp. 218-32.
2. Wright, Last Stand of Chinese Conservatism, p. 50.

the title. It was a dangerous gamble, but one which promised enormous financial and political rewards if it succeeded.

Unfortunately for Oboi and his following, the K'ang-hsi Emperor was much more than a ritually acceptable figure, and even as a young boy he began to display qualities of exceptional leadership. In the late 1660s he stepped forward as a forceful heir to the Ch'ing dynasty. Relying on a small group of supporters, led by Songgotu and Mingju, the K'ang-hsi Emperor began to assert his influence and to exhibit his brand of leadership, continuing to protect Manchu traditions while trying to conciliate dissident Chinese subjects. In the last years of the 1660s a fierce contest between the Oboi faction and the Songgotu-Mingju faction dominated the court at Peking. At stake was the leadership and the future of the Manchu dynasty.

THE FRAGMENTATION OF THE JOINT REGENTS' FACTION AND THE HARBINGERS OF THE OBOI FACTION, 1665-1666

Well before the full-scale emergence of the Oboi faction in 1667, tensions had developed within the Joint Regents' faction. Oboi tried to become primus inter pares, increasing his personal power while still assisting the other regents in the joint formulation of policy. By the middle of the 1660s, as was mentioned above, Oboi had already appointed several of his family and associates to posts within the banner hierarchy. The fragmentation of the Joint Regents' faction and the transition to the Oboi faction were greatly accelerated by two major developments: the appointment of Soni's granddaughter as Empress of the K'ang-hsi Emperor in 1665 and the banner relocation affair of 1666-67.

The Hsiao-ch'eng Empress

Since the main focus of this study has been the policies of the regents themselves, we have had little occasion since the introductory chapter to refer to developments within the Forbidden City. After the Grand Empress Dowager Hsiao-chuang assisted the regents in the forgery of the Shun-chih Will in early 1661, she retired from direct interference in government matters and devoted herself to the child emperor. When the emperor's own mother, the Hsiao-k'ang Empress, died in March 1663, Hsiao-chuang became responsible for the upbringing and education of the K'ang-hsi Emperor, who was then only nine years old. Hsiao-chuang also had the powerful function of making decisions on matters which directly affected the emperor himself. In this role the Grand Empress Dowager could exert her influence on court politics through indirect and often devious channels. On the occasion of the death of the Hsiao-k'ang Empress in 1663, for example, she excused the young boy from participating in the funeral procession to Manchuria and from immediate involvement in the political world; she announced: "The Emperor is young in age. How can he assume the heavy responsibilities left to him by the imperial ancestors? It is not appropriate for him to depart from the

Forbidden City to personally escort the Empress' casket. . . . Although the Emperor is to be spared in accordance with my motherly orders, he still weeps in grief unceasingly."[3] But surely behind this ostensible rationale for keeping the emperor secluded in Peking was the Grand Empress Dowager's desire to prevent the regents and others from prying the emperor away from her control.

One of the important prerogatives of the Grand Empress Dowager was that of offering advice to the emperor on the choice of an empress. During the Shun-chih period, one may recall, the emperor ignored the suggestions of his mother and instead took Hsiao-hsien as his imperial bride. Unlike his father, however, the K'ang-hsi Emperor was fastidious in his adherence to the Chinese virtue of filiality. In October 1665 the Grand Empress Dowager suggested Soni's granddaughter as a possible mate; the marriage ceremony took place on 16 October 1665, and the young girl was given the name, "the Empress Hsiao-ch'eng." The marriage contract, probably written under orders from the Grand Empress Dowager, exalted the new empress and indirectly honored her family:

> She is the virtue, love, and happiness of the generations. She is the beginning of the flowering of the imperial influence. She is tender and beautiful in her entire being. She will proclaim the teachings of feminity throughout the six palaces. She will bring motherly rectitude to the ten thousand countries. Thus I accept the maternal orders of the Empress Dowager and by means of this contract and these gifts I establish her as my Empress.[4]

By arranging this marriage, the Grand Empress Dowager Hsiao-chuang made a substantial impact on the world of Peking politics. First of all, speaking for the emperor himself, she had clearly indicated a preference for Soni over the other regents. As mentioned before, of the four regents Soni was the most experienced in both military and civil matters and seemed to be the most aware of the delicate problems confronting the Ch'ing dynasty. Soni, moreover, advocated the early return of the government to the emperor's personal control.[5] In an edict of 1667, a few months before Soni's death, the elderly regent was singled out as an outstanding servant of the Ch'ing ruling house:

> In the time of T'ai-tsu [Nurhaci] the Regent and Earl Soni was appointed to the Mi-shu yüan where he worked very diligently. Under T'ai-tsung [Abahai] he was entrusted with important matters both

3. KH Shih-lu, ch. 8, pp. 13a-b.
4. Ibid., ch. 16, p. 17a.
5. At the time when the emperor took over personal control of the government in 1667, an entry in the "Veritable Records" noted that Soni requested the emperor to follow this course (ibid., ch. 23, p. 4a).

at the court and abroad. He devoted his abilities to the fullest extent and was totally loyal and honest. When T'ai-tsung died, he remembered fully the gracious treatment he had received from the imperial ancestors. He remained steadfast in his loyalty and did not worry about his own life. He worked diligently for the Imperial House. Under the Shih-tsu Emperor [Shun-chih] he again was entrusted with important matters both at court and abroad and worked with diligence and sincerity.

When Shih-tsu died, because of Soni's diligent and long service as a high official and his constant loyalty and sincerity, he was entrusted with a task of the highest magnitude. In the Imperial Will he was designated as a Regent. He respectfully obeyed the imperial orders and remained loyal and sincere. From morning to night he was loyal and genuine. He devoted his strength to this task.[6]

Secondly, the appointment of the Hsiao-ch'eng Empress marked the beginning of an intimate relationship between Soni's family and the K'ang-hsi Emperor. The Empress Hsiao-ch'eng gave birth to two of the emperor's children. The first, born in 1669, died in infancy. The empress died in 1674 giving birth to the second child, Yin-jeng, who was designated as heir apparent to the Manchu throne.[7] Furthermore, Soni's son, Songgotu (d. 1703), became one of the emperor's most trusted Manchu officials in the latter third of the seventeenth century. Songgotu, initially an imperial bodyguard, was appointed vice-president of the Board of Civil Office in 1668 and a Grand Secretary one year later. He was also a key figure in the purge of the Oboi faction in 1669. During the 1680s, the K'ang-hsi Emperor entrusted him with Sino-Russian diplomatic relations, and Songgotu was one of the two chief negotiators for the Ch'ing at Nerchinsk in 1689.[8]

Thirdly, and most importantly for our purposes, the marriage of the emperor in 1665 had the immediate effect of alienating Oboi and Ebilun. According to the list of crimes drawn up against Oboi and Ebilun in 1669, the appointment of the Hsiao-ch'eng Empress had "filled their hearts with envy and jealousy" and both of them had "dared to submit memorials asking [that this event] be prohibited."[9] In a personal sense, the selec-

---

6. Ibid., ch. 21, pp. 13a-b. Soni was subsequently granted the rank of duke of the first class; although Soni tried to refuse this honor, the emperor insisted that he keep the rank (ibid., ch. 21, pp. 24b-25a, and ch. 22, pp. 1a-b, 4b-5a).

7. Yin-jeng, however, did not succeed to the throne and was eventually degraded and placed in confinement by the K'ang-hsi Emperor. Biography of Yin-jeng in Hummel, pp. 924-25. Biographies of the Hsiao-ch'eng Empress in T'ang, Ch'ing huang-shih ssu-p'u, ch. 2, pp. 10b-11a; Chang Ts'ai-t'ien, Ch'ing lieh-ch'ao hou-fei chuan-kao, ch. shang, pp. 79a-82b. Gabula, the father of the Hsiao-ch'eng Empress, was a chamberlain of the Imperial bodyguard (PCTC [1795], ch. 317, passim; Hummel, p. 664).

8. Hummel, pp. 663-66.

9. KH Shih-lu, ch. 29, pp. 8a-b, 10b.

tion of Soni's granddaughter as empress was an affront to the other regents, who were understandably angry. But politically as well, the imperial wedding had serious implications. The event was the first major
intrusion of the Grand Empress Dowager into court politics since the
death of the Shun-chih Emperor. The growth of imperial influence, particularly in league with Soni and Songgotu, obviously meant the decline
of the political power of the other regents. The advent of the Hsiao-
ch'eng Empress, therefore, intensified the disintegration of the Joint Regents' faction and drove Oboi and the other unfavored regents to more
devious means of retaining power.

As partial compensation for his damaged prestige, Oboi tried his
own version of bedchamber warfare. Early in 1667 Oboi's nephew,
Na-er-tu, the son of Baha, was wed to the second daughter of the Shun-
chih Emperor. Na-er-tu gained the title of Imperial Son-in-law (Hosoi
Efu) and established for the first time a marital tie between Oboi's
relatives and the imperial family. Oboi, who probably contrived this
relationship, had brazenly shown that Soni was not the only regent who
could graft his family onto the imperial tree. But Na-er-tu's wedding
held only superficial satisfaction for Oboi and did not change the balance
of power in Peking. [10]

The Banner Relocation Affair, 1666-1667

Stung by the emperor's marriage in late 1665 and yet confident of the
growing strength of his own faction, Oboi devised a scheme which would
mark a decisive break with the regents Soni and Suksaha, elevate his
status in Manchu ruling circles, and test the power of the Oboi faction.
Essentially, Oboi's plan called for a mass transfer of the troops of his
own banner, the Bordered Yellow, from their military farm lands located
primarily south of Peking to areas in northeastern Chihli then held by
troops of the Plain White Banner. In order to understand the significance
of Oboi's scheme, we must explore the background of banner land allotments.

Before the conquest in 1644, both Nurhaci and Abahai had appropri-
ated farm lands in conquered areas of southern Manchuria and granted
them to imperial princes, military commanders, and to banner troops. [11]
Under this system each of the banners was given a fixed geographical
location on the points of the compass. The most honored position was
the north, presumably because that was the direction of the Manchu home-

10. T'ang, Ch'ing huang-shih ssu-p'u, ch. 4, p. 10a. Na-er-tu was the seventh son of Baha. In 1669, when Baha was degraded along with the others of the
Oboi faction, Na-er-tu was also degraded and returned to the ranks of the commoners. But in 1676 he was exonerated and given the title of Junior Preceptor.
The date of his death is unknown (PCST, ch. 1, p. 6a). The second daughter of
the Shun-chih Emperor was born in 1652. She died at the age of thirty-three sui
in 1685.
11. Mo, Man-tsu shih lun-ts'ung, pp. 106-7.

land, and the two Yellow Banners were placed there. The White Banners were located to the east; the Red Banners, to the west; and the Blue Banners, the least significant of the eight, to the south. [12]

When Dorgon came to Peking in 1644, he faced the task of relocating the thousands of banner troops (wai tso-ling) in farming lands. In order to offer protection to the imperial capital and to keep the bulk of the bannermen under close surveillance, Dorgon decided to grant them plots of land in the metropolitan province of Chihli. Unlike Manchuria, most of Chihli was heavily populated and there were relatively few fertile areas which could be occupied by bannermen without displacing Chinese residents. Dorgon thus resorted to a technique called "land enclosure" (ch'üan-ti) whereby Chinese were forced to vacate their land and homes and were given land grants in other areas of northern China. Major land enclosures occurred three times in the Dorgon regency, and the total amount of land involved amounted to almost a million hsiang (one hsiang equals a little less than an acre). [13]

Dorgon's land enclosures brought strong resentments from both Chinese and Manchu subjects. Chinese often found that their new land was neither as large nor as fertile as their previous property and that they had lost the income from a year's harvest during their move. Manchus suffered because they lacked skill in Chinese agricultural techniques and were sometimes unable to eke out a living on the small and over-cultivated plots in Chihli province. Many bannermen also complained that they were granted land of such poor quality that cultivation was altogether impossible. Although the Chinese had little redress for their grievances, the early Ch'ing rulers endeavored to satisfy the complaints of the Manchu residents. Bannermen were permitted either to hand over their land to the government in return for fixed monthly allowances of money and grain, or they could choose to move to new locations.[14] In 1664, for example, 26,450 banner troops were each granted approximately five acres of new land in various prefectures around Peking. [15]

Another issue which caused distress was Dorgon's departure from the Nurhaci-Abahai system of locating the Eight Banners according to the four cardinal directions. Dorgon himself was a member of the Plain White Banner and consequently placed Plain White bannermen to the ex-

12. Hummel, p. 600; Hsieh Pao-chao, Government of China, pp. 63-64.

13. A good study of the land enclosure question in the early Ch'ing period is Ma, "Manchu-Chinese Social and Economic Conflicts," pp. 335-40. Other accounts are available in Mo, Man-tsu shih lun-ts'ung, pp. 106-9; Hsiao I-shan, 1: 400-402.

14. When bannermen chose to return their land to the state, this land was then either granted to other bannermen who had complained of the quality of their holdings or it was returned to the Chinese (Ma, "Manchu-Chinese Social and Economic Conflicts," p. 339). As time went on, more and more of the banner land fell into Chinese hands, either through the above-mentioned process or by bannermen selling or mortgaging their lands to Chinese farmers (ibid., pp. 349-50).

15. KH Shih-lu, ch. 11, pp. 2b-3a; PCTC (1795), ch. 62, pp. 19b-20b.

treme north and east of Chihli province just below the Great Wall. For his own residence Dorgon chose the town of Yung-p'ing, only fifty miles to the southwest of Shanhaikwan. Not only did the Plain White Banner thus hold the position of honor, but it also controlled access to the major coastal route to Manchuria through the pass at Shanhaikwan. Probably as retribution to those members of the Bordered Yellow Banner who had supported Haoge as the successor to the Manchu throne in 1643, Dorgon allotted the Bordered Yellow Banner only a few areas north of Peking and concentrated most of these bannermen south of Peking in Shun-t'ien, Pao-ting, and Ho-chien prefectures.[16]

Early in 1666 Oboi submitted a memorial which called for a land exchange between the Bordered Yellow and Plain White Banners and additional land enclosures in northeastern Chihli for the Bordered Yellow Banner. Oboi's ostensible justifications for this plan were to rectify the unjust land grants made by Dorgon and to provide those of his own banner with more fertile plots.[17] But behind the surface rationale Oboi had several subtle motives in mind. First, by asserting the superiority of his own banner at the expense of the Plain White, the banner relocation affair would effectively constitute a break with Suksaha, whose banner was the Plain White. Oboi and Suksaha had never been close friends, and, according to the "Veritable Records," they "argued with each other every time that they discussed matters."[18] Secondly, Oboi probably calculated that the banner relocation plan, if successful, would place him in a position remarkably similar to that of the powerful Dorgon. Not only would Oboi's banner hold the ground once held by Dorgon, but Oboi himself would emerge as the dominant figure in the regency just as Dorgon had twenty years earlier. Thirdly, Oboi's scheme was an ideal test case to measure his own strength and that of his faction. If his opposition within the regency, the court, and the imperial apartments was unable to frustrate his blatant and arrogant act, then Oboi could proceed freely to extend his grasp over the Ch'ing government.

During the months of February to May 1666 Oboi tried to force his banner relocation scheme through regular channels in the metropolitan

16. Hummel, p. 600. The actual locations of the two banners were as follows: the Plain White Banner occupied the districts of T'ung-chou, Yung-p'ing, Tsun-hua, San-ho, Feng-jun, Luan-chou, Lo-ting, Chi-chou, and Yü-t'ien; the Bordered Yellow Banner occupied Pao-ting, Ho-chien, Cho-chou, Shun-yi, Mi-yün, Huai-jou, P'ing-ku, Hsiung-hsien, Ta-ch'en, Hsin-an, Jen-chiu, Su-ning, and Jung-ch'eng. These place names have been collected from various entries in the KH Shih-lu and from Hsiao I-shan, 1:394-96. In spite of the fact that the Bordered Yellow Banner was given an inferior position in symbolic terms, it received by far the most land in the allotments of the 1640s. In all the Bordered Yellow Banner received 257,115 hsiang, while the Plain White Banner received only 131,477 hsiang (PCTC [1795], ch. 69, pp. 1a-4a).

17. Oboi's memorial is not available in any of the standard sources, but it is mentioned in KH Shih-lu, ch. 18, pp. 3b-4b.

18. Ibid., ch. 18, p. 4a.

government. From the first he faced stiff resistance. On February 18 the Manchu president of the Board of Revenue, Sunahai, a member of the Plain White Banner and a former member of Dorgon's bodyguard, submitted a memorial of protest: "This land has already been allotted for several years. Moreover, when [bannermen] received commoners' land-holdings in the third year of the K'ang-hsi reign, an imperial rescript was promulgated prohibiting further enclosures. I request that [Oboi's] document concerning the Eight Banners be rejected."[19] For the time being Oboi chose to ignore Sunahai's opposition and instead convened a joint session of the Council of Deliberative Officials, the Nine Ministers, and the Censorate to discuss his proposal. Prince Giyešu, who served as spokesman for the joint session of the three bodies, tried to circumvent Oboi's plan by focusing attention on the land holdings of the Eight Banners in general rather than on the lands held by the Bordered Yellow and Plain White Banners in particular. On February 24 Prince Giyešu announced that there were over 50,000 acres of banner lands which had been inundated by sand or flooded over, and he suggested that metropolitan officials be commissioned to make a careful investigation of the banner lands.[20]

Oboi, seeing an opening in Giyešu's suggestion, created a special banner land investigation commission headed by Prince Wen-ch'i, who evidently had agreed to tailor the commission's report to promote the regent's scheme.[21] On 24 April 1665 Wen-ch'i delivered his obviously biased findings to the court: "We have investigated the lands of each banner which have been rendered impossible to cultivate because of inundation by flood water or by sand. Of these the most unbearable [land] is that of the Bordered Yellow Banner."[22] Oboi, delighted with Wen-chi's report, issued an imperial rescript:

Now the land of each of the banners which cannot be cultivated has been pointed out. On the basis of the memorial of the lieutenant-generals and others which was derived from a personal investigation [we may conclude] that the Bordered Yellow Banner suffers most severely. . . . We must order the Bordered Yellow Banner to move and live in the land which has not yet been enclosed around Yung-p'ing prefecture.[23]

19. Ibid., ch. 18, pp. 4a-b.
20. Ibid., ch. 18, pp. 5a-b.
21. Ibid., ch. 18, p. 5b.
22. Ibid., ch. 18, p. 15a; PCTC (1795), ch. 62, pp. 21a-22a. Wen-ch'i was a prince and a grandnephew of Nurhaci. Wen-ch'i's greatest accomplishments were his military victories in the 1670s in dealing with the Rebellion of the Three Feudatories (CSLC, ch. 3, pp. 34b-35a). On Wen-ch'i's report to the court, see Liu, p. 55.
23. KH Shih-lu, ch. 18, pp. 15b-16a. The details of the land transfer were worked out in a memorial of the Board of Revenue dated 12 May 1666. This docu-

The initial resistance to the regent's plan had failed, and it was apparent that Oboi had pushed the issue through the metropolitan bureaucracy with surprising ease. During the latter half of 1666, however, opposition to Oboi hardened. Three of the officials designated to implement the banner relocation orders endeavored to thwart the regent's design. Board President Sunahai was sent from Peking to oversee the relocation of the two banners, but after a little more than a month he returned without carrying out his orders.[24] The two highest provincial officials in Chihli, Governor-general Chu Ch'ang-tso and Governor Wang Teng-lien, both pursued dilatory tactics and submitted memorials of protest. Chu Ch'ang-tso pointed out the suffering and inequities caused by previous enclosures and transfers:

> With respect to the land which has been transferred or enclosed, there is great variety between that which is fertile and that which is barren. Among the troops there is considerable disagreement about whether their land [grants] are generous or stingy. There is suffering among those impoverished commoners whose land has been enclosed and they complain that they have been left without a livelihood. Their lives are almost empty.[25]

Governor Wang Teng-lien agreed with the governor-general and implored the court to "spare those of the two banners who have lived peacefully and worked in eastern Chihli for a long time and prevent those myriad commoners from moving."[26]

After watching his opponents dominate the stage for several months, Oboi finally resorted to the familiar techniques of purge and terror. On 12 December 1666 he issued an order for the arrest and trial of Sunahai, Chu Ch'ang-tso, and Wang Teng-lien. On January 14 of the following year, the Board of Punishments delivered its verdict: both Chu and Wang were to be flogged a hundred strokes and, except for their concubines, all of their property was to be confiscated.[27] Dissatisfied with the leniency of the Board's decision, Oboi pronounced his own sentence:

---

ment, which was probably written under Oboi's orders, called for a virtual exchange of the lands of the Bordered Yellow and Plain White Banners as well as additional allotments of both populated and unpopulated lands in northern Chihli to the Bordered Yellow Banner. In essence, the Bordered Yellow Banner would keep only its previous holdings in four hsien north of Peking and would occupy all those holdings of the Plain White Banner in northern and northeastern Chihli. The Plain White Banner would then be moved to the former Bordered Yellow Banner areas south of Peking. The pretense of interest in the conditions of the lands of the other banners was dropped as Oboi noted that such matters could be considered at a later date (KH Shih-lu, ch. 18, pp. 18a-19b; PCTC [1795], ch. 62, pp. 22a-23b).

24. KH Shih-lu, ch. 20, pp. 11b-12a.
25. Chu Ch'ang-tso's memorial quoted in Liu, p. 57.
26. CSLC, ch. 6, p. 9b. See also Liu, p. 57.
27. KH Shih-lu, ch. 20, pp. 17a-b.

In the matter of distributing the land, they did not act in accordance
with their commission and they submitted reckless memorials. . . .
All of them have committed crimes of the greatest magnitude. Sunahai, Chu Ch'ang-tso, and Wang Teng-lien are to be immediately executed by strangulation and their property is to be confiscated. [28]

With his primary enemies eliminated, Oboi proceeded to carry out the
banner relocation scheme. During the early months of 1667, 46,000
Bordered Yellow bannermen moved to the north and west of Peking and
resettled on 203,000 hsiang of land formerly held by the Plain White Banner and by unfortunate commoners. At the same time 22,361 troops of
the Plain White Banner were transported southward and occupied 111,805
hsiang below Peking. [29]

In the banner relocation affair, Oboi not only proved his ability to
manipulate the Ch'ing government to his own ends, but he also swept
away the facade of unity within the Joint Regents' faction. Although Suksaha was the obvious victim, the banner transfer augmented the tension
between Oboi and Soni which had grown from the appointment of the Hsiao-
ch'eng Empress. According to one of Soni's biographers, "Soni was extremely upset about this matter; both he and Suksaha saw that Oboi's
power was becoming stronger every day and they could not tolerate this."[30]
But Soni, elderly and infirm, was very close to his death, which occurred
in August 1667. And since Ebilun refrained from opposing Oboi, the only
regent who could muster effective resistence was Suksaha. Before he
dared to confront Suksaha directly, however, Oboi had to expand his political power. The extension of the Oboi faction was the first task.

THE OBOI FACTION AT ITS HEIGHT, 1667-1668

In late March and early April of 1667 the Oboi faction suddenly grasped
some of the most prestigious posts in the empire. On March 16 Bambursan, a grandson of Nurhaci and one of Oboi's closest adherents, was ap-

---

28. Ibid., ch. 20, p. 18a. For other documents relating to the trial and execution of Oboi's opponents in this matter, see ibid., ch. 20, pp. 14b-15b. Two
days after Oboi's verdict was announced, Oboi also made an attack on a man called
Ying-wu-er-tai. Ying-wu-er-tai, who had died several years earlier, had been a
president of the Board of Revenue and had been entrusted with making the original
locations of the banners in Chihli under the Dorgon regency. Furthermore, he
had been a clansman of Sunahai. Consequently, Oboi posthumously stripped Ying-
wu-er-tai of all his ranks and titles (ibid., ch. 20, pp. 18b-19b).

29. Ibid., ch. 20, pp. 20a-b; Ma, "Manchu-Chinese Social and Economic
Conflicts," p. 340. In 1669 the K'ang-hsi Emperor endeavored to rectify the banner relocation cruelties. In an edict to the Board of Revenue, he asked that all
those unjustly removed from their land be permitted to return and that in the future all enclosures of the commoners' land be prohibited (ibid., ch. 30, pp. 8a-
b). Sunahai, Chu Ch'ang-tso, and Wang Teng-lien were all acquitted posthumously,
regular funerary rites were conducted in their memories, and each was given a
title to be inherited by his offspring (ibid., ch. 31, p. 7a).

pointed Grand Secretary of the Department of the Secretariat (Mi-shu yüan).[31] Eight days later, Oboi initiated a full-scale "capital evaluation" (ching-ch'a), and he ordered the removal of four board presidents, six vice-presidents, a sub-chancellor of the Grand Secretariat, a vice-president of the Censorate, and the director of the Court of Judicature and Revision.[32] By this massive purge Oboi not only struck back at former opponents, but he also left openings at the highest levels of the metro-politan bureaucracy which could be filled by his own followers. On March 28 three of the Oboi faction were named as board presidents (Asha, Ka-ch'u-ha, and Marsai), and three became vice-presidents (T'ai-pi-t'u, Mai-yin-ta, and Lodo). On April 1 Ata and Becingge, who later became Oboi's appointees to the governorships of Shansi and Shensi, took over the jobs of director of the Court of Judicature and Revision and director of the Banqueting Court.[33]

Through his former appointments to banner posts and through his metropolitan appointments of March–April 1667, Oboi had moved the dagger of factionalism close to the heart of the imperial government. Over the next two years Oboi used his factional leverage to the fullest, assiduously trying to gain absolute political power as Dorgon had in the 1640s.

According to the list presented in the "Veritable Records," there were thirty-nine men associated with the Oboi faction (including Oboi and Ebilun).[34] Of the thirty-nine, two were Mongols, two were Chinese bannermen (Liu Chih-yüan and Liu Kuang), and the rest were Manchus. Several of the faction were relatives of Oboi: his three brothers (Jobtei, Murma, and Baha), his son (Namfe), three nephews (Foron, Namo, and Sai-pen-te), and two in-laws (La-hu and Lambu). Nine of the Oboi faction were members of the Bordered Yellow Banner, five were designated as Imperial Clansmen, and the rest were scattered among the other seven banners. When the faction was at its strongest (1667-68), the followers of Oboi held an impressive array of positions: one Grand Secretary, one sub-chancellor, four board presidents, three vice-presidents, two governors, eight lieutenant-generals, two deputy lieutenant-generals, three Manchu generals-in-chief, and three chamberlains of the Imperial Body-guard.[35]

30. CSK, ch. 255, p. 3b.

31. KH Shih-lu, ch. 21, p. 9a.

32. Ibid., ch. 21, pp. 12a-b.

33. Ibid., ch. 21, pp. 12b-14a, passim. These sudden appointments to high metropolitan posts marked a change from the 1661-66 period when Oboi had but one follower in these posts. See Appendix 2.

34. The list of those involved in the Oboi faction is taken from KH Shih-lu, ch. 29, pp. 3b-28b, passim. This includes all of those specifically designated as associates of Oboi and all those who participated in the activities of the faction whether or not they were punished for their participation. It is quite possible that the number of members exceeded thirty-nine, but we must rely on the Shih-lu, which is the only solid source on this matter.

35. This information is taken from the biographical sections in CSK, CSLC, KCCH, and PCTC, as well as from the lists of officials in CS and PCTC. In a

These numerical assessments, however, fail to present a complete picture of the nature of the Oboi faction. The group was an informal and loose coalition of men who, either out of family loyalties or self-interest, had chosen to serve the ambitions of the regent Oboi. In the eyes of the commission which later prosecuted the Oboi faction, the real leadership of the group lay in the hands of Oboi and ten other Manchus: Asha, Bambursan, Ebilun, Jobtei, Ka-ch'u-ha, Marsai, Mai-yin-ta, Murma, Saipen-te, and T'ai-pi-t'u. Many of the remaining twenty-eight were implicated only because they had gained high position through Oboi's influence or because they had been involved tangentially in one or another of Oboi's factional activities. A large number of them were obscure and insignificant figures who undoubtedly would have been forgotten in Chinese history had they not been sucked into the whirlpool of factionalism.[36]

The common bond which brought the Oboi faction into a somewhat coherent group was the quest for personal gain and personal power. Power itself, and the very immediate personal prestige and benefits that power could produce, became the goals rather than the tools of the Oboi faction. In order to illustrate the scope of activities undertaken by the Oboi faction, we shall focus on Oboi himself and three of his prominent followers, Ebilun, Bambursan, and Marsai.

The primary source of information about the activities of Oboi during the late 1660s is the record of his crimes compiled in 1669 under the direction of Prince Giyešu.[37] In this document there is a list of thirty transgressions committed by the regent, but these generally fall into two categories: state crimes and personal crimes.

The most heinous of Oboi's state crimes, of course, were his formation of a faction and his interference in government affairs. Major policy decisions, according to Giyešu, were made within this faction itself: "All affairs of state were first privately decided within this group and then their orders were carried out. He took officials of the boards and departments and held private discussions of matters with them before they submitted memorials" (p. 7a). Furthermore, as we have already seen in the banner relocation incident, Oboi would brook no opposition, and he "closed

---

few cases one man held more than one of these posts and thus he is included more than once in these numerical assessments.

Oboi was careful to hold absolute control over his own banner. All three of the lieutenant-generals of the Bordered Yellow Banner were from his faction: Chinese, Liu Chih-ytian and Liu Kuang; Manchu, Murma; and Mongol, T'ai-pi-t'u.

36. KH Shih-lu, ch. 29, pp. 3b-28b, passim. The ten leading members of the Oboi faction, with the exception of Ebilun, Jobtei, Marsai, and Mai-yin-ta, were executed for their crimes.

37. The various crimes of Oboi listed in this section do not include the major crimes such as Oboi's reaction to the appointment of the Hsiao-ch'eng Empress, the banner relocation affair, and the execution of Suksaha. Prince Giyešu cited these, but they have been treated at length elsewhere in this chapter. For the complete list of Oboi's crimes see KH Shih-lu, ch. 29, pp. 6a-10a. For the crimes of Ebilun see ibid., ch. 29, pp. 10a-11b. For Bambursan, see ibid., ch. 29, pp. 12a-14a. Page numbers given in the text refer to these lists.

up the avenue of words. " On one occasion, when three of the lieutenant-
generals of the Mongol Banners failed to comply with Oboi's desires,
he refused to allow the lieutenant-generals of the Mongol Banners to participate in the meetings of the Council of Deliberative Officials (pp. 8b,
9a).

Also among Oboi's state crimes was his contemptuous treatment of
the emperor and the Grand Empress Dowager. Even after the K'ang-hsi
Emperor began to assert political influence in August 1667, Oboi refused
to show proper respect: "In the Emperor's presence, he loudly scolded
the high officials of the boards and departments. Moreover, he intercepted memorials directed to the Emperor" (p. 8b). One of Oboi's crimes
was his obstinate refusal to obey an imperial order concerning the Grand
Empress Dowager: "When the Emperor was making an imperial tour at
Hai-tzu [a park in the Imperial City], he ordered Oboi to submit a clear
memorial to the Grand Empress Dowager. But he did not obey the imperial order and on the contrary he told the Emperor to memorialize himself" (pp. 9b-10a).

Turning to the category of personal crimes, we find that Oboi was
accused of trying to dominate the regency through symbolic as well as
political acts: "In the Will of the former Emperor, Oboi's name was
listed after that of Ebilun, but he was unwilling to obey respectfully.
Whenever they sat in a row, all sat to the right of Ebilun, including Ka-
ch'u-ha of his own clique. Whenever memorials were submitted, Oboi's
name was always listed first" (p. 9b). In addition, Oboi committed one
transgression which seems to reflect an unstable personality: "Because
his own horse was stolen, Oboi seized the keeper of the Imperial Stables
and several horse merchants. He personally endorsed a decision to exe-
cute them and he confiscated their property and made it his own" (p. 9a).
On another occasion, Oboi forced a man named Kesig to move his father's
grave on the grounds that it obstructed his own family's burial site (p. 10a).

Through the list of Oboi's crimes prepared by Prince Giyešu comes
a vague picture of the personality of the regent. Certainly he "coveted
and monopolized state affairs and political power" (p. 8a). But beyond
his political ambition, Oboi seems to have been an insecure individual.
His violent reactions to criticism, his snappy retort to the emperor, and
his petty concern for recognition all seem to reinforce this conclusion.
Oboi had been a remarkable general, but he was less comfortable as a
political leader. His ambition brought him close to the summit of the political world, but his military background had left him with a narrow mind
and the conviction that criticism was tantamount to insubordination.

Unlike his forceful co-regent, Ebilun was a passive man, apparently
incapable of asserting himself for either good or evil. His military record was the least distinguished of the four regents, and in politics as well
he seems to have tagged along at every stage. When Prince Giyešu compiled the "Crimes of Ebilun, " he was hard pressed to find any crimes
which Ebilun had himself committed. Of the twelve crimes which Giyešu
eventually selected, most accused Ebilun of tolerating or assisting Oboi

in his evil designs. For example, Crime Nine recounted the case where Oboi executed the keeper of the Imperial Stables and observed that "Ebilun was aware of this matter but he did not raise his head" (p. 11a). The only crime which was attributed solely to Ebilun was his illegal appointment of one of his inexperienced personal subordinates, Urgei, to a post in the metropolitan government (p. 10b).

Ebilun may well have shared Oboi's dreams of personal glory, but he was unable to achieve his ambitions through his own efforts. He lacked the political drive characteristic of the other regents. That he succeeded in achieving high status at all was probably due largely to his inherited position as son of the illustrious Eidu. Ebilun was an untalented branch of a remarkable Manchu family.

Prince Bambursan was the most influential member of the Oboi faction next to Oboi himself. In terms of the number of charges levied against the high-ranking members of the Oboi faction—an indication of degree of guilt rather than numerical accuracy—Bambursan was second only to Oboi, with twenty-one crimes. Unfortunately, Bambursan's career prior to the 1660s has been neglected by his own biographers. We know only that his father, Tabai, was the sixth son of Nurhaci, and that Bambursan inherited the title of Prince of the Blood of the Sixth Degree (fu-kuo kung). One may surmise that he had a relatively undistinguished background and, like many others in the Oboi faction, he allied himself with the regent in hopes of personal advancement. Suddenly in early 1667 Bambursan was appointed as chamberlain of the Imperial Bodyguard and Grand Secretary of the Mishu yüan.[38]

Serving Oboi in a sycophantic fashion, Bambursan was able to use his new position as Grand Secretary to satisfy the regent's lust for prestige. He flattered Oboi by regularly submitting requests for increasing Oboi's titles and distinctions (p. 12b). In the autumn of 1667 both Oboi and Ebilun were granted dukedoms of the first class. These titles, however, were recorded only in the Manchu language in the "Basic Record of Nobility" (Pen tz'u-chüeh). Grand Secretary Bambursan thus ordered a Chinese translation of this work "so as to make widely known the splendors of the Regents" (p. 12b).

Using his influence as a prince, Grand Secretary, and chamberlain, Bambursan interceded for the Oboi faction throughout the upper metropolitan bureaucracy. He authorized the appointment of several officials who were sympathetic to Oboi's cause. On Bambursan's orders, Isha, the son of Marsai, was placed in the Registry of the Grand Secretariat, where he could transmit information relating to state documents to Oboi and others in his faction (p. 13a). Bambursan, furthermore, was able to protect pro-Oboi officials who had been accused of criminal acts. When the censor Yü To was prosecuted for submitting an inaccurate memorial, Bambursan interceded and demanded a pardon (pp. 12a-b).

Marsai, in contrast to Bambursan, was a well-known figure in Manchu

38. CSK, ch. 255, p. 8b. Biography of Tabai in CSLC, ch. 3, p. 38b.

military and political circles long before his association with the Oboi faction. From his father, a distinguished general who had participated in the Manchu conquest, Marsai had inherited several titles, including that of baron. In 1658 Marsai assisted Lodo, later an associate of Oboi, in the command of several thousand troops to suppress a loyalist revolt in Kweichow. A year later, Marsai moved to Kiangnan, where he aided in the defense of the province against Cheng Ch'eng-kung and earned the title of Viscount of the First Class. In 1663, having become deputy lieutenant-general of the Manchu Plain White Banner, Marsai accompanied Murma and Tuhai in the successful expedition against the Li Lai-heng Rebellion. Sometime in the mid-1660s, however, Marsai linked his fortunes with the Oboi faction, and in March 1667 he became president of the Board of Works. In the following year he became president of the Board of Revenue and lieutenant-general of the Mongol Plain White Banner.[39]

Marsai's appointment as president of the Board of Revenue on 31 January 1668 caused considerable furor in Peking. First of all, this marked a departure from the pattern of dyarchy, since Marsai became the third president while the Chinese and Manchu incumbents, Wang Hung-tso and Ma-hsi-na, were retained. In naming Marsai as the third president of this board, Oboi pointed back to the Shun-chih reign, in which there had been two Manchu presidents and one Chinese president during the years of 1650-53.[40] But over the years of 1653-67 the dyarchic system had been preserved, and Oboi's return to the triple presidency was an obvious attempt to augment the political strength of his faction. The Board of Revenue was an enormously powerful institution, controlling most of the financial affairs of the empire, and thus Marsai's appointment was a considerable asset for the Oboi forces. Moreover,

---

39. CSLC, ch. 6, pp. 13a-14a. In the late 1660s, Marsai, in addition to his activities in the Oboi faction, seemed to perform his official duties with diligence and competence. See, for example, his several memorials on river conservancy in 1669 in the KH Shih-lu, ch. 27, pp. 12b-13b, 22a-b, 22b-23a, 23a-24a.

40. When the Board of Revenue was first established at Mukden in 1631, a prince was in charge and beneath him were four "presidents": two Manchus, one Chinese, and one Mongol (see chapter 2). In 1644 it was decided that there would be no set number of presidents in this particular board. In 1649, however, Dorgon extended the dyarchic pattern (one Manchu, one Chinese) to the Board of Revenue. With the succession of the Shun-chih Emperor to control of the government in 1651, the triple presidency (two Manchus, one Chinese) was instituted. But from 1653 to 1668 there were only two presidents, one Manchu and one Chinese. After Oboi was removed in 1669, the K'ang-hsi Emperor returned to the pattern of dyarchy in the Board of Revenue (HTSL, ch. 19, pp. 15b-17a [pp. 5310-11]).

There was also a triple presidency in the Board of Rites and the Board of Punishments during 1650-53, but Oboi did not reinstitute this pattern during his regency (HTSL, ch. 19, pp. 11b-12a [p. 5308], and ch. 20, p. 3b [p. 5316]).

On Marsai's appointment to the presidency of the Board of Revenue in 1668, see KH Shih-lu, ch. 24, p. 30a.

Marsai quickly took the upper hand in the Board of Revenue. The Chinese president, Wang Hung-tso, like the former Manchu president, Sunahai, was outspoken in his opposition to the schemes of Oboi and his following.[41] In September 1668 Bambursan, always a useful hatchet-man for Oboi, charged Wang Hung-tso with neglect of his responsibilities and with using the seal of the Board of Revenue to pilfer silver from the imperial treasuries. Wang was thus dismissed from his post.[42]

After occupying the presidency of the Board of Revenue for a little over a year, Marsai became ill and died. But even in death Marsai was an object of controversy. Oboi canonized Marsai with the posthumous designation, "loyal and diligent" (chung-mei). Since Marsai obviously was not worthy of such veneration, the K'ang-hsi Emperor tried to countermand Oboi's orders. But Oboi would not be swayed, and he ignored the emperor's pleas. For the time being Marsai was officially recognized as a Ch'ing saint.[43]

THE EMERGENCE OF IMPERIAL SUPPORT

While the Oboi faction grew rapidly both in numbers and in influence during the years of 1667 and 1668, several Manchu and Chinese courtiers began to look to the emperor himself as the only possibility for breaking Oboi's stranglehold over the imperial government. The Joint Regents' faction of the early 1660s had pursued policies which were appealing to the Manchu conquest elite, while the Oboi faction was welcomed only by those few persons directly connected with Oboi himself. The banner relocation affair had proved that Oboi was willing to alienate not only the Chinese elite but Manchu bannermen as well in his quest for personal power. The K'ang-hsi Emperor thus became a personification of political stability, racial harmony, and imperial legitimacy to many Manchus as well as Chinese.

41. Wang Hung-tso was a chü-jen from Yunnan and had become a financial specialist under the late Ming and the early Ch'ing. At first he served as a department director and later as a vice-president in the Board of Revenue. In 1658 he became president of that board, a post which he held until 1661 and again from 1664 to 1668. In 1669-70 he served as president of the Board of War. Wang died in 1674 (CSLC, ch. 78, pp. 48b-49b; CSK, ch. 269, pp. 1a-2a).
According to one of Marsai's biographers, the other Manchu president of the Board of Revenue, Ma-hsi-na, was a member of the Oboi faction (CSLC, ch. 6, p. 14a). If this is true, then both Manchu presidents in 1668 were followers of Oboi and the only anti-Oboi figure was Wang Hung-tso.
42. KH Shih-lu, ch. 26, pp. 19a-b, and ch. 29, p. 13b; CSLC, ch. 6, p. 14a, and ch. 78, p. 49b. Wang was replaced by Huang Chi, a chin-shih from Hangchow. It is probable that Huang was appointed to this post by the K'ang-hsi Emperor who later named Huang to several board presidencies and as Grand Secretary (Hummel, p. 337).
43. KH Shih-lu, ch. 28, pp. 14b-15a, and ch. 29, p. 8b; CSLC, ch. 6, p. 14b. When Oboi was removed in mid-1669, Marsai's posthumous title and designation were retracted (KH Shih-lu, ch. 29, pp. 15a, 17b).

The Forerunners of Imperial Control (August 1666–August 1667)

On 30 August 1666 a memorial from a metropolitan censor named Chang
Wei-ch'ih set the pro-K'ang-hsi movement into motion:

> I humbly recollect that the Shun-chih Emperor took over personal
> control of the government in the eighth year of his reign when he had
> reached the age of fourteen [sui]. At present the Emperor has been
> enthroned for six years and his age is exactly the same. I humbly
> request that an auspicious day be selected for the Emperor to assume
> personal control of the government.
>   Imperial Endorsement: Let the memorial be entered and made
> known. [44]

For several months after Chang submitted his memorial, the emperor
and his advisers waited quietly and presumably looked for an appropriate
time to act on Chang's suggestion.

In early April 1667, immediately after Oboi carried out his "metropolitan evaluation" and placed several followers in high office, the emperor started to assert his power. During the months of April, May, and
June, the emperor began to issue his own edicts, which were quite different in tone and substance from those drafted by his regents. On 4 April,
for example, the following edict was directed to the Six Boards and the
Censorate:

> In metropolitan evaluations, virtue and ability should be the cri-
> teria for the retirements, promotions, and transfers of the officials
> of the boards and the departments. Using proper criteria we must
> endeavor to make known the loyal and the honest and those who work
> diligently for the dynasty. The officials of the boards and depart-
> ments clearly know those among their subordinates who are virtuous
> and those who are not. Those who are upright, virtuous, and able
> should be recommended immediately so that they may be selected
> and appointed. Those who are without ability and who are degenerate
> must be immediately impeached and punished. . . .
>   It is the responsibility of the Censorate and the censorial officials
> to maintain discipline. This work is essential to the dynasty. They
> must immediately draw up forthright criticisms. On matters of dis-
> loyalty and corruption, they must immediately secure the facts and
> submit impeachments. [45]

Such thinly veiled attacks on the Oboi faction were designed not only to
condemn the regent and his appointees, but they also indicated the presence of the emperor himself and promised a very different sort of administration in the future. In another edict in late June the emperor was

44. Ibid., ch. 19, p. 16a.
45. Ibid., ch. 21, pp. 15a–b.

portrayed as a man of boundless humanity who was deeply concerned
about the plight of the commoners:

> The common people are the basis of the dynasty. We must enable
> them to possess the necessities of life in their homes so that they
> may live and work in happiness and peace. Only then can we be
> praised as a rule of great tranquility. Recently I have heard that
> in Chihli and the other provinces many commoners are without homes
> and that sickness and suffering has brought great disorder. Such
> conditions bring great grief to me! This is either caused by officials
> who are greedy and cruel . . . or by the fact that the laws are not
> suitable. [46]

In July the demand for the K'ang-hsi Emperor to assume personal
control reached a new peak as Hsiung Tz'u-li, an assistant reader in the
Hung-wen yüan, submitted an extraordinary memorial. Hsiung Tz'u-li,
a chin-shih of 1658, was a young man just over thirty years of age when
he presented his memorial to the emperor. Although Hsiung became an
immensely influential official during the later seventeenth century, in
1667 he was a minor metropolitan figure and it required considerable
fortitude for him to offer his suggestions and criticisms to the throne at
a time when the Oboi faction was in full sway. [47]

Hsiung's memorial,[48] which was submitted on 27 July, developed the
themes of the earlier imperial edicts, indirectly chastised the Oboi faction, and laid out much of the conceptual framework for the later K'ang-
hsi reign. First of all, Hsiung echoed the complaints of the Chinese
peasant:

> The commoners are compelled to do hard work throughout the
> year. They have barely enough property to support their parents
> and to raise their families. In the summer they are taxed and then
> again in the autumn they must pay the harvest tax. They are always
> being hurried and forced about. The local officials double the regu-
> lar taxes and in addition [demand] various other payments. (p. 12a)

Hsiung contrasted the peasants' suffering with the extravagance of the
wealthy urban population and pleaded for frugality throughout the empire:

> I have observed that today's habits and customs are wasteful and
> excessive. . . . One fur, and the needs of a man of moderate means

---

46. Ibid., ch. 22, p. 6a.
47. Hummel, pp. 308-9; CSLC, ch. 7, pp. 48a-50b. Hsiung's memorial may
have been drafted in cooperation with the emperor's own advisers since so much
of the document reflected sentiments later expressed by the emperor himself.
48. See KH Shih-lu, ch. 22, pp. 11b-17a. Page numbers for specific quotes
are given in the text.

are expended. One feast, and the annual needs of a man are dissipated. Chariot-drivers wear clothing fit for nobles. Actresses
wear headdresses fit for ladies. This is the basis of hunger and
cold and this is the origin of crime. Actions based on the teaching
of propriety must begin with the nobles and with the Emperor's
retinue. (pp. 15b-16a)

According to Hsiung's argument, such evils were caused by corrupt and
incapable officials:

Opportunists follow no rules and precedents in making changes. They
are quick to see the advantages in front of their eyes and they measure these closely in order to facilitate their own private interests.
. . . In the morning they make rules and in the evening they abolish
them. Thus the people overflow the court when they gather for trials.
At present, affairs have reached a state of urgency. (pp. 13a-b)

With an obvious slap at Oboi, whose distrust of the Chinese scholar-elite
was well known, Hsiung wrote:

Those who raise questions are called wild and depraved. Those who
fulfill their duties are seen as impulsive and belligerent. The honest
and peaceful are dismissed as affected. The upright are laughed at
as perverted and decadent. Those who are cultivated in ethics and
in the way of righteousness, and those who search for deep meaning
in books, are ridiculed as orthodox Confucians. (p. 14a)

Hsiung suggested a number of tentative solutions for these flaws. He
stressed the need for "virtuous and able officials" and called for the impeachment and dismissal of the "degenerate and incompetent." He advised the emperor to look first to the metropolitan bureaucracy on the
theory that "the inner officials serve as a measure for the four cardinal
directions" (p. 13a). Hsiung also insisted that there must be equality between Manchu and Chinese officials and that both must share in important
governmental deliberations:

Reprimand Manchu and Chinese officials alike. [Tell them to] be
humble and sincere, to act with propriety, and to be honest in holding office. What is right is to be called right, and what is wrong is
to be called wrong. The Chinese officials must not act in a subordinate fashion towards the Manchu officials in the course of their work.
The high officials of the boards must not show partiality in deliberat-
ing over appointments. (p. 14a)

Finally, and perhaps most important in the light of the policies toward
education and scholarship in the later K'ang-hsi period, Hsiung Tz'u-li
called for an emphasis on Confucian teaching and on the use of Confucian

scholars in key political posts. Hsiung felt that all potential officials should be evaluated on the basis of their comprehension of the Confucian principles. He was careful to urge that both relatives of high officials and "scholars in retirement" (Ming loyalists) should be measured on educational grounds: "Treat the sons and brothers of the dukes, nobles, and high officials in the same fashion [as the ordinary scholars]. There are some among the scholars in retirement and the recluses who comprehend the Classics and are upright in conduct. . . . When men such as this can be of assistance to the dynasty, how can we treat them as insignificant?" (pp. 15a-b).

Hsiung's memorial was a passionate entreaty for the assertion of imperial control and for the promotion of Confucian principles and racial harmony. Hsiung had written an eloquent overture to the K'ang-hsi reign. Oboi, however, failed to see the matter quite that way. According to a biographer, when Oboi read Hsiung Tz'u-li's memorial, he remarked, astutely enough, "this is a criticism of me."[49] Accordingly, Oboi tried to restrict the right of lower-ranking officials to submit memorials of impeachment.[50] Oboi probably would have punished Hsiung Tz'u-li had the latter not secured the protection of the emperor.[51]

The Emperor's Government (August 1667)

The final decision to permit the emperor to assume personal command of the state was made in August 1667, about a month after Hsiung Tz'u-li presented his famous memorial. By this time the Oboi faction had extended its control throughout much of the upper echelons of the civil and military establishment. On 12 August, moreover, Soni died after a lengthy illness, and thus the one regent who had been inclined to represent imperial interests and to mitigate against the Oboi group had disappeared from the scene. Soni's death, along with the growth of Oboi's power, convinced the Grand Empress Dowager and the emperor's advisers to urge the K'ang-hsi Emperor to assert his influence.

The public proclamation of this decision, announced on 21 August, is a revealing statement:

> Formerly in the third month, the Regent Soni and others requested that the Emperor take over personal control of the government. But the Emperor remained in the inner [apartments] and did not come forth.
>
> On this matter he issued an imperial proclamation: "I am still too young. The matters of the empire are very complex and I am not yet capable of handling them. I wish that you would wait for several years."

49. CSLC, ch. 6, p. 11b.
50. KH Shih-lu, ch. 29, p. 8b.
51. Ibid., ch. 29, p. 8b. As one of Oboi's crimes, Giyešu accused him of intending to harm Hsiung Tz'u-li. The implication is that Hsiung was not maligned because the emperor or someone close to the emperor intervened.

The Regents submitted memorials on several occasions and yet
the Emperor refused three times. The Regents' memorials said:
"When the Shun-chih Emperor was fourteen <u>sui</u>, he assumed control
of the government. Today the Emperor's age and his virtue are the
same. The affairs of the empire must be controlled in a generous
fashion. We make our request earnestly."

The Emperor took the Regents' memorials to the Grand Empress
Dowager. The Grand Empress Dowager issued an edict: "The Emperor is still young. He needs your help and that of others in administering the government. How can he take over the affairs of the
empire on his own? You must wait one or two years and then memorialize again."

The Regents memorialized once again: "If the Emperor takes
over the ten thousand matters, we will still assist him in administration."

The Grand Empress Dowager issued an edict in which she gave
her approval. [52]

Like the Shun-chih Will, this announcement was a fabrication designed to
provide legitimacy for a new regime. But unlike the Shun-chih Will, this
announcement now made Oboi and the other two regents the victims rather
than the beneficiaries of a forgery. While Soni probably did request the
emperor to take command, it is equally probable that Oboi, Ebilun, and
Suksaha took a dim view of this prospect.

A major feature of this statement was that the regents would continue
"to assist" the emperor in administration. This was a tacit admission
that the emperor and his supporters were not yet ready to oust the Oboi
faction. Instead the emperor had merely asserted his presence and his
eventual intention to dominate the government without such "assistance."
Over the next two years the emperor would work behind this facade of
cooperation to bolster his own strength and to prepare for an assault
against his erstwhile assistants. [53]

In the matter of K'ang-hsi's taking over the government, the Grand
Empress Dowager Hsiao-chuang evidently held the ultimate decision-
making power. But supporting the emperor and the Grand Empress Dowager was a new faction led by Songgotu and Mingju. Songgotu and Mingju
shared two important characteristics which influenced their factional
activities. They were both young men who began their rise to power after
the conquest in 1644. Raised in Peking, they were prominent figures in
a new generation of Manchus who might be called the post-conquest Man-

52. Ibid., ch. 23, pp. 2b-3a.
53. The policy of cooperative government was set forth in even clearer terms
in a proclamation of 25 August 1667: "The empire is very large and the problems
of government are very troublesome. The burdens [of governing] and offering
counsel must also lie with the Regents, the Princes, and the metropolitan and provincial, civil and military, officials of all ranks" (ibid., ch. 23, pp. 4a-b).

chu elite. While retaining strong attachments to Manchu tradition and
to the martial arts, the post-conquest elite was more familiar with Chinese language and culture than were those in the preceding generations
of the conquest elite. Furthermore, they recognized the need for greater
Sino-Manchu cooperation to overcome the racial hatreds of the conquest
period. A second characteristic of Songgotu and Mingju was that both
began their careers in the Imperial Bodyguard. Although both received
concurrent appointments in the civil bureaucracy during 1666-69, they
kept their positions of imperial bodyguards of the first class.[54] In seeking support for the K'ang-hsi Emperor, therefore, they naturally turned
to their fellow officers in the Imperial Bodyguard.

The formation of this bodyguard clique provided the K'ang-hsi group
with sufficient military power to move against Oboi. The bodyguard
clique also provided loyal personnel who could be appointed to key civil
and military posts to counteract the influence of the Oboi faction. In the
years 1668-70, before and after the removal of Oboi himself, several
imperial bodyguards of the first rank received high appointments. Mingju
was named president of the Board of Punishments (1668) and president of
the Censorate (1669). Songgotu became a vice-president in the Board of
Civil Office (1668) and then was appointed a Grand Secretary one year
later. Songgotu's cousin, Shuai-yen-pao (the son of Hife), was elevated
from first-rank bodyguard to vice-president of the Board of Civil Office
and later to Director General of Grain Transport during the summer of
1669. Shortly after Oboi's removal, other first-rank bodyguards received similar appointments: Ch'a-ha-la was elevated to vice-president
of the Board of Works, Amuhūlang to vice-president of the Li-fan yüan,
Garu to Minister of the Imperial Household, Pan-ti to vice-president of
the Board of War, and Po-lo-t'e to vice-president of the Li-fan yüan.[55]
This bodyguard clique constituted the power base for the Songgotu-Mingju

54. An interesting episode occurred in Songgotu's career during the summer
of 1669. In June Songgotu requested to be relieved of his post of vice-president
of the Board of Rites and to remain only as an imperial bodyguard of the first
class. Then in September 1669 he was suddenly elevated to the position of Grand
Secretary. See ibid., ch. 31, pp. 6b-7a. A possible explanation is that Songgotu wanted to work solely with the Imperial Bodyguard during the crucial transition period after the conviction of Oboi. By the end of the summer when the new
K'ang-hsi regime was firmly in power, then Songgotu may have been willing to
move into more prestigious posts outside the Imperial Bodyguard.

55. I am indebted to Jonathan Spence for his suggestion of the role of imperial bodyguards in the K'ang-hsi reign and for pointing out the large number of
imperial bodyguards who rose to prominence immediately after the demise of the
Oboi faction. In Spence's new book on the K'ang-hsi Emperor, the activities of
bodyguards in the factionalism of the late K'ang-hsi years are revealed in great
depth. See Spence, Emperor of China, chapters 2 and 5, passim.

For the appointment of these bodyguards in the transitional era after the fall
of the Oboi faction, see ibid., ch. 29, pp. 18a-b; ch. 30, pp. 4a, 4b, 10a-b; ch.
36, pp. 1b, 7a.

faction and permitted the emperor and the Grand Empress Dowager to extend their influence into the metropolitan bureaucracy (as we shall see later in this chapter).

Another important representative of the post-conquest elite supporting the K'ang-hsi Emperor was Prince Giyešu (1645-97). Giyešu was a great-grandson of Nurhaci. His grandfather, Daišan, was one of the four major princes selected to aid Nurhaci in governmental affairs, and it was Daišan who was most influential in engineering the succession of Abahai in 1626 and of Fu-lin (the Shun-chih Emperor) in 1643. Giyešu inherited the family's princely title and, probably because of his close relationship with the K'ang-hsi Emperor, emerged as the spokesman for the Council of Deliberative Officials at the end of the Oboi era. Since Giyešu was a young man in his early twenties during these years, it is difficult to estimate how much power he actually possessed. It is possible that he was merely a figurehead for the imperial faction who could use his position in the Council to publicize and legitimize the decisions made by the Grand Empress Dowager and her cohorts. In any case, Giyešu, along with Songgotu, was given much of the credit for the purge of the Oboi faction in 1669. During the revolt of the Three Feudatories, Giyešu was commander-in-chief of the Ch'ing forces in the southeast, and he effected the defeats of both Keng Ching-Chung and Cheng Ching.[56]

The imperial faction of the 1660s, therefore, found its spokesman in Prince Giyešu, its authority in the Grand Empress Dowager, and its political and military power in Songgotu, Mingju, and their bodyguard allies. In one respect, this new faction perpetuated a key characteristic of the Dorgon, Jirgalang, and Joint Regents' factions which had preceded them. They retained a strong commitment to the martial values of the Manchu tradition and looked to a vigorous expansion of the Ch'ing empire. Songgotu, Mingju, and Giyešu all served as prominent military commanders later in the seventeenth century.[57] The biggest differences, however, were the youthfulness of the Songgotu-Mingju faction and the dominating influence of the K'ang-hsi Emperor himself. Although its power base was Manchu, the Songgotu-Mingju faction found many allies among the Chinese officialdom. With the assistance of these allies, the new faction proved willing to placate the dissident Chinese elite. The K'ang-hsi Emperor realized the explosive situation created by Sino-Manchu racial tensions and endeavored to satiate some of the Chinese dreams expressed in Hsiung Tz'u-li's memorial.

56. Hummel, pp. 270-71; CSLC, ch. 1, pp. 5a-7a.

57. It is clear that Mingju, Songgotu, and Giyešu shared the usual Manchu interest in martial matters and in the expansion of the Manchu empire. As mentioned elsewhere, Mingju was one of the first to advocate the use of Ch'ing forces against the feudatory princes, and Giyešu distinguished himself in the campaigns that followed. Songgotu, although he advised the emperor to adopt conciliatory measures towards the feudatory princes, proved himself a forceful Manchu negotiator at Nerchinsk and later participated in the operations against Galdan.

The Trial and Execution of Suksaha (August-September 1667)

In the two weeks immediately after the K'ang-hsi Emperor achieved
nominal control of the government, the court witnessed a very strange
series of events. The regent Suksaha submitted a curious memorial and
then was censured by the emperor, tried by the Council of Deliberative
Officials, and finally sentenced to death. Furthermore, there seems to
have been some degree of unanimity between the Oboi faction and the
Songgotu-Mingju faction on this matter. Suksaha not only opposed the
Oboi faction, but he also jealously guarded his role as regent and resisted efforts to return governmental control to the emperor. Both Oboi
and the emperor's supporters agreed, therefore, that Suksaha was a
dangerous element and that his political power should be eliminated.

On 31 August Suksaha presented an unusual memorial in which he
berated himself with almost masochistic pleasure and, in the light of
later testimony, implied disapproval of the emperor's new role as head
of state:

> My talents are common and my knowledge is superficial. But
> the former Emperor looked upon me and appointed me a high offi-
> cial. From morning to night I suffered great anxiety and dreaded
> to be entrusted with such great favor. When the former Emperor
> died, I wanted to be buried with him, an act which would completely
> demonstrate my sincerity and my stupidity. I never expected that
> when the Imperial Will was promulgated, my name would be listed
> among the Regents. I was torn apart, not knowing whether to live
> or die. By the Imperial Will this fool was given another life. . . .
> Unfortunately in the past one or two years, I have become quite ill
> from being involved in worldly problems. Thus I have been unable
> to fully devote my efforts before the Emperor. This is a crime
> from which I cannot escape.
>
> Now that you have come to rule the administration personally, I
> humbly beg you to be astute and perceptive. Order me to guard the
> tomb of the former Emperor. By this my life will be perpetuated.
> And thus I can give a slight token of repayment for the Emperor's
> care and I can also exert myself in a small way. [58]

The K'ang-hsi Emperor, puzzled and annoyed by Suksaha's memorial,
replied:

> Suksaha has memorialized and asked that he be permitted to guard
> the tombs so that his life will be perpetuated. I do not know why he
> should be compelled to reside there. Why is he unable to perpetuate
> his life here? How can one perpetuate life by guarding the tombs?
> On this matter which the Emperor cannot untangle, let the Council
> of Deliberative Officials deliberate and memorialize. [59]

58. KH Shih-lu, ch. 23, pp. 7a-b.   59. Ibid., ch. 23, pp. 7b-8a.

On 2 September the emperor approved the Council's suggestion that Suksaha be arrested and interrogated. The Council held an immediate hearing at which not only Suksaha but also Oboi, Ebilun, and other members of the Oboi faction presented testimony relevant to the case. On point after point Oboi and his associates accused Suksaha of conspiring against the K'ang-hsi Emperor and of other criminal acts. Then on 4 September Prince Giyešu outlined the Council's case against Suksaha in the form of twenty-four crimes which the regent was alleged to have committed. According to Prince Giyešu, the real intent of Suksaha's memorial was a gesture of protest against the emperor's assumption of political authority. To clarify this accusation, Giyešu referred to a statement which Suksaha reputedly had made to Bambursan: "The Duke of Chou served as Regent to Ch'eng-wang. It was not until the fourteenth year of the Ch'eng-wang period, when the Emperor was over twenty _sui_, that he took personal command of the government." Furthermore, Suksaha apparently had refused to participate in a counsel session called by the emperor toward the end of August. When the orders were repeated, Suksaha reportedly replied, "I will not go."[60]

Somewhat pressed to make the list of crimes against Suksaha reach the impressive figure of twenty-four, Prince Giyešu pounced upon some fairly trivial incidents in Suksaha's career. Crime Twelve, for instance, concerned Suksaha's use of one of the emperor's own bricks to heat his soup. Although Suksaha himself denied that it was an imperial brick, testimony from a man named Siteku indicated that it was indeed the emperor's brick and that Suksaha, but a regent himself, had encroached on imperial prerogatives (pp. 12a-b). Crime Twenty-three alleged that Suksaha had taken the dynastic record of the Hung-wu Emperor of the early Ming period and brought it to his own house for private perusal. Deftly using the art of implying guilt through circumstantial evidence, Giyešu concluded, "what matters undertaken by Hung-wu did he wish to imitate?" (p. 16a).

After reviewing the twenty-four crimes, the Council of Deliberative Officials recommended that Suksaha be stripped of all ranks and honors and executed by slicing. Also slated for execution in the Suksaha affair were his brother, Belhetu, four of his sons, and three nephews. Several of Suksaha's associates and clansmen were to suffer the loss of their

---

60. Ibid., ch. 23, pp. 7a, 13b-14a. Suksaha's contemptuous treatment of the emperor and his opposition to the emperor's new political role were the major themes of Giyešu's list of crimes against him. I have only cited two examples; for further information, see ibid., ch. 23, pp. 8b-16b, passim.

Four of the crimes levied against Suksaha dealt with his pretension to have been the Shun-chih Emperor's closest associate. According to Giyešu's report, Suksaha claimed that the former emperor had permitted Suksaha alone to find an auspicious imperial burial location and had promised Suksaha that he would be buried near the emperor. Suksaha was also reputed to have said that he alone was present when the Shun-chih Emperor died. During the funeral procession, Suksaha rode alongside the emperor's casket while the other regents followed several _li_ to the rear (ibid., ch. 23, pp. 10a-11b).

ranks and offices. Suksaha's property was to be totally confiscated and his wives and other children sent to the Imperial Household to work as servants (pp. 16b-17b).[61]

The emperor accepted the verdict of the Council with the minor modification that only Suksaha and one of his sons would be executed, and by beheading rather than by slicing. The emperor's approval, however, was prefaced by the explanation that Oboi forced him to sanction the harsh purge of Suksaha, his family, and associates:

> The Emperor is aware that Oboi loathes Suksaha and that the two have often wrangled and have become enemies. In league with his faction of Bambursan and others [Oboi] has committed several crimes and truly wants to sentence [Suksaha] to the most severe punishments.
>
> [The Emperor] was determined not to permit his request. But Oboi disputed the matter in the presence of the Emperor and submitted forceful memorials for several days.[62]

It is my belief that this preface was not attached to the original document but was added at a later date under the emperor's orders in order to shift the guilt for Suksaha's execution to Oboi and his faction. One finds it difficult to imagine that the emperor would have called attention to the "several crimes" of Oboi and Bambursan almost two years before he ventured to remove them from power.

There are several reasons to believe that the emperor and the Songgotu-Mingju faction not only welcomed the execution of Suksaha, but even helped to engineer his trial and execution. Suksaha had always been an opportunist and, if there is any veracity to his twenty-four crimes, he did not want to relinquish his political influence as regent. Second, Suksaha's case, like the case against the Oboi faction in 1669, was reviewed by Prince Giyešu, a close associate of the emperor. Third, no fewer than thirteen of the twenty-four accusations levied against Suksaha dealt directly with his contempt for the K'ang-hsi Emperor and his desire to prevent the emperor from taking personal control. Fourth, even when the Suksaha affair was reconsidered in July 1669, several weeks after Oboi's removal, Suksaha himself was still declared guilty.[63] Finally, the removal and execution of Suksaha was a logical way in which to test the strength of the Songgotu-Mingju faction. If the emperor and his advisers could successfully unseat Suksaha, they could move with greater confidence against Oboi later on.

---

61. At least three of Suksaha's sons, however, survived this purge. All three of them inherited ranks formerly held by Suksaha (PCST, ch. 22, p. 4a).

62. KH Shih-lu, ch. 23, pp. 17b-18a.

63. Ibid., ch. 30, pp. 4b-5a; CSLC, ch. 6, p. 6a. The others among Suksaha's family and associates, however, were exonerated (KH Shih-lu, ch. 30, p. 9a).

THE OBOI FACTION AND THE SONGGOTU-MINGJU FACTION:
SHIFTING BALANCE OF POWER

The events of the spring and summer of 1667 had marked an important
turning point in seventeenth-century Chinese politics. The Joint Regents'
faction, the last bastion of Manchu conservatism, was fractured by the
deaths of Soni and Suksaha and by the rapid growth of the Oboi faction.
To counterbalance the ambitions of Oboi and his supporters, the K'ang-
hsi Emperor had asserted personal control of the government on the advice of the Grand Empress Dowager and of the small but potent Songgotu-
Mingju faction. Hsiung Tz'u-li, a minor metropolitan bureaucrat, had
called for a reign of virtue and harmony to rectify the terror and dissen-
sion of the early 1660s. Hsiung's memorial, amplified by the earlier
edicts concerning virtuous officials and a humane government, promised
a K'ang-hsi regime which would understand and nurture the Chinese elite.
But the emperor and his advisers had also displayed their tough and
courageous features. It was in July 1667, one will recall, that Wu San-
kuei's temporary resignation was accepted. In the same year the strength
of the banner forces was increased as the emperor's faction anticipated
an eventual showdown with the feudatory princes. In short, many of the
key characteristics and personalities of the later K'ang-hsi reign became
evident during 1667. Before the emperor could open his renowned chapter
in Chinese history, however, he had to come to grips with Oboi. [64]

The Revision of the "Veritable Records" of the Shun-chih Reign:
A Barometer of Factionalism

On the day that the verdict against Suksaha was announced (4 September),
the Chinese president of the Board of Rites, Huang Chi, requested that
the "Veritable Records" (Shih-lu) of the Shun-chih reign be compiled and
revised.[65] The revision of the dynastic records gained special significance
in the late 1660s. A conflict developed between the Oboi faction and the
emperor's faction over whom to select as compilers of the Shun-chih
Shih-lu. The appointment of the compilers during the years 1667-69,
therefore, provides a useful barometer for measuring the shifting balance
of factional power.

On 21 October, two months after the emperor had assumed political
responsibility, the first appointments were announced.[66] The chief com-

---

64. In late August and early September 1667 the K'ang-hsi Emperor took
special pains to honor the regents by citing their long service and by granting
them new honors. On 29 August, a few days before Suksaha's trial, the emperor
praised Suksaha, Ebilun, and Oboi as "loyal and sincere" and asked that the Council of Deliberative Officials grant them honors. On 8 September both Ebilun and
Oboi received dukedoms of the first class. Although the two regents tried to refuse this honor, the emperor insisted (KH Shih-lu, ch. 23, pp. 5a-b, 19b, 22b, 24a).
This is probably to be interpreted as an effort on the part of the emperor to allow
the regents to retire with honor.
    65. Ibid., ch. 23, p. 18a.
    66. Ibid., ch. 24, pp. 2a-3a.

piler was none other than Oboi's accomplice, Grand Secretary Bambursan. Although the great majority of those selected to assist Bambursan were not associated with either faction, two were among the emperor's closest allies. Mingju was named as an assistant compiler and Hsiung Tz'u-li was appointed a Chinese reviser.[67] In the following month Oboi decided to offset the influence of Mingju and Hsiung Tz'u-li by appointing three of his followers, Budari, Uksai, and Mušu, as assistant compilers of the Shun-chih Shih-lu.[68] By the end of 1667, therefore, the appointments to the Shih-lu revision project reflected the dominance of the Oboi faction in Peking politics.[69]

During the year of 1668, however, the Songgotu-Mingju faction gained support and strength. Although Oboi maintained his earlier hold over several metropolitan posts, new faces began to appear at the top of the Peking bureaucratic hierarchy. By early 1669 the emperor could claim support from the following high-ranking statesmen: Grand Secretary Duikana; Board Presidents Tu Li-te, Huang Chi, Mingju, and Wang Hsi; Vice-Presidents Songgotu, Ts'ai Yü-jung, Mishan, and Wu Cheng-chih; and President of the Censorate Feng P'u.[70]

As a symbolic gesture of his increased influence, the emperor appointed a new chief compiler of the Shun-chih Shih-lu on 19 October 1668. Grand Secretary Duikana was selected to replace Bambursan.[71] By this point, some eight months before the ouster of Oboi, the Songgotu-Mingju faction had gained the upper hand in Peking.

The K'ang-hsi Emperor, His Father, and His Future

The K'ang-hsi Emperor was not content to devote himself solely to the

---

67. There were several Chinese appointed to this commission who later became important officials in the 1670s and 1680s. Among these were Li Wei, Wei I-chieh, and Fan Cheng-mo.

68. KH Shih-lu, ch. 24, p. 9b. Oboi had appointed these three members of his faction as sub-chancellors of the Inner Three Departments on 11 November 1667. Thus they had the proper credentials to participate in the revision of the "Veritable Records" (ibid., ch. 24, p. 7b).

69. On 6 January 1668, Bambursan was also appointed Chief Compiler of the Shih-lu for the Abahai reign (ibid., ch. 24, p. 24b). The T'ai-tsung shih-lu, first compiled in 1652-55, was revised during the years of 1673-82. The Chief Compiler during the latter period was Tu Li-te (Hummel, pp. 3, 78).

70. I have listed these officials after an examination of their biographies. All of them held very high metropolitan posts during the 1670s, and many were particularly favored by the emperor himself. In contrast to this growing strength of the imperial faction, there were only six members of the Oboi faction holding high metropolitan offices in early 1669: Bambursan, Ka-ch'u-ha, Asha, Ch'i-shih, T'ai-pi-t'u, and Mai-yin-ta (CS, 4:2545).

71. KH Shih-lu, ch. 27, p. 3b. On 5 May 1669, Tu Li-te, who had just been appointed a Grand Secretary, became Chief Compiler in place of Duikana. Biography of Duikana in CSLC, ch. 6, pp. 24a-b; biography of Tu Li-te in Hummel, p. 778. On 4 October 1669, Songgotu himself became the Chief Compiler (KH Shih-lu, ch. 31, p. 9b).

problems of power politics during 1668 and early 1669. He was fully
aware of the damaging effects wrought by the forged Shun-chih Will. The
Imperial Will had not only portrayed his father as a weak and corrupt
sovereign, but it had authorized the regime of the four regents and had
sanctioned their pro-Manchu and anti-Chinese policies. The emperor
was determined to rescue his father's reputation and thus provide a different sort of legacy for the K'ang-hsi reign.

On 22 February 1668 the emperor dedicated a funerary tablet to his
father on which he had inscribed a lengthy tribute to the virtues of the
Shun-chih Emperor.[72] The K'ang-hsi Emperor portrayed his father as
a brilliant military leader and an exceptionally virtuous scholar:

> The deceased Emperor surpassed all in his divine wisdom. He
> brought the ten thousand countries fully into his grasp. He exalted
> [the virtues of] filiality and humanity. In military affairs he made
> great achievements and in scholarship he was virtuous. He balanced
> the two vital powers [of yin and yang] and he surpassed the thou-
> sand ancients. (ch. 25, p. 4a)

Not only had the Shun-chih Emperor combined scholarship (wen) and the
military arts (wu), but he had also "treated Manchus and Chinese according to one system, and he did not give greater weight to either the
military or the civil" (ch. 25, p. 6b). Furthermore, "the basis of his
rule was the common people. . . . He enforced the laws strictly, and
none dared to kill and rob the commoners" (ch. 25, p. 5a). Finally, the
Shun-chih Emperor had been very attentive to his duties. He "opened
and scrutinized every memorial." For his advisers he "chose both Manchu and Chinese scholarly officials." He had even bothered to construct
a special office where officials of the Hanlin Academy could gather and
prepare to offer advice to the throne (ch. 25, p. 6a).

The emperor probably was aware that there was some truth in the
regents' portrait of his father, but K'ang-hsi needed a new image for
the future of the Ch'ing dynasty. What better technique than to pose as
a filial son celebrating the virtues of an illustrious father. Now the task
was to carry his father's dreams to realization.

As the year of 1668 wore on, more and more of the imperial edicts
and imperial decisions bore the distinctive mark of the K'ang-hsi Emperor. He inaugurated a campaign to seek out official corruption and incompetence. Unlike most other emperors, whose orders on such matters
were often ignored, K'ang-hsi went on a local inspection tour and announced:

> I have made a personal tour of the capital area and its vicinity. I
> observed that the magistrate of T'ung-chou, Ou-yang Shih-feng, and

72. For this tribute and for later edicts mentioned below, see KH Shih-lu;
chuan and page numbers are given in the text.

the assistant magistrate, Li Cheng-chieh, are inferior and incompetent. Moreover, Colonel T'ang Wen-yao is not at all adept in military matters. Let them all be removed from office. (ch. 28, p. 11a)

In late June the emperor called for a strict application of laws and, displaying his sense of humor, ordered Oboi to head a commission to "investigate the handling of criminal cases" (ch. 26, p. 6b). When a famine occurred in Kansu, he directed the Board of Revenue to select two "honest and able officials" to go to the disaster area and meet with the local officials; he also insisted that "no matter what the cost, money and rations must be distributed and housing must be found for the starved people" (ch. 25, pp. 19a-b). Revealing a puritanical strain, the emperor prohibited gambling on the grounds that it caused the people to neglect their occupations and brought ruin to their homes and property (ch. 26, pp. 8b-9a).

At the same time K'ang-hsi began to repudiate some of the most famous policies of the Oboi regency. In October 1668, in an act calculated to win the affection of the Chinese elite, he restored the "eight-legged essay" to the examination system. In December he ordered a relaxation of the coastal evacuation policy and sent a special commission to Kwangtung to assure that the displaced persons were returned to their homes. In the spring of 1669 the case against Ferdinand Verbiest was reconsidered, and the Jesuit once again became assistant director of the Imperial Bureau of Astronomy.

THE DEATH OF OBOI

After months of careful preparation, assuring his own political strength and publicly outlining his goals, the K'ang-hsi Emperor finally denounced Oboi on 14 June 1669:

> I know that Oboi is an elderly official, that his name was included in the Imperial Will, and that he was highly respected. I had hoped that he would alter his wicked ways and repent his crimes. But now he has greedily collected bribes and his rebellious clique has grown daily. . . . The proofs of their wickedness are almost innumerable. (ch. 29, pp. 4b-5a)

The emperor then ordered that Oboi be arrested and interrogated by a commission headed by Prince Giyešu. On 26 June Giyešu produced the lengthy document enumerating the crimes of Oboi and his associates discussed earlier, and he recommended the death penalty for twenty-five members of the Oboi faction, including Oboi himself, Ebilun, Bambursan, and Marsai.

After hearing Prince Giyešu's report and considering his verdict, the emperor chose leniency. Oboi would not suffer the excruciating death by slicing, but instead would be removed from office, deprived of all property, and imprisoned. Ebilun, since "he was not involved in the formation of the clique," would lose his title of Grand Preceptor, but his son would inherit his rank of duke of the first class. Only seven members of the Oboi faction—Bambursan, Murma, Asha, Ka-ch'u-ha, T'ai-pi-t'u, Sai-pen-te, and Namo—were to be executed, on the grounds that their crimes were "unforgivable." As for the rest, the emperor deemed them "triv-ial and insignificant men," and refrained from punishing them at all (ch. 29, pp. 17a-18b). With Oboi out of the way and eight of his powerful hench-men eliminated (Marsai died earlier in 1669), the emperor had effectively crushed the Oboi faction, and he could afford to be lenient with the others.

But what about the fate of Oboi? Although he most likely died in con-finement, a number of stories have circulated concerning his arrest and death. According to one historian:

> Emperor Kang Hsi dared not issue an edict to send Grand Secretary Ngau Bei [Oboi] to execution. He called him in for a private audience. He then hid several strong men in the court dressed as boys playing hide-and-seek in the courtyard of the palace. When the powerful minister came in, he was caught by those "boys" and executed in the back yard before his execution was officially ordered. [73]

Another story holds that one day the emperor was in the imperial study (nan shu-fang) waiting with several palace attendants for Oboi's arrival. When Oboi entered, the attendants grabbed him, held his hands behind his back, and forced him to kneel. Then he was commanded to "warm his hands" by holding a tea bowl which had been boiled in water to make it hot. When Oboi dropped the bowl, the attendants pushed him prostrate on the floor. The emperor then cried out, "Oboi is powerful but disre-spectful," and ordered that he be punished. [74]

A third story claims that the emperor became enraged at Oboi when, on New Year's Day of 1669, the regent appeared at court wearing an em-peror's garb with the minor exception of a velvet knot instead of the im-perial pearl on his hat. The emperor then went to the Grand Empress Dowager's apartments to ask how to eliminate the pretentious regent. While visiting the Grand Empress Dowager, the emperor saw a eunuch casting dice. "Kang Hsi seized the cup, paused an instant as if invoking supernatural aid, and made a cast. The numbers came out all different, whereupon the Grand Empress Dowager, delighted, exclaimed: 'You need not be afraid of him any longer.'" The story goes on to observe that a week before Oboi was arrested, he feigned illness. Lying on his bed and covered by a sable robe, Oboi was visited by the emperor. Sud-denly one of the emperor's aides pulled the robe aside and discovered a concealed dagger. The emperor merely smiled and remarked, Ao Pai [Oboi] is indeed a true Manchu warrior; he keeps his weapons by his side,

73. Hsieh Pao-chao, Government of China, p. 39.
74. Shang, p. 138.

even when on a bed of illness, that he may rise at any moment to defend his Emperor." Shortly thereafter Oboi was arrested and was given imperial permission to commit suicide. But, so the story proceeds, before Oboi could take his own life, a palace wrestler strangled him in prison. To celebrate this event, the emperor decreed that on every New Year's Day dice would be thrown to determine the omens for the coming year. This custom, however, is said to have been corrupted in the later years of the dynasty by eunuchs who fixed the dice to invariably forecast good fortune.[75]

All of these stories are probably as false as they are imaginative. They were born of a desire to bring a spectacular close to Oboi's career. To the Jesuit fathers, to the Chinese elite, to the displaced commoners living on the southeastern coast and in Chihli, and to the officials in Peking who opposed his faction, Oboi had become an embodiment of evil. For such a figure to die quietly in prison was unthinkable.

In spite of the contempt for Oboi in the popular memory, during the eighteenth century he was recognized officially for his military achievements. In 1713 the K'ang-hsi Emperor recalled Oboi's illustrious career as a soldier, and posthumously granted him the rank of baron. At first this rank was held by Oboi's grandnephew, Su-hei, but it was later inherited by Oboi's grandson, Dafu. When Dafu became a deputy lieutenant-general in 1727, he impressed the Yung-cheng Emperor at an audience. The emperor therefore restored Oboi's dukedom and granted it to Dafu. The revived dukedom was given the appellation, "military excellence" (ch'ao-wu). After Dafu was killed in 1731 while fighting against the Ölöd Mongols, the ch'ao-wu dukedom remained in his family for a half-century. In 1780, however, the Ch'ien-lung Emperor, citing the crimes of the Oboi faction, reduced the former regent's hereditary rank to that of baron.[76]

Ebilun and his family, unlike Oboi, suffered no permanent disgrace either in the popular memory or in court records. Recognizing that Ebilun had been only marginally involved in the Oboi faction, the K'ang-hsi Emperor restored his dukedom in 1670 and permitted him to return to the court. When Ebilun died in 1674, he was given a state funeral and received the rather appropriate posthumous name, "reverent but cautious" (k'o-hsi). One of his daughters, at first an imperial concubine, became an empress in 1677, and after her death in the following year she was called the Hsiao-chao Empress. Several of Ebilun's sons and their descendants achieved high military and civil offices during the latter part of the seventeenth century and throughout the eighteenth century. One of his sons, Alingga, served as president of the Li-fan yüan; a grandson

75. Backhouse and Bland, Annals and Memoirs, pp. 243-45.
76. Hummel, p. 600; PCST, ch. 1, p. 6b; CSLC, ch. 6, p. 12b. The descendants of Oboi's three brothers, particularly those of Baha, included many relatively prominent figures in military and court circles (PCST, ch. 1, pp. 5b-6a, 6a, 7b).

became president of the Board of Punishments, another was a Grand
Secretary and a Grand Councillor, and a third served as a governor-
general. In 1852 the Hsien-feng Emperor gave one of his commanders,
Saišangga, the sword of Ebilun as a symbol of authority while Saišangga
was leading troops against the Taiping rebels.[77]

77. Hummel, pp. 220-21; PCST, ch. 5, pp. 7a-9a. On the Hsiao-chao Empress, see T'ang Pang-chih, Ch'ing huang-shih ssu-p'u, ch. 2, p. 11a; Chang
Ts'ai-t'ien, Ch'ing lieh-ch'ao hou-fei chuan-kao, ch. shang, pp. 82b-85a.

9   The Oboi Regency and the K'ang-hsi Reign

With the Oboi faction crushed in 1669 and the four regents all dead by the mid-1670s, a new era dawned in Ch'ing China. Gone were many of the policies of the regency. The "eight-legged essay" system was revived and bannermen were once again permitted to take the regular civil examinations. The dyarchic Manchu-Chinese balance was restored in the Grand Secretariat. The land taken from the commoners in Oboi's banner relocation scheme was returned to them and unfortunate statesmen who were executed under Oboi's orders were posthumously honored. Jesuit fathers such as Verbiest and Gerbillon became close assistants of the K'ang-hsi Emperor and provided useful technical and diplomatic advice. Ming loyalist scholars, the object of sharp attacks during the regency, were slowly drawn into the Ch'ing fold by the various appeasement tactics of the K'ang-hsi Emperor. The cautious military expeditions of the Oboi period were replaced by the emperor's full-scale campaigns against the feudatory princes, against the Russians in Manchuria, against the Chengs on Taiwan, and against the Ölöd Mongols under Galdan. [1]

What then did the K'ang-hsi Emperor inherit from the Oboi regency? In light of the emperor's repudiation of so many of the policies and personalities of the Oboi era, it is surprising how many items were retained. Building on the foundation laid by his regents, the emperor expanded the Imperial Household into a large personal bureaucracy. The Council of Deliberative Officials continued to act as an imperial advisory board composed primarily of Manchus who reviewed major policy decisions. The

---

1. The K'ang-hsi Emperor began initiating many of his changes in policies and personnel immediately after the removal of Oboi. Of the forty-five top metropolitan positions, for example, only sixteen appointees remained in office by the end of 1669. Of the twelve board presidents in February 1669, only two held their same positions by the end of the year (CS, 4:2452). During the summer of 1669, moreover, the K'ang-hsi Emperor firmly established his hold over the banner hierarchy. To establish his control over Oboi's own banner, the Bordered Yellow, K'ang-hsi appointed new lieutenant-generals and deputy lieutanant-generals in both the Manchu and Chinese divisions of the Bordered Yellow Banner (KH Shih-lu, ch. 29, pp. 6a-b, and ch. 30, pp. 4a-b, 8b). In September he named a new lieutenant-general of the Mongol Bordered Yellow Banner (ibid., ch. 31, p. 13b). New appointments to the banner leadership continued throughout the year of 1669, with the emperor devoting special attention to the Three Imperial Banners. See PCTC (1795), ch. 320, 323, 326, passim.

Later in his regime the K'ang-hsi Emperor made reference to poor appointments during the Oboi regency. In 1684 the emperor observed that "the tu-fu are

rigorous k'ao-ch'eng evaluation system, revived by the regents to measure performance on the basis of tax collection and local order, was
perpetuated under the K'ang-hsi reign. In spite of the restoration of the
"eight-legged essay," the emperor maintained the examination quotas at
considerably lower levels than under the Shun-chih period. As mentioned
earlier, the emperor followed Oboi's example and appointed several Manchus to posts in the upper provincial bureaucracy. The regents' system
of military governorships in Manchuria was kept intact until the very end
of the Ch'ing dynasty. The K'ang-hsi Emperor even ordered a temporary
return to the regents' coastal evacuation policy during the campaign a-
gainst Cheng Ching in the late 1670s and early 1680s.

    In terms of specific policies and institutions, therefore, a great deal
of the Oboi regency was incorporated into the fabric of the K'ang-hsi
reign as a whole.² To explore the more basic differences between the
emperor and his regents, one must look beyond these specifics into the
realm of personality and attitude. Over the preceding chapters it has
been argued that both the regents and the K'ang-hsi Emperor were proud
and protective of their Manchu heritage. Common to both the emperor
and his regents was their desire to maintain the unity, purity, and superiority of the Manchu race and their commitment to realizing the Manchu dream of the conquest and consolidation of the Chinese empire. Both
cherished the Manchu military tradition and insisted upon maintaining
military values among the Manchu people. Also common to both was a
willingness to experiment and innovate, particularly when they were dealing with problems of government.

    The differences between the emperor and his four regents, in terms
of style of leadership and policymaking, were functions of their personalities and backgrounds. The regents, with the possible exception of Soni,

---

the high officials who oversee the provinces, and they thoroughly understand those
matters which affect the people's lives. During Emperor Shih-tsu's reign, those
who held such positions could still be categorized among the virtuous. But when
we came to the regency period, and began to appoint such men as Chang Ch'ang-
k'ang, Pai Ju-mei, Chang Tzu-te, Chia Han-fu, Ch'ü Chin-mei, and Han Shih-
ch'i, then the bandits came, disturbed the countryside, and brought great suffering to the commoners. Today's tu-fu, while I feel they are somewhat better than
before, still have similar propensities and the change has not been complete"
(KH Shih-lu, ch. 114, pp. 8b-9a). From a review of the biographies of the officials mentioned by K'ang-hsi, it is apparent that all of them were impeached and
punished for improprieties while serving as governors or governors-general.
See CSLC, ch. 7, pp. 45a-46a, and ch. 78, pp. 60a-61a; KCCH, ch. 154, pp. 24a-
25a; Ch'ien I-chi, Pei-chuan chi, ch. 61, pp. 10b-11b, and ch. 62, pp. 2a-b.
    2. Other similarities between the regents and the K'ang-hsi Emperor are made
apparent in Jonathan Spence's work on the K'ang-hsi Emperor. The emperor, for
instance, was adamant about specificity in memorials on military matters and
shared his regents' concerns about the role of eunuchs in Peking. The emperor's
execution of the Ming loyalist scholar, Tai Ming-shih, also reminds one of the regents' prosecution of the Ming History Case. For these matters, see Spence,
Emperor of China, chapters 2 and 6, passim.

had lived immersed in the Manchu military tradition. They were raised
in Manchuria as elite members of a warrior community. During their
youth they had awaited the day when they could participate in battles a-
gainst the Chinese. The wealthy Chinese scholar-official class became
more than a military enemy for the young Manchus. This class came to
represent the antithesis of the Manchu ideal; they were perceived as
soft scholars and aesthetes, untoughened by the demands of warfare.

Although the four Manchus never were entrusted with the formulation
of overall plans for the conquest, they were well-schooled as soldiers
and tacticians. As high-ranking military subordinates imbued with a
deep sense of mission, they produced superb records on the field of battle during the 1630s and 1640s. After the conquest, however, the future
regents found themselves powerless throughout the Shun-chih period.
Worst of all, the Shun-chih Emperor seemed to allow his personal life
and the court to slip back into habits of late Ming China. The four Manchus quietly waited in the wings for the moment when they could take the
stage and reveal their own visions for Manchu China.

When the regents took command in 1661, therefore, they were products not only of a Manchu value system, but also of the hatreds, frustrations, and desires of their own careers. Their preoccupation with military matters forced them to view government and society from a soldier's
perspective. Chinese as well as Manchus were expected to act with military discipline and to perform military feats. The regents' inexperience
in the planning of military strategy, however, rendered them incapable
of venturing very far beyond the strategic guidelines established in the
Shun-chih years. Radical in their adherence to military values, the regents were conservative in their military operations and foreign policies.
The regents also exhibited strong suspicions about the Chinese elite.
They had come to China with distorted images of this elite, and they had
been further embittered by what they saw as the sinophilic tendencies of
the Shun-chih Emperor. Finally, they were frustrated and antagonized
by their minimal political influence during the Shun-chih reign and were
left with a lust for political power.

The K'ang-hsi Emperor, on the other hand, was reared in a very
special and controlled environment.[3] He spent at least part of his youth
living with his nurses in a palace outside the Forbidden City and away
from the corrupting pressures of the court. His early education and development seem to have been largely influenced by his remarkable grand-
mother, the Grand Empress Dowager Hsiao-chuang. During his early
years the emperor became fluent in Manchu and learned to read and write
Chinese well enough to deal efficiently with state documents. Under the
Grand Empress Dowager's tutelage the K'ang-hsi Emperor learned respect for Manchu military traditions and for riding, archery, and the
hunt. But, judging from the nature of his later regime, it is evident that

---

3. The following information is taken from Hummel, pp. 301, 328; and Spence,
"Seven Ages of K'ang-hsi," pp. 205-11.

the young emperor also received some tutoring in Chinese philosophy
and history. He was guided to respect certain aspects of Chinese civi-
lization and was informed of the traditional responsibilities of a Chinese
emperor.

Although the K'ang-hsi Emperor was a proud and unabashed Manchu
like his regents, he also took several steps calculated to soothe Chinese
resentments and to win Chinese support. Acting in the traditional role
of the Chinese emperor, in 1670 the K'ang-hsi Emperor issued his famous Sheng Yü (The Sacred Edict of K'ang-hsi), in which he posed as a
paternal figure concerned for his flock and laid out sixteen maxims for
moral behavior. In 1679, following Hsiung Tz'u-li's memorial, he held
the po-hsüeh examination to bring Ming loyalist scholars into his administration. Likewise he patronized the arts and letters and sponsored
several compilation projects such as the K'ang-hsi tzu-tien (The K'ang-
hsi Dictionary) and the Ch'üan T'ang-shih (Complete T'ang Poems).
Even a hall in one of the palaces of Peking was set aside for the use of
artists, architects, and technicians in his court.[4] In short, the K'ang-
hsi Emperor avoided the sinophobia of Oboi and the other regents, and
instead deftly manipulated Chinese tradition to create a more peaceful
atmosphere within China.

A large segment of the emperor's career, however, can only be explained by his unique combination of political genius and Manchu military
vitality. In many respects he was tougher and more imaginative than
his regents in seeking similar goals. He reminds us of Nurhaci and Abahai, even of Chinggis Khan, in his search for governmental efficiency
through innovation and in his quest for security through military expansion. Avoiding the usually isolated role of the emperor, he embarked on
six Southern Tours to gain firsthand information about conditions at the
provincial and local levels. He relied on his own bondservants and on
the more informal and efficient "palace memorial" system to alleviate
the problems of slow and distorted communication between the provinces
and the capital. In order to preserve Manchu traditions and military
toughness, he spent most summers at his palace in Jehol beyond the
Great Wall, and in the autumns he personally led banner troops on rugged hunting expeditions.[5] He also prohibited Chinese emigration to Manchuria, in an effort to maintain the ethnic homogeneity of the Manchu
homeland.

Furthermore, the K'ang-hsi Emperor must be ranked with Nurhaci
and Abahai as an empire-builder. Through his carefully planned and
forcefully executed military operations he extended Ch'ing imperial control to southern and southwestern China, to the island of Taiwan, to much
of the territory of the northern and western Mongols, and to the frontiers
of northern Manchuria. The K'ang-hsi Emperor, therefore, did not for-
sake the visions of his forebears, nor even the aspirations of his regents,

4. Hummel, p. 329.
5. Spence, Ts'ao Yin, p. 52.

as he held the throne of the Ch'ing dynasty. He was not just an exceptional emperor; he was an exceptional Manchu emperor, many of whose accomplishments would have been applauded enthusiastically by his regents. His acts of conciliation toward the Chinese were not akin to those of the Shun-chih Emperor; rather, they were acts of a versatile ruler who remained intensely loyal to the Manchu tradition, while seeking a more harmonious relationship with the Chinese.

The emperor's regents, by contrast, lacked K'ang-hsi's versatility. They shared the Manchu side of his character, but were unable to anticipate his complexity. The only exception was Soni, whose activities and offspring made significant contributions to the transition between early Ch'ing and high Ch'ing. But on the whole the regency reflected the obsession for Manchu dominance which characterized most of those in the conquest elite. The regents emphasized the Manchu elements of the early Ch'ing state and society, while the Chinese elite and Chinese institutions were considered subordinate, sometimes even dangerous, factors. Having conquered on horseback, they sought to rule from horseback. While the regents were in the saddle, they took the Ch'ing state for its last ride towards exclusive Manchu dominance. The K'ang-hsi Emperor, who was willing to play the role of good Confucian emperor for political mileage, found it easier to dismount from the horse of conquest and to sit upon the Chinese throne.

Appendix 1
The "Death" of the Shun-chih Emperor and the Forgery of His Will

The events which occurred during the first days of February 1661 have been a source of debate among Chinese historians. The basic issue is whether or not the Shun-chih Emperor actually died on 5 February or whether he retired to a Buddhist monastery where he spent the remaining years of his life. Several imaginative tales have been written about the "retirement" of the Shun-chih Emperor and about the mysterious visits of the K'ang-hsi Emperor and the Grand Empress Dowager to the "strange monk of Wu-t'ai."[1] Hsiao I-shan, while unwilling to fully support the retirement thesis, has concluded that retirement and death from illness are both credible possibilities.[2] Meng Sen, on the other hand, made an extensive study of this problem and concluded that the emperor definitely died of smallpox in early February. Meng's evidence for this contention rests on two diaries (nien-p'u) of close imperial attendants, the subchancellor Wang Hsi and the monk Hsing-ts'ung. Both of them saw the emperor personally in early February and both record a daily decline in his condition.[3] Although these nien-p'u do not constitute proof of Shun-chih's death in early 1661, Meng would seem to have circumstantial evidence on his side, and, until further information is uncovered, we had best assume that Shun-chih died on 5 February.

It is certain, however, that Shun-chih did leave his own Imperial Will, and almost certain that this document was later rewritten and expanded before being made public. On 1 February Wang Hsi was called to the emperor's bedside and was asked to take down imperial edicts and instructions as well as to read "secret sealed memorials" to the emperor. On 4 February Wang Hsi and Margi, another subchancellor, were called again to the emperor's couch.[4] According to Wang Hsi, the emperor ordered them to record his Will for transmission to the officials of the court. In

1. See Johnston, "Romance of an Emperor," pp. 1-24, 180-94; Backhouse and Bland, Annals and Memoirs, pp. 235-38.
2. Hsiao I-shan, 1: 405.
3. See Meng, "Ch'ing-ch'u san ta i-an k'ao-shih,", pp. 456-57.
4. The official account of the drafting of the Will, as well as biographical accounts, indicates that these two officials were given the responsibility for making the drafts. See KH Shih-lu, ch. 1. pp. 4b-5a. Also see CSK, ch. 256, pp. 5b-7a, and ch. 279, p. 8a; Hummel, p. 819; Johnston, "Romance of an Emperor," pp. 190-91.
Wang Hsi was a chin-shih (1647) who was given the responsibility of assisting the emperor in the composition of edicts in the early 1650s. He was especially respected for his ability to translate Chinese into Manchu, and he had taught Manchu in the Department of Dynastic History in the late 1640s. During the 1650s

Wang Hsi's biography there is the following account: "[Wang Hsi] fell to
the ground, swallowing his tears, and said that his brush could not record
the Emperor's edict. But then he exerted himself and restrained his grief
and pain. He made the first draft in front of the imperial couch."[5] When
the draft was completed, the emperor ordered his subchancellors to "receive and cherish" the Imperial Will and to draw up a finished proclamation. It is unclear whether they worked together or separately in fulfilling
these instructions. Wang Hsi reports that he went to the Ch'ien-ch'ing
Gate, where he concealed himself behind a folding screen to edit and read
the draft. He mentions that he reviewed his final draft three times and
finally, at sundown, felt that it was in accordance with Shun-chih's stipu-
lations.[6] The finished Will was then taken by Margi to an imperial bodyguard, named Chia-pu-chia, who was in attendance on the Grand Empress
Dowager. Chia-pu-chia in turn submitted it to the Grand Empress Dowager,
probably in the evening of 4 February.[7] The regents and the emperor's
mother, therefore, had roughly a day in which to alter the document to their
own interests.

The probable extent of the forgery has been described elsewhere in
this book, but it is worth mentioning that Meng Sen felt that only those
sections of the Imperial Will dealing with financial extravagance, limited
contact with officials, and unwillingness to accept criticism were possibly
genuine.[8] In his nien-p'u, Wang Hsi recorded his astonishment at the
final Will which was read at court on the evening of 5 February and said
"that he dared not speak the truth on what had happened."[9] Meng Sen,

---

he held several positions: Diarist (with the responsibility of giving daily lectures
to the emperor), subchancellor in the Grand Secretariat, expositor of the academy,
chancellor of the Imperial Academy, vice-president of the Board of Rites (1858),
and president of the Board of Rites (1660) (Hummel, p. 819; CSK, ch. 256, pp. 5b-
7a; KCCH, ch. 4, pp. 1a-32a).

Margi was a Manchu of the Plain Yellow Banner whose ancestors had offered
their allegiance to Nurhaci in the early seventeenth century. Like Wang Hsi,
Margi was a skilled translator and gained chü-jen status in the translator's examination (fan-i) in 1651. In 1652 he was awarded the chin-shih and became a
compiler of the First Class. By imperial edict which cited his translating ability, Margi became a Reader in the Department of Literature and Conduct (1653).
In 1654 he was made a subchancellor and was entrusted with the revision of the
"Veritable Records" for the Nurhaci and Abahai reigns. Margi was also involved
in several military campaigns in the late 1650s. During the Oboi regency he
served as vice-president of the Board of Punishments (1666) and then as governor-
general of Kiangnan and Kiangsu (1668). He also played a role in the suppression
of the Rebellion of the Three Feudatories in the 1670s. He died in 1689 (CSK, ch.
279, pp. 8a-9a; CSLC, ch. 10, pp. 1a-2b).

5. CSK, ch. 256, p. 5b.
6. Meng, "Ch'ing-ch'u san ta i-an k'ao-shih," p. 457.
7. KH Shih-lu, ch. 1, p. 4b.
8. Meng, Ch'ing-tai shih, p. 128.
9. Ibid., p. 128.

offering additional evidence of the forgery, has noted that the emperor
did attend Wu Liang-fu's tonsuring on 31 January 1661, and concluded
that it is highly improbable that Shun-chih would have turned against his
eunuchs in his Will dictated four days later.[10] Once again, as in the
matter of Shun-chih's death, we are left with strong circumstantial evidence on the forgery to which we must give credence until contrary evidence is discovered.

A skeptic might ask: if the Imperial Will of the Shun-chih Emperor
was a forgery, why then did the K'ang-hsi Emperor leave it in the "Veritable Records"? The most likely explanation is that K'ang-hsi knew that
the Will was a forgery and left it in for personal and political reasons.
K'ang-hsi, never known as a man of modest ego, probably realized that
this tarnished portrait of his father would make K'ang-hsi himself the
first strong Ch'ing emperor to rule China proper. It is also possible
that K'ang-hsi assumed that the Chinese officialdom, knowing full well
that the extant Will was forged, would applaud K'ang-hsi's edict to his
father in February 1668. Finally, since the Will expressed many widely
held opinions of the Manchu conquest elite, K'ang-hsi could have concluded that it was not worth alienating that elite by altering the "Veritable
Records." In short, by leaving the forged Will in the Ch'ing chronicle
and writing his own testimony to his father in 1668, K'ang-hsi left two
distinct images for his own reign, one Manchu and one Chinese. And by
seeking to fulfill both images, K'ang-hsi sought to elevate himself in the
eyes of both groups.

10. Ibid., pp. 128-29.

Appendix 2
Career Patterns of Key
Metropolitan Statesmen, 1661–1666

Considering the absence of studies on career patterns of Manchu and Chinese officials in the early Ch'ing period, it is useful to consider those who served as Grand Secretaries, board presidents, presidents of the Censorate, and presidents of the Li-fan yüan in the years of 1661-66. Since these men had made their way to the top of the bureaucratic ladder, they exemplify the criteria for political success in the early years of the Ch'ing dynasty. The careers of thirty-nine of these statesmen are presented in table A, at the end of this appendix. Fourteen of these were Manchus, twenty-two were Chinese degree-holders, two were Chinese bannermen (one of these also held the chin-shih degree), and two were Mongols. The reason for the greater number of Chinese is not that they dominated the bureaucracy at the expense of the Manchus, but rather that the rate of turnover was higher among the Chinese officials.

In general the evidence presented in table A indicates that the highest metropolitan posts in 1661-66 were held by men who had emerged as officials in the 1630s and 1640s, reached the acme of official success during the 1650s and 1660s, and had retired or died by the time of the Rebellion of the Three Feudatories. The Manchus in these key posts, unlike most in the conquest elite, reflected a wealth of both military and civil experience and were not just conquerors fresh from battle. The Chinese incumbents were almost all chin-shih degree-holders with substantial backgrounds at the metropolitan level dating from the 1640s. The majority of these statesmen, both Manchu and Chinese, avoided becoming embroiled in the factionalism of the late 1660s and neither supported nor obstructed the ambitions of Oboi. Competence and maturity, then, characterized both the Manchu and Chinese high official elite in these years.

The Manchus who held these high offices represented all eight of the banners in a relatively equitable division. Although many of the Manchus had begun their careers in the military service, almost all of them had been appointed to major metropolitan posts before becoming presidents or Grand Secretaries. Five of the Manchus had been board vice-presidents, and one had been a subchancellor in the Inner Three Departments. None of the fourteen Manchus studied is known to have stepped out of a purely military career into the highest echelons of the Peking bureaucracy without some previous exposure to civil administration. These Manchus generally followed one of two different career patterns: a combination military-civil route or a predominantly civil route.

Sunahai will serve as an example of the first type, the combination of military and civil experience. Sunahai was a member of the Plain

White Banner. During the Dorgon regency he served as one of Dorgon's personal bodyguards and as a subchancellor in the Inner Three Departments. In the late 1640s Sunahai accompanied the Manchu Prince Haoge on the campaign in which Chang Hsien-chung was finally exterminated. In 1649 he participated in a military expedition led by Ajige against a loyalist rebellion in the city of Ta-t'ung, Shansi. A year later Sunahai translated the Chinese dynastic history, Record of the Three Kingdoms (San-kuo chih), into Manchu and was given hereditary ranks for his accomplishment. He became vice-president of the Board of Civil Office in 1653 and three years later was also given the position of deputy lieutenant-general of the Manchu Bordered Red Banner. At the end of the Shun-chih period he became president of the Board of Works (1660) and later in the same year was transferred to the presidency of the Board of War. In this latter post Sunahai oversaw the implementation of the famous coastal evacuation policy whereby the population of much of the China coast was evacuated to prevent trade with the troops of Cheng Ch'eng-kung (Coxinga). Sunahai was appointed Grand Secretary and president of the Board of Revenue under the Oboi regency. Unlike most of his Manchu peers, Sunahai became a staunch opponent of the Oboi faction. In 1666, when Oboi ordered a massive banner land transfer in order to place the troops of his own banner in the best location, Sunahai refused to follow the regent's orders. Oboi retaliated by bringing the recalcitrant Sunahai to trial and sentencing him to execution by strangulation.[1]

An example of the second type of Manchu career pattern, the predominantly civil route of the post-conquest Manchu elite, was that of Duikana. Duikana's biography, except for his lack of an examination degree and his racial background, reads like that of many early Ch'ing Chinese political figures who were competent administrators and who climbed to the top of the bureaucratic ladder in a regular series of persistent steps. He was first appointed as a second-class secretary in the Board of Works (1645) and later as department director in the same board (1652). In 1661 he became a senior vice-president in the Censorate and was transferred to vice-president of the Board of Punishments in the following year. He was elevated to Manchu president of the Board of Punishments in 1665 and submitted a memorial which condemned the self-enslavement of Chinese to Manchu bannermen; the memorial was approved and followed. Three years later he became a Grand Secretary and was appointed as a compiler of the "Veritable Records" for the Shun-chih reign. The K'ang-hsi Emperor cited Duikana for his admirable service and made him president of the Board of Civil Office. Duikana retired in 1674 and died in the following year.[2]

For the Chinese political aspirant the chin-shih degree remained the mandatory prerequisite for top metropolitan posts. All but two of the twenty-three Chinese examined held the chin-shih; one of the others was

1. Biographies of Sunahai in CSK, ch. 255, p. 5a; CSLC, ch. 6, pp. 6a-7a.
2. Biography of Duikana in CSLC, ch. 6, pp. 24a-b.

a chü-jen; and the last held no degree but was a Chinese bannerman.
Although the date of receipt of the chin-shih extended as far back as 1613,
well over half had received the highest degree in the 1640s. Of the nineteen Chinese whose backgrounds are known, only eight had served under
the Ming and only three of these had held high Ming posts. The majority
of the Chinese were first appointed to a Ch'ing post in the Dorgon period
(1643-50), and only two had served the Manchus prior to the conquest.
Like the Manchus, most of the Chinese were appointed as Grand Secretaries or board presidents between 1650 and 1666, and the length of official service averaged about thirty to thirty-five years for both racial
groups. Only one of the Chinese, Wang Hung-tso, is known to have openly opposed the Oboi factionalism. Wang was eventually ousted from his
post as president of the Board of Revenue for his resistance to the designs
of Oboi and his subordinates. As a group, the Chinese seem to have been
a little younger than the Manchu statesmen; over half of them endured into
the 1670s, while only four Manchus evidenced similar longevity.

Wei Chou-tso is a fairly typical example of the Chinese metropolitan
statesman during this period. Born in Shansi, Wei received his chin-shih
in 1637 and served as a department director in the last years of the Ming.
When Li Tzu-ch'eng took Peking in early 1644, Wei renounced his allegiance to the Ming and acted as an official under Li's short-lived regime.
After the Manchu conquest Wei once again shifted sides and was appointed
a department director in the Board of Civil Office. In 1653 he was made
a vice-president in the Board of Punishments on the recommendation of
the famous Chinese bannerman, Hung Ch'eng-ch'ou. As vice-president,
he distinguished himself by submitting memorials on such topics as the
punishment of robbers and the reform of the official evaluation system.
He was raised to president of the Board of Works in 1654 and was given
the title of Grand Guardian of the Heir Apparent. Four years later he was
transferred to the presidency of the Board of Civil Office and was appointed as Grand Secretary. On three occasions (1659, 1661, and 1664) he was
entrusted with the task of serving as chief examiner in the metropolitan
examinations. In 1660 Wei Chou-tso and the Manchu Grand Secretary Ba-
hana were responsible for the revision of the Law Codes (lü-li), and Wei
was given the hereditary title of viscount. Later, in 1667, he was appointed a compiler of the Shun-chih Shih-lu. After a retirement of three years
for illness, Wei returned as Grand Secretary in 1672 and submitted memorials on the selection of officials and the reform of the financial administration. He died in 1675 and was accorded funerary honors appropriate
for an official of his high station. Wei's career is indicative of the high
rewards which the Manchus bestowed on those Chinese who served the
Ch'ing loyally and capably.[3]

3. Biographies of Wei Chou-tsou in CSK, ch. 244, pp. 9a-10a; CSLC, ch.
79, pp. 41b-43a.

TABLE A. Statistics on Key Metropolitan Officials of 1661-66

	Manchu	Chinese	Mongol
Types of officials investigated *	14	23	2
Positions held, 1661-66			
Grand Secretary	6	11	.....
Board President	11	20	1
President of Censorate	4	6	.....
President of Li-fan yüan	2	.....	2
Banner allegiances			
Plain Yellow	2	.....	.....
Bordered Yellow	2	1	.....
Plain White	1	.....	2
Bordered White	2	1	.....
Plain Red	2	.....	.....
Bordered Red	1	.....	.....
Plain Blue	3	.....	.....
Bordered Blue	1	.....	.....
Highest examination degrees held by the			
Chinese officials			
Chin-shih (by year in which degree was earned)			
1613	.....	2	.....
1616	.....	1	.....
1619	.....	1	.....
1628	.....	2	.....
1634	.....	1	.....
1637	.....	1	.....
1643	.....	5	.....
1646	.....	6	.....
1647	.....	2	.....
Chü-jen	.....	1	.....
No degree	.....	1	.....
(Total)	.....	(23)	.....
Chinese who served under the Ming **			
High positions	.....	3	.....
Low positions	.....	5	.....
No service until after 1644	.....	11	.....
Unknown	.....	4	.....
Previous experience ***			
Grand Secretariat			
Subchancellor	3	7	.....
Other	.....	6	.....
Six Boards			
Vice-president	5	13	.....
Other	3	4	.....
Censorate			
Vice-president	1	3	.....
Other	1	3	.....
Provincial			
Tu-fu	.....	1	.....
Other	.....	3	.....

TABLE A (continued)

	Manchu	Chinese	Mongol
Previous experience (continued)			
Imperial Bodyguard			
Chamberlain	1	.....	.....
Other	3	.....	.....
Banner Officer Corps			
Captain or above	5	.....	.....
Major role in campaigns of conquest or			
consolidation	5	.....	1
Unknown	3	1	1
First appointment as Ch'ing official			
1620s	2	1	1
1630s	2	1	.....
1640–43	1	.....	.....
1644–50	4	15	.....
1651–60	.....	.....	.....
1661–66	.....	.....	.....
Unknown	5	6	1
First appointment as Grand Secretary or			
Board President			
1620s	.....	.....	.....
1630s	.....	1	.....
1640–43	.....	.....	.....
1644–50	.....	2	.....
1651–60	7	13	1
1661–66	7	7	1
Total years of service as an official			
11–15	.....	1	.....
16–20	.....	2	.....
21–25	3	3	.....
26–30	1	1	.....
31–35	1	6	.....
36–40	3	4	1
Over 40	1	3	.....
Unknown	5	3	1
Total years of service as Grand Secretary or			
Board President			
Fewer than 5	2	4	.....
5–10	6	5	1
11–15	3	4	.....
16–20	2	6	1
21–25	.....	2	.....
26–30	.....	2	.....
Unknown	1	.....	.....
Oboi faction			
Opponent	3	1	.....
Adherent	1	.....	.....
No information	10	22	2

TABLE A (continued)

	Manchu	Chinese	Mongol
Later service as high official****			
1669-75	2	4	.....
1676-80	.....	1	.....
1680s	1	4	.....
1690s	.....	.....	.....
1700s	.....	1	.....
No further service after 1660s	11	13	2
Date of death			
1660s	8	7	2
1670s	3	7	.....
1680s	.....	3	.....
1690s	1	2	.....
1700s	.....	1	.....
Unknown	2	3	.....

SOURCES: PCTC, PCTC (1795), CSK, CSLC, KCCH, Hummel, PCST, and CS.

* Of the twenty-three Chinese investigated, two were Chinese bannermen. One of these bannermen also held the chin-shih degree and thus was a member of the Chinese official elite.

** High positions are those of governor-general, governor, board vice-president, or above. Low positions are all those beneath these, down to district magistrate.

*** Every time that one of the officials investigated had held a post listed in this section, his name was entered. There are, therefore, a number of cases where a man has several entries in this section.

**** Entries were made only next to the latest date that a man held high positions under the late K'ang-hsi reign. High officials include only board presidents, Grand Secretaries, and lieutenant-generals.

Appendix 3
Provincial Appointments and
Administration in the Oboi Regency

Table B, given at the end of this appendix, provides an analysis of fifty-two governors and governors-general during the 1661-66 period. In addition to indicating the regents' adherence to the Dorgon compromise in the highest provincial appointments, table B also shows the considerable civil administrative experience which the tu-fu brought to their posts. Of the thirty-eight for whom we have information about their backgrounds in official service, eight had been presidents or vice-presidents of the Six Boards; eight had been Grand Secretaries or sub-chancellors; six had been vice-presidents of the Censorate; seventeen had held provincial posts of magistrate or above; and twenty-eight had held minor metropolitan posts (beneath vice-president). Twenty-nine of the tu-fu had been governors-general or governors prior to 1661 and were reappointed during the Oboi period.

Turning to the financial commissioners and judicial commissioners, one finds a nearly even division between Chinese bannermen and regular Chinese officials. A survey of forty-four financial commissioners (rank 2B) who held office during the first eight years of the K'ang-hsi reign indicates that eighteen were Chinese bannermen. Among forty-seven judicial commissioners (rank 3A) studied, twenty-one were Chinese bannermen.[1] Among the ranks of these officials, moreover, there was a much higher percentage of degree-holders than among the governors-general and governors. Thirty of the ninety-one examined were chin-shih recipients, and over half (53 of 91) held degrees of kung-sheng or above.

In the lower-ranking provincial posts there were considerably fewer appointments of Chinese bannermen. Of thirty prefects (rank 4B) in the

---

1. These figures on financial commissioners and judicial commissioners are taken from the lists of officials provided in the provincial gazetteers. In the case of the financial commissioners the provinces checked were Anhwei, Chekiang, Fukien, Honan, Hunan, Kiangsu, Kwangsi, Kweichow, Shansi, Shantung, Shensi, and Szechwan. Chihli was not included because there were no financial commissioners appointed in that province until 1669. The other provinces were eliminated because of inadequate information in provincial gazetteers. The same provinces were studied for information on the judicial commissioners with the exception of Fukien, which was omitted for lack of information about the dates during which the post was held.

In 1668 there were four Manchus appointed as financial commissioners and two as judicial commissioners. The significance of these Manchu appointments is discussed in chapter 5. Appointees were recorded as Chinese bannermen when they were listed as coming from Chinese Manchuria or when they were specifically listed as bannermen.

province of Kiangnan during 1661-68, nineteen were from Chinese official elite backgrounds and only eleven were recorded as members of
the Chinese banners.[2] There were 178 magistrates in Kiangnan during
the same years; of these only twenty-five were Chinese bannermen,
while the remainder were of the Chinese official elite. Similarly, at
the magisterial level, there was a predominance of examination degrees. Of the magistrates in Kiangnan, no fewer than 139 (or 78 percent) held degrees of kung-sheng and above; 40 (or 22 percent) were
chin-shih; and 49 (or 27 percent) were chü-jen.[3]

Although the regents carefully followed Dorgon's policy in appointments, they did make major changes in provincial administrative and
gographical divisions during their regime. As explained in chapter 5,
they increased the numbers of governors-general from nine to twenty.
This numerical expansion permitted the regents to introduce their own
appointees without dismissing the governors-general who had served
during the late Shun-chih period. It also allowed them greater supervision of military operations through their new appointments. In 1662
the regents made it clear that these governors-general were to assume
the key role in military matters and that governors were to devote themselves exclusively to civil concerns.[4]

In late 1665, however, the number of governors-general was reduced to eleven (including the director-general of River Conservancy).
Only four provinces, Hukuang, Szechwan, Fukien, and Chekiang, retained the former system of one governor-general to a province. In
most other cases, two provinces were combined under one governor-
generalship. In north China the three provinces of Chihli, Shantung,
and Honan were combined under a single governor-general's jurisdiction.[5]

2. Chiang-nan t'ung-chih, ch. 106-8, passim. There were thirty-four prefects in Kiangnan during the Oboi period, but four of these were listed in the provincial gazetteer without information about whether they were Chinese bannermen or regular Chinese officials. Twenty-five of these prefects were recorded
as degree-holders. Five held the chin-shih, five the chü-jen, fourteen the kung-
sheng; and one the sheng-yüan.

3. Information on the magistrates of Kiangnan is from ibid. Of the 178 magistrates, eighteen were listed in the gazetteer without any information about
whether they were Chinese bannermen or regular Chinese officials.

The Szechwan provincial gazetteer was examined for magistrates during the
same period. The results of this survey were strikingly similar to those in
Kiangnan. There were 194 magistrates in 1661-68: 163 were regular Chinese
officials, 24 were Chinese bannermen, 2 were Manchus, and 5 were listed without information in the gazetteer. Of those whose degrees were listed (169), 58
were chin-shih, 39 were chü-jen, 65 were kung-sheng, 4 were chien-sheng, and
3 were sheng-yüan (Ssu-ch'uan t'ung-chih, ch. 103-5, passim).

4. KH Shih-lu, ch. 6, p. 12a; Fu Tsung-mao, Ch'ing-tai tu-fu chih-tu, p.
96; Kessler, "Ethnic Composition of Provincial Leadership," p. 491.

5. KH Shih-lu, ch. 15, pp. 14a-b; Fu Tsung-mao, Ch'ing-tai tu-fu chih-tu,
pp. 10-20; Yang Yü-liu, Chung-kuo li-tai ti-fang hsing-cheng chü-hua, p. 308;
Chao Ch'üan-ch'eng, Ch'ing-tai ti-li yen-ko piao, pp. 15, 68, 91, 101.

There are several explanations for these changes. First, by 1655 there was relative peace throughout the empire, and the governors-general, whose primary role under the regency was military, were not needed in such profusion. Secondly, as mentioned in chapter 5, the governors-general had not all been loyal adherents of the Manchu court, and consequently the regents may have thought that by lessening their numbers they would reduce corruption and disobedience. Thirdly, the preservation of the single governor-generalship system in the provinces of Hukuang, Szechwan, Fukien, and Chekiang, was probably an effort to keep close tabs on the feudatories as well as on the China coast. The combination of three provinces under one governor-general in north China was most likely designed to provide more unified military control in the metropolitan area.

TABLE B. Statistics on Governors-general and Governors, 1661-66

	Governors-general	Governors
Positions held *		
Chinese bannermen	21	24
Chinese official elite	1	6
Banner allegiances		
Plain Yellow	2	3
Bordered Yellow	4	2
Plain White	2	4
Bordered White	5	1
Plain Red	2	3
Bordered Red	.....	5
Plain Blue	2	3
Bordered Blue	4	1
Unknown	.....	2
Highest examination degree		
Chih-shih	2	3
Chü-jen	.....	3
Kung-sheng	3	8
Sheng-yüan	.....	1
None **	17	15
Previous experience ***		
Grand Secretariat (Inner Three Departments)		
Grand Secretary	1	.....
Subchancellor	5	2
Other	6	5
Six Boards		
President	1	.....
Vice-president	3	4
Other	9	8
Censorate		
Vice-president	4	2
Metropolitan censor	.....	3
Provincial censor	1	3

TABLE B (continued)

	Governors-general	Governors
Previous experience (continued)		
Provincial administrators		
Prefect or above	4	8
Magistrate	3	2
First appointment as Ch'ing official		
1636-43	5	1
1644-49	13	12
1650-60	.....	3
Unknown	4	14
First appointment as governor or governor-general		
1644-49	1	.....
1650-60	13	15
1661-66	8	15
Later service as an official		
1669-75	.....	8
1676-80	4	2
1680s	2	1
1690s	.....	.....
None after 1660s	16	8
Unknown	.....	11
Date of Death		
1660s	9	5
1670s	4	7
1680s	2	3
1690s	3	.....
1700s	1	.....
Unknown	3	15

SOURCES: CS, PCTC, PCTC (1795), CSK, CSLC, KCCH, and Yen, Ch'ing-tai cheng-hsien lei-pien. In some cases provincial gazetteers were consulted for additional information.

* This selection of fifty-two tu-fu includes almost all of the incumbents during the 1661-66 period; a few were excluded because of lack of biographical information. In cases where a man served both as governor and governor-general, he is listed only once, under governors-general.

** All those whose biographies give no listing of an examination degree are listed in this category.

*** Only posts held prior to first appointment as tu-fu are listed in this category. Every time that an official had held a post listed in this section, his name was entered. There are, therefore, a number of cases where a man has more than one entry in this section.

Appendix 4
Economic Policy in
the Oboi Regency

To Soni, Suksaha, Ebilun, and Oboi, as well as to all of the early Ch'ing rulers, the procurement of revenue was a task of paramount importance. First of all, the regents needed income to cover the usual operating expenses of the empire: compensation of officials, public works and river conservancy, military supply and wages, imperial buildings and celebrations, the imperial family and the emperor's retinue, and so forth. Secondly, the regents also had to devote a considerable portion of the budget to underwriting military campaigns and to keeping the banner troops at wartime levels of preparedness. In southeastern, southern, and southwestern China, as well as in the barren lands of northern Manchuria, the dynasty faced strong threats, and the regents had to be ready to meet them. A third reason for the regents' concern about revenue was symbolic: increased tax income indicated that the Ch'ing dynasty was spreading its control over the empire and bringing peace and stability to its subjects. The regents were anxious to show that the Manchus could rule China as smoothly, efficiently, and prosperously as a regime of purely domestic origins.

While economic statistics presented in traditional Chinese sources are seldom reliable as accurate assessments, it is evident that the Ch'ing treasury was far from solvent when the regents assumed control of the government. In 1664 the regents issued an edict citing the deficits for the period of 1644–60 as totaling twenty-seven million taels in silver and over seven million shih of rice.[1] A few years earlier a censor noted that the annual military expenditure for the province of Yunnan, the headquarters of Wu San-kuei, totaled nine million taels, while the annual revenue for the entire empire was only 8,750,000 taels.[2]

The causes of the economic problems during the early Ch'ing period were several. In the four decades preceding the Oboi regency the Chinese people had suffered extraordinary losses of land, life, and property. The rebellions of Chang Hsien-chung and Li Tzu-ch'eng and the conquest battles of the Manchus destroyed huge amounts of cultivated land and brought death to tens of millions of Chinese. Throughout most of the Ming period the land tax registers amounted to over 700,000,000 mou, but by 1645 the total had dwindled to 405,000,000 mou. The official registers of adult males (ting) had also shrunk drastically to slightly over

---

1. KH Shih-lu, ch. 12, pp. 13a–15a. For further information on this deficit, see Hsieh Pao-chao, Government of China, pp. 199–201.
2. SC Shih-lu, ch. 136, p. 22a.

ten million taxable persons.[3] The drop in these tax registers meant, of course, a substantially smaller annual income for the early Ch'ing as compared to the Ming period. In the first few decades of the Ch'ing dynasty, moreover, several millions of taels were lost to the Ch'ing treasuries through tax remissions to areas plagued by droughts and floods and to areas devastated by military conflicts.[4] Finally, the heavy palace expenditures of the late Shun-chih reign contributed to the drain on the Ch'ing treasury.

The demands placed on these shrunken Ch'ing resources, particularly military demands, were exceptional. During the 1640s and 1650s the consolidation of the Chinese empire under the Manchus was a slow, and very costly, operation. When the regents established their regime in February 1661, the arduous defensive campaign to protect the China coast from Cheng Ch'eng-kung's invasion was less than a year's history, and the battles against the Ming Prince of Kuei (Chu Yu-lang) were still raging in the southwest. The establishment of the three semi-independent feudatories under Shang K'o-hsi, Keng Chi-mao, and Wu San-kuei during the 1650s had already begun to cost the Manchus dearly by the early 1660s. Wu San-kuei in particular had established a small empire in the southwestern provinces of Yunnan and Kweichow. The expense of maintaining Wu's regime, already considerable by 1660, amounted to twenty million taels annually by 1670.[5]

Expenditures for military operations remained high throughout the Oboi regency, to the dismay of many Chinese civil officials. One official complained that:

> With respect to the wealth of the empire, there are no areas more
> flourishing than the East and the South, and yet there are no areas

---

3. These figures on the land and ting registers are taken from Ho, Studies on the Population of China, pp. 35, 236.

4. In spite of their obsession for tax receipts, the regents, whether because of the pervasiveness of the Confucian ideal or because of their own humanity, were relatively generous in granting tax remissions. In the first year of the regency, all land taxes in arrears from 1658 and earlier were exempted from payment; in 1663 the date for exemptions was moved forward to 1661 (Hu-nan t'ung-chih, ch. 54, p. 1394; Hu-pei t'ung-chih, ch. 49, p. 1335). When a serious famine developed in Shensi in 1655, the regents issued a sympathetic rescript which rescinded the tax quotas for the afflicted regions (KH Shih-lu, ch. 14, pp. 18a-19a). In Hukuang, where the rebellion of Li Lai-heng raged during the Oboi years, tax remissions were granted every year from 1661 to 1668 (Hu-pei t'ung-chih, ch. 49, p. 1335). The regents also endeavored to systematize the tax remission procedures; in 1665 it was decided that when a disaster was reported, three-tenths of the taxes would immediately be rescinded, the remainder to be exempted when an investigation was conducted and completed (KH Shih-lu, ch. 14, p. 24b). As observed in chapter 6, the regents granted tax remissions to all those who were evicted from their homes along the China coast in the famous coastal evacuation policy designed to reduce the supplies to Cheng Ch'eng-kung.

5. Hummel, p. 879.

more depleted than the East and the South. In the case of Yunnan's military supplies, they are exhausted by ten million plans; and in Fukien and Chekiang, by a million strategies. [6]

In 1667 a provincial censor in Hukuang, Su Chen, expressed similar sentiments: "The reason for the insufficiency of the dynasty's revenue is [the amount spent] in caring for the troops. Speaking in terms of annual expenditures, scattered items account for twenty percent and military expenses account for eighty percent." [7]

Another cause of the financial deficit was official corruption. Many local officials levied large amounts of illegal taxes from village residents and others withheld taxes which should have been remitted to Peking. In some cases corruption in tax collection extended even to the highest provincial officials. [8] Often local officials, in collusion with the local elite, deliberately falsified land tax registers in order to lighten payments for the elite and to assure bribes for the officials. [9] In other cases chaotic and antiquated systems of tax registration made the remission of accurate tax receipts virtually impossible. [10] To make matters still worse, illegal minting of coinage was a prevalent crime in the 1660s. [11]

Tax evasion was another substantial cause of early Ch'ing economic woes. The nonpayment of taxes either by default or by actual refusal by force had been fairly common during the reign of the Shun-chih Emperor. [12] In June 1661 the extraordinary number of 13,517 members of the local elite in Kiangnan were accused of tax evasion. This Kiangnan Tax Case was the most famous example of tax evasion under the regency, and it is investigated in detail in chapter 5 of this volume.

Part of the solution to the regents' economic troubles had been achieved through the military consolidation of the late 1640s and 1650s. As the Ch'ing leaders gradually extended their control across the empire and suppressed dissident elements in the society, the land tax registers and _ting_ registers showed increasing gains. By 1661 the land tax registers had expanded to almost 550,000,000 _mou_ or close to 150,000,000 _mou_ in excess of the officially recorded land in 1645. By 1660 the _ting_ total had reached 19,000,000 adult males, or close to double the 1651 figures. [13] The relative peace of the 1660s also assisted the regents in

6. Memorial of Chi Chen-i in SC Shih-lu, ch. 136, p. 4b.

7. KH Shih-lu, ch. 24, p. 3b.

8. For memorials and edicts describing the corruption of officials entrusted with tax collection in the 1660s, see KH Shih-lu, ch. 12, pp. 13a-15a; ch. 12, pp. 3a-4a; and ch. 26, pp. 12b-13b.

9. Ibid., ch. 8, pp. 4a-b.

10. Ibid., ch. 8, pp. 16a-b; ch. 9, pp. 21a-b.

11. The high number of punishments outlined for illegal minting in the 1660s attests to the prevalence of this crime (HTSL, ch. 220, pp. 15b-16b [pp. 8022-23]).

12. Hsiao Kung-chuan, Rural China, pp. 139-40.

13. These figures are from Ho, Studies on the Population of China, pp. 35, 102.

their quest of financial solvency. Without the burdens of supporting large-scale military campaigns, the Ch'ing treasury was given a short breathing-spell in which to recover for the gigantic military efforts which would come in the late seventeenth century: the suppression of the Rebellion of the Three Feudatories, the conquest of Taiwan, and the defeat of Galdan in Outer Mongolia.

Nevertheless, the rational and forceful efforts of the regents to alleviate their financial problems must also be given considerable credit for lessening the economic burdens of the early Ch'ing. In an attempt to augment the revenue for military needs, the regents revived a late Ming tax system called the lien-hsiang (training rations). Under this Ming system the land tax was increased by approximately 10 percent per mou of land, and the revenues from this surtax were collected separately and allotted solely for military expenditures. It was hoped that the lien-hsiang income would add 5,000,000 taels annually to the regular income.[14]

In order to decrease official corruption in tax collection and in order to bring a halt to tax evasion, the regents resorted to strong admonitions and stern punishments. Several edicts were issued outlining penalties for all officials who tampered with tax registers, levied illegal or excessive taxes, or withheld imperial tax revenues.[15] The penalty of death was prescribed for all those involved in cases of illegal minting. All of the local officials in the area, whether or not they were aware of the private minting operations, were to be punished by fines and demerits in rank.[16] In specific cases of tax evasion, such as the Kiangnan Tax Case of 1661, the principals were executed, while others were degraded, fined, or deprived of their property.

The regents also endeavored to reduce bureaucratic expenditures and to increase the efficiency of the tax system. According to accounts in local gazeteers uncovered by Ch'ü T'ung-tsu, the wages for all clerks serving under chou and hsien magistrates were eliminated entirely in 1662.[17] In order to circumvent illegal taxation by yamen runners and and local clerks, an order in 1661 stipulated that taxpayers personally deliver their taxes to the magistrate's yamen.[18] In 1662 orders were issued to simplify the tax registration and collection procedures by combining the land tax and the ting revenues. Under this system only the military revenues would be collected separately, while the rest was to be

14. KH Shih-lu, ch. 4, p. 9b, and ch. 5, pp. 19b-20a.

15. Ibid., ch. 14, pp. 20a-b, and ch. 21, pp. 3a-b; HTSL, ch. 172, pp. 16a-17a (pp. 7354-55); Hsiao Kung-chuan, Rural China, p. 111; Hsieh Pao-chao, Government of China, p. 193.

16. HTSL, ch. 220, pp. 15b-16b (pp. 8022-23); Ch'ing-ch'ao wen-hsien t'ung-k'ao, ch. 14, pp. 4971-72.

17. Ch'ü T'ung-tsu, Local Government in China, p. 45. While this decision may have been a temporary economic boon to the Manchu regents, unsalaried clerks probably cost the Ch'ing far more heavily in the long run through increased corruption.

18. Hsiao Kung-chuan, Rural China, p. 96.

sent directly to the Board of Revenue in Peking.[19] Perhaps the most
effective of all the techniques adopted by the regents in the economic
field was the reintroduction of the k'ao-ch'eng system and the conse-
quent evaluation of officials on the basis of tax receipts rather than relying on more nebulous categories of administrative ability.[20]

These various measures taken during the Oboi regency did help to
soften the economic crisis and at the same time showed the regents' tendency to rely on tough and innovative devices to achieve their ends. But
the early Ch'ing economic problems were closely related to provincial
and military questions. As long as the provincial officialdom was of
dubious loyalty and major military challenges were left unsettled, the
Ch'ing house could not achieve economic security. So in their economic
policies, as in their provincial and military policies, the regents provided not total answers but partial solutions, leaving a base on which
the K'ang-hsi Emperor could build.

19. Ch'ing-ch'ao wen-hsien t'ung-k'ao, ch. 2, p. 4863. The effort to combine the land and ting taxes into a single system was a continuation of the Ming
"single whip" reform.

20. The regular evaluation system was also supplemented by regulations which
promised awards for supporting military operations. In 1664, for example, it was
stipulated that officials who contributed one hundred horses to the army were to receive two merit points towards promotion in rank (KH Shih-lu, ch. 11, p. 11b).

Glossary of Characters

This glossary is limited to the names and terms of major importance to this book. Omitted from this glossary are: (1) many names and terms that appear only once in the notes; (2) offices or titles that appear in Brunnert and Hagelstrom, Present Day Political Organization of China (BH); (3) characters for persons, organizations, and books that appear in the index to Hummel, Eminent Chinese; and (4) all place names. Most place names may be found in the map at the beginning of this book or in G. M. H. Playfair, The Cities and Towns of China (Shanghai, 1910).

Amuhūlang	阿穆瑚瑯	Chang Wei-ch'ih	張維赤
An-k'un	安坤	ch'ao-wu	超武
Asha	阿思哈	chen	鎮
Ata	阿塔	chen (imperial pronoun)	朕
Baha	巴哈	chen shen min chih	朕甚憫之
Bambursan	班布爾善	Ch'en Shen	陳慎
Becingge	白清額	Ch'en Yung-ming	陳永命
beile	貝勒	cheng-fa	征伐
Belhetu	白爾赫圖	ch'eng-cheng	承政
Budari	布達禮	ch'eng-chih	稱職
Ceke	車克	Ch'eng I-ts'ang	程翼倉
Ch'a-ha-la	查哈喇	chi-mi	覊縻
Chang Feng-ch'i	張鳳起	Chi-shih	濟世
Chang Shang-shien	張尚賢	ch'i-hsin-lang	啟心郎
Chang Ts'un-jen	張存仁	chia-chang	家長

Chia-pu-chia 賈卜嘉

Chiang Kuo-chu 蔣國柱

chien-kuan Feng-t'ien 兼管奉天
fu-yin shih-wu ta-ch'en 府尹事務大臣

Chih-wen kuan 置文館

Chin 金

Chin Ai-tsung 金哀宗

Chin Hsi-tsung 金熙宗

Chin T'ai-tsu 金太祖

Chin T'ai-tsung 金太宗

ching-ch'a 京察

Ching-hai chiang-chün 靖海將軍

Ching-nan Wang 靖南王

Ch'ing 清

Chou 周

Chou Yu-te 周有德

Chu Ch'ang-tso 朱昌祚

chu-fang tso-ling 駐防佐領

Ch'üan T'ang-shih 全唐詩

ch'üan-ti 圈地

chün-chih 軍制

chün-kung hsü-hsü 軍功卹敘

chün-tsui i-fa 軍罪議罰

chung 忠

chung-mei 忠毎

Chung-kuo 中國

Cokto 綽克託

Daso 達索

Duikana 對喀納

er-ch'en 貳臣

er-shih-ssu ya-men 二十四衙門

fan-Ch'ing fu-Ming 反清復明

Feng Shuang-li 馮雙禮

Feng-t'ien chiang-chün 奉天將軍

Foron 佛淪

Garu 噶祿

gūsai ejen 固山額真

Hai-ch'eng kung 海澄公

Hai-tzu 海子

Hife 希福

Hou Yü-kung 侯余公

Hsi Piao 洗彪

hsi-shan k'ou 西山寇

hsiang 晌

hsiang-hsien 鄉賢

hsiang-yüeh 鄉約

Hsiao Chen 蕭震

Hsin Man-chou 新滿洲

hsün-an yü-shih 巡按御史

hsün-tsang 殉葬

Huang Ming-piao 黃明標

Huang-Ming shih-kai　皇明史概

hui-t'ui　會推

Hung-wen yüan　宏文院

i　夷

i-chao　遺詔

i-cheng ta-ch'en　議政大臣

i-cheng wang　議政王

i-fa　議罰

Isha　伊思哈

Jobtei　趙布太

jou-yüan　柔遠

ju-ch'en　濡臣

Junta　準塔

Ka-ch'u-ha　噶褚哈

kai-t'u kuei-liu　改土歸流

K'ang-hsi tzu-tien　康熙字典

k'ao-ch'eng　考成

k'ao-man　考滿

Karantu　喀蘭圖

Kesig　克什克

k'o-hsi　恪僖

k'o-shui　課稅

Koro Baturu Loosa　科羅巴圖魯勞薩

k'u-miao　哭廟

kuan　管

kuan-chih　官制

kuan pu-shih　管部事

Kuei Wang　桂王

Kung Pang　龔榜

Kuo Shih-ching　郭士景

Kuo-shih yüan　國史院

La-hu　剌祜

Lambu　蘭布

Li Cheng-chieh　李正潔

li-hsing　理刑

Li Kuo-ying　李國英

Li Lai-heng　李來亨

Li Ta-tseng　李大增

Li T'ang-i　李唐裔

Li T'ien-yü　李天浴

Li T'ing-shu　李廷樞

Liang Hua-feng　梁化鳳

Liao　遼

Liao T'ai-tsu　遼太祖

lien-hsiang　練餉

Lin T'ien-ching　林天擎

Liu Cheng-hsüeh　劉正學

Liu Cheng-tsung　劉正宗

Liu Chih-yüan　劉之源

Liu Fang-ming　劉芳名

Liu Kuang　劉光

Liu Wen-hsiu　劉文秀

Liu-yü　六論

Lodo　羅多

Lu Ch'ung-chün　盧崇峻

lu-hsün　錄勳

Lu Kuang-hsü　陸光旭

Lu Ming-ch'en　盧明臣

lun　論

Mai-yin-ta　邁音達

Margi　麻勒吉

Marsai　馬爾賽

meng-hui　盟會

meng-ku ya-men　蒙古衙門

Mergen　墨爾根

Mi-shu yüan　秘書院

Ming　明

Ming-shih chi-lueh　明史紀略

Moro　莫洛

mou　畝

Mou Yun-lung　牟雲龍

Murma　穆里瑪

Mušu　穆舒

Na-er-tu　訥爾都

Namfe　納穆福

Namo　訥莫

nei-san-yüan　內三院

nien-p'u　年譜

Ning-ku-t'a chiang-chün　寧古塔將軍

Ou-yang Shih-feng　歐陽世逢

pa-ku wen-chang　八股文章

pa ta-ch'en　八大臣

pa ya-men　八衙門

p'an　判

Pan-ti　班迪

pao-i tso-ling　包衣佐領

Pen tz'u-ch'üeh　本辭爵

piao　表

pien-fang　邊方

pin-k'o　賓客

p'ing　平

p'ing-ch'ang　平常

P'ing-hsi Wang　平西王

P'ing-nan Wang　平南王

po-hsüeh hung-ju　博學宏詞

Po-lo-t'e　博羅特

Sai-pen-te　塞本德

San-kuo chih　三國志

shang-san-ch'i　上三旗

shen-chin　紳衿

Shen T'ien-fu　沈天甫

Sheng-yü　聖諭

shih　食

shih cha-er-ku-ch'i　十扎爾固齊

shih-san ya-men 十三衙門

Shih Tao-ch'i 赫搖旗

Shuai-yen-pao 帥顏保

Siteku 席特庫

Sohon 索渾

Solgo 索爾和

Su-hei 蘇赫

Sun T'ing-ch'üan 孫廷銓

Suna 蘇納

Sunahai 蘇納海

ta-chi 大計

Ta-Chin Shih-tsung pen-chi 大金世宗本記

T'ai-pi-t'u 泰壁圖

Tanka (Tan-k'ou) 蜑寇

tang 黨

T'ang Wen-yao 唐文耀

t'ao-jen 逃人

Tejin 特晉

t'i 體

Ti-pao 邸報

tien 殿

t'ien-hsia 天下

T'ien-hsia sui te-chih ma-shang, pu-k'o-i ma-shang chih. 天下雖得之馬上不可以馬上治

T'ien ming 天命

T'ien-ch'i 天啟

t'ien-tzu 天子

ting 丁

Ts'ao Pien-chiao 曹變蛟

ts'an-cheng 參政

ts'e 策

tsou-hsiao an 奏銷案

tsui 最

tsung-ping 總兵

Tung-i 佟義

tzu-ch'en 自陳

tzu-tao 子道

Uksai 吳格塞

Urgei 吳爾喀

wai-ch'a 外察

wai tso-ling 外佐領

wang 王

Wang Hsien-tso 王顯祚

Wang Hung-tso 王宏祚

Wang Lai-jen 王來任

Wang Teng-lien 王登聯

Wei Chou-tso 衛周祚

wen 文

wen-ch'en 文臣

Wen-ch'i 溫齊

wu 武

wu ching 武經

wu ta-ch'en 五大臣

yang 陽

Yang Er 楊二

Yang Hsi 楊熙

Yang San 楊三

yen-kuan 言官

yin 陰

Yü To 俞鐸

yü-yung chien 御用監

Yüan 元

Yüan T'ai-tsu 元太祖

yung 用

Yung-li 永曆

Works Cited

In this list I have refrained from subdividing the works cited into such categories as primary sources and secondary works. Rather than endeavor to explain this practice, I refer my readers to Jonathan Spence, Ts'ao Yin, p. 308, where he discusses the difficulty of separating Chinese works into "primary" and "secondary" material.

Backhouse, Edmund, and Bland, J. O. P. Annals and Memoirs of the Court of Peking. Boston, 1914. BH.

H. S. Brunnert and V. V. Hagelstrom. Present Day Political Organization of China. Revised by N. Th. Kolessoff; translated by A. Beltchenko and E. E. Moran. Shanghai, 1912.

Bosmans, Henri. "Ferdinand Verbiest, Directeur de L'Observatoire de Peking, 1623-1688." Revue des questions scientifiques, January–April, 1912, pp. 224-30.

Bowra, E. C. "The Manchu Conquest of Canton." The China Review 1 (Hongkong, 1872-73): 86-96, 228-37.

Boxer, C. R. "The Rise and Fall of Nicholas Iquan (Cheng Chih-lung)." T'ien-hsia Monthly 2 (1940-41): 401-39.

_____. "The Seige of Fort Zeelandia and the Capture of Formosa from the Dutch, 1661-1662." Transactions and Proceedings of the Japan Society, 1926-27, pp. 16-47.

_____. South China in the Sixteenth Century. London, 1953.

Campbell, William. Formosa under the Dutch. London, 1903.

Chang Chung-li. The Chinese Gentry. Seattle, 1955.

Chang Hao. Liang Ch'i-ch'ao and Intellectual Transition in China, 1890-1907. Cambridge, Mass., 1971.

Chang Te-ch'ang. "The Economic Role of the Imperial Household in the Ch'ing Dynasty." The Journal of Asian Studies 31, no. 2 (February 1972): 243-73.

Chang T'ien-tse. Sino-Portuguese Trade from 1514-1644. Leiden, 1934.

Chang Ts'ai-t'ien 張采田 .   Ch'ing lieh-ch'ao hou-fei chuan-kao
　　清列朝后妃傳稿 [Draft Biographies of the Ch'ing Em-
　　presses and Concubines, listed by Reigns]. 2 chüan. N.p., 1929.

Chao Ch'üan-ch'eng 趙泉澄. Ch'ing-tai ti-li yen-ko piao 清代地理
　　沿革表 [Tables of Changes in Administrative Areas in the
　　Ch'ing Dynasty]. Peking, 1955.

Che-chiang t'ung-chih 浙江通志 [The Gazetter of Chekiang Province].
　　280 chüan. N.p., n.d. Reprint (4 vols., with continuous pagina-
　　tion), Shanghai, 1934.

Ch'en Chieh-hsien 陳捷先 . "Chiu Man-chou tang shu-lüeh" 舊滿洲
　　檔述略 [An Introduction to The Old Manchu Archives]. In
　　Chiu Man-chou tang 舊滿洲檔 [The Old Manchu Archives],
　　pp. 1-56. Reprint, Taiwan, 1969.

_____. "Hou-Chin ling-ch'i peile lueh-k'ao" 後金領旗貝勒
　　略考 [A Brief Study of the Banner-Governing Beile in the Later
　　Chin Dynasty, 1616-1635]. Ku-kung wen-hsien 故宮文獻
　　[Ch'ing Documents at the National Palace Museum (Quarterly)]
　　1, no. 1 (December 1969): 43-48.

_____. Man-chou ts'ung-k'ao 滿洲叢考 [Studies on the Early
　　Ch'ing Dynasty]. Taipei, 1965.

_____. "Tuo-er-kang ch'eng 'Huang-fu she-cheng wang' yen-chiu"
　　多爾袞稱皇父攝政王研究 [A Study of Dorgon's Title
　　"Imperial Father Regent"]. Ku-kung wen-hsien 故宮文獻
　　[Ch'ing Documents at the National Palace Museum (Quarterly]
　　1, no. 2 (March 1970): 1-19.

_____. "The Value of the Early Manchu Archives." In Ch'en and
　　Sechin, pp. 58-80.

Ch'en and Sechin.
　　Chieh-hsien Ch'en and Jaqchid Sechin, eds. Proceedings of the
　　Third East Asian Altaistic Conference, 17-24 August 1969.
　　Taipei, 1969.

Ch'en Teng-yüan 陳登原 . Chin Sheng-t'an chuan 金聖歎傳 [Biog-
　　raphy of Chin Jen-jui]. Hongkong, 1935.

Chen, Vincent. Sino-Russian Relations in the Seventeenth Century. The
　　Hague, 1966.

Ch'en Wen-shih 陳文石 . "Ch'ing-jen ju-kuan ch'ien ti nung-yeh sheng-
　　huo, T'ai-tsu shih-tai" 清人入關前的農業生活太祖

時代 [The Agrarian Livelihood of the Ch'ing Peoples before the Conquest, the T'ai-tsu Period]. Ta-lu tsa-chih 大陸雜誌 [Continental Magazine] 22, no. 8, pp. 8-13.

_____. "Man-chou pa-ch'i niu-lu ti kou-ch'eng" 滿洲八旗牛彔的構成 [The Evolution of the niru in the Manchu Eight Banners]. Ta-lu tsa-chih 大陸雜誌 [Continental Magazine] 31, no. 9, pp. 14-18.

Cheng T'ien-t'ing 鄭天挺. Ch'ing-shih t'an-wei 清史探微 [Studies in Ch'ing History]. N.p., 1946.

_____. "Tuo-er-kang ch'eng huang-fu chih i-ts'e" 多爾袞稱皇父之臆測 [An Opinion about Dorgon's Title "Imperial Father"]. Kuo-hsüeh chi-k'an 國學季刊 [Journal of National Studies] 6, no. 1 (1936): 1-14.

Chi-fu t'ing-chih 畿輔通志 [The Gazetteer of the Metropolitan Province]. 300 chüan. N.p., 1872. Reprint (8 vols., with continuous pagination), Shanghai, 1934.

Chiang.

Chiang Jih-sheng 江日昇. T'ai-wan wai-chi 臺灣外集 [Collection of Documents Relating to Taiwan and Foreign Affairs]. 30 chüan. N.p., 1704. Reprint (3 vols., with continuous pagination), Taiwan, 1960.

Chiang-nan t'ung-chih 江南通志 [The Gazetteer of Kiangnan (Kiangsu and Anhwei)]. 200 chüan. N.p., 1736.

Ch'ien I-chi 錢儀吉. Pei-chuan chi 碑傳集 [Collection of Epitaphs and Biographies]. 160 chüan. N.p., 1893.

Chin-liang 金梁. Man-chou lao-tang pi-lu 滿洲老檔秘錄 [A Secret Record from the Old Manchu Archives]. 2 vols. Peiping, 1929.

Ch'ing-ch'ao wen-hsien t'ung-k'ao 清朝文獻通考 [Imperial Encyclopedia of the Ch'ing Dynasty]. 300 chüan. N.p., 1787. Reprint, Shanghai, 1936.

CS.

Ch'ing-shih 清史 [History of the Ch'ing Dynasty]. 8 vols. Taipei, 1961.

CSK.

Ch'ing-shih kao 清史稿 [Draft History of the Ch'ing Dynasty]. 536 chüan. Peking, 1928.

CSLC.

    Ch'ing-shih lieh-chuan 清史列傳 [Ch'ing Dynasty Biographies].
    80 chüan. N.p., 1928. Reprint (10 vols.), Taipei, 1962.

Ch'ü T'ung-tsu. Local Government in China under the Ch'ing. Cambridge,
    Mass., 1962.

Chung, A. L. Y. "The Hanlin Academy in the Early Ch'ing Period (1644-
    1795)." Journal of the Hongkong Branch of the Royal Asiatic Society
    6 (1966): 100-119.

Ch'ung-ming hsien-chih 崇明縣志 [The Gazetteer of Ch'ung-ming Dis-
    trict]. 20 chüan. N.p., 1760.

Corradini, Piero. "Civil Administration at the Beginning of the Ch'ing
    Dynasty." Oriens Extremus 9 (December 1962): 133-38.

d'Orleans, P. J. Histoire des deux conquerans tartares qui ont subjugue
    la Chine. Paris, 1688.

du Halde, Jean Baptiste. Description géographique, historique, chrono-
    logique, politique, et physique de l'empire de la Chine. 4 vols.
    Paris, 1735. English translation by R. Brookes. The General
    History of China. 4 vols. London, 1741.

Dunne, George H., S. J. Generation of Giants: The Story of the Jesuits
    in China in the Last Decades of the Ming Dynasty. Notre Dame,
    Ind., 1962.

Fa-shih-shan 法式善. Ch'ing-pi shu-wen 清秘述聞 [Examinations
    and Examiners in the Ch'ing Dynasty]. 16 chüan. N.p., 1798.

Fairbank, John K., ed. The Chinese World Order. Cambridge, Mass.,
    1968.

_____. Trade and Diplomacy on the China Coast. 2 vols. Cam-
    bridge, Mass., 1953. Reprint (2 vols. in one), Cambridge, Mass.,
    1964.

Fairbank, John K., and Teng Ssu-yu. Ch'ing Administration: Three
    Studies. Cambridge, Mass., 1960.

Fang, "Early Manchu Military Forces."
    Fang Chao-ying. "A Technique for Estimating the Numerical
    Strength of the Early Manchu Military Forces." Harvard Journal
    of Asiatic Studies 13 (1950): 192-215.

Fang and Tu.
    Fang Chao-ying and Tu Lien-che 房兆楹，杜聯喆. Tseng-

chiao Ch'ing-ch'ao chin-shih t'i-ming pei-lu 增校清朝進士題名碑錄 [Record of the Chin-shih Degree-Holders in the Ch'ing Dynasty]. Taipei, 1966.

Farquhar, David M. "The Origins of the Manchus' Mongolian Policy." In Fairbank, Chinese World Order, pp. 198-205.

Fletcher, Jesoph F. "China and Central Asia, 1368-1884." In Fairbank, Chinese World Order, pp. 206-24.

Franke, Chinese Examination System.
Wolfgang Franke. The Reform and Abolition of the Traditional Chinese Examination System. Cambridge, Mass., 1960.

Fu-chien t'ung-chih 福建通志 [The Gazetteer of Fukien Province]. 278 chüan. N.p., 1829-35.

Fu Lo-shu. A Documentary Chronicle of Sino-Western Relations (1644-1820). 2 vols. Tucson, 1966.

_____. "The Two Portuguese Embassies to China during the K'ang-hsi Period." Toung Pao 43 (Leiden, 1955): 75-94.

Fu Tsung-mao 傅宗懋. "Ch'ing-ch'u i-cheng ta-ch'en t'i-chih chih yen-chiu" 清初議政大臣體制之研究 [A Study of the i-cheng System of the Early Ch'ing]. Kuo-li cheng-chih ta-hsüeh hsüeh-pao 11 (May 1965): 245-94.

_____. Ch'ing-tai Chün-chi ch'u tsu-chih chi chih-chang chih yen-chiu 清代軍機處組織及職掌之研究 [A Study of the Organization of the Grand Council and Its Functions under the Ch'ing]. Taipei, 1967.

_____. Ch'ing-tai tu-fu chih-tu 清代督撫制度 [The tu-fu System of the Ch'ing Period]. Taipei, 1963.

Gasster, Michael. Chinese Intellectuals and the Revolution of 1911. Seattle, 1969.

_____. "Reform and Revolution in China's Political Modernization." In Wright, China in Revolution, pp. 67-96.

Golder, F. A. Russian Expansion on the Pacific, 1641-1850. Cleveland, 1914.

Goodrich, L. Carrington. The Literary Inquisition of Ch'ien-lung. Baltimore, 1935.

Greslon [Grelon], Adrien. <u>Histoire de la Chine sous la domination des Tartares</u>. Paris, 1671.

Harvey, G. E. <u>History of Burma</u>. N.p., 1925.

Ho, Ping-ti. <u>The Ladder of Success in Imperial China</u>. New York, 1962.

_____. <u>Studies on the Population of China, 1368-1953</u>. Cambridge, Mass., 1959.

Howorth, Henry Hoyle. <u>History of the Mongols, from the 9th to the 19th Century</u>. 4 vols. London, 1876-1927.

Hsiao I-shan.

    Hsiao I-shan 蕭一山. <u>Ch'ing-tai t'ung-shih</u> 清代通史 [Comprehensive History of the Ch'ing Period]. 5 vols. Peking, 1923.

Hsiao Kung-chuan. <u>Rural China: Imperial Control in the Nineteenth Century</u>. Seattle, 1960.

Hsieh Kuo-chen.

    Hsieh Kuo-chen. "Removal of the Coastal Population in the Early Tsing Period." Translated by T. H. Chen, in <u>Chinese Social and Political Science Review</u> 15 (1930-31): 559-96.

Hsieh Kuo-chen 謝國楨. "Chuang-shih shih-an ts'an-chiao chu-jen k'ao" 莊氏史案參校諸人考 [Notes on the Case of Chuang T'ing-lung]. <u>T'u-shu-kuan-hsüeh chi-k'an</u> 圖書館學季刊 [Library Studies Journal] 4, no. 3-4 (Peking. 1930): 423-27.

_____. <u>Ming-Ch'ing chih chi tang-she yun-tung k'ao</u> 明清之際黨社運動考 [An Examination of the Parties and Societies in the Ming-Ch'ing Period]. Shanghai, 1935.

Hsieh Pao-chao. <u>The Government of China (1644-1911)</u>. Baltimore, 1925.

Hsü K'o 徐珂. <u>Ch'ing-pai lui-ch'ao</u> 清稗類鈔 [Categorized Documents on the Ch'ing Dynasty]. 48 <u>ts'e</u>. Shanghai, 1917.

HT.

    <u>Ch'in-ting ta-Ch'ing hui-tien</u> 欽定大清會典 [The Ch'ing Statutes]. 100 <u>chüan</u>. Shanghai, 1899. Reprint (in 1 vol., with continuous pagination), Taiwan, 1963.

HT (1690).

    <u>Ch'in-ting ta-Ch'ing hui-tien</u> 欽定大清會典 [The Ch'ing

Statutes]. N. p. , 1690.

HTSL.

    Ch'in-ting ta-Ch'ing hui-tien shih-li 欽定大清會典事例 [The Collected Statutes of the Ch'ing Dynasty]. 1220 chüan. Shanghai, 1899. Reprint (in 19 vols. , with continuous pagination), Taiwan, 1963. In footnote citations, page numbers from the 1963 edition are given in parentheses following the page numbers from the 1899 edition.

Huang Pei. "A Study of the Yung-cheng Period, 1723-1735: The Political Phase." Ph.D. dissertation, University of Indiana, 1964.

Hucker, Charles O. The Censorial System of Ming China. Stanford, 1966.

_____. "Governmental Organization of the Ming Dynasty." Harvard Journal of Asiatic Studies 21 (1958): 1-66. This article is reprinted in Studies of Governmental Institutions in Chinese History, edited by John L. Bishop, pp. 57-124. Cambridge, Mass. , 1968.

_____. The Traditional Chinese State in Ming Times, 1368-1644. Tuscon, 1961.

Hu-nan t'ung-chih 湖南通志 [The Gazetteer of Hunan Province]. 228 chüan. N.p. , 1885.

Hu-pei t'ung-chih 湖北通志 [The Gazetteer of Hupei Province]. 172 chüan. N.p. , 1911. Reprint (in 3 vols. , with continuous pagination), Shanghai, 1921.

Hummel.

    Arthur W. Hummel, ed. Eminent Chinese of the Ch'ing Period. 2 vols. Washington, D.C. , 1943-44. Reprint (2 vols. in one), Taipei, 1964.

Johnston, R. F. "The Romance of an Emperor." The New China Review 2 (1920): 1-24, 180-94.

Kahn, Harold L. Monarchy in the Emperor's Eyes. Cambridge, Mass. , 1971.

K'ai-p'ing hsien-chih 蓋平縣志 [The Gazetteer of K'ai-p'ing District]. 18 chüan. K'ai-p'ing, 1930.

Kanda Nobuo 神田信夫 . "Shinsho no bairoku ni tsuite" 清初の 貝勒について [On the Beile in the Early Ch'ing Dynasty]. Tōyō gakuhō 東洋學報 [Reports of the Oriental Society] 43, no. 4 (March 1958): 1-23.

_____. "Shinsho no gisei daijin ni tsuite" 清初の議政大
臣について [On the Deliberative Ministers in the Early Ch'ing
Dynasty]. In Wada hakhushi kanreki kinen Toyoshi ronso
和田博士還曆紀念東洋史論叢 [Essays on Asian
History in Commemoration of Dr. Wada's Sixty-First Birth-
day], pp. 171-85. Tokyo, 1951.

KCCH.

Kuo-ch'ao ch'i-hsien lei-cheng 國朝耆獻類徵 [Biogra-
phies of the Elderly and Distinguished in the Ch'ing Dynasty].
720 chüan. N.p., 1890. Reprint (in 25 vols., with continuous
pagination), Taiwan, 1966.

Keene, Donald R. The Battles of Coxinga. London, 1951.

Kessler, Lawrence D. "Chinese Scholars and the Early Manchu State."
Harvard Journal of Asiatic Studies 31 (1971): 179-200.

_____. "Ethnic Composition of Provincial Leadership During the
Ch'ing Dynasty." The Journal of Asian Studies 28, no. 3 (May
1969): 489-511.

KH Shih-lu.

Ta-Ch'ing Sheng-tsu Jen huang-ti shih-lu 大清聖祖仁皇帝
寶錄 [The Veritable Records of the K'ang-hsi Reign]. 300
chüan. Tokyo, 1937.

K'u-miao chi-lüeh 哭廟紀略 [A Record of the K'u-miao Affair]. In
T'ung-shih 痛史 [A History of Suffering], edited by Lo-t'ien-
chü-shih 樂田居士. Shanghai, 1911. Vol. 2.

Ku Yen-wu 顧炎武. "Shu Wu P'an er-tzu shih" 書吳潘二子事
[On the Matter of Wu Yen and P'an Ch'eng-chang]. In Pei-chuan
chi-pu 碑傳集補 [Addenda to the Pei-chuan chi], edited by
Min Er-ch'ang 閔爾昌, ch. 35, pp. 23b-28b. Peiping, 1931.

Kuang-lu and Li Hsüeh-chih 廣祿, 李學智. "Lao Man-wen yüan-
tang yü Man-wen lao-tang chih pi-chiao yen-chiu" 老滿文
原檔與滿文老檔之比較研究 [A Comparative Study
of the Old Manchu Original Archives and the Old Manchu Ar-
chives]. Chung-kuo tung-ya hsüeh-shu yen-chiu chi-hua wei-
yüan-hui nien-pao 中國東亞學術研究計劃委員會
年報 [Bulletin of the China Council for East Asian Studies],
no. 4 (Taipei, June 1965): 1-165.

Kuei-chou t'ung-chih 貴州通志 [The Gazetteer of Kweichow Pro-
      vince]. 46 chüan. N.p., 1741.

Lattimore, Owen. Inner Asian Frontiers of China. New York, 1940.
      Paperback reprint with new introduction, Boston, 1962.
      _____. Manchuria: Cradle of Conflict. New York, 1932.
      _____. The Mongols of Manchuria. New York, 1934.

Lee, Robert H. G. The Manchurian Frontier in Ch'ing History. Cam-
      bridge, Mass., 1970.

Lifton, Robert Jay. Revolutionary Immortality. New York, 1969.

Li Hsüeh-chih. "An Analysis of Questions Relating to the Imperial
      Succession During the Reign of Nurhaci." In Ch'en and Sechin,
      pp. 174-81.

Li Tieh-tseng. The Historical Status of Tibet. New York, 1956.

Liao-yang hsien-chih 遼陽縣志 [The Gazetteer of Liao-yang Dis-
      trict]. 40 chüan. N.p., 1927.

Liu.
      Liu Chia-chü 劉家駒. Ch'ing-ch'ao ch'u-ch'i ti pa-ch'i
ch'üan-ti 清朝初期的八旗圈地 [The Allotted Land Policy
for the Eight Banners in the Early Ch'ing Dynasty]. Taipei, 1964.

Ma Feng-ch'en. "Manchu-Chinese Social and Economic Conflicts in
      the Early Ch'ing." In Chinese Social History, edited by E-tu Sun
      and John de Francis, pp. 333-51. Washington, D.C., 1956.

Mancall, Mark. "The Ch'ing Tribute System: An Interpretive Essay."
      In Fairbank, Chinese World Order, pp. 63-89.
      _____. Russia and China: Their Diplomatic Relations to 1728.
      Cambridge, Mass., 1971.

Man-chou shih-lu 滿洲寶錄 [The Veritable Records of the Manchus].
      Peking, 1927. Reprint (in 1 vol., with continuous pagination),
      Taipei, n. d.

Man-wen lao-tang 滿文老檔 [Old Manchu Archives]. Edited by Toyo
      Bunko. 7 vols. Tokyo, 1955-64.

MCSL.
      Ming-Ch'ing shih-liao 明清史料 [Historical Materials on the
      Ming and Ch'ing Dynasties]. Shanghai and Taiwan, 1930 ff. Reprint,
      Taiwan, 1965.

Meng Sen 孟森. "Ch'ing-ch'u san ta i-an k'ao shih" 清初三大
疑案考實 [An Examination of Three Great Cases in the Early
Ch'ing Period]. In Meng, Ch'ing-tai shih, pp. 449-550.

_____. Ch'ing-tai shih 清代史 [Essays in Ch'ing History].
Edited by Wu Hsiang-hsiang 吳相湘. Taipei, 1960.

_____. Ming-Ch'ing shih lun-chu chi-k'an 明清史論著集刊
[Collection of Writings and Discussions of Meng Sen on Ming
and Ch'ing History]. Taipei, 1961.

_____. "Pa-ch'i chih-tu k'ao-shih" 八旗制度考實 [An Exam-
ination of the Organization of the Eight Banners]. In Meng,
Ch'ing-tai shih, pp. 20-100.

_____. "Shu Ming-shih ch'ao-lüeh," 書明史鈔略 [On the Ming-
shih ch'ao-lüeh]. In Meng, Ming-Ch'ing shih lun-chu chi-k'an,
pp. 141-47.

_____. "Tsou-hsiao an" 奏銷案 [Taxation Case Reported to the
Board of Revenue]. In Meng, Ming-Ch'ing shih lun-chou chi-
k'an, pp. 434-52.

Michael, Franz. The Origin of Manchu Rule in China. Baltimore, 1942.
Reprint, New York, 1965.

Ming-shih 明史 [History of the Ming Dynasty]. 302 chüan. N.p., 1739.
Reprint (in 6 vols., with continuous pagination), Taipei, 1962.

Mo Tung-yin 莫東寅. Man-tsu shih lun-ts'ung 滿族史論丛 [Col-
lected Essays on the History of the Manchu Race]. Peking, 1958.

Morgan, Evan. "Times and Manners in the Age of the Emperor K'ang-
hsi." Journal of the North China Branch of the Royal Asiatic
Society 69 (1938): 23-45.

Nan-hsün chih 南潯志 [The Gazetteer of Nan-hsün District]. N.p.,
1929.

Nivison, David. S. "Ho-shen and His Accusers: Ideology and Political
Behavior in the Eighteenth Century." In Confucianism in Action,
edited by David S. Nivison and Arthur F. Wright, pp. 209-43.
Stanford, 1957.

Novikov, Boris. "The Anti-Manchu Propaganda of the Triads, ca. 1800-
1860." In Popular Movements and Secret Societies in China,

1840-1950, edited by Jean Chesneaux, pp. 49-63. Stanford, 1972.

Okada Hidehiro 岡田英弘. "Ch'ing T'ai-tsung chi-wei k'ao-shih" 清太宗繼位考實 [A Study of Ch'ing T'ai-tsung's Succession to the Throne]. Ku-kung wen-hsien 故宮文獻 [Ch'ing Documents at the National Palace Museum (Quarterly)] 3, no. 2 (March 1972):31-37.

Parsons, James B. The Peasant Rebellions of the Late Ming Dynasty. Tuscon, 1970.

PCST.
Pa-ch'i Man-chou shih-tsu t'ung-p'u 八旗滿洲氏族通譜 [Genealogy of the Manchu Clans in the Eight Banners]. 80 chüan. N.p., 1745.

PCTC.
Pa-ch'i t'ung-chih 八旗通志 [General History of the Eight Banners]. 342 chüan. N.p., 1739.

PCTC (1795).
Pa-ch'i t'ung-chih 八旗通志 [General History of the Eight Banners]. 342 chüan. N.p., 1795.

Pfister, Louis. Notices biographiques et bibliographiques sur les Jesuites de l'ancienne mission de Chine, 1552-1773. In Variétés Sinologiques, no. 59 (Shanghai, 1932), and no. 60 (Shanghai, 1934).

Pien-i tien 邊裔典 [Regulations on the Frontier Tribes]. In Ku-chin t'u-shu chi-ch'eng 古今圖書集成, ch. 209. Shanghai, 1934.

Ponsby-Fane, R. A. B. "Koxinga: Chronicles of the Tei Family." Transactions and Proceedings of the Japan Society 34 (London, 1937):62-132.

Rankin, Mary B. Early Chinese Revolutionaries: Radical Intellectuals in Shanghai and Chekiang, 1902-1911. Cambridge, Mass., 1971.

Reid, John. "Peking's First Manchu Emperor." Pacific Historical Review, June 1936, pp. 130-46.

Rockhill, William W. China's Intercourse with Korea from the Fifteenth Century to 1895. London, 1905.

Ross, John. The Manchus; or, the Reigning Dynasty in China, Their Rise and Progress. London, 1880.

SC Shih-lu.

    Ta-Ch'ing Shih-tsu Chang huang-ti shih-lu 大清世祖章皇帝 實錄 [The Veritable Records of the Shun-chih Reign]. 144 chüan. Tokyo, 1937.

Shan-tung t'ung-chih 山東通志 [The Gazetteer of Shantung Province]. 200 chüan. N.p., 1911. Reprint (in 5 vols., with continuous pagination), Shanghai, 1934.

Shang.

    Shang Yen-liu 商衍流. Ch'ing-tai k'o-chü k'ao-shih shu-lu 清代科舉考試述錄 [The Recommendation and Examination Systems of the Ch'ing Period]. Peking, 1958.

Shen-yang hsien-chih 瀋陽縣志 [The Gazetteer of Shen-yang District]. 15 chüan. N.p., 1917.

Shen Yün 沈雲. T'ai-wan Cheng-shih shih-mo 臺灣鄭氏始末 [A Complete Account of the Chengs on Taiwan]. N.p., n.d. Reprint (in 1 vol., with continuous pagination), Taipei, 1958.

Sheng-ching t'ung-chih 盛京通志 [The Gazetteer of Sheng-ching]. 130 chüan. Peking, 1778. Reprint (in 3 vols., with continuous pagination), Taipei, 1965.

Spence, Jonathan D. Emperor of China: Self-Portrait of K'ang-hsi. New York, 1974.

    _____. "The Seven Ages of K'ang-hsi (1654-1722)." The Journal of Asian Studies 26, no. 2 (February 1967):205-11.

    _____. To Change China. Boston, 1969.

    _____. Ts'ao Yin and the K'ang-hsi Emperor: Bondservant and Master. New Haven and London, 1966.

Ssu-ch'uan t'ung-chih 四川通志 [The Gazetteer of Szechwan Province]. 204 chüan. N.p., 1816.

Su-chou fu-chih 蘇州府志 [The Gazetteer of Soochow Prefecture]. 150 chüan. N.p., 1883.

T'ai-tsung shih-lu.

    T'ai-tsung Wen huang-ti shih-lu 太宗文皇帝實錄 [The Veritable Records of the T'ai-tsung Reign]. 20 chüan. Shanghai, 1936. Reprint (in 2 vols., with continuous pagination), Taipei, n.d.

T'ang Pang-chih 唐邦治. Ch'ing huang-shih ssu-p'u 清皇室四譜

[Four Genealogies of the Ch'ing Imperial House]. 4 chüan. N.p.,
1923.

Tayama Shigeru 田山茂. Shin-jidai ni okeru Moko no shakai seido
清時代に於ける蒙古の社会制度 [Mongol Social
Systems in the Ch'ing Period]. Tokyo, 1954.

T'ieh-ling hsien-chih 鐵嶺縣志 [The Gazetteer of T'ieh-ling District].
20 chüan. N.p., 1931.

Tsao Kai-fu. "The Rebellion of the Three Feudatories against the Manchu Throne in China, 1673-1681: Its Setting and Significance."
Ph.D. dissertation, Columbia University, 1965.

Wada Sei. "Some Problems Concerning the Rise of T'ai-tsu, the Founder
of the Manchu Dynasty." In Memoirs of the Reserach Department
of the Toyo Bunko, no. 16 (Tokyo, 1957):35-73.

Wakeman, Frederic, Jr. "High Ch'ing: 1683-1839." In Modern East
Asia: Essays in Interpretation, edited by James B. Crowley,
pp. 1-28. New York, 1970.

Wang Chung-han 王鍾翰. Ch'ing-shih tsa-k'ao 清史雜考 [Inves-
tigations on Ch'ing History]. Peking, 1957.

Wang Fu-chih 王夫之. Yung-li shih-lu 永曆實錄 [The Veritable
Records of the Yung-li Reign]. In Ch'uan-shan ch'üan-chi 船山
全集 [The Collected Works of Wang Fu-chih]. Vol. 12, 26 chüan.
N.p., 1840-42. Reprint, Taipei, 1965.

Wang Hsiu-ch'u. "A Memoir of a Ten Days' Massacre in Yangchow."
T'ien-hsia Monthly 4 (1937):515-37.

Wang, John Ching-yu. Chin Sheng-t'an. New York, 1972.

Watt, John. The District Magistrate in Late Imperial China. New York,
1972.

_____. "Theory and Practice in Chinese Administration: The Role
of the Ch'ing District Magistrate in Historical Perspective." Ph.D.
dissertation, Columbia University, 1967.

Wei Yuan 魏源. Ta-Ch'ing sheng-wu chi 大清聖武記 [Record of
the Military Achievements of the Ch'ing Dynasty]. 14 chüan. N.p.,
1844. Reprint (in 1 vol., with continuous pagination), Taipei, 1962.

Wiens, Harold J. China's March towards the Tropics. Hamden, Conn.,
1954.

Willhelm. Hellmut. "The Po-hsüeh Hung-ju Examination of 1679." Journal of the American Oriental Society 71 (1950):60-66.

Wills.

John E. Wills, Jr. "Sino-Dutch Trade and Diplomacy: A Chronicle, 1662-1690." Ph. D. dissertation, Harvard University, 1966.

Wright, Mary C., ed. China in Revolution: The First Phase, 1900-1913. New Haven, 1968.

_____. The Last Stand of Chinese Conservatism: The T'ung-chih Restoration, 1862-1874. Stanford, 1957.

Wu, Silas H. L. Communication and Imperial Control in China: Evolution of the Palace Memorial System, 1693-1735. Cambridge, Mass., 1970.

_____. "The Memorial Systems of the Ch'ing Dynasty (1644-1911)." The Harvard Journal of Asiatic Studies 27 (1967):7-75.

Wu Wei-yeh 吳偉業. Lu-ch'iao chi-wen 鹿樵紀聞 [Recollections of a Recluse]. 2 chüan. N.p., n.d. Reprint, Taipei, 1961.

Yang Kuang-hsien 楊光先. Pu te i 不得已 [I Could Not Do Otherwise]. N.p., n.d. Reprint, n.p., 1929.

Yang Pin 楊賓. Liu-pien chi-lüeh 柳邊紀略 [A Record of the Willow Palisade Border Area]. In Liao-hai ts'ung-shu 遼海叢書, ts'e 117, 5 chüan. Dairen, 1939.

Yang Ying 楊英. Ts'ung-cheng shih-lu 從征實錄 [A Veritable Record of Accompanying the Battles (of Cheng Ch'eng-kung)]. N.p., n.d. Reprint (in 1 vol., with continuous pagination), Taipei, 1958.

Yang Yü-liu 楊予六. Chung-kuo li-tai ti-fang hsing-cheng ch'ü-hua 中國歷代地方行政區劃 [Local Administrative Divisions in Chinese History]. N.p., 1957.

Yen Mao-kung 嚴懋功. Ch'ing-tai cheng-hsien lei-pien 清代徵獻類編 [Chronological Lists of High Officials in the Ch'ing Period]. 25 chüan. N.p., 1931.

Yün-nan t'ung-chih-kao 雲南通志稿 [Draft Gazetteer of Yunnan Province]. 216 chüan. N.p., 1835.

Zi, Etienne. "Pratique des examens litteraires en Chine." Variétés Sinologiques, no. 5 (Shanghai, 1894).

Index